Leading Corporate Citizens

Vision, Values, Value Added

Leading Corporate Citizens

Citizens

VISION, VALUES, VALUE ADDED

Sandra Waddock

Boston College
Carroll School of Management

**McGraw-Hill
Irwin**

Boston   Burr Ridge, IL   Dubuque, IA   Madison, WI   New York   San Francisco   St. Louis
Bangkok   Bogotá   Caracas   Kuala Lumpur   Lisbon   London   Madrid   Mexico City
Milan   Montreal   New Delhi   Santiago   Seoul   Singapore   Sydney   Taipei   Toronto

McGraw-Hill Higher Education ⊗

*A Division of The **McGraw-Hill** Companies*

LEADING CORPORATE CITIZENS: VISION, VALUES, VALUE ADDED
Published by McGraw-Hill, an imprint of The McGraw-Hill Companies, Inc. 1221 Avenue of the
Americas, New York, NY, 10020. Copyright © 2002, by The McGraw-Hill Companies, Inc. All rights
reserved. No part of this publication may be reproduced or distributed in any form or by any means,
or stored in a data base or retrieval system, without the prior written consent of The McGraw-Hill
Companies, Inc., including, but not limited to, in any network or other electronic storage or
transmission, or broadcast for distance learning.
Some ancillaries, including electronic and print components, may not be available to customers
outside the United States.

This book is printed on acid-free paper.

1 2 3 4 5 6 7 8 9 0 FGR/FGR 0 9 8 7 6 5 4 3 2 1

ISBN 0-07-245390-7

Publisher: *John E. Biernat*
Senior Sponsoring editor: *Andy Winston*
Editorial coordinator: *Sara E. Strand*
Marketing manager: *Lisa Nicks*
Project manager: *Scott Scheidt*
Production supervisor: *Gina Hangos*
Coordinator freelance design: *Mary L. Christianson*
Freelance cover designer: *Kristyn Kalnes*
Supplement coordinator: *Susan Lombardi*
Compositor: *Carlisle Communications, Ltd.*
Typeface: *10.5/12 Times Roman*
Printer: *Quebecor World Fairfield Inc.*

Library of Congress Cataloging-in-Publication Data
Waddock, Sandra A.
    Leading corporate citizens : vision, values, value added / Sandra Waddock.
        p. cm.
    Includes index.
    ISBN 0-07-245390-7 (alk. paper)
    1. Social responsibility of business. 2. Values. 3. Human ecology. 4. Common good. 5.
Citizenship. I. Title.
HD60.W33 2002
658.4'08—dc21

                                            2001030065

www.mhhe.com

For Ben
With love,
Mom
Boston 2001

Brief Contents

Contents

PART 2

Leading Corporate Citizens with Vision, Values, and Value Added

4. Personal and Organizational Vision   83

5. Values in Management Practice: Operating with Integrity   115

Preface

Take a look at the business press these days. It seems hard to escape a great deal of talk about companies becoming good corporate global citizens. But just what is corporate global citizenship and how do corporations achieve it? *Leading Corporate Citizens* explores what it takes to make a company into a leading corporate citizen and some of the pathways toward the type of personal leadership that such citizenship implies.

Leading Corporate Citizens is about corporate responsibility—what I call responsible practice—and about stakeholders and the implicit, inextricable relationships between companies and their stakeholders. The book uses a framework of vision, values, and value added to lead us toward this vision of corporate citizenship. Vision is personal, organizational, and even societal. Vision encompasses the ways in which our work together in an organization, a corporation, will make a difference in the world around us. Values are what we stand for as individuals, as organizations, as society. This book illustrates how we can instill in our organization the constructive values to which stakeholders are willing to make a commitment. *Leading Corporate Citizens* is about having a positive and constructive vision supported by values that contribute to productive sources of value added for the enterprise. It is about personal and organizational insight, vision, and learning as the ongoing activities that inform day-to-day practice. It is about balance in our lives, individual and organizational, and balance among what I call the spheres of activity in society, all in ways that are ecologically sustainable.

Leading Corporate Citizens is about responsible practice and the associated bottom-line benefits. It is countercultural in the sense that it opposes a short-sighted, narrowly focused perspective on the purpose and roles of the firm and deliberately sets a difficult, long-range target that is in the interests of all. It is not necessarily about organizations that exist today as much as it is about organizations as they need to exist to build a better world tomorrow. It is about what works and in that sense, it is intended to be a practical guide to action for leaders.

The premise of *Leading Corporate Citizens* is to work with what is best in capitalism while preserving or enhancing a sense of the collective good that sustains us in our communities, families, and working lives. It is about an integrated wholeness rather than fragmentation, an attempt to focus on the truly big picture so that when leaders of the future make decisions, they will be well aware of the impacts of those decisions. It is also about paying attention to the soft stuff that is actually the hard stuff—to the qualitative as well as quantitative impacts and results of company actions, to the subjective as well as objective aspects of the lives we lead in organizations and societies today.

In *Leading Corporate Citizens,* I try to present a positive vision of the corporation in society, in all its manifest roles and with all of its impacts. Deliberately and even somewhat idealistically (my Pollyanna nature coming through full force), I intend to take us toward a new paradigm of the organization, one that does, in fact, take into account its responsibilities towards multiple stakeholders while achieving multiple positive bottom lines in the long term. At the same time, I try to present some of the dominant critiques of the corporation so that managers are exposed to them and understand that there are two sides to the currently dominant paradigm of shareholder capitalism that might be somewhat (albeit not fully) alleviated by stakeholder capitalism.

Not all corporations today achieve this vision of responsible practice, of living vision and values that result in value and values added. In fact most probably don't, but many companies do show evidence of partially achieving it and some are working hard toward this vision. And, as *Leading Corporate Citizens* attempts to demonstrate, the rewards for those that do can be significant over the long term.

STRUCTURE OF THE BOOK

Leading Corporate Citizens is structured into four parts, the first of which provides "A Context for Leading Corporate Citizens." Chapter 1, "Corporate Global Citizenship: Vision, Values, Value Added," provides one of the core frameworks of the book: the idea that guided by inspirational vision and a set of principles or core values a company can add value. This chapter also introduces the relational stakeholder perspective that guides much of the vision of the book itself. Chapter 2, "Spheres of Influence: The Ecological Underpinning," focuses quite literally on the ground beneath our feet, the natural environment on which human civilization depends for its very existence and on which businesses depend for the raw materials used in the production of goods and services. Chapter 3, "The Three Spheres of Human Civilization," rounds out the context in which businesses operate by arguing that human civilization, built upon the natural environment, can be described in three spheres: economic, political or governmental, and civil society. Each of these spheres has specific types of goals and a set of values that determines the nature and type of enterprise that tends to arise in that sphere.

The second part of the book is called "Leading Corporate Citizens with Vision, Values, and Value Added." This chapter takes the framework of vision, values, and value added sketched out in the first chapter and elaborates each element of that framework. Chapter 4, "Personal and Organizational Vision," argues that vision that inspires meaning and commitment, both personally and organizationally, is necessary to bring out the best in all of us. This chapter further takes a developmental perspective on both individuals and organizations, making the case that relatively higher levels of cognitive, moral, and emotional development are needed to cope with the complexity and relative chaos of today's organizations if they are, in fact, to become leading corporate citizens. Chapter 5, "Values in Management Practice: Operating with Integrity," argues that integrity, in all senses of the word—honesty and forthrightness, operating from a principled base, and soundness and wholeness—is needed to bring vision to life in a way that engenders stakeholder commitment and the best possible performance. This chapter also argues for responsible practice as the basis of sound—and ultimately profitable—operations. The theme of value added is carried forward in chapter 6, which tries to synthesize the evidence for linking vision, values, and value added, showing that not only is responsible practice the right thing to do but that ultimately it is the more effective—and profitable—way to go.

The third part of the book, "Leading Corporate Citizens and their Stakeholders," articulates the specific practices that leading corporate citizens can employ with respect to their stakeholders, the natural environment, and society at large to get to the value added discussed in the previous section. Chapter 7, "Stakeholders: The Relationship Key," discusses the boundary-spanning, stakeholder related functions found inside leading corporate citizens and highlights the specific practices that can be considered to be current "best practice" within each of the stakeholder arenas found in most companies. Chapter 8, "Measuring Multiple Bottom Lines: Getting to Value Added" tries to make real the ways in which the nontraditional (nonfinancial) bottom lines associated with different stakeholders can—and are—being measured both by external research groups, analysts, and critics, and by companies themselves when they want to improve performance. Chapter 9, "Ecological Thinking in the Global Village," takes the word ecological in two senses. First, the chapter provides some insight into the ways in which humans—and businesses in particular—impact the natural environment, and how the negative aspects of those impacts might be lessened and certainly need to be attended to. Then the chapter turns to the ecology of human civilization, addressing the ways in which cross- or multisector collaboration can be developed to address societal needs more holistically than they can be addressed from any one sphere of human civilization.

The final part of *Leading Corporate Citizens* is "Leading Corporate Citizens into the Future." This section moves us into the emerging norms and standards that are impacting business operations throughout the world today—and that are likely to have even more impact in the future. Chapter 10, "Global Standards—Global Village," explicitly addresses the emergence of global standards for business practice, as well as human and labor rights, and illustrates some of the reasons why companies wishing to be leaders in corporate citizenship should set and live up to internal and external standards of responsibility. Chapter 11, "Values Added: Global Futures," highlights some practical and creative ways in which leading corporate citizens can begin to think about—and anticipate—the future, making that future appear less chaotic and unpredictable. Finally, chapter 12, "Leading Global Futures: The Emerging Paradigm of Leading Corporate Citizenship," attempts to pull all of this thinking together in what one reviewer said was certainly not the typical ending to a book such as this. Using Gareth Morgan's idea of "imaginization," this final chapter takes the reader on a tour of the new paradigm organization—the leading corporate citizen. In this tour, chapter 12 attempts to illustrate what it would be like in such an entity, how it would feel, and why, in the end, it might be important to move in that direction.

In the end, *Leading Corporate Citizens* is about leadership on two levels. The first level is the individual manager/executive's leadership—and the courage needed to take the long-term perspective implied in becoming a good citizen, attending to responsibilities and relationships inherent when interdependencies with stakeholders are acknowledged. The second level is that of the corporation, much maligned as a citizen in some parts of the world, but ultimately guided by individuals who must themselves live in the world created by these powerful organizations. What I can hope is that some new awareness—mindfulness—of the need to be responsible for the impacts that corporate decisions have on multiple stakeholders is generated by this book. In the end, after all is said and done, it is our own integrity as human beings and as leaders of corporate citizens, it is in knowing that we did our best, that will matter.

ACKNOWLEDGMENTS

Thanks are in order, so many that I scarcely know where to begin and I know I will forget many important contributors to my ideas and knowledge.

For inspiration, community, and intellectual genesis of some of the ideas embedded in this book, I am grateful to my colleagues and friends in the Boston College Leadership for Change (LC) Program—as well as for our participants, now too numerous to name. The guides in LC to a positive vision of the corporation are many. From Sociology are Severyn Bruyn, Charlie Derber, Paul Gray, and Eve Spangler. From Boston College's Carroll School of Management (for LC and so much more) are Judy Clair, Joe Raelin, and Bill Torbert; and our business partners over the years, Robert Leaver, Bill Joiner, Charlene O'Brien, Neil Smith, and, of course, LC founder and inspiration, Steve Waddell, and our director Rebecca Rowley.

I would like to thank my longtime co-author and colleague Sam Graves for his friendship, support, and our work together. It has been a source of much pleasure to work with him over the years. In many ways our work together provides the ultimate foundation for this book to the point where it probably could not have been written without the research partnership we have shared.

Intellectual debts are much more difficult to repay. For all the authors cited in this book and so many more, I thank you for your ideas and vision. I hope your ideas have inspired mine in ways you find acceptable. Particular debts are owed to those who once taught and continue to teach me. From Boston University, where I did my graduate work (although most are now elsewhere), I thank mentor and now friend Jim Post, and John Mahon, Dave Brown, and Jerry Leader in particular. Stan Davis, who was at BU when I was there, also taught me the critical question: "so what?"

Other colleagues at Boston College have been supportive of the type of integrative thinking about teaching, community-collaborative relationships, and general integration of scholarship with the world about us: Mary Walsh from the School of Education, Fran Sherman from the Law School, Jean Mooney from the School of Education, Robbie Tourse from Graduate School of Social Work, Jim Fleming, School of Education, and Mary Brabeck, Dean of School of Education. Your work in outreach scholarship is truly an inspiration underpinning this book.

My business in society colleagues are probably too numerous to mention by name lest I forget someone important. To all of you I say, your work continues to inspire and provide a source of stimulation that will yet help us build a better world. I do want to acknowledge by name a few business in society friends beyond those from BU named above. Your work has been particularly helpful, in part because the ideas and hard work has helped to shape the field and the ideas expressed here, and in part because each of you has in your own way, been supportive of me and my small efforts. So, thanks to Lee Preston (U. of Maryland), Bill Frederick (Emeritus, U. of Pittsburgh), Ed Epstein (formerly Berkeley, now dean at St. Mary's University), Ed Freeman (Darden, U. of Virginia), Jeanne Liedtka (Darden, U. of Virginia), Diane Swanson (Kansas State) and Donna Wood (U. of Pittsburgh).

Over the years, the leaders of SIM and IABS, International Association of Business in Society have also provided the "ground" on which some of these ideas could be tested and developed. Let me also acknowledge the key roles played in both my personal and intellectual development by Dawn Elm (St. Thomas), Jeff Lenn (George Washington), Jeanne Logsdon (New Mexico), Archie Carroll (Georgia), and Rich Wokutch (Virginia Tech), and so many others with whom I have exchanged ideas over the years. All those sessions at all those meetings, all those articles you have written, all that work: it all helps.

Reviewers of this book, some of whom I know by name and others not, are owed a particular debt of gratitude. Especially those of you who reviewed the whole manuscript know how much it benefited from your comments: Jerry Calton (University of Hawaii, Hilo), Melissa Baucus (Utah State), and Linda Treviño (Penn State), Dawn Elm (St. Thomas), Joel Reichart (Fordham), Anne Lawrence, and Afseneh Nahavandi (Arizona West). Special thanks are owed to Larry Lad (Butler U.), doctoral colleague, friend, and co-conspirator on this path. And to Judy Clair (Boston College), for talking through so many of these ideas—and particularly for helping me think more creatively about teaching through our work together in Leadership for Change and on mindful management, not to mention your friendship.

The mistakes and problems that remain, of course, remain mine. The good stuff I owe to you all and many others.

To my son Benjamin Waddock Wiegner, I give thanks for being, for talking, for challenging, and for all the love he gives. This one's for you, Ben.

PART ONE

A Context for Leading Corporate Citizens

CHAPTER 1

Corporate Global Citizenship:

VISION, VALUES, VALUE ADDED[1]

I want to challenge you to join me in taking our relationship to a still higher level. I propose to that you [corporate leaders] . . . and we, the United Nations, initiate a global compact of shared values and principles, which will give a human face to the global market.

Globalization is a fact of life. But I believe we have underestimated its fragility. The problem is this. The spread of markets outpaces the ability of societies and their political systems to adjust to them, let alone to guide the course they take. History teaches us that such an imbalance between the economic, social and political realms can never be sustained for very long. . . .

We have to choose between a global market driven only by calculations of short-term profit, and one which has a human face. Between a world which condemns a quarter of the human race to starvation and squalor, and one which offers everyone at least a chance of prosperity, in a healthy environment. Between a selfish free-for-all in which we ignore the fate of the losers, and a culture in which the strong and successful accept their responsibilities, showing global vision and leadership.

—KOFI ANNAN, SECRETARY-GENERAL, UNITED NATIONS

CORPORATIONS ARE CITIZENS OF THE WORLD

When corporate activities transcend national boundaries, as those of many corporations do today, it is increasingly clear that they exert multiple influences on local conditions. In return, corporations are influenced by those local conditions. Because many corporations, particularly transnational corporations, have great wealth and access to enormous resources, sometimes in excess of that of entire smaller nations, they wield great power. It is this power that draws the attention of critics and friends alike. This power makes it imperative that firms operate with integrity with respect to all of their stakeholders and that there be a balance among the economic, political, and civil sectors of society if the health of all is to be sustained. Kofi Annan makes this very clear in the opening paragraphs of this chapter.[2]

Too often managers forget this reality as they attempt to grow the bottom line or the top line. Yet the typically unrecognized reality is that corporations—all organizations, in fact—are built on the basis of the corporations' relationships with those who can affect or are affected by the company and the operating practices corporations develop to achieve business results. These relationships with employees, customers, owners, suppliers, local communities, governments—that is, the company's stakeholders[3]—and the treatment of the natural environment can make or break a company in the modern world.

Citizenship, corporate and individual, cannot be separated from the day-to-day operating practices that structure stakeholder relationships for companies. Corporate citizenship is an integral part of the whole corporation as it exists in whole communities and whole societies, with whole people operating within. Corporations, as the last statement makes clear, are what Ken Wilber termed "holons"; that is, both wholes in and of themselves and parts of something larger. As holons, they are embedded in and affect the web of relationships that constitute societies, just as biological systems are also interrelated webs.[4] Or as Chris Marsden and Jörg Andriof recently argued:

> Corporate citizenship needs to be perceived not as a bolt-on activity but as something which pervades the whole of a company's operations. It should also be seen not always as a business cost, a trade-off against additional profits, but more often as a significant contributor to long-term business success and entirely coincident with the goal of profit maximisation.[5]

The embeddedness of corporations in society, their existence as socially constructed holons in economic, political, and societal contexts, means that increasingly careful attention needs to be given to the role of corporations as global citizens. Being a corporate global citizen implies that companies must understand themselves in all three contexts, that is, as global entities, as corporations, and as citizens. Specifically, corporations are:

GLOBAL. Corporations increasingly operate in diverse national and local contexts, cultures, and political landscapes, with a diverse array of peoples whose basic human dignity demands respect.

CORPORATE. Corporations are legal entities granted a social contract or charter by the societies within which they operate, which can (theoretically) be revoked by those societies if the "public" responsibilities of the corporation are not met.

CITIZENS. As citizens, corporations are members of a state or polity with explicit duties and responsibilities to the stakeholders that exist within its societal holon which need to be met if the corporation is to sustain its charter and retain its privileges and rights.

Corporate citizenship by these definitions, then, involves more than meeting the discretionary responsibilities of philanthropy, volunteerism, and otherwise doing "social good." This broad understanding of citizenship means paying attention to operating policies and practices, to outcomes and implications of corporate activities, and developing a "living" set of policies, practices, and programs that help a company achieve its vision and values. The following definition of corporate responsibility and corporate global citizenship will guide us throughout this book:

> Good corporate citizens live up to clear constructive visions and core values. They treat well the entire range of stakeholders who risk capital in, have an interest in, or are linked to the firm through primary and secondary impacts through developing respectful, mutually beneficial operating practices and by working to maximize sustainability of the natural environment.

Given this definition, let's start with a proposition: The fundamental purposes of the corporation include *but go far beyond* generating shareholder wealth. Indeed, wealth and profits are simply important by-products of the firm's efforts to create a product or service for customers that adds sufficient value so that customers are willing to pay for it. These goods and services are produced through the good offices of employees, managers, suppliers, and allies, using a wide range of forms of capital.

Capital of course includes financial resources supplied by the owners or shareholders. Equally important, "capital" encompasses not only the intellectual and human capital provided by employees, but also gaining customer trust and loyalty that products or services will meet expectations and add value, which is a form of social capital. In today's world of strategic and cross-sector alliances and supplier partnerships, there is also a form of social capital required within business relationships. Further, capital includes the infrastructure and social relations supplied by the communities where the company is located, and the social contract written or unwritten by a range of local, state, and national governments that have provided the social—and legal—basis on which the firm's existence is premised.

All of these "capitals" are supplied to the firm by stakeholders. A *stakeholder,* generally, is any individual or group who is affected by or can affect an organization.[6] We will discuss what stakeholding means in significant detail below.

Despite the prevailing idea that the purpose of the firm is to maximize shareholder wealth (and it is absolutely essential that companies *do* produce wealth to survive), corporations are considerably more than profit-maximizing efficiency machines because of their numerous impacts. Corporations are inherently and inextricably embedded in a *web of relationships,* relationships with stakeholders, that create the context in which they do business, that establish the vision for achieving their purposes, and that enable the productive activity of the enterprise to be successfully accomplished. Without these stakeholders, the corporation cannot survive nor can it begin to make a profit, never mind maximize profits. Indeed, we could make the argument, as this book does, that the corporation is nothing more and nothing less than constituted of its primary relationships.

Profits Are a By-Product . . .

Therefore, we begin with this premise: Profits are essential to corporate success and indeed survival. Profits are critical to sustaining democratic capitalism, but they are a by-product of the many relationships on which a corporation or any other organization depends for its legitimacy, power, resources, and all kinds of capital investments. This perspective, which differs from the perspective of traditional economics about the firm (which says that the one and only purpose of a firm is to maximize profits or shareholder wealth), is called the stakeholder capitalism concept of the firm.

In this stakeholder view, stakeholder relationships and the operating practices (policies, processes, and procedures) that support those relationships are the basis of corporate global citizenship. Much is being written about corporate global citizenship these days. In 1997, for example, the Hitachi Foundation produced a report called *Global Corporate Citizenship—Rationale and Strategies,* authored by David Logan, Delwin Roy, and Laurie Regelbrugge, which provides a rationale for how companies should act responsibly in the global arena. In this report, corporate citizenship is defined as follows:

> Today the phrase leading companies are using to define their relationship with the wider society is "corporate citizenship." It implies a responsibility to provide useful goods and services while operating legally, acting ethically, and having concern for the public good. Corporate citizenship is a multifaceted concept that brings together the self-interest of business and its stakeholders with the interests of society more generally.[7]

This broadly focused approach means that corporate citizenship actually goes way beyond traditional arenas of philanthropy, partnership, and strategic community relations. Although citizenship is commonly identified with partnership with nongovernmental or social agencies around "social" issues, or with community involvement that has a strategic business purpose such as volunteer or in-kind giving programs, it is indeed much more expansive in its scope.[8] For example, one approach to corporate citizenship, as well as to corporate "social" responsibility, takes the perspective that the social responsibilities—and by extension, citizenship activities—are discretionary for the firm, to be met only when more fundamental issues of economic, legal, and ethical responsibilities have been met.[9]

The dominant interpretation of the neoclassical economics model suggests that the corporation should maximize wealth for one stakeholder, the owners or shareholders. Conformance to existing law and meeting ethical responsibilities come next, especially in the view of neoclassical economist Milton Friedman. In his classic article attacking the concept of social responsibility, "The Social Responsibility of Business Is to Make a Profit," Friedman stated:

> [T]he doctrine of "social responsibility" taken seriously would extend the scope of the political mechanism to every human activity. It does not differ in philosophy from the most explicitly collectivist doctrine. It differs only in professing to believe that collectivist ends can be attained without collectivist means. That is why in my book *Capitalism and Freedom,* I have called it a "fundamentally subversive doc-

trine" in a free society, and have said that in such a society, "there is one and only one social responsibility of business—to use its resources and engage in activities designed to increase its profits so long as it stays within the rules of the game, which is to say, engages in open and free competition without deception or fraud."[10]

The basis for the assertion by Friedman and other economists that shareholders are the only important stakeholder is that owners have taken a risk with their investments in the firm and thus are owed a profit. But this view is arguably too constricted to be useful in today's world where it is increasingly recognized that other stakeholders are equally important to the survival and success of the firm and that they too make significant investments in the welfare of the firm.

Recent thinking about corporate citizenship has significantly broadened in scope, recognizing that citizenship inherently involves the rights and duties of membership. Chris Marsden and Jörg Andriof of the University of Warwick, in the United Kingdom, summarized this perspective:

> As Peter Drucker [said] . . . citizenship is more than just a legal term, it is a political term. "As a political term citizenship means active commitment. It means responsibility. It means making a difference in one's community, one's society, one's country." Drucker might have added, in today's global economy, "one's world." Good corporate citizenship, therefore, is about understanding and managing an organisation's influences on and relationships with the rest of society in a way that minimises the negative and maximises the positive.[11]

This book, therefore, will focus on broadening your understanding of the risks, ties, and investments in the firm made by a broad range of stakeholders, encompassing owners but going well beyond them as companies attempt to live out their responsibilities through their operating practices. *Operating practices* are the policies, procedures, and processes that companies develop to implement their day-to-day business activities and relate to their stakeholders, both internal and external. These operating practices are developed with respect to stakeholders and as they exist in relationship not only to the economic sector of society, but also to the political and civil sectors as well. The book will also focus on the rewards inherent in developing relationships with stakeholders based on mutual respect, dignity, and constructive values as opposed to merely exerting power or influence over them.

Stakes and Stakeholders

Let's start by considering the definition of a stake and therefore a stakeholder, one who holds a stake, in more detail. The word "stake" can have one of three different general meanings, each representing a different type of relationship between the stakeholder and the entity in which a stake exists. A *stake* is, among other definitions, a *claim* of some sort—for example, a claim of ownership based on a set of expectations related to principles of ethics, such as legal or moral rights, justice or fairness, the greatest good for the greatest number, or the principle of care. These ethical bases will be explored further in Chapter 4.

Claim
) Investment
) Bond

Second, a stake can signify that a stakeholder has made an *investment,* thereby putting some sort of capital at *risk.*[12] In this usage, a stake is an interest or a share in some enterprise or activity, a prize as in a horse race, a share or perhaps a grubstake for which the provider expects a return for the risk taken. Typically, the type of risk under consideration relates specifically to the type of capital invested. Thus, for example, owners invest financial capital in the firm, while communities may invest *social capital*—or relationships built upon trust and association—in the firm's local presence or create infrastructure to support the firm's activities. Employees invest their human capital, their knowledge, and their intellectual energies, all forms of "capital," in the firm. Customers invest their trust as part of the firm's franchise and hence their willingness to continue to purchase the goods and services produced by the firm. Suppliers may invest in specific technology, equipment, or infrastructure so that they can enhance their relationship to the firm over time and make the bonds tighter.

This brings us to the third meaning of stake embedded in stakeholder relationships: a *bond* of some sort, such as a tie or tether, something that creates *linkages* between two entities, such as tangible linkages that bind two (or more) entities together (e.g., contracts or long-term relationships for purchasing supplies) or intangible linkages such as emotional ties or loyalty. Bonds can come about because of some tangible or intangible investment or risk taken by the stakeholder in a specific enterprise or activity, which then creates an ongoing relationship. Alternatively, an intangible bond can come about because a stakeholder *identifies* in some way with the organization and therefore feels an association with the organization that potentially creates one of the other types of stakes, a claim or a risk.[13] The box below summarizes the previous discussion.

The Bases of Stakeholding

Stake as:	Stake is based on:
• Claim	• Legal or moral right
	• Consideration of justice/fairness
	• Utility (greatest good for the greatest number)
	• Care
• Risk	• Investment of capital including
1. Owner	1. Financial capital
2. Community	2. Social/infrastructure capital
3. Employee	3. Knowledge/intellectual/human capital
4. Customer	4. Franchise (trust) capital
5. Supplier	5. Technological, infrastructure capital
• Bonds (tether, tie)	• Identification (process)
• Each type of stake creates a relationship that, when constructive and positive, is:	• Mutual
	• Interactive
	• Consistent over time
	• Interdependent

Stakeholder Relationships

Notice that each of the types of stakes identified above creates a *relationship* between the stakeholder and the organization in which there is a stake.[14] For example, owners are clearly stakeholders. The stakeholder-owner, who makes an investment thereby creates a relationship with the organization in which the investment is made. Similarly, the stakeholder who puts something at risk for possible benefit through an enterprise creates a relationship with that enterprise, as communities do when they invest in local infrastructure such as roads, sewers, and other local services that support a firm's activities. Bonds of identity also create ongoing relationships. The important point, then, is that whichever meaning we use to define a stake, being a stakeholder creates an ongoing and interactive relationship between the stakeholder and enterprise or activity in which one has a stake.[15] The stakeholder perspective conceives of the firm inherently as a set of linkages among stakeholders, a network of relationships.[16]

Stakeholder relationships also create a boundary around managerial responsibilities so that corporations do not have to become responsible for all of the problems of society, but only for those that they create or those that affect them. Thus, when we think about corporate responsibility, we can think of it in terms of the *public responsibility of managers,* which is limited to the areas of primary and secondary involvement of their enterprises.[17] The principle of public responsibility, which was developed by scholars Lee Preston and James Post, comes about in part because companies are granted "charters" to incorporate by the states in which they are established and in part as a result of the impacts that companies have on their various constituencies. It also is a result of the fact that corporations, indeed all organizations, are part of and intersect with other aspects of society.

The scope of managers' public responsibilities is quite wide given the resources that companies, particularly multinational companies, command and the resulting power they hold. According to Preston and Post, management's responsibilities are limited by the organization's primary and secondary involvement, both of which contain stakeholders to whom the firm must pay attention if it hopes to succeed. Primary involvement arenas are related to the primary mission and purpose of the firm as attempts to live out its vision in society. Thus, "Primary involvement relationships, tested and mediated through the market mechanism, are essential to the existence of the organization over time."[18]

Primary involvement arenas are those that affect *primary stakeholders,* that is, those stakeholders without whom the company cannot stay in business.[19] For most companies, primary stakeholders include owners, customers, employees (at least in virtual organizations), suppliers, and allies. Although some people believe that the environment is a stakeholder because it supplies the raw materials necessary to the company's existence,[20] we will take the perspective that *the environment is an essential underpinning to all human civilization,* an underpinning that needs to be healthy for human civilization to survive.[21]

But managerial public responsibilities do not end with primary involvement arenas; they extend also to arenas of *secondary involvement,* which includes those arenas and relationships that affect or are affected by the firm's activities. *Secondary stakeholders,* by extension, are those who affect or are affected by the company's activities in an indirect or by-product way. Secondary stakeholders may not be in direct transactions with the corporation or necessary to its survival, but because they can impact the firm or are affected by the firm's activities, it is important that the needs and interests of secondary stakeholders be taken into consideration in much the way that those of primary stakeholders are.[22] Thus, the governments that create the rules of the game by which companies operate, as well as the communities that supply the local infrastructure on which companies depend, can be considered secondary stakeholders.

Stakeholders interact with—or in the case of primary stakeholders actually constitute—organizations; that is, they are in relationship to an organization or company. Thus, for example, activists may attempt to influence corporate environmental policy but may not be in a position to put the company out of business, making them secondary stakeholders. Similarly, towns and cities located downstream from a company may feel the impact of its polluting a river that flows through, and in this way they are secondary stakeholders. Firms ignore these impacts at their peril because, as the next section suggests, such secondary stakeholders can be demanding or dangerous when their needs are urgent, when for a variety of reasons they have power, or when they are awakened into action if they have been inactive (dormant). Figure 1.1 shows the interrelationships of primary and secondary stakeholders of the corporation.

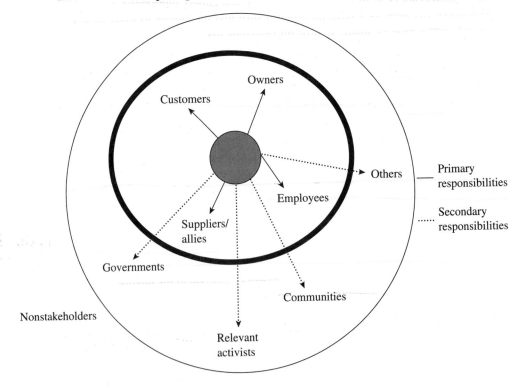

FIGURE 1.1.   Primary and Secondary Stakeholders of the Corporation

Stakeholder Status

What is it that gives stakeholders their status as stakeholders and how can managers determine how important or salient a given stakeholder actually is to a company? Ronald Mitchell, Brad Agle, and Donna Wood have provided a model that helps with this determination.[23] They identified three primary bases from which stakeholders can potentially operate: *power,* which is based on stakeholders' capacity to influence the firm's behavior (or be influenced by the firm's behavior); *legitimacy,* which is based on contract, exchange, legal title, legal right, moral right, at-risk status, or moral interest in the harms and benefits of a company's actions; and *urgency,* which is based on compelling demands. When none of these attributes is present, the party is not considered to be a stakeholder.

Stakeholders having all three attributes are called *core* or *definitive stakeholders;* primary stakeholders generally fall into this category. Stakeholders who have legitimacy and power are termed dominant stakeholders though there is no particular urgency to their claim, interest, or relationship. Employees would be in this category if relationships with them were good, as would suppliers, communities, governments, and of course owners. Given an urgent situation that demands attention, any one of these stakeholders quickly becomes definitive, demanding corporate attention. Stakeholders with power and urgency are called *dangerous* or *coercive stakeholders,* because they have an urgent cause and the power to exert their will upon the corporation or make significant demands upon it (e.g., an activist group picketing outside the gates). Finally, stakeholders with legitimacy and urgency, but not power, are termed *dependent stakeholders* because they depend upon others with power (e.g., governments, courts, or unions) to make their voice heard to the corporation (e.g., the victims of an oil tanker spill like that of the *Exxon Valdez*). The box below indicates how stakeholder status can shift over time.

It is clear that businesses need to pay attention consistently over time to the policies and relationships that they develop with primary stakeholders. Some stakeholders, on the other hand, have only one attribute present and thus may not be perceived as important to the firm. But managers might also want to pay attention to some of

---

Airline Rage and the Internet Shift Stakeholder Status

An example can illustrate not only how important it is for companies to pay attention to the demands of stakeholders, but also how they can shift over time. Airline passengers frequently feel ill treated by the airline companies, resulting in feelings of frustration, resentment, and anger, but in the past they had little impact on the behavior of the airlines. Although passengers were core to the airline companies' existence, the airlines perhaps saw them as having urgency and even legitimacy but very little power. The advent of the Internet has changed that situation dramatically. Numerous websites have been developed that create vehicles through which passenger complaints can be forwarded to the Federal Aviation Authority, which regulates the airline industry. Especially as information technology advances, it is clear that companies will find it hard and harder to "write off" stakeholders.

—MELISSA BAUCUS, *Xavier University*

these secondary stakeholders. Stakeholders with one attribute are classified as either dormant (i.e., having only power, which may be unused unless circumstances warrant, such as the media), discretionary (i.e., having only legitimacy, such as beneficiaries of a firm's philanthropy), or demanding (i.e., having only urgency, such as a disgruntled former employee or a terrorist).

Corporate Responsibility and Citizenship

Taking a practice-based stakeholder view of the corporation significantly alters the approach to the firm and its responsibilities, broadening the understanding of those to whom a firm is accountable. It moves the conversation directly toward the quality and nature of the *relationships* that companies develop with stakeholders and the assessment of the impacts of corporate activities on those stakeholders. Such a perspective moves our thinking away from a largely descriptive and even instrumental (or usefulness) perspective on stakeholder relationships. We move in this book toward a more normative model[24]—that is, a model of the way, in the best of worlds, stakeholder relationships *ought* to be, as the quotation in the chapter opening by Kofi Annan, Secretary General of the United Nations, suggests.

In support of this perspective, the Business Roundtable (BRT), a major association for business leaders, issued a "Statement on Corporate Responsibility" as long ago as 1980, even before the term "stakeholder" itself became popularized. In this statement, the BRT argued that "it is clear that a large percentage of the public now measures corporations by a yardstick beyond strictly economic objectives."[25]

BRT and later theorists about corporate responsibility and stakeholder theory argued that in addition to returning profits and wealth to shareholders, corporations had allegiances to other constituencies, which we now call stakeholders: "Corporations operate within a web of complex, often competing relationships which demand the attention of corporate managers."[26] Among the stakeholders to whom the BRT says managers must pay attention are customers, employees, communities, suppliers, and society at large as well as, of course, shareholders.

Indeed, the *corporation* can be defined as consisting of a system of primary stakeholder groups,[27] or, alternatively, a corporation is simply a network of relationships with stakeholders. Customers, employees, owners, and suppliers are stakeholders that would be classified as primary stakeholders. Notably, without any one of these stakeholders, the corporation would cease to exist, hence it is undeniably embedded in this web of relationships. Managers who understand the critical importance of sustaining healthy and positive relationships with all of these stakeholders, as well as others specific to the individual organization, can readily make the link to understanding corporate responsibility more broadly than do neoclassical economists, who chose to focus solely on the owner-stakeholder. In the words of the BRT, which are even truer today when the impact of businesses frequently has global scope:

> [The corporation's] economic responsibility is by no means incompatible with other corporate responsibilities in society. In contemporary society all corporate responsibilities are so interrelated that they should not and cannot be separated.

The issue is one of defining, and achieving, responsible corporate management which fully integrates into the entire corporate planning, management, and decision-making process consideration of the impacts of all operating and policy decisions on each of the corporation's constituents. Responsibility to all these constituents *in toto* constitutes responsibility to society, making the corporation both an economically and socially viable entity. Business and society have a symbiotic relationship: The long-term viability of the corporation depends upon its responsibility to the society of which it is a part. And the well-being of society depends upon profitable and responsible business enterprises.[28]

In other words, responsible leaders and mangers cannot operate with blinders on with respect to the impacts that their actions have on any and all of their stakeholders, especially if they hope to do well over the long term. Gaining the respect and commitment of employees, customers, suppliers, communities, and relevant government officials, as well as owners, is essential to productivity and performance. Because corporations are part of and interdependent with the communities and societies in which they operate, they need to actively engage with their stakeholders. Maintaining positive stakeholder relationships involves establishing constructive and positive relationships with them, and being constantly aware of both the status and health of each stakeholder group, if they hope to succeed long term. These relationships, then, are the essence of corporate global (or local) citizenship.

Interactive and Dialogue-Based Stakeholder Relations, Not Management

Respect for the "other" in any relationship is at the heart of good stakeholder relations. While it is frequently true that companies have a great deal of power because they command significant resources, they still need to recognize the importance of maintaining good relationships with their stakeholders to experience outstanding long-term performance. Recent research, for example, shows that when companies score highly in *Fortune*'s reputational ratings, they are also consistently high performers with respect to their primary stakeholders.[29] Further, companies that are more responsible also appear to perform better financially, thus creating a virtuous circle.[30]

Reactive Stance

Companies' stakeholder relationships can evolve in one of three ways: reactively, proactively, or interactively.[31] When companies or their managers act reactively, they may not be paying very much attention to what is going on outside the company's boundaries. When they are in a reactive mode, companies may deny their responsibility for establishing and maintaining positive policies toward stakeholders, engage in legal battles to avoid responsibility, or do the bare minimum to meet the letter but not the spirit of the law.[32] Reaction puts the company and its managers on the defensive, rather than in a more positive mode. Because managers have failed to anticipate problems from stakeholders, they may find themselves wondering how things evolved in such a negative fashion.

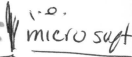

i.e.
micro suft

Proactive Stance

Better, but probably still insufficient to establish truly positive stakeholder relationships, is the stance that companies sometimes take when they work to proactively anticipate issues arising from external stakeholders. They may do this by establishing one of any number of "boundary-spanning functions" to cope with their external relations.

Boundary-spanning functions are those that cross organizational boundaries, either internally or externally, and attempt to develop and maintain relationships with one or more stakeholder groups. For example, modern multinational corporations typically will have at least some of the following functions: public affairs, community relations, public relations, media relations, investor relations, employee relations, government relations, lobbyists, union relations, environmental officers, issues management, and in one recent instance, a vice president for corporate responsibility. The traditional approach to attempting to "manage" stakeholders implied by the Mitchell, Agle, Wood framework discussed earlier is more compatible with the reactive and proactive stances than with the emerging approach to *developing relationships* with stakeholders through dialogue and mutual engagement implied by the interactive stance discussed next.

Interactive Stance

Even a proactive stance with respect to stakeholders falls short of the ideal unless the company's boundary-spanning functions are managed interactively and with respect for the claims, risks, and bonds that stakeholders have. Stakeholders, as we have noted, exist in relationship to the firm, embedded in a network that makes them interdependent to some extent on the firm while the firm is interdependent on them for its success. Thus, arguably the firm's best stance to show ongoing respect for its stakeholders is a mutual and interactive one that is consistent over time and that acknowledges both the mutuality of the relationship and the interdependence of the two entities.

Such constructive and positive relationships between organizations and their stakeholders are built upon a framework of *interaction, mutual respect,* and *dialogue,* as opposed to "management" or dominance. That is, progressive companies no longer attempt to "manage" or dominate their stakeholders. Rather, they have recognized the importance of engaging with them in a relationship based on respect and dialogue or talking *with* each other, rather than talking *at* or *to* each other, which can be more one-sided. Building this relationship is not a state or a one-time thing, but a long-term evolving *process* that requires commitment, energy, a willingness to admit mistakes, and capacity to change when problems arise.

Sustaining—or even fully implementing—such a complete set of principles and maintaining ongoing dialogues with stakeholders to support the principles in a complex and tension-filled world is incredibly difficult. Arguably, having a guiding vision underpinned by values is a critical key to long-term success, not only for the corporations, but also for the societies in which they operate. Developing and implementing visions guided by positive end values means focusing on balancing the

Leading Citizen: Royal Dutch Shell and the Dialogue Process

One company that has embarked on a significant effort to develop such a dialogue with its stakeholders is the Royal Dutch/Shell Group.[33] Perhaps because Shell got into somewhat serious reputational difficulties around the sinking of the Brent Spar 40-story-high oil platform in the North Atlantic and the execution of activists in Nigeria, the company has established a whole series of operating principles and interactive dialogues with key stakeholder groups. These problems threatened Shell's legitimacy as a company. Rather than acting reactively or even proactively, Shell has responded interactively, by attempting to establish ongoing dialogue with stakeholders affected by company activities. In addition, the company has articulated a clear set of standards and principles that illustrate the values in which it believes. The company appears to be making a sincere effort to forward the idea that there need not be a trade-off between principles—or values—such as treating stakeholders well and making money.

In *Profits and Principles—Does There Have to Be a Choice?*[34] a first-ever report on its internal transformation to attempt to become stakeholder-friendly, Royal Dutch/Shell sets forth nine principles that the company expects managers to live up to and that define the dialogical process the company hopes to establish with its stakeholder groups (see Table 1.1).

Shell is far from perfect, and indeed the business—oil—within which it operates, is itself problematic as a limited ecological resource from an environmentalist perspective. Further, the process of implementing these principles is only at its beginning. Nonetheless, the principles articulated reflect a clear vision and set of guiding principles. The principles identify a philosophy that appears to underpin a genuine effort—necessary to achieving good global citizenship—to articulate, define, and then systematically implement a guiding vision and set of core values on which the company's relationships with its numerous stakeholders can rest. Such an internal examination, which needs to be undertaken by managers who are themselves visionary and personally aware, is a critical first step toward achieving citizenship.

For these reasons, Royal Dutch/Shell's principles are worth reviewing, as is Shell Group's ongoing struggle to implement them broadly in its diversified and dispersed enterprise (see Table 1.1). Further information on Royal Dutch/Shell's initiatives in this respect can be found at the company's website: http://www.shell.com/. See especially the "Tell Shell" e-mail facility meant to enhance stakeholder dialogue.

TABLE 1.1.   Principles Articulated by Royal Dutch/Shell Group

Principle 1: Objectives
The objectives of the Shell companies are to engage efficiently, responsibly, and profitably in the oil, gas, chemicals, and other selected businesses and to participate in the search for and development of other sources of energy. Shell companies seek a high standard of performance and aim to maintain a long-term position in their respective competitive environments.

Principle 2: Responsibilities
Shell companies recognize five areas of responsibility:
To shareholders. To protect shareholders' investment, and provide an acceptable return.
To customers. To win and maintain customers by developing and providing products and services which offer value in terms of price, quality, safety, and environmental impact, which are supported by the requisite technological, environmental, and commercial expertise.

TABLE 1.1.   Continued.

To employees. To respect the human rights of their employees, to provide their employees with good and safe conditions of work, and good and competitive terms and conditions of service, to promote the development and best use of human talent and equal opportunity and employment, and to encourage the involvement of employees in the planning and direction of their work, and in the application of these principles within their company. It is recognized that commercial success depends on the full commitment of all employees.

To those with whom they do business. To seek mutually beneficial relationships with contractors, suppliers, and joint ventures and to promote the application of these principles in so doing. The ability to promote these principles effectively will be an important factor in the decision to enter into or remain in such relationships.

To society. To conduct business as responsible corporate members of society, to observe the laws of the countries in which they operate, to express support for fundamental human rights in line with the legitimate role of business and to give proper regard to health, safety, and the environment consistent with their commitment to contribute to sustainable development.

These five areas are seen as inseparable. Therefore, it is the duty of management to continuously assess the priorities and discharge its responsibilities as best it can on the basis of that assessment.

Principle 3: Economic Principles

Profitability is essential to discharging these responsibilities and staying in business. It is a measure both of efficiency and of the value that customers place on Shell products and services. It is essential to the allocation of the necessary corporate resources and to support the continuing investment required to develop and produce future energy supplies to meet consumer needs. Without profits and a strong financial foundation, it would not be possible to fulfil the responsibilities outlined above.

Shell companies work in a wide variety of changing social, political, and economic environments, but in general they believe that the interests of the community can be served most efficiently by a market economy.

Criteria for investment decisions are not exclusively economic in nature but also take into account social and environmental considerations and an appraisal of the security of the investment.

Principle 4: Business Integrity

Shell companies insist on honesty, integrity, and fairness in all aspects of their business and expect the same in relationships with all those with whom they do business. The direct or indirect offer, payment, soliciting, and acceptance of bribes in any form are unacceptable practices. Employees must avoid conflicts of interest between their private financial activities and their part in the conduct of company business. All transactions on behalf of a Shell company must be accurately and fairly in the accounts of the company in accordance with established procedures and must be subject to audit.

Principle 5: Political Activities

Of companies. Shell companies act in a socially responsible manner within the laws of the countries in which they operate in pursuit of their legitimate commercial objectives.

Shell companies do not make payments to political parties, organisations, or their representatives or take any part in politics. However, when dealing with governments, Shell companies have the right and the responsibility to make their position known on any matter which affects themselves, their employees, their customers, or their shareholders. They also have the right to make their position known on matters affecting the community where they have a contribution to make.

Of employees. Where individuals wish to engage in activities in the community, including standing for election to public office, they will be given the opportunity to do so where this is appropriate in the light of local circumstances.

Principle 6: Health, Safety, and the Environment
Consistent with their commitment to contribute to sustainable development, Shell companies have a
systematic approach to health, safety, and environmental management in order to achieve continuous
performance improvement.
To this end, Shell companies manage these matters as any other critical business activity, set targets for
improvement, and appraise and report on performance.

Principle 7: The Community
The most important contribution that companies can make to the social and material progress of the
countries in which they operate is in performing their basic activities as effectively as possible. In addition,
Shell companies take a constructive interest in societal matters which may not be directly related to the
business. Opportunities for involvement—for example, through community, educational, or donations
programmes—will vary depending upon the size of the company concerned, the nature of the local society,
and the scope for useful private initiatives.

Principle 8: Competition
Shell companies support free enterprise. They seek to compete fairly and ethically and within the framework
of applicable competition laws; they will not prevent others from competing freely with them.

Principle 9: Communications
Shell companies recognise that, in view of the importance of the activities in which they engage and their
impact on national economies and individuals, open communication is essential. To this end, Shell
companies have comprehensive corporate information programmes and provide full relevant information
about their activities to legitimately interested parties, subject to any overriding considerations of business
confidentiality and cost.

Source: Royal Dutch/Shell Group, *Profits and Principles—Does There Have to Be a Choice? The Shell Report 1998* (London, 1998).

interests of multiple stakeholders. These stakeholders are individuals and organizations operating in the economic sector, and also those stakeholders operating in two
other sectors, the political and civil or social sectors. In addition, companies face an
in creasing imperative to balance human stakeholders' interests with the need for a
healthy ecological environment.

LEADING CHALLENGES:
A NEW PARADIGM OF CORPORATE CITIZENSHIP

Fundamentally, corporate global citizenship cannot evolve into constructive stakeholder relationships without the active participation of effective, aware, and progressive leaders. Aware leaders have thought deeply about their own values and vision, as
companies themselves must do, by knowing what they stand for. As a result, they are
prepared for the complex world they must face. Being prepared won't necessarily

lessen the complexity or the difficulty of decisions. But awareness does help leaders make the right decisions when challenges are high, as they inevitably are in a complex social and political environment. Particularly in an era when activists and other stakeholders can mobilize nearly instantaneously and globally, awareness of and response to the demands of leading a corporate citizen is a must. In effect, this mobilization is what happened in 1999 in Seattle when activists disrupted the World Trade Organization from meeting.

That is the goal of this book: to help leading citizens understand the real world of complex dilemmas that leaders face, to help them understand the multiple perspectives that are embedded in every decision, and to build awareness of the impacts and implications of each of those decisions on the people—the stakeholders—whom they affect.

A Context for Leading Corporate Citizens

The first three chapters, including this one, explore the context in which businesses operate today. In the next chapter, we will look at the spheres of human civilization as they are built upon a healthy ecological environment. In Chapter 3 we will continue to explore the interrelationship of the corporation as it exists within the economic sphere with organizations and enterprises that exist in the political and civil or societal spheres of activity in human civilization.

Leading Corporate Citizens
with Vision, Values, and Value Added

Mere understanding of the need for balance among the spheres, however, is insufficient to guide organizations successfully. Both individuals and organizations need clear and constructive visions embedded with what are here called constructive end values to get the kinds of value-added that sustain a business over time. Successful leaders develop personal vision and awareness, growing intellectually, emotionally, and morally so that they can cope with the complexity and challenges of the global business arena. Higher levels of individual and organizational awareness and development, ongoing learning, and empowerment are also necessary for organizations to succeed in the complexity of the modern world, as we shall see in Chapters 4 to 6. There we will explore the realities and linkages among vision (Chapter 4), values (Chapter 5), and value-added (Chapter 6).

Leading Corporate Citizens and Their Stakeholders

Chapters 7 to 9 provide significant evidence that developing positive operating practices with respect to multiple stakeholders is likely to be the key to organizational success in the future. We will explore relationships with stakeholders directly by assessing the links companies create with their many stakeholders so they can get to value-added (Chapter 7). Then we will explore how an emphasis on multiple bottom lines rather than a single bottom line can be productive (Chapter 8). In taking this approach, we will learn not only that the "soft stuff" is really the "hard stuff," but also that it can be and is being measured.

We will explore the ways in which operating with integrity adds value—and values—to business enterprise through living up to articulated visions as well as established codes promoting respect and human dignity (Chapter 8). In Chapter 9 we will assess the "ecology" of global citizenship, exploring the implications of corporate activities on both the natural environment and sustainability, and moving toward an understanding of what a broader awareness of the impact of economic activities on the environment means for long-term economic development. The intersection of the knowledge economy, blurring of boundaries with increased technological connectivity, and need for respecting human dignity will serve as a foundation for this exploration.

Leading Corporate Citizens into the Future

The exploration of vision, values, and value-added provides a framework for businesses to operate with integrity amid complexity and change, that is, living up to codes of conduct and emerging standards globally (Chapter 10) and operating with values-added (Chapter 11), rather than in a purposely value-neutral stance. Finally, we will focus on developing an integrated vision of what a new paradigm corporation would look like if it were fully implemented (Chapter 12). How and where would individuals fit in? How does this new paradigm organization look, feel, and act? How can we manage effectively and efficiently, doing the right thing and doing things right, for the future?

NOTES TO CHAPTER 1

1. Some of the thinking in this chapter owes a debt to my paper with Neil Smith, "Relationships: The Real Challenge of Corporate Global Citizenship," *Business and Society Review,* Spring 2000, 105(1): 47–62.
2. Kofi Annan, "Business and the U.N.: A Global Compact of Shared Values and Principles," World Economic Forum, Davos, Switzerland, January 31, 1999. Reprinted in *Vital Speeches of the Day* 65 (February 15, 1999), pp. 260–261. For further information on The Global Compact, see http://www.unglobalcompact.org/.
3. The classic reference is R. Edward Freeman's *Strategic Management: A Stakeholder Approach* (New York: Basic Books, 1984), and also William M. Evan, and R. Edward Freeman, "A Stakeholder Theory of the Modern Corporation: Kantian Capitalism," in *Ethical Theory and Business,* ed. by T. Beauchamp and N. Bowie (Englewood Cliffs, NJ: Prentice Hall, 1988). Max Clarkson identifies stakeholders as primary and secondary, depending on the level of risk they have taken with respect to the organization; see Max B. E. Clarkson, "A Stakeholder Framework for Analyzing and Evaluating Corporate Social Performance," *Academy of Management Review,* 20 (1995), pp. 1, 92–117.
4. See, for example, the works of Ken Wilber, *A Brief History of Everything* (Boston: Shambala Publications, 1996); *The Eye of Spirit: An Integral Vision for a World Gone Slightly Mad* (Boston: Shambala Publications, 1998); and *The Marriage of Sense and*

Soul: Integrating Science and Reason (New York: Random House, 1998). For a discussion of the web that constitutes life and the ways in which all matter is interrelated, see Fritjof Capra, *The Web of Life* (New York: Anchor Doubleday, 1995).

5. Chris Marsden and Jörg Andriof, "Towards an Understanding of Corporate Citizenship and How to Influence It," *Citizenship Studies* 2, no.2 (1980), pp. 329–30.

6. R. Edward Freeman, *Strategic Management: A Stakeholder Approach* (New York: Basic Books, 1984).

7. David Logan, Delwin Roy, and Laurie Regelbrugge, *Global Corporate Citizenship—Rationale and Strategies* (Washington, DC: The Hitachi Foundation, 1997), p. iii.

8. Indeed, Logan et al., *Global Corporate Citizenship,* take this very perspective, cited above.

9. See Archie B. Carroll, "A Three-Dimensional Conceptual Model of Corporate Social Performance," *Academy of Management Review* 4 (1979), pp. 497–505. Carroll more recently restated his perspective, expanding the model to global corporate citizenship in "The Four Faces of Corporate Citizenship," *Business and Society Review: Journal of the Center for Business Ethics at Bentley College,* 1–7, pp. 100–101.

10. Milton Friedman. "The Social Responsibility of a Business Is to Increase Its Profits," *New York Times Magazine,* September 13, 1970.

11. Chris Marsden and Jörg Andriof, "Towards an Understanding of Corporate Citizenship and How to Influence It," *Citizenship Studies* 2, no.2 (1980), pp. 329–30.

12. See Clarkson for an extended discussion of stakes; see also Ronald K. Mitchell, Bradley R. Agle, and Donna J. Wood, "Toward a Theory of Stakeholder Identification and Salience: Defining the Principle of Who and What Really Counts," *Academy of Management Review,* 22, no. 4 (October 1997), pp. 853–86.

13. For a perspective on this, see Tammy MacLean, "Creating Stakeholder Relationships: A Model of Organizational Social Identification—How the Southern Baptist Convention Became Stakeholders of Walt Disney," paper presented at the 1998 Annual Meeting of the Academy of Management, San Diego, CA.

14. Thanks are owed to Max B. E. Clarkson for providing a basis for thinking about corporate social performance in terms of stakeholder relationships. See his article, "A Stakeholder Framework for Analyzing and Evaluating Corporate Social Performance."

15. See, for example, R. Edward Freeman's *Strategic Management: A Stakeholder Approach* (New York: Basic Books, 1984); and Evan and Freeman, *A Stakeholder Theory of the Modern Corporation.* See also Clarkson, "A Stakeholder Framework for Analyzing and Evaluating Corporate Social Performance," pp. 92–117, and, more recently, Mitchell, Agle, and Wood, "Toward a Theory of Stakeholder Identification and Salience," pp. 853–86.

16. See Evan and Freeman, 1988.

17. The concepts of primary and secondary involvement come from Lee E. Preston and James E. Post's classic book, *Private Management and Public Policy: The Principle of Public Responsibility* (Englewood Cliffs, NJ: Prentice Hall, 1975).

18. Ibid., p. 95.

19. This is Clarkson's definition, p. 106; however, the distinction goes back to Freeman.

20. For example, Mark Starik, "Should Trees Have Managerial Standing? Toward Stakeholder Status for Non-Human Nature," *Journal of Business Ethics* 14 (1995), pp. 204–17.

21. See, for example, Robert A. Phillips and Joel Reichart, "The Environment as a Stakeholder? A Fairness Based Approach," *Journal of Business Ethics* 23 (January 2000), pp. 183–97.

22. Again, see Clarkson, p. 107.
23. Mitchell, Agle, and Wood, "Toward a Theory of Stakeholder Identification and Salience," pp. 853–86. Their model has been somewhat modified by Steven L. Wartick and Donna J. Wood in *International Business and Society* (Malden, MA: Blackwell Press, 1998) in the fashion incorporated into this discussion.
24. For background on descriptive, instrumental, and normative branches of stakeholder theory, see Thomas Donaldson and Lee E. Preston, "The Stakeholder Theory of the Corporation: Concepts, Evidence, and Implications," *Academy of Management Review* 20 (January 1995), pp. 1, 65–91.
25. See New York Business Roundtable, "The Business Roundtable, Statement on Corporate Responsibility," October 1981, p. 152. Thomas G. Marx, *Business and Society,* Economic, Moral, and Political Fundamental Text and Reading. Prentice-Hall. The term stakeholder entered the popular parlance in 1984 with the issuance of Freeman's seminal book *Strategic Management: A Stakeholder Approach,* cited above.
26. Business Roundtable, p. 153.
27. Clarkson, p. 110; see also Freeman, 1984.
28. Business Roundtable statement, cited in Marx, p. 157.
29. Note that this linkage is the basis of the instrumental argument for positive stakeholder relationships, as discussed by Donaldson and Preston, cited above.
30. See, for example, S. A. Waddock and S. B. Graves, "Quality of Management and Quality of Stakeholder Relations: Are They Synonymous?" *Business and Society* 36, no. 3 (September 1979), pp. 250–79, and Waddock and Graves, "The Corporate Social Performance—Financial Performance Link," *Strategic Management Journal* 18, no. 4, pp. 303–19.
31. See Preston and Post, *Private Management and Public Policy,* for a discussion of this framework.
32. See also Clarkson's "postures," which are different from those outlined here, p. 109.
33. For the story of this transformation, see Philip H. Mirvis, "Transformation at Shell: Commerce and Citizenship," *Business and Society Review* 105, no. 1 (January 2000), pp. 63–84.
34. Royal Dutch/Shell Group, *Profits and Principles—Does There Have to Be a Choice?* The Shell Report, London, 1998; see also www.shell.com.

CHAPTER 2

Spheres of Influence:

THE ECOLOGICAL UNDERPINNING

Even at present population levels, nearly a billion people go to bed hungry each night. Yet the soils on which we depend for food are being depleted faster than nature can regenerate them, and one by one the world's once most productive fisheries are collapsing from overuse. Water shortages have become pervasive, not simply from temporary droughts but also from depleted water tables and rivers taxed beyond their ability to regenerate. We hear of communities devastated by the exhaustion of their forests and fisheries and of people much like ourselves discovering that they and their children are being poisoned by chemical and radioactive contamination in the food they eat, the water they drink, and the earth on which they live and play.

As we wait for a technological miracle to resolve these apparent limits on continued economic expansion, some 88 million people are added to the world's population every year. Each new member of the human family aspires to a secure and prosperous share the planet's dwindling bounty. . . . Bear in mind that population projections are produced by demographers based only on assumptions about fertility rates. They take no account of what the planet can sustain. Given the environmental and social stresses created by current population levels, it is likely that if we do not voluntarily limit our numbers, famine, disease, and social breakdown will do it for us well before another doubling occurs.

—DAVID KORTON, *When Corporations Rule the World*

ECOLOGICAL BALANCE AND HUMAN CIVILIZATION

Modern business activities occur in an intensely, even hyper, competitive, and relatively newly globalized environment.[1] Change is considered to be a constant and there is ever-increasing pressure for enhanced productivity and performance. For businesses, growth and efficiency come by way of dog-eat-dog competition where the winner takes all in terms of market share and "maximized" profits for shareholders.

Without diminishing the importance of competition—and competitiveness—for corporate success, we can add another perspective. Consider that companies operate in a sphere or sector of activities we can call the economic sphere. This sphere has all of the imperatives of growth, efficiency, productivity, and competition inherent in the current capitalistic paradigm, which, with the fall of Communism and the rapid evolution of e-commerce, now is operating at some level in most free societies in the world. We know, however, that the economic sector cannot operate independent of society. The economic system is a creature of and created by society. And human civilization, of which economic activities are a part, depends upon a healthy natural environment or ecology.

There is more to society than its economic base. Living well—the "good life," by almost anyone's definition—has important elements of long-term sustainability in terms of community and ecological health. The need for balancing economic, social, and political interests—the three spheres of influence in human civilization—with ecological sustainability is becoming ever clearer as industrialization and development progress. Living the good life in the future may mean significant shifts in both our understanding of what that good life is and could be. Many "good conversations" on what the good life is are needed so we can begin to understand how the elements that comprise the civilized world can be brought together in better balance than has been achieved in the past century of industrialization. Very likely, the future will hold more emphasis on community, spirit and togetherness, meaningful work, and potentially less on production of material goods that are unsustainable at a global level so that the good life can be balanced equitably among all human societies.

Broadly speaking, human activities can be categorized into three main spheres. There is the *economic sphere,* where the production of goods and services occurs. Complementing and necessary to the economic sphere is the *political* or *public policy sphere,* which is the domain of governments that set the "rules of society" and at least in theory work toward the public interest at all levels. Then there is the *civil society sphere,* which encompasses the relationships and activities generated by families and friendship communities, associations, not-for-profit organizations, educational institutions, religious organizations, and other nongovernmental organizations (NGOs) in developing human civilization.

The success of any one of these sectors requires that there be an appropriate balance of power and interests among all of them as well with the ecological surround on which they depend. As will be discussed below, the imperatives and goals of each sector differ in important ways that influence how they relate to each other.

To complete this picture and provide for an integrated view of what is frequently called the "global village"—that is, the world of communities in which we all live and to which we are all connected—we must deeply understand the critical role of the *ecological* or *natural environment.* The ecological environment forms the essential foundation on which all else rests. Without the diversity inherent in the natural environment, without its sustaining resources, which provide raw materials for production, and without appropriate balance in human activities to protect those natural resources, industry and human society quite literally cannot sustain themselves.

In that sense we are dependent on this foundation of ecology and the web of life[2] that it supports for our very existence.

The Spheres of Activity

To summarize, there are three spheres of activity in human civilization—economic, political, and civil society underpinned by a natural environment or ecological surround. Together these spheres define human society. We will focus on the ecological surround in this chapter, and discuss the three spheres of human civilization in the next chapter:

ECONOMIC SPHERE. This sphere encompasses businesses and profit-generating enterprise, associated supplier relationships that produce the goods and services upon which human civilization depends.

POLITICAL OR PUBLIC POLICY SPHERE. This sphere encompasses governmental bodies at the local, state, national, regional, and global (international) levels that create the rules by which societies operate and establish what is meant within and between societies by the public interest.

CIVIL SOCIETY SPHERE. This sphere encompasses all other organized forms of activity, such as nongovernmental organizations (NGOs), nonprofit enterprise, schools, religious organizations, political organizations, families, and civic and societal enterprise and generates the civilizing relationships and sense of community that characterize human society. This sector is sometimes called the third or independent sector as well as civil society.

NATURAL OR ECOLOGICAL ENVIRONMENT. The environment underpins and supports all else, providing sources of raw materials for sustaining human civilization and healthy societies. A healthy ecology is essential to the long-term health of all of human civilization.

Each of these spheres (which will sometimes be called sectors) intersects and overlaps to some extent with all the others, hence they must be viewed together as a *system*, inextricably and unavoidably interwoven with one another. What happens in one sphere or sector inevitably affects what happens in all of the others. Global corporate citizenship needs to be understood as a system characterized by ecological interdependence and mutuality among entities operating in the different spheres, as Figure 2.1 indicates and which we will discuss in more detail below.

The Need for Balance

Just as nature requires a balance among elements to sustain any healthy ecological environment, so too must it be when we think about corporate global citizenship as part of the social ecology. Balance among the interests of all three important sectors

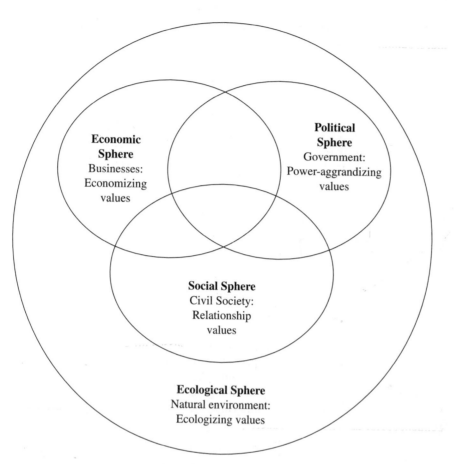

FIGURE 2.1.   Spheres of Influence: Economic, Political, Social, Ecological

of human civilization is a paramount concern. In sustaining this balance among sectors and with the natural world, we must also marry competition and competitiveness with cooperation and collaboration in the process that biologists call *symbiosis*. Competition *and* collaboration, with sustainability, are necessary and important to societal—and business—health and success. The physicist Fritjof Capra perhaps expressed it best:

> The recognition of symbiosis as a major evolutionary force has profound philosophical implications. All larger organisms [and organizations], including ourselves, are living testimonies to the fact that destructive practices do not work in the long run. In the end the aggressors always destroy themselves, making way for others who know how to cooperate and get along. Life is much less a competitive struggle for survival than a triumph of cooperation and creativity. Indeed, since the creation of the first nucleated cells, evolution has proceeded through ever more intricate arrangements of cooperation and coevolution.[3]

Mastering systems thinking, which we will consider in this chapter, is a critical element of creating continually improving and learning enterprises.[4] An integrative and systems approach is essential if we are to conceive of operating businesses, as well as governments and civil society enterprise, in sustainable ways, giving due consideration to the "seventh generation" out, as our Native American ancestors would have noted.

SYSTEMS THINKING: THE NEED TO INTEGRATE THE ENVIRONMENT

Western philosophy and science underpin the capitalist economic system in which much of the developed world lives today. Western science, including the "science" of economics, tends to approach its subjects by taking them apart and reducing them to their smallest elements. Once the smallest elements or fragments have been understood and taken apart, the Western approach hopes to reintegrate the pieces and thereby figure out how the integrated whole works. This approach derives from thinkers like René Descartes (1596–1650), is premised on the physics of Isaac Newton (1642–1727), and is empiricist in its orientation in that it seeks external evidence in coming to its conclusions.

But this approach, which essentially reduces things to their fundamental parts or atomistic elements, also separates the material elements (body) from nonmaterial aspects of the world, like consciousness, emotions, aesthetic appreciation, and spirituality. In simple terms, Western thinking has largely separated and broken into fragmented parts the mind and body, with little mention at all of heart and spirit, of community and meaning, none of which are directly observable. It has in some respects done much the same thing to the environment, making some people forget (or ignore) our interdependency with nature. Additionally, technological advances have sometimes made "progress" seem inevitable, as if a solution to whatever problems arise were always just around the corner. The Western approach has a major drawback in that it tends to lessen our ability to think about the system as a whole, which for many people may have lessened their ability to think about the ecological impacts of business actions.

The fragmented or atomistic approach, however, has come under severe criticism in recent years, for reasons that the quote from Peter Senge highlights in his influential *The Fifth Discipline*[5] (see box). Many people now believe that a more integrated approach, in part ecologically based and in part based on an integration of mind and body (or material and nonmaterial), better speaks to the long-term needs of human beings and the communities and organizations to which they belong. Such an approach will be particularly critical in the technologically complex and ecologically resource-constrained future where an understanding of the impacts of one part of the system on the other will be increasingly necessary.

This systemic approach to leading corporate citizenship has been fueled by the development of theories of chaos and complexity which are beginning to shed greater light on the behavior of complex systems, a set to which human systems clearly belong. It has been further advanced by quantum physics, astrophysics, and biology's new understanding of the nature of matter and the interconnectedness among all living things, as well as between living and nonliving matter.[6]

Such developments have highlighted the need for a more integrated approach to understanding the impact of human beings, and the economic organizations they create, on the world and in particular on the natural environment. In management circles this new approach has generated a great deal of thinking about progressive enterprise, or what this book terms new paradigm organizations and what others call learning organizations.

Holons

Systems thinking focuses on wholes, or more accurately, holons—whole/parts—and the interrelationships and interdependencies among them.[7] A *holon* is anything that is itself whole and also a part of something else, according to Ken Wilber. For example, a neutron is an entity, a whole, and it is also a part of an atom. A hand is an entity in itself and also a part of an arm, which is part of a body, and so on. In social systems, an individual (whole) is part of a family (whole) that is part of a community, and so on. In organizations, individuals are part of departments, which are units of divisions, which are parts of the corporate entity, which are part of their industry whole, which in turn is part of society. Holons, whole/parts, are integrally linked to the other holons of which they are a part. When something shifts in one holon, the others are affected as well because they are interdependent. *Domino effect*

We can think of holons as being nested within each other. Each holon is nested within the next level of holon, assuring both the interconnectedness and interdependence of each to the other. In system terms this means that anything that affects one part of the system also affects (at some level and in some way) the whole system. When we begin to think about systems in this way, our perspective on the corporation is changed: No longer can we consider that a company operates independently of its impacts on stakeholders. Because the company and its stakeholders are part of

---

Systems Thinking

A cloud masses, the sky darkens, leaves twist upward, and we know that it will rain. We also know that after the storm, the runoff will feed into groundwater miles away, and the sky will grow clear by tomorrow. All these events are distant in time and space, and yet they are all connected within the same pattern. Each has an influence on the rest, an influence that is usually hidden from view. You can only understand the system of a rainstorm by contemplating the whole, not any individual part of the pattern.

Business and other human endeavors are also systems. They, too, are bound by invisible fabrics of interrelated actions, which often take years to fully play out their effects on each other. Since we are part of that lacework ourselves, it's doubly hard to see the whole pattern of change. Instead, we tend to focus on isolated parts of the system, and wonder why our deepest problems never seem to get solved.

Source: Peter Senge, *The Fifth Discipline, The Art and Practice of the Learning Organization* (New York: Doubleday, 1991), pp. 6–7.

the larger holon of the communities, societies, and global village in which they are nested, they must, by this way of thinking, impact each other reciprocally.

Thus, for example, a company might think of itself as separate from a nonprofit organization to which it has given money in the past. When the company withdraws funding—cuts off the nonprofit organization, in a sense—the company's leaders may believe that they have ended their impact and responsibility. But the withdrawal of funding creates shifts in the financial stability of the nonprofit organization that have multiple ramifications both within the nonprofit and on the clients it serves. While the company may believe that it is immune from these impacts, there may be subtle shifts in employee morale or important customers may find out about the withdrawal of funds and cease doing business with the firm. No actions take place within holons without such impacts.

Another example might be an employee—a holon as individual—who quits the firm to go to a dot-com company or is fired without due process. It may seem that there are few system effects in these cases, but think about it: An employee who is no longer present (whether for the dot-com or by virtue of being let go) leaves a gap. Someone has to pick up the work that individual did, morale may be affected, new individuals may be brought in to replace the person, or other employees may have more work to do. There are system effects because the removal of this individual has created new relationships and "gaps" that didn't exist before. One reason that we tend to ignore these effects is that some of the ramifications are subtle. They are not necessarily immediately physical or quantifiable but relate rather to attitudes, how people feel about their work or organization, and what meaning they attach to their work.[8]

The general approach in the Western world has also been to look for data, empirical evidence, and the facts that are believed to comprise reality—that is, to focus on "objective" data. Rather than looking at realities that are more subjectively experienced (or in collective settings, intersubjectively), the typical Western approach is to focus on the material evidence that can be gathered to support the case. But thinkers like Peter Senge (and ecologists like Thomas Gladwin, physicists like Fritjof Capra, and management thinkers like Margaret Wheatley, among many others)[9] propose that is important to incorporate not only the objective data that can be observed when we consider, for example, individual or company behaviors, or individual or societies as systems, but also to focus on the nonmaterial—that is, the elements of consciousness and conscience, of emotion and feelings, of meaning and meaningfulness, of spirit and indeed of spirituality—if the work of enterprise is to be approached holistically at least when we are considering sentient beings.

Integrating the Subjective and Objective

Ken Wilber has constructed an integrative developmental framework for understanding the world's systems.[10] He noted that the Western tradition has focused almost exclusively on objective, empirically observable elements of individual and collective systems. Wilber generated a two-by-two matrix (see Figure 2.2) in which he placed individual and collective "exterior" or observable elements (i.e., that which is "objective") on the right-hand side. On the left-hand side, he placed the interior, nonobservable and subjective aspects of the world of living beings. To fully

	Left-hand Side	**Right-hand Side**
	Interior	**Exterior**
Individual	Subjective Intentional Realm of "I" experienced	Objective Behavioral Realm of "It" observed
Collective	Intersubjective Cultural Realm of "We" experienced	Interobjective Social Realm of "It(s)" observed

FIGURE 2.2. Wilber's Framework for Understanding Holons

understand anything, Wilber said, we must understand all four quadrants. Complete understanding of something sentient encompasses: (1) interior (or nonobservable elements that we must ask about, such as thoughts, feelings, meanings, aesthetic appreciation) and (2) exterior (observable elements). Both interior subjective elements and external objective elements also contain (3) individual and (4) collective aspects. Wilber termed these "I," "we," and "it" categories (by collapsing both individual and collective objective elements into one category of observable behaviors).

As we move through this book, we must keep in mind that to really understand anything human, including business life and decisions, requires dealing with all four ways of viewing the world. We are all familiar with traditional data gathering and observation that focus on the importance of objective information, whether individual or group. For example, we know about traditional financial measurement for individuals (i.e., pay) and companies (i.e., profits). At the same time, subjective individual aspects or what individuals experience and are conscious of, and the subjective collective aspects or what the group experiences and is conscious of, are also meaningful in creating visionary organizations, as we will see in the next three chapters.

Attitudes matter, for example, as does employee, customer, and supplier/ally morale and the sense of community generated within a company. As we shall see in Chapter 4, the meaning that attaches to organizational vision can be an important motivator and element of long-term success, even though it is not directly measurable. Recognizing this so-called soft side of management, recent scholars and business leaders have increasingly emphasized these arenas. More attention is now being put on individual and organizational vision and values, the meaning of work, and organizational culture as parts of the competitive mix that, properly leveraged, enhances organizational success. Leading corporate citizens now stress the importance of relationships and the trust inherent in what is coming to be called social capital, which we shall discuss in Chapter 6.

By taking an integrative and holistic systems perspective, we can reshape the way that each of us views our impact on the world and the world's impact on us.

Systems thinking is a discipline for seeing the "structures" that underlie complex situations and for discerning high from low leverage change. That is, by seeing wholes we learn how to foster health. . . . [Systems thinking and the related disciplines of personal mastery, mental models, shared vision, and team learning] are concerned with a shift of mind from seeing parts to seeing wholes, from seeing people as helpless reactors to seeing them as active participants in shaping their reality, from reacting to the present to creating the future.[11]

A Sustainable Starbucks?

It sometimes seems as though there is a Starbucks on every corner. Indeed, the company now has more than 2,800 coffee shops throughout the United States, the United Kingdom, Canada, and Asia, sells its coffee in a wide range of restaurants, businesses, airlines, hotels, and universities, and through mail-order and on-line catalogs. Ubiquitous as it has become, Starbucks seems well on its way to achieving its goal of establishing itself as the most recognized and respected brand in the world. So, how does a company that has achieved such market dominance by selling coffee (and related) products move toward sustainability in its growing operations?

In 1998 Starbucks formed a partnership with Conservation International (CI) intended to support growers of shade grown coffee and promote cultivation that protects biodiversity, encourages use of environmentally sustainable agricultural practices, and helps the farmers earn more money. This partnership, which was renewed and upgraded in the summer of 2000, permits CI to work in five coffee-growing projects in Latin America, Asia, and Africa. The expansion represents an effort to replicate the success of the initial project, started in 1998, in the El Triunfo Biosphere Reserve Sierra Madre de Chiapas, which CI considers to be one of the world's most important biodiversity "hotspots." Through a program called "Conservation Coffee," Starbucks enables CI to help small farmers grow coffee in the buffer zone of the reserve under the shade of the forest canopy. Growing coffee in the shade helps protect the reserve's forests, streams, and wildlife, while providing substantial income benefits for the farmers.

The year 2000 partnership will enable CI to expand its work into more ecological hotspots, while building on Starbucks's commitment to the development of sustainable agriculture. In addition, the project will develop sourcing guidelines that incorporate sound environmental management practices, while providing a fair livelihood to farmers, and seek to engage other industry leaders in the sustainable coffee-growing effort.

Sources: Starbucks website, http://www.starbucks.com; The Standard, http://www.thestandard.com/companies.

ECOLOGY: THE BIOLOGICAL BASIS OF CITIZENSHIP

Why do companies like Starbucks move toward sustainable practices? Let us begin to understand the overall system in which businesses operate at its foundation: the natural environment. With the earth's population at nearly six billion people and projected to double within the next century (if trends don't change), there is an increasing imperative to understand the impact of human beings on the ecology that sustains them. One organization that has taken a creative and systemic approach to understanding ecological sustainability and the role of business in it is The Natural Step (TNS), a Swedish organization.

Thinking Systemically about Ecology: The Natural Step Framework.[12]

Founded in 1989 by Dr. Karl-Henrik Robert, The Natural Step works to develop a consensus describing basic understanding of the ecological environment and the role of humans in that environment, and the ways in which humans are threatening not only other forms of life on earth, but also themselves, by permitting activities that result in deteriorating natural conditions.[13] Dr. Robert, joined by John Holmberg, a Swedish physicist, defined a set of important *system conditions* based on the laws of thermodynamics and natural cycles that form the framework for environmental sustainability of The Natural Step.

Sustainability, as the biologist Humberto Maturana noted, is critical not only to the environment, but also to human beings, and particularly to the environment's capacity to sustain healthy and successful human civilization. The environment, Maturana pointed out, will go on in one form or another. Given the reality of serious ecological degradation (see Chapter 9 for additional discussion of some of the ecological problems facing the planet), the real question is not whether the earth will survive or not. It will. *The real question is, Can human society survive?* Hence the importance of assuring that business leaders have a better understanding of ecological sustainability than they previously have had.[14]

TNS's framework, while somewhat radical relative to current economic thought, is aimed at helping individuals and organizations understand ecology systemically so that the use and abuse of natural resources can be reduced and newer sustainable approaches to production developed. In addition, TNS hopes to help focus the development of new, less resource intensive, technologies, and provide a common language and set of guiding principles for sustainable enterprise. Although TNS has only recently been introduced into the United States, Canada, the United Kingdom, Japan, and Australia, the name and approach of TNS is a household word in Sweden.

TNS highlights some of the problematic aspects of human economic development on the ecology. Because of the impact of the six billion people currently alive on earth, multiple ecological systems, including croplands, wetlands, the ozone layer, forests, fisheries, and groundwater, are facing serious trouble. Visible garbage is filling up landfills and various pollutants accumulate less visibly in the atmosphere. The ozone hole is increasing, with negative consequences for human life.

Rain forests continue to be depleted with an almost unimaginable impact on world ecology because not only do rain forests provide fresh water but also they cleanse the atmosphere. Some ecologists believe that a sustainable number of people on earth would be between one and two billion.

According to environmentalist Paul Hawken, "We are far better at making waste than at making products. For every 100 pounds of product we manufacture in the United States, we create at least 3,200 pounds of waste. In a decade, we transform 500 trillion pounds of molecules into nonproductive solids, liquids, and gases."[15] Clearly, if we believe that the earth's resources are limited and that demands upon the system cannot be sustained at this rate of "progress" over time, then a new approach to productivity is necessary. TNS's framework provides a set of system conditions that, according to the scientists who originally created the system in Sweden (and others where it is being replicated throughout the world), will be needed to prevent the world from "hitting a wall" of unsupportable demands on the natural environment. The box on the next page lists the system conditions for sustainability developed in Sweden.

The TNS system is aimed at sustainable development. *Sustainable development* can be defined as "a process of achieving human development . . . in an inclusive, connected, equitable, prudent, and secure manner," according to ecological scholar Thomas Gladwin and his colleagues.[16] Gladwin has defined five elements that represent a set of *constraints* on *human development,* similar to those that TNS produced for the material world.

Inclusiveness connotes an expansive view of the space, time, and component parts of the observed ecology, embracing both ecological and human conditions in the present and the future. *Connectivity* means understanding the inherent interconnectedness and interdependence of elements of the world and problems in the world. *Equity* means a fair distribution of resources and property rights within and between generations. Putting these latter two together suggests greater comprehension of the unavoidable links between, for example, creating better ecological health and efforts to reduce poverty or the gap between rich and poor.

Prudence means taking care of the resources of the world, much as is suggested by the TNS constraints. In practice, being prudent means keeping ecosystems and socioeconomic systems healthy and resilient, avoiding irreversible losses of ecological or other resources, and—as the TNS constraints also indicate—keeping human activities within the earth's regenerative capacity. Finally, *security* focuses on the sustainability of human life, that is, ensuring "a safe, healthy, high quality of life for current and future generations."[17] Table 2.1 lists these constraints.

Thinking systemically about the natural environment leads to important questions about the impact of human civilization and economic development on the natural environment. Later in this book, we will consider some of the ecological problems that have arisen as a result of human and economic development, technological advances, and the process of industrialization. For now, however, it is important to recognize that thinking systemically about ecology fundamentally means thinking in new ways about the relationships that exist between human beings and the enterprises they create and the rest of the natural world.

Indeed, thinking about ecological sustainability may mean putting aside traditional (i.e., Western) ways of viewing the relationship of human beings to the natural world, especially if companies are to be truly global citizens in a sustainable world. It may even mean shifting our perspective away from an anthropomorphic (human centered) or technocentric (technologically oriented) worldview beyond even an ecocentric (ecological) worldview.[18] It may mean a wholly new approach to

---

The Natural Step's Four System Conditions for Ecological Sustainability

1. *Substances from the earth's crust must not systematically increase in nature.*

In a sustainable society, human activities such as the burning of fossil fuels and the mining of metals and minerals will not occur at a rate that causes them to systematically increase in the ecosphere. There are thresholds beyond which living organisms and ecosystems are adversely affected by increases in substances from the earth's crust. Problems may include an increase in greenhouse gases leading to global warming, contamination of surface and groundwater, and metal toxicity, which can cause functional disturbances in animals. In practical terms, the first condition requires society to implement comprehensive metal and mineral recycling programs, and decrease economic dependence on fossil fuels.

2. *Substances produced by society must not systematically increase in nature.*

In a sustainable society, humans will avoid generating systematic increases in persistent substances such as DDT, PCBs, and freon. Synthetic organic compounds such as DDT and PCBs can remain in the environment for many years, bioaccumulating in the tissue of organisms, causing profound deleterious effects on predators in the upper levels of the food chain. Freon, and other ozone-depleting compounds, may increase risk of cancer due to added UV radiation in the troposphere. Society needs to find ways to reduce economic dependence on persistent human-made substances.

3. *The physical basis for productivity and diversity of nature must not systematically be diminished.*

In a sustainable society, humans will avoid taking more from the biosphere than can be replenished by natural systems. In addition, people will avoid systematically encroaching upon nature by destroying the habitat of other species. Biodiversity, which includes the great variety of animals and plants found in nature, provides the foundation for ecosystem services that are necessary to sustain life on this planet. Society's health and prosperity depend on the enduring capacity of nature to renew itself and rebuild waste into resources.

4. *We must be fair and efficient in meeting basic human needs.*

Meeting the fourth system condition for ecological sustainability is a way to avoid violating the first three system conditions. Considering the human enterprise as a whole, we need to be efficient with regard to resource use and waste generation in order to be sustainable. If one billion people lack adequate nutrition while another billion have more than they need, there is a lack of fairness in meeting basic human needs. Achieving greater fairness is essential for social stability and the cooperation needed for making large-scale changes within the framework laid out by the first three conditions.

To achieve this fourth condition, humanity must strive to improve technical and organizational efficiency around the world, and to live using fewer resources, especially in affluent areas. This system condition implies an improved means of addressing human population growth. If the total resources throughput of the global human population continues to increase, it will be increasingly difficult to meet basic human needs as human-driven processes intended to fulfill human needs and wants are systematically degrading the collective capacity of the earth's ecosystems to meet these demands.

Source: The Natural Step's Four System Conditions, http://www.naturalstep.org/what/what_cond.htm

TABLE 2.1. Constraints on Sustainable Human Development

Inclusiveness:	Expansive view of space, time, and elements of ecology (present and future).
Connectivity:	Understanding inherent interconnectedness and interdependence of world's elements and problems.
Equity:	Fair distribution of resources and property rights (within and between generations).
Prudence:	Taking care of world's resources so they are healthy and resilient.
Security:	Sustainability of health and high-quality human life for present and future generations.

Source: Thomas N. Gladwin, James J. Kennelly, and Tara-Shelomith Krause, "Shifting Paradigms for Sustainable Development: Implications for Management Theory and Research," *Academy of Management Review* 20, no. 4 (October 1995), pp. 874–908.

economic development focused on sustainability. The box on page 35 illustrates the efforts of two corporations forming strategies for sustainable development.

If we can manage this shift of perspective successfully, we can perhaps achieve a more integrated perspective. A fully integrative perspective would synthesize the three critical spheres of civilization—economic, political, and societal—with the ecological and also integrate the subjective and intersubjective elements of emotions, intuition, aesthetics, and culture, among others, into our perspective. The result would be a better understanding of the values that underpin each sphere of activity, as will be discussed below, and their integration with the others into an ecologically sustainable and holistic worldview. Working through this integration will be the topic of the remainder of this chapter.

INTERSECTING SPHERES OF HUMAN CIVILIZATION, NATURE, AND ASSOCIATED VALUES

The previous sections highlighted the importance of taking a systemic view of the relationship between business institutions and their impact on the natural environment. As noted at the outset, human civilization is comprised of three distinct spheres of activity that depend on the bounty of the natural environment: the economic sphere in which businesses operate, the political sphere where multiple levels of governmental activities take place, and the civil society sphere which incorporates many activities associated with "civilizing" human beings and building relationships founded in community. Figure 2.1 illustrates the overlapping, connected, and interdependent relationship that exists among these spheres of activity and influence.

In a pioneering work relating business values to biophysics and biochemistry, William Frederick outlined three important "value clusters," two of which dominate business or economic activities in the economic sphere.[19] The first and probably the dominant value for business corporations in the United States is economizing. *Economizing* means the prudent and efficient use and processing of resources needed to live well. What Frederick means by economizing is that the primary purpose—and indeed, the imperative—of business is to create goods and services as efficiently as possible.

The second value cluster that Frederick said underpins business activity is *power aggrandizing* or augmenting and preserving the power of managers and the organization itself.[20] Power aggrandizing means that businesses (as well as other forms of organizations, particularly governments), have a tendency to accumulate and control resources and power over time, making themselves increasingly influential.

These two value clusters exist to a significant degree in a state of tension with the third value cluster of ecologizing. *Ecologizing* is the tendency of evolutionary and natural processes to "interweave the life activities of groups in ways conducive to the perpetuation of an entire community."[21] Ecologizing, effectively, means using resources in ways that sustain life and energy, meaning (as with nature) that nothing goes to waste. Viewed ecologically, what is waste to one part of the system becomes, in effect, food for another part of the system. Unfortunately, many businesses have not yet taken this perspective on their activities in the world. The business value clusters are summarized in the box on the next page, while the box below highlights some business efforts to move toward ecological sustainability.

Sustainability in Action

Sara Schley and Joe Laur reported several initiatives of major corporations that were attempting to become leading citizens by employing the principles of The Natural Step and gaining bottom-line benefits for doing so, although none of these companies was operating sustainably at the time. Here is an excerpt from their report:

A number of pioneering companies around the globe have begun to employ strategies for sustainable development. Already, they have seen substantial contributions to the bottom line via cost savings and revenue generation. For example, McDonald's Sweden is now composting food scraps that it formerly paid to have disposed of, and is selling this compost at a profit. The company has also reduced its packaging waste and has advertised this progress on its new, biodegradable tray covers.

The New England Power Company has opened a new coal ash recycling facility (coal ash is a waste product of the power production process and costs $15 per ton to dispose of in landfills). The ash is now being recycled via a patented process at a production rate of 20–25 tons per hour. New England Power is selling the recycled ash at a profit as a cement substitute in the manufacture of concrete. The material makes the concrete stronger, easier to pour, more resistant to saltwater, and less expensive to produce than the standard cement currently used in concrete. . . .

Source: Sara Schley and Joe Laur, "The Sustainability Challenge: Ecological and Economic Development" (Cambridge, MA: Pegasus Communications, 1997), from http://www.seedsys.com/article.

When we take a very broad perspective on the three spheres of human civilization (which we will discuss in considerably more detail in Chapter 3), and their relationship to nature, we can see that the values Frederick identified may provide different guiding imperatives for the different spheres of activity. For example, Frederick noted that both economizing and power aggrandizing are central to economic sector activities. If, however, we look at the broader societal system in which businesses operate in our three-sphere societal model, we note that the major form of "currency" in the political sector is power, probably even more so than in business, while the major emphasis in the business sector is economizing. Thus, if we think about the value clusters that Frederick has identified at the more macro level of human civilization viewed through the lens of the sphere systems, we note that each sphere of activity also has a dominant value cluster. The dominant values of business center on economizing (with contributions from power aggrandizing). Businesses rightly focus on efficiency of production of the goods and services they are in business to generate.

In contrast, the activities of the governmental or political sphere tend to focus on the garnering and use of power to accomplish their objectives, since governments are in the business of setting the rules of the game for society. Thus, the dominant values of the political sphere or governments are those of power aggrandizing.

Civil society, in contrast, tends to focus on developing organizations and institutions that "civilize" society, building relationships and community. Thus, the values of the civil society sphere, which are not addressed in Frederick's model, are more congruent with relationship and community building.

As we have seen above, natural processes tend to waste nothing, suggesting that nature, which provides ecological underpinning for all of this human activity, is dominated by ecologizing values.

Table 2.2 shows the major values associated with activities in each of the three spheres of human civilization plus nature, with what Frederick called X-values added. X-values are the values that individuals bring with them into any institutional or organizational setting; hence they are related to individuals. Further, human society has developed a set of technological values that have fostered industrial development over the past centuries.

Economizing values, dominant within businesses, emphasizes keeping the system whole and efficient as well as continually growing. Given these values, it is not

Frederick's Value Clusters

Economizing:	the prudent and efficient use and processing of resources needed to live well.
Power aggrandizing:	augmenting and preserving the power of managers and the organization itself.
Ecologizing:	the evolutionary and natural processes that interweave with life activities of groups so that they are conducive to the perpetuation of an entire community.

Source: William C. Frederick, *Values, Nature, and Culture in the American Corporation* (New York: Oxford University Press, 1995).

TABLE 2.2. Dominant Values within Each Sphere of Activity

Business Values	Political (and Business) Values	Civil Society	
Economizing values	*Power-aggrandizing Values*	*Relationship Values*	*E*
Economizing (Efficiency)	Hierarchical (rank-order) organizing	Care	Lin
Growth	Managerial decision power	Connectedness	Div
Systemic integrity	Power-system equilibrium	Community	Hom ..auc succession
	Power aggrandizement	Civility	Community

Other Values that Influence the Spheres

Technological Values	*X-Factor Values (Individual)*
Instrumental pragmatics	Personal, idiosyncratic,
Cooperative-coordinative relations	role-conditioned values
Technical expertise	
Public openness	
Participatory leveling	

Source: Adapted from William C. Frederick, *Values, Nature, and Culture in the American Corporation* (New York: Oxford University Press, 1995).

surprising that businesses tend to focus on efficiency and growth at almost any cost. These emphases are the natural by-products of the business system that modern society has created.

Power-aggrandizing values, which are present in business and dominate in the political (public policy) sphere, focus on maintaining hierarchy (bureaucracy) through managerial decision-making capacity that helps to keep the power system stable or in equilibrium, and continued power enhancement. Given the dominance of these values in the public policy sphere where governments at all levels operate, perhaps it is understandable that governments focus on the acquisition and use of power. Efficiency is not government's imperative, as the product or output of governments has more to do with establishing the rules by which societies operate than with producing goods and services.

Civil society includes all of the social institutions other than business and governmental bodies that sustain the "fabric" of society. Civil society is dominated by values of relationship. These values emphasize the importance of building and sustaining relationships through what Nell Noddings terms an ethic of care, building connectedness, and fostering civility through the building of community.[22]

The *natural environment is* dominated by ecologizing. Activists in that arena choose values of ecologizing, which focus on linkage or connectedness and maintenance of diversity as well as use of resources so that nothing is wasted. Natural processes evolve consistently while maintaining a regularity of pattern.

X-factor values are those particular personal values, based on their own backgrounds, that individuals bring with them to any organization. *Technological values,* which drive business activity, are pragmatic in that they use various instruments to achieve their ends. Additionally, technologists learn to value "coordinative, integrative, and cooperative relationships among tool users." Also valued by technology users are technical expertise, truth telling and honesty, and a value Frederick called participatory leveling, which is the tendency of advanced technology to create participatory and democratic environments; hence these values make up the technological value cluster.[23]

The dominant values within the spheres of activity form a kind of "imperative" for activities within each sphere that guides activities of organizations within that sphere, at least to the extent that this is the way humans have operationalized that sphere to date. Thus, business organizations are justifiably driven toward economizing ends of efficiency, given the way human societies have to this point in time framed business activities. Similarly governments and political bodies are driven by a power imperative. Civil society, it appears, is driven more by the values of relationship and care that tend to "civilize" humanity through relationships, while the ecological environment is driven by principles of ecologizing. Given the differences in values dominant in each of the spheres of activity, it is not hard to understand why issues of sustainability have been relatively neglected in management thinking until quite recently, when environmental degradation has become more obvious.

LEADING CHALLENGES: BALANCING THE TENSION OF VALUE CLUSTERS

Unfortunately, as the discussion on sustainability above illustrates, the dominant values of business, "economizing" or efficiency followed by power aggrandizing, are not always aligned with values of relationship and ecologizing directed at community building or environmental sustainability.[24] Nor are the dominant business values necessarily entirely consistent with the values of "civilizing" or civility that seem to dominate the relationship-oriented civil society, though of course all of the value clusters exist to some extent within each sphere of activity.

The differences in dominant values create a constant dynamic and interactive tension among organizations operating in different spheres, making continued efforts by actors within each sphere to find appropriate balance between competing goals and interests in the sphere essential to human societies. The result is a contested world of constant change and continued evolution. The "contest" among human-centered values of civility, nature-centered values of ecologizing, industry-centered values of economizing, and politics-centered values of power aggrandizing creates the need to continue to strive for balance among the spheres in order that humans—as well as other living beings—can live in a healthy world.

It takes significant awareness and a capacity to think systemically, rather than atomistically, for leaders of corporate citizens to fully understand the relationship between business enterprise and nature. The differences in underlying values and their associated imperatives create significant tensions among organizations operating in the different spheres of activity—and leading corporate citizens must somehow come to balance these tensions. As we move forward, we will explore some of the ways that companies are actually working through and with this need for balance among the spheres of human civilization—and with nature itself.

The next chapter will explore the imperatives of each sphere in greater detail to see how we might think about creating balance among them through leading corporate citizens. In later chapters we will then explore the role of vision and values to improve corporate performance and add value for a broad set of stakeholders.

NOTES TO CHAPTER 2

1. See Richard D'Aveni, *Hyper-Competition: Managing the Dynamics of Strategic Maneuvering* (New York: Free Press, 1994).
2. For a marvelous and accessible description of the interconnectedness of living and material entities, see Fritjof Capra's *The Web of Life* (New York: Anchor Doubleday, 1995).
3. Ibid. p. 243.
4. Peter M. Senge, *The Fifth Discipline: The Art and Practice of the Learning Organization* (New York: Doubleday, 1991).
5. Senge. pp. 6–7.
6. For some insight into these topics, start with James Gleick, *Chaos: Making a New Science* (New York: Viking; Stuart Kauffman, *At Home in the Universe: The Search for the Laws of Self-Organization and Complexity* (New York: Oxford University Press, 1995); Capra, *The Web of Life;* Humberto R. Maturana and Francisco J. Varela, *The Tree of Knowledge: The Biological Roots of Human Understanding,* rev. ed. (Boston: Shambala Press, 1998); and Senge's *Fifth Discipline.*
7. The term *holon* is from Arthur Koestler and is extensively developed in Ken Wilber's works. *Sex, Ecology, Spirituality: The Spirit of Evolution* (Boston: Shambala Press, 1995); and *The Eye of Spirit: An Integral Vision for a World Gone Slightly Mad* (Boston: Shambala Press, 1998) and *A Brief History of Everything* (Boston: Shambala Press, 1996).
8. Thanks to Reviewer #2 for these examples.
9. Thomas N. Gladwin, James J. Kennelly, and Tara-Shelomith Krause, "Shifting Paradigms for Sustainable Development: Implications for Management Theory and Research," *Academy of Management Review* 20, no. 4 (October 1995), pp. 874–907; Fritjof, Capra, *The Turning Point: Science, Society, and the Rising Culture* (New York: Bantam Books, 1983); and Margaret J. Wheatley, *Leadership and the New Science: Learning about Organization from an Orderly New Universe* (San Francisco: Berrett-Koehler, 1992).
10. See Wilber, various books, note 7.
11. Senge, p. 69.
12. Information on The Natural Step can be found at http://www.naturalstep.org/.
13. This reference is based on a talk by Humberto Maturana at the 1998 annual meeting of the Society for Organizational Learning. A version of this talk by Maturana and Pille Bunnell titled "Biosphere, Homosphere, and Robosphere: What Has That to Do with Business?" is available at the SoL website, http://www.sol-ne.org/res/wp/maturana/index.html.
14. The information in this section is based on The Natural Step website, TNS Framework, http://www.naturalstep.org/what/what_frame.html.

15. Quoted in The Natural Step website.
16. Gladwin, Kennelly, and Krause, pp. 874–907.
17. President's Council on Sustainable Development, quoted in Gladwin, p. 1. Much of the discussion in these paragraphs is based on the Gladwin article.
18. Gladwin, Kennelly, and Krause developed these terms.
19. William C. Frederick uses a biological and evolutionary basis to develop these value sets in his pathbreaking book, *Values, Nature, and Culture in the American Corporation* (New York: Oxford University Press, 1995). Much of the discussion in this section is adapted from Frederick; however, the application to other spheres is the author's.
20. Frederick, p. 92.
21. Ibid., p. 9.
22. Nell Noddings, *Caring: A Feminine Approach to Ethics and Moral Education* (Berkeley: University of California Press, 1984).
23. Frederick, pp. 201–203.
24. Ibid.

CHAPTER 3

The Three Spheres of Human Civilization

All human systems and ecosystems require balance: competition with co-operation, selfishness and individualism with community and social concern, material acquisitiveness with thirst for knowledge and understanding, rights with responsibilities and the striving for love, justice, and harmony. . . . Natural systems never maximize single variables, such as profit or efficiency. Thus, we can infer that maximizing behavior on the part of any individual or firm is shortsighted and destructive of the larger system. . . .

Grassroots globalists and their organizations are often spurned by governments as amateurs, agitators, or troublemakers. Even the United Nations has warmed only slowly to citizen organizations. They are now emerging as a third, independent sector in world affairs—challenging the domination of global agendas by nation states and transnational corporations. The global civil society, newly interlinked on the Internet and by millions of newsletters, increasingly driving agendas of nations and corporations, which still refer to citizens groups as nongovernmental organizations (NGOs). Many grassroots globalist leaders retort that governments and corporations are NCOs (noncivil organizations). Global concerns have been on the agendas of grassroots civic groups, including churches and other organizations that have worked for food aid, peacemaking, education, culture, and youth exchange, since the turn of [the twentieth] century.

—Hazel Henderson, Building a Win-Win World.

. . . [It] is clear that the large American corporation today is more rather than less responsive to the social demands of its external environment. But these exercises in social responsibility no longer represent managerial discretion—corporate executives' sharing of the fruits of market power with stakeholder groups in order to assure labor peace and enhance their position in the community and in society. Instead, they reflect the explicit demands made by government regulation, and firms' efforts to go beyond regulation in ways that integrate these requirements into their strategic and business planning so as to enhance competitiveness and profitability, rather

than simply raising costs. Government regulations and court decisions have limited the scope of managerial decision making; today's managers are continuously seeking ways to convert these societal restrictions into competitive opportunities.

MARINA V. N. WHITMAN, New World, New Rules:
The Changing Role of the American Corporation.

Human civilization depends on a healthy ecological environment for its sustenance and maintenance; the environment or ecological system, as the last chapter illustrates, underpins all we do and are, providing essential elements of earth, air, and water, not to mention the raw materials of productive processes. But human society is itself a complex system, which requires balance among several competing sets of influences and activities, some of which today seem out of balance.

To understand human civilization from an integrated perspective, we will explore in this chapter the necessary balance among three spheres that encompass human activity: economic, political, and civil society, recognizing, as the last chapter discussed, the need for a healthy ecology underpinning all. Figure 3.1 shows the spheres also introduced in the last chapter and illustrates a balance among all of the spheres and with their grounding of nature. The ecological or natural environment sphere, highlighted in Figure 3.1, was the topic of the previous chapter. In this chapter, we will discuss in detail the three spheres of *human* civilization (see Figure 3.2): the economic sphere, the political sphere, and the civil society sphere. Figure 3.2D illustrates the type of imbalance that some observers suggest is happening today.

Each of these spheres of human activity has, as noted in Chapter 2, a dominant emphasis, such as production of goods and services for the economic sphere, and

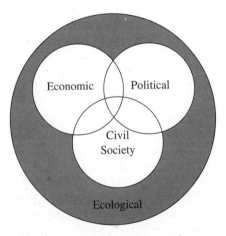

FIGURE 3.1.   Balanced Spheres of
Activity: The Natural Environment

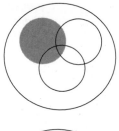

3–2A. The Economic Sphere
Highlighted

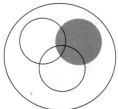

3–2B. The Political Sphere
Highlighted

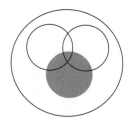

3–2C. The Civil Society
Sphere Highlighted

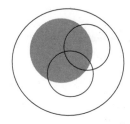

3–2D. An Unbalanced
and Dominant
Economic Sphere

FIGURE 3.2.   Three Spheres of Human Civilization in
and out of Balance

underlying values imperative. In the economic sphere, to be discussed first (Figure
3.2A), the focus is on the production of goods and service, with a driving imperative of economizing, that is, efficient use of resources. This chapter will explore both
the benefits and drawbacks of activities in the economic sphere. In the political
sphere, that of governments, the rules of societies are established and an infrastructure is created that sustains and governs each society. The political sphere (Figure
3.2B) is dominated by power aggrandizing values. Finally, the civil society sphere
(Figure 3.2C) emphasizes the building and maintenance of community and is driven
by values of relationship and civilizing.

Each of these spheres of activity will be discussed below. Obviously, there is
much more activity within each sphere than can be reasonably discussed here. We

will, however, try here to provide a synthesis of key features within the sphere to better understand how leading corporate citizens can provide goods and services efficiently using their imperative of economizing, while still operating with integrity and responsibly with respect to the other spheres. Because vast differences exist among nations, particularly in the national ideologies that guide political and cultural decisions, we will begin our exploration of the three spheres of human society by gaining an understanding of national ideologies, then move to the discussion of the three spheres of human activity.

IDEOLOGY

National ideology is a shared system of beliefs or "the collection of ideas that a community uses to make values explicit in some relevant context."[1] Values as used in this definition are "timeless, universal, noncontroversial notions that virtually every community everywhere has always cherished,"[2] including justice, economizing, and respect. In other words, at the core of every society are what we will term end values (see Chapter 5). When combined with the specific context or historical development of a community, these values constitute its unique identity, typically an identity that members of a given community or state want to preserve. Thus, although ideology at its extreme can be a source of dissension or differences, in milder and healthier forms, ideology helps people to establish an important sense of place and identity—or community.

Ideology, according to George Lodge and Ezra Vogel, has five components, which are listed in Table 3.1. These components involve the ways that human beings are perceived and, in particular, their perceived relationship to the broader community, as well as what types of formal and informal policies and culture exist to manifest those relationships. Ideology also involves the perception of nature and reality, and determines what type of government is considered appropriate within a given culture or nation.

Lodge and Vogel identified two "ideal-type" ideologies, which can be placed at either end of a continuum, with most real-world ideologies somewhere in between the two ends. On the one end of the continuum is *individualism,* an ideology in which individuals are the ultimate source of value and meaning, with community interests defined through self-interested competition (i.e., what Adam Smith means by free-market competition in its ideal state). On the other end of the continuum is *communitarianism,* a system in which the interests of the community are considered more important and meaningful than those of individuals.

Individualism

Individualism is the atomistic notion that a community is no more than the sum of the individuals in it.[3] Under an individualistic system, property rights take precedence and the best government is thought to be a limited government. Individualism also emphasizes competition and materialism, to the extent that it focuses on satis-

TABLE 3.1. Components of Ideology

1. The relationship between the human beings and the community, the individual, and the group; and the means to individual fulfillment and self-respect.
2. The institutional guarantees and manifestations of that relationship, such as property rights.
3. The most appropriate means of controlling the production of goods and services.
4. The role of the state.
5. The prevailing perception of reality and conception of nature, concerning, for example, the role of science and the functions of education.

Source: George C. Lodge and Ezra F. Vogel, *Ideology and National Competitiveness: An Analysis of Nine Countries* (Boston: Harvard Business School Press, 1987), p. 9.

faction of consumer desires. Newtonian science, with its fragmentation and atomization, undergirds thinking about nature in individualistic systems. The United States is probably the most individualistic country in the world, though there is considerable tension even there between the values of individualism and those that favor community.[4] Individuals holding more radical views on individualism tend to separate economic, political, and civil society spheres and want to keep them separate through a laissez-faire approach to government and a celebration of free competition, limited government, and equality of opportunity. Ultimately, this individualism is captured in Thomas Jefferson's immortal phrase "life, liberty, and the pursuit of happiness," which is embedded in the U.S. Constitution.[5]

Communitarianism

At the other end of the continuum of ideologies is communitarianism, which serves in many ways as a counterpoint to individualism. Communitarianism is characterized by an emphasis on community, with the belief that the community is something organic and whole in itself, comprised of more than the sum of its parts. Under communitarian systems, people believe that the needs and interests of the community take precedence over those of individuals, and that survival, justice, self-respect, and other human values depend on recognition of community needs. Communitarian cultures focus on equality of outcomes or results, frequently using hierarchy to achieve equitable outcomes. They also value consensus, rather than the more contractual arrangements preferred in individualistic societies.

Rather than emphasizing property and individual rights, communitarian societies tend to emphasize the rights and duties of membership, placing community needs first in priority. Communitarian societies frequently have active, planning-oriented governments (though they can be either democratic or more authoritarian in form). Scientifically, communitarian societies tend to take a more holistic (rather than atomistic) view of nature and the world around them, seeing interdependence among societal elements rather than independence. Japan and many other Asian nations lean toward the communitarian end of the continuum of ideology.

Impact of Ideology

Understanding where a nation falls on this ideological continuum is important for managers and leaders because the cultural differences that manifest themselves as a result of ideological differences can determine the proper approach to business within a society. For example, managers in more communitarian countries may need to see a potential business partner as part of their community and to develop a trusting relationship with future partners over an extended period of time before they are able to work together. Managers from more individualistic nations may want to outline a contractual agreement immediately, as soon as it can be signed off on by the lawyers. Such a tactic might well alienate managers who ordinarily build business on the relationship and trust that comes from knowing and trusting each other over time in the communitarian environment.

Further, cultural differences that manifest themselves as a result of differing ideologies may be deeply valued by people within that society. Attempts by multinational corporations or any other entity, such as an intergovernmental organization, to do business in ways that contradict or subvert the prevailing ideology may be met with discontent and resistance at best and downright rebellion at worst. Most peoples care deeply about their own cultures and beliefs that derive from ideology. Embedded as they are within their own ideological perspective, people find it difficult to accept a radically different perspective unless they are capable of "holding" in their own heads multiple perspectives simultaneously (for more on holding multiple perspectives simultaneously, see the discussion of cognitive development in Chapter 4).

Without deep understanding of differences in ideology and their cultural manifestations, it is easy for leaders of corporate citizens to get themselves and their companies into trouble inadvertently, or to step on the toes of actors in the political or civil society spheres unintentionally. Managers are constantly faced with the paradoxes and tension inherent in the individualism-communitarian continuum, especially in a world that is highly interconnected electronically and where many companies work in a global context. Although global standards about respecting human dignity and taking care of the natural environment exist, there is a natural "tension of the opposites" that requires careful balancing when dealing with communities other than one's own. For example, the attitude toward government as policy makers differs radically depending on whether one is in a country that is based largely on individualistic or communitarian values.[6]

Individualistic countries like to "keep government off our backs," as the saying goes in the United States. People in individualistic countries believe that the less government there is, the better. Government's role is viewed as protection of property and rights, enforcement of contracts, and ensuring that markets are free so competition can be fostered. Intervention by government is frowned upon, except when there is a crisis, and business-government relations are typically adversarial at best. In individualistic countries, public policy is viewed as best developed through the play of contesting parties in the public policy arena, rather than through centralized control over public policy making.

USA

Communitarian nations differ greatly from individualistic countries in their respect for and attitude toward government, as in Japan. Communitarian nations view government as prestigious and authoritative, even authoritarian at times.[7] Because the interests of community are placed over those of individuals, the function of governments in more communitarian nations is seen as defining and meeting community needs and interests as a first priority. Because the focus in such countries emphasizes membership in the community, governments play important roles in determining what constitutes such membership and what duties and rights membership entails. Although communitarian countries believe that consensus is important, there may be little hesitation to force consensus from either an authoritarian central government or a coercive grassroots movement when the interests of the community as a whole are at stake. Relations between business and government in communitarian countries tend to be more collaborative and cooperative than they are in more individualistic nations.

The Need for Both/And

Of course no nation is fully individualistic or fully communitarian. There is always a tension of the oppositions or a tug of war at work because healthy societies require both individual and community. The United States, for example, has struggled to sustain community over the years in the face of the dominant ideology of individualism. Economist Adam Smith's "invisible hand" of the free market, which will be discussed in more detail below, is supposed to result in a better society for all, not an amoral, cutthroat, free-for-all where consequences of actions are not taken into account.

Western philosophy and culture generally tend to be more rooted in individualism, while Eastern philosophies and cultures tend to be more communitarian in nature, although there are vast differences among nations in both parts of the world. For example, individualistic nations tend to govern through numerous laws and regulations, while communitarian nations tend to establish longer-term priorities and help the nation's enterprises "develop" toward meeting those priorities and goals. The role of contracts is also different; individualistic nations rely upon contracts to do business while communitarian nations seek trusting, long-term relationships as a basis of doing business.

Whichever ideology holds sway in a given country, it is easy to see that not only public policy but also what is considered acceptable corporate behavior will be greatly influenced by the ideology and culture of the nation. Other key differences among nations that affect culture and business performance will be discussed in Chapter 10. In applying thinking about ideology to leading corporate citizens, we can see that companies face a significant tension between the need for fostering entrepreneurial (and individualistic) efforts to innovate while sustaining a community engaged in the common purposes of the firm. This tension can be healthy or problematic, depending on how far a company goes toward an individualistic or communitarian philosophy, as there is always some need for balance.

This book argues, as does philosopher Robert Solomon, that excellent perform-ance in companies requires a commitment to integrity and balancing these types of tensions, as well as care and compassion for people in the company.[8] Being caring and compassionate inherently demands just this type of balance between the needs of individuals and the need for a community that works together toward some com-mon goal.

THE ECONOMIC SPHERE

Many observers believe that business is the most powerful institution in society to-day. Certainly it is the most dominant in terms of size and impact on human lives as well as the ecology, including other living beings, particularly in the industrialized nations of the world. Indeed, some transnational corporations control more re-sources than many small countries, leading some observers to think that the entire system is out of balance, looking more like Figure 3.2D than 3.2A.

Corporate power inevitably leads to a great deal of responsibility for leading corporate citizens, particularly because corporations have been granted rights simi-lar to those granted to persons (in the United States). Corporate decisions, after all, impact not only other businesses, but also the other sectors that comprise society: the political sphere and the civil society sphere, as the intersection of the spheres il-lustrates. The following sections will explore the origins and nature of business en-terprise as we know it today, as well as the necessary and important relationships of a business with a multiplicity of stakeholders. The following two sections will ad-dress the imperatives in the other important societal sectors, recognizing constantly that all three spheres of influence and activity depend for their health and well be-ing on a healthy ecological system.

The present business model is premised on economizing values of efficiency, continued growth, and the interplay of supply and demand in what are supposed to be free markets, as well as by power-aggrandizing values, which were discussed in the previous chapter. At the core of the economic model is the value cluster of "econ-omizing;" that is, "prudent, careful, sometimes deliberately calculated, rational where possible actions of individuals, groups, and organizations that are intended to produce net outputs or benefits from a given amount of resource inputs."[9] Given these dominant values, it not surprising that companies and their managers seek out ways of conserving precious resources and continuing to grow, or that they use power-aggrandizing techniques to consolidate their resources and strengthen their influence on the markets they serve. It is also not surprising that, when feasible, they place costs outside of their own systems—a process called externalizing costs—to appear more efficient.

Since we have argued that companies are comprised of their primary stake-holder relationships, it seems that to survive and be successful, leading corporate cit-izens need to maintain good relationships with their stakeholders. That is the core of the model of citizenship presented in this book.

The Corporation and Its Stakeholders

Let us think about these relationships for a moment. Companies are typically sta
and financed by owners who, in the current thinking of many business leaders,
considered to be the dominant (and sometimes only important) stakeholder. We I
already seen in Chapter 1, however, that other stakeholders are critical to the suc
of companies as corporate citizens and that they too have placed various form
their capital at risk, are invested in, or tied in relationship to companies. For example, *employees* as stakeholders develop, produce, and deliver the company's products and services. The existence of companies is also contingent upon the goodwill
and continued purchases of *customers*. Companies also depend upon the earth for
raw materials (ultimately) and *suppliers and allies or partners,* who produce the raw
materials necessary for the company to generate its own goods and services.
Relationships with these stakeholder groups constitute any leading corporate citizen's *primary stakeholder relationships.*

There are also critical *secondary stakeholder relationships* without which most
companies could not survive. For example, companies rely upon *governments*—local, state/provincial, national, and increasingly international—to create the rules of
society that make trading, economic, and political relationships feasible over time.
Corporate citizens rely upon their local *communities* for an educated workforce and
the infrastructure (e.g., roads, local services, and zoning regulations) that make production of goods and services possible. And there are other critical secondary stakeholders that depend on the particular circumstances of the company and the nature
of its business.

Economic development is positive not only because it supplies these goods and
services, but also because it provides jobs to consumers throughout the developed
world.[10] Rosabeth Moss Kanter, who studies large corporations, believes that "The
world is becoming a global shopping mall in which ideas and products are available
everywhere at the same time. This puts the power of choice in the hands of customers, changing the terms of competition forever."[11]

Although some critics decry the materialism (and imbalance in the social system, as Figure 3.2D suggests) inherent in such a consumerist approach to the global
economy, the competitive dynamics on which it rests are undeniable. Rapid change,
intensifying competition, multiple new competitors in most product and service domains, and global connectedness have reshaped the economic—and social—environment in which people in the developed world live today.

Processes of Globalization and the Competitive Environment

Processes of globalization, which Kanter identified as mobility, simultaneity, bypass,
and pluralism have created a wholly new competitive environment.[12] *Mobility* means
that capital, people, and ideas transcend boundaries, flowing across them by many
means, such as individuals traveling from place to place or, increasingly, electronically

through the Internet and technological means. *Simultaneity* means that goods and services become available everywhere and all at once at a pace that Stan Davis and Christopher Meyer described as "blur."[13] *Bypass* suggests that there will be alternative routes to get goods and services to their purchasers, thereby reducing dependencies among the otherwise interconnected stakeholders. For example, while some companies may once have relied on local providers for supplies and equipment, increasingly they are using the Internet to find the lowest-cost supplier and purchasing such supplies on line, bypassing local companies. Finally, *pluralism* means that processes of decentralization will continue to devolve responsibility on the smallest, most entrepreneurial units possible, a trend that has been evident in the United States for some years. This movement toward pluralism suggests that huge bureaucratic companies, with many layers of management and enormously complex internal relationships, may eventually be replaced by smaller, more entrepreneurial and autonomous or semiautonomous units, even down to individual employees becoming contractors for their own services.

Competing successfully in this hypercompetitive economic context means, according to Kanter, that companies need to become "world class." Being world class in turn demands that companies and their leaders need to maintain awareness of the leading edge concepts that guide progressive companies. Such world-class companies, "leading corporate citizens" in our terms, need to stay connected technologically, within their communities, and in their industries with all of their stakeholders. Finally, companies need to continue to develop competence among all of their important stakeholders by investing in ongoing learning throughout the enterprise.[14]

With all of the change implied by the globalization process, staying connected to stakeholders, fostering individual and corporate citizenship and civic engagement, and maintaining community, whether inside the organization or outside in society, would appear to be more important than ever. Without ties to local communities and the *relationships* that sustain them, it is difficult for companies to be accountable for the decisions they make. Simultaneously, *balance* among the three spheres of activity in human society—economic, political, and civil—becomes a paramount concern, as does providing appropriate mechanisms to assure accountability for decisions taken in the interests of remaining or becoming competitive and world class.

As we shall see below, the rise of modern capitalism and the relatively rootless transnational corporation (i.e., its activities transcend national boundaries or even a "home" country) poses some dangers to ecological sustainability, as well as to sources of community and relationships locally. Leaders of corporate citizens need to learn to pay attention to the balance needed to keep human societies healthy and businesses successful.

The Capitalist Market System Past and Present

Corporate citizenship responsibilities, although frequently overlooked, derive directly from the origin of the corporate form itself, which is based in a legal charter granted wherever a company operates. This government-granted "charter" gives a company the right to do business and receive certain legal benefits. In particular, incorporation means that the corporation itself is treated as a "person" that can be sued. In addition to the corporation's being viewed as a person, individual managers are now increasingly being held liable for corporate acts. As a result, corporate leaders need to pay careful attention to the legal and ethical issues facing them within the company, and make decisions on the company's behalf that will withstand both public and legal scrutiny. In effect, the corporate charter and subsequent court decisions have granted companies the right to be treated as a legal person.

In the United States, early corporations were granted charters through state legislatures, but only for a limited period of time and with limited powers. Charters were considered "legal fictions with no claim to a natural place in the order of things or in the spontaneous associations or contracts of private parties."[15] Over time, however, U.S. courts made decisions that granted to companies the rights of a legal person. These rights include freedom of speech, which is powerfully used in advertising, the media, and corporate political action committees (PACs), which are entities established by corporations to lobby legislators and take other political actions on the organization's behalf. Prior to these decisions, however, corporations were considered to be instruments to forward the public interest, rather than instruments operated primarily for private gain. There is a significant movement today, highlighted by protests against the World Trade Organization when it attempted to meet at the end of the 20th century in Seattle, to return the corporation to its roots and its public responsibilities.

Neoclassical Economics

Today's market system, frequently termed the free market or free market capitalism, is based on a number of assumptions. Derived from the ideas of the Scottish economist Adam Smith (1723–1790), the concept of a free market is today expressed in the neoclassical economic system. The premise of neoclassical economics is that a multitude of small buyers will "demand" and receive goods and services from a multitude of small producers. No one buyer or supplier will, under this model, be able to command a significant portion of the market or influence the market price. Over time, with many transactions, demand and supply will reach a point of equilibrium and balance.[16]

Another assumption of the neoclassical model is that information is readily available to all participants in the market (i.e., there are no trade secrets or proprietary knowledge). Further, sellers bear all the costs of producing goods and services; that is, such costs are internalized rather than externalized. Full cost accounting— that is, fully accounting for *all* of the costs associated with the production of goods and services, including those costs today not typically included, such as the cost of using up raw materials or creating pollution—would thus be employed. When costs are not included in a full costing system, they are externalized.

Externalizing costs, such as the costs of pollution or extracting irreplaceable environmental resources, means that those costs are borne not by the producer of the good or service, but elsewhere, typically by the general public through tax assessments. The costs, however, remain in the system somewhere, even if they are borne not by the organization that produces them but by, for example, taxpayers.

Additionally, the free market model of neoclassical economics assumes, following the English economist David Ricardo's (1772–1823) theory of comparative advantage, that investment capital remains within national borders and international trade is balanced. Finally, the model assumes that savings are invested in productive capital.[17]

Failed Assumptions of Neoclassical Economics

Think about these assumptions. Very few of them actually apply to today's economies, which means that to some extent the balance implied by the "free" market is somewhat mythical in the complex global economic arena. For one thing, most modern industries, instead of comprising numerous small buyers and sellers, are oligopolies comprised of a few very large corporations, some of which control more resources than many countries. This reality means that some companies do indeed command significant portions of the market and are quite capable of influencing the market price.

Further, most large corporations have numerous trade secrets and much closely held proprietary information that they use to their competitive advantage. Indeed, that is often the very source of competitive advantage (in addition, of course, to the knowledge capital of employees). Many costs are externalized. The whole thrust of the economizing value that is the business imperative is to foster as much externalization of costs as possible in order to preserve efficiency and enhance productivity. But because "the costs are in the system somewhere,"[18] they will be paid for somewhere, frequently, as noted above, by taxpayers.

Finally, there is an almost obsessive attention to increasing shareholder wealth in the current system with little regard for other stakeholders, which in the United States, is of course, related to the dominance of the individualistic ideology discussed at the outset of this chapter. Most shareholders or "owners" in modern large corporations are distantly removed from any strategic or operational details because they own only a small fraction of the millions of company shares outstanding and have little voice in and no impact upon corporate affairs. The emphasis on maximizing shareholder wealth means that too frequently corporate resources are used to generate short-term improvements in share price, while long-term and societal needs are put aside, bringing us back to the question of balancing societal—not just economic—needs. The shareholder wealth or finance capitalism model thus pays little regard to building productive assets in the underlying business, in part because accountability for corporate actions is limited and corporate power is high.[19]

The Public Responsibilities of the Corporation

An alternative perspective suggests that companies have public as well as private responsibilities. While setting public policy is a part of the political sphere, corporations and their leaders, by virtue of the charter granted to them by the state, do have public responsibilities that need to be recognized explicitly. Public responsibilities revolve around understanding the impacts that companies have on their stakeholders and in the broader societies in which they operate. In return for the right or license to operate granted by states and nations to companies, as corporate citizens companies need to respect the rights of other stakeholders, treat them fairly and justly, and avoid harm wherever possible. We will discuss these stakeholder-related responsibilities in more detail in Chapter 4.

In a seminal book about the "principle of public responsibility" for the private corporation, Lee Preston and James Post described the scope of managerial responsibility based on the extent of impacts of corporate actions, decisions, and behavior.[20] Updating Preston and Post's ideas to include stakeholder considerations, it is clear that corporate leaders today need to be concerned about the impacts that they have on both primary and secondary stakeholders.

Primary Responsibility

Preston and Post described two levels of managerial responsibility, primary and secondary. *Primary responsibility* has to do with the business of the organization, whatever it is, that is, "the role that defines its nature and social purpose and that provides the basis for exchange relationships between it and the rest of society."[21] Primary responsibilities, then, have to do with the impacts and outcomes of corporate decisions and actions with respect to primary stakeholders, including employees, customers, owners, and—at least for many companies that operate through a network structure—suppliers and allies. In addition, because of their close ties, key secondary responsibilities—business responsibilities—need to be met with respect to other important stakeholders, including local communities where the company has operations or does business, and the governments that establish the rules of society that impact the firm.

Essentially, these primary and secondary responsibilities have to do with proper treatment of stakeholders, with granting them appropriate respect for their positions and the same dignity that one would accord in any long-term working relationship that one hoped to sustain over time. But these responsibilities are essentially private responsibilities because they have to do with the day-to-day business practices involved in producing goods and services and their impacts. Indeed, as argued above, the primary stakeholder relationships effectively *constitute* the firm.

Secondary Responsibilities

The secondary responsibilities of the corporation have to do with its historical and continuing "public" character (even though some of this character has been denied in recent times). According to Preston and Post, the *secondary responsibilities* of the firm are "all those relationships, activities, and impacts of the organization that are ancillary or consequential to its primary involvement activities," including the use of its products or services, and the externalities associated with production processes.[22]

Within these secondary responsibilities are relationships with secondary stakeholders, that is, those that may not immediately impact or be impacted by the firm's activities. Thus, a company has a responsibility for the social welfare of its retirees through operation of a decent pension plan that will support them. It is responsible for the education of local school children to the extent that they represent the workforce of the future on whom the company and its affiliates depend. It is responsible for the sustainability of the ecological environment because the company itself depends on that environment for its own resources. The health of the community is also intertwined with the ecology, so the company's activities might have significant ecological impacts. Secondary—and public—responsibilities are those associated with the broader and less direct societal impacts of the firm's operations.

Together, primary and secondary responsibilities encompass all of the arenas and stakeholders to whom corporate leaders should pay attention in their decision-making capacity. Stakeholder impacts, particularly secondary impacts, also determine the extent to which economic activities in our three-sphere model intersect with the political and civil society spheres of activity. The more overlap in a given stakeholder arena, the more responsibility a company has for its actions with respect to that stakeholder. Of course, corporations, like all of human society, depend on an ecology that supports human life at its base.

Today, the business system itself can be viewed as an ecological system, with no clear boundaries between one type of enterprise and the next, interconnected and interdependent, and working as much from collaboration as from competition.[23] Such businesses recognize that they coevolve with their competitors, suppliers, customers, and other stakeholders, rather than operating independently. By taking a systems perspective on this coevolution and recognizing their interdependency with stakeholders in the other spheres of society, leading corporate citizens can learn to tap new opportunities early because they are in constant dialogue with these key stakeholders, who frequently operate in the political and civil society spheres. But they also need to recognize that these other stakeholders play important roles in the balancing act of sustaining human civilization.

Rethinking Public Responsibilities

As noted above, shareholders (owners) today in America and increasingly throughout the world are the stakeholders to whom leaders are believed to owe their primary allegiance and the "maximization" of wealth. In the minds of many corporate leaders, other stakeholders' needs and interests are considered secondary when they are considered at all.

This narrowness of perspective, which derives from the individualistic ideology, has significant consequences for other important stakeholders, those who are too frequently left out of consideration when companies take actions on behalf of shareholders/owners, and whose needs would be better considered in a communitarian logic. For example, when companies cut costs in the interests of achieving more profitability or when they acquire companies simply because they desire more power, their executives may be thinking only of shareholder wealth rather than the consequences for employees, customers, or local communities. During the 1990s employee loyalty, commitment, and morale were eroded by numerous and reoccurring downsizings, restructurings, and reengineerings, which leave resources stretched and change a constant. This erosion of loyalty becomes critical when companies face, as they do at the start of the third millennium, personnel shortages. Communities suffer the consequences of companies moving long-standing facilities to lower wage countries, leaving a wreckage of unemployed workers, devastated small businesses who relied on patronage from bigger businesses, and eroded community tax bases and infrastructure. One clear example is the cost-cutting, massive employee layoffs, and numerous failed acquisitions and subsequent divestitures of General Electric Corporation under the leadership of Jack Welch.[24] Welch (now retired) has been touted as the CEO of the 20th century because his leadership made GE's stock price soar; however, little attention is given to some of the by-products of the layoffs and other cost-cutting moves that accompanied this profitability. A balanced approach suggests that both types of issues need consideration.

Other indicators of problems with the current business model might be noted. Air and water pollution, toxic waste dumping, and other negative by-products of production are created by a corporate system that finds it more efficient to gain competitive advantage through externalizing such costs rather than assuming them within product costs. With adequate regulatory protections, such externalization may be the most efficient means of achieving certain types of productivity. In developing nations, transnational enterprises emphasize low-cost production in what some term a "race to the bottom"[25] that pits nation against nation and leaves too many people working in sweatshop conditions with little if any dignity or freedom.[26]

Dot-com companies pose another whole set of issues related to corporate citizenship. Characterized by extremely rapid growth, immense wealth for relatively young entrepreneurs, intense competitive pressure, and little profit at least in the early stages of their lives, dot-com companies (or e-commerce) need to grow into better understanding of their responsibilities to stakeholders other than owners.[27] In addition, some dot-com companies are "virtual" companies, meaning that employees, customers, and suppliers meet only online rather than face-to-face. The citizenship implications of such virtual organizations have yet to be clarified.

Still, it is clear that leading corporate citizens today demands more rather than less of tomorrow's executives. Leaders must take into consideration the impacts of their decisions on the wide range of stakeholders interdependent with them in the societal holon, that is, incorporate at least a modicum of communitarian thinking into their individualism and entrepreneurial efforts. Taking this perspective on the public responsibilities of the corporation seriously means that corporations are probably not responsible for, nor should they take responsibility for, arenas of political/public policy and civil life for which organizations operating in those spheres have responsibility.

Because of the amount of power that transnational corporations have accrued in recent years, it is critically important that actors within each of the other two spheres of human civilization (as well as activists on behalf of the natural environment) have relatively equal access to shaping the future of societies. It is to these important other spheres and the ways in which they can and should balance corporate power and resources we now turn.

THE POLITICAL SPHERE

The political sphere is comprised of governments and governmental organizations (GOs) on multiple levels. Governments exist at multiple levels. They operate locally, administering towns and cities. They operate at a state, provincial, or regional level. And they operate at the level of the nation-state. Increasingly, they operate between governments at the intergovernmental organization (IGO) level. Each of these levels has responsibility for setting the rules of society, which affect the economic and civil spheres (as well as the political) at their level.

Public policy makers, whether elected or appointed to public office, at least in democratic societies, are charged with responsibility for "the public interest" or the "common good." In democratic societies, the public good is, at least in theory, determined either directly by the public or by elected officials chosen to represent the public. In the United States, governments tend to be comprised of three branches. One is the executive branch, comprised of the lead public official (i.e., the president, governor, or mayor, depending on the level) and the regulatory agencies that imple-

---

An Ounce of Prevention:
Ford and 3M Seek to Balance Short-Term Profits and Long-Term Problems

In May 2000 two major corporations made startling announcements that rocked the business world—and highlighted companies' growing awareness of the need to balance short-term profits with long-term environmental and corporate sustainability. William C. Ford, chairman of Ford Motor Company, acknowledged that sports utility vehicles (SUVs)—which account for more than 20 percent of the company's U.S. sales—contribute more to global warming, emit more exhaust, and endanger other motorists more than standard cars. Ford said that the company would continue to make SUVs to fill consumer demand, but that it would seek ways to mitigate the environmental damage caused by the vehicles. Almost simultaneous with this announcement, Ford became involved in a massive recall effort for the Firestone tires on its Explorer models of SUVs. The recall involved the recall of more than six million tires in some 16 countries, and illustrates the complexity of becoming a leading corporate citizen.

The week after Ford's statement on the SUVs and pollution, the 3M Company announced that it will voluntarily phase out many of its popular Scotchgard products. Company researchers found that a chemical used to protect fabrics, carpet, and leather from staining tends to accumulate in human and animal tissue. Over time, this chemical could potentially pose a health or environmental risk.

In both of these cases, corporate leaders emphasized the link between environmental and health issues and long-term profitability. Ford told reporters that he didn't want his company to appear to follow the cigarette companies' lead by continuing to manufacture a dangerous product. The enormous financial judgments levied by juries against tobacco companies may have served as an additional incentive for 3M and Ford to burnish their public images through these recent displays of corporate responsibility.

Sources: "Ford's SUV Shocker," Salon.com, May 13, 2000; "3M Agrees to Phase Out Some Scotchgard Products" by Cat Lazaroff, Environment News Service, May 17, 2000. Produced by "Leverage Points for a New Workplace, New World!" An e-bulletin, from Pegasus Communications. The information on the Ford recall is from Tim Dobbins, "US Seeks More from Ford on Tire Swaps," Reuters News Service, August 31, 2000.

ment laws. The legislative branch is comprised of elected representatives of the people and is generally responsible for creating the laws by which citizens, be they individual or corporate, must abide. The third branch is the judicial branch, which consists of the court system, and is charged with enforcing the laws.

The Common Good

In theory, the critical role of institutions in the political sphere is to determine what actions, policies, and rules are in the public interest or the common good and to set the rules of society that foster that common good. These rules are frequently called rules of the game or what we will call rules of society(ies). Such rules are implemented through *public policy* or the combination of decisions and actions taken by elected and appointed public officials.[28] The *public interest* or *common good* is the particular standards and values that people in a society generally agree are in the best interests of that society. In most democratic nations, the common good is underpinned by values such as social justice, equity and fairness, and human dignity.

The political or governmental sphere, as earlier noted, is dominated by *values of power aggrandizing* in developing its institutions, standards, and policies, since there is no currency that represents the bottom line as can be found in business. Governmental organizations, as a result, have a distinct tendency to organize themselves bureaucratically, following rules and procedures, and creating hierarchies and sets of regulations for constituents to follow, partly as a result of the underlying value of power aggrandizing. In spite of this tendency toward power aggrandizing, governmental leaders in most democratic nations are charged with determining and implementing the (current) view of the common good as defined by the contest of forces that result from the pluralistic interests inevitably found in any society.

Governments create and implement the rules of societies through what is called the *public policy process*. According to Preston and Post, "Public policy refers to widely shared and generally acknowledged principles directing and controlling actions that have broad implications for society at large or major portions thereof."[29] A nation's political structure and constitution determine the public policy process and its outcomes, which in turn dictate how laws, court, and executive decisions are to be made. The public issues that are dealt with through public policy decisions and rulings constitute the public policy agenda, which may or may not represent majority opinion at any given time even in democratic nations.[30] The United States has three branches of government, the executive, the legislative, and the judicial, that form a system in which there are natural checks and balances in an effort to assure that no one branch gains too much power or gets out of control.

In the United States, the *public policy arena*—that is, the arenas where debates about what public policy should be—is filled with competing interests and contested values from numerous different groups each of which wants some say in setting the public policy agenda. All of these competing interests would like to have their point of view and their best interests represented in the law, regulations, and court decisions in a system that is called pluralism. But only some interests can actually be represented in laws and regulations at any given time. Thus, an important task of public policy makers is to determine which, among the many competing interests at play at any given time, should receive attention and priority. Obviously, both the public policy agenda and public policy itself shift over time as societal interests and needs change.

Of course, in a pluralistic society, where there are many points of view and many interests that need to be represented, it is difficult to determine the public interest or the common good. This variety of interests creates a contest of sorts that the public policy process, when it works well, is meant to help sort out. Citizens who wish to have "voice" on a given matter tend to band together in associations, activist groups, or other organizations so that their voices become more powerful—and thus better able to be heard by government officials. The Internet and other forms of electronic communication are facilitating the formation of such civic and political associations, which can form voting blocs, create newsletters, form protest movements, generate lobbying activities, or engage in numerous other forms of political action.

Recognizing the value of such activities, many companies have banded together in industry, trade, and other economic associations. Some observers even claim that such associations can be a foundation for developing what is called a "civil economy," that is, an economy in which free market forces are regulated by the forces of community and self-interest that seek the good of the whole. Indeed, in some respects, this seeking of the common good is what Adam Smith sought in developing the theory of free markets. Although the reality of markets is that they are not entirely free, their power to produce goods and services that do benefit humanity is real. That power, however, needs to be tempered by active involvement from officials whose primary duty is to act on behalf of a public interest defined by some sort of democratic process.

Most nations have at least three levels of government to which businesses need to pay attention: local community or municipal, state or provincial, and national. In the future, we can expect that intergovernmental agencies will play an increasingly important role in setting the rules of societies, particularly when there is a need for rules that go across national boundaries.

Why Government?

There is a good deal of cynicism in the United States today about government, in part because of its power-aggrandizing tendencies, which can sometimes result in seemingly immovable bureaucracies, overburdensome regulations, and excess spending without as much success in reaching national priorities as many consider desirable. In part, the cynicism exists because of what linguist Deborah Tannen called the "argument culture," in which issues tend to be polarized and all aspects of the lives and actions of public officials are closely scrutinized for flaws and inconsistencies.[31]

Whatever their problems, governments do play a socially essential role in creating the rules of the society that permit corporate and market activity to develop, enable markets to be "free," and provide for trust in the system of trading relationships that constitute world economies. In addition, they set the rules that govern society itself, including the social discourse, types of organizations and activities permitted in civil and economic realms, and national or state priorities. Governments also serve to protect and indeed in many respects define the public good or the public interest, particularly in democratic societies where, at least in principle, the general public has some say—or voice—in fostering public policy decisions.

Governments, when they work on behalf of citizens (which is not always the case in dictatorships), protect citizens from harmful actions that might result if there were no socially accepted rules to follow. In addition, they have an important role in protecting public goods and dealing with externalities that impact or are created by business operations.

Public Goods

Public goods, as opposed to the public good defined above, are shared, generally indivisible, and external benefits that accrue to all citizens from actions taken by others.[32] Typically, people cannot use goods unless they are willing to pay for them, but when goods are public, they are available to all whether or not they are willing or able to pay. For example, when a company installs pollution equipment, everyone in the neighborhood benefits even though they have not paid for the installation. Thus, the company has generated a public good; however, it has potentially also incurred a cost that other companies do not have and may as a result have put itself at somewhat of a competitive disadvantage in doing so. Typical public goods are clean air, clean water, parks, and highways that, once available, are shared by the entire public.

Externalities

Externalities are the reverse of public goods in that they are public "bads." Thus, if that same company refuses to install the pollution-control equipment, everyone downwind suffers from the pollution created. Externalities then are the shared and usually indivisible costs that accrue to people or organizations even when they do not take the deleterious actions themselves. Common forms of externalities include most forms of pollution, which are shared by all in the form of undrinkable water or dirty air. The problem, as we have discovered with pollution and other externalities, is that the costs do not disappear because they are externalized. These costs remain somewhere in the system, typically in the public arena where the general public, rather than the customers of the polluting business, has to pay. The "Boss Hog" case illustrates some of the externalities of hog farming.

The Prisoner's Dilemma

Dealing with externalities and public goods raises what is called the prisoner's dilemma, which makes obvious why rules and regulations are sometimes necessary. In a prisoner's dilemma situation, the gain of one party occurs at the cost of another party as well as to the system as a whole. In a typical framing of the prisoner's dilemma, a dictator captures two of the "regular suspects" for a heinous crime that has been committed, without knowing which, if either, committed the crime. Separating the suspects, the dictator tells each that if she or he implicates the other, the dictator will be able to greatly reduce the sentence of the squealer, setting her or him free, while the other will face hanging or life in prison. If neither confesses or

In 1999 swine production contributed $1 billion to the North Carolina economy, surpassing tobacco. This industry has experienced explosive growth under the stimulus of franchises offered by large meat-processing corporations, like Murphy Family Farms, which give growers a set price for the output of their mass-production operations. Many of the estimated 10 million porkers who populate the eastern lowland counties of the state spend their lives confined to pens in huge, high-tech facilities that deliver food to the front and dispose of waste at the rear via conveyor belts. Since a hog produces four times the volume of waste as a human being, one corporate hog farm can generate a waste stream equivalent to that of a city of 250,000 people. The traditional method for dealing with this prodigious outflow has been to dig a waste lagoon, followed by spraying the liquefied waste on nearby fields as an organic fertilizer.

By the mid-1990s the increasing number and size of these "swine factories" in North Carolina was generating a political backlash against the *externalities* imposed on neighboring communities by corporate hog farm practices. Beyond the obvious "public bad" of a downwind stench and the incremental impact of acid rain from evaporating ammonia, the waste lagoon and field spray system create a nitrogen-rich effluent carried by rain into nearby streams. Excessive nitrogen in the streams feeds the bloom of algae, turning the streams emerald green. When this algae collects in wetlands near the ocean, it dies and sinks to the bottom. Bacteria, feeding on the dead algae, rob the water of oxygen, causing periodic fish kills near fishing and tourist areas. The failure of one industry to recognize and "internalize" its externality costs imposes an economic burden upon other industries, while also negatively impacting society and the ecological system.

In the summer of 1995, public concern about the negative environmental impacts of corporate pig farming reached new heights in the soggy, smelly aftermath of Hurricane Floyd. Torrential rains in June swelled the state's more that 3,600 waste lagoons to near overflowing, weakening their retaining walls and threatening a deluge of liquid waste upon downstream fisheries and communities. Many hog farmers illegally drained excess lagoon waste into streams and swamps to prevent a breach in their dikes. In the end, Hurricane Floyd washed out 50 waste lagoons and drowned more than 30,000 hogs. Defenders of corporate hog farm practices sought to divert public blame and political retribution by claiming that this environmental calamity was an "Act of God." A critic in the state legislature countered that this was a "sign from God" that conventional methods for dealing with the industry's societal mess were inadequate and had to change.

State politicians, previously concerned with promoting economic development and highly sensitive to the political clout and campaign contributions of "Boss Hog," responded to public pressure for increased regulatory controls and oversight. In 1997 the General Assembly imposed a temporary moratorium on new hog farms and stepped up regulatory oversight of swine operations. In 1999 Governor Jim Hunt decreed that existing waste lagoons must be phased out over 10 years. The following year, Democratic State Attorney General Mike Easley, in charge of the regulatory crackdown, ran for governor on a platform calling for more balance between the push for economic growth and the pull for corporate accountability and environmental sustainability.

The search is on for a new, more sustainable swine waste processing technology, at an estimated cost to taxpayers and hog farmers of at least $400 million. One of the most promising approaches is a bacterium that reduces the waste to amino acids that can be reconstituted as animal feed. In the end, the solution to this problem will be political, rather than scientific. Some have called upon the government to promote a "systems" solution by creating a market for the processed swine waste, whether as compost, animal feed, or crab bait. This would give the farmer some added income to cover the higher cost of managing manure. Many hog farmers have borrowed heavily to finance expansion at a time when overproduction has driven the price of pork bellies below the break-even point for many producers. A more sustainable industry may also be a smaller industry, with limits to growth to accompany limits on waste.

Source: Jerry Calton, University of Hawaii, Hilo. This case is based on the Raleigh *News-Observer* investigative series entitled "Boss Hog" which won the 1996 Pulitzer Prize for public service journalism. For an in-depth look at this "messy" issue, go to the website: http://www.nando.net/sproject/hogs/.

squeals, then both will face, say, three years in prison. Whoever confesses faces 20 years in prison. Then the dictator goes to the other prisoner with the same message.

Obviously, the best "system" outcome is that neither prisoner confesses, both face the reduced three-year sentences, but neither hangs nor faces life in prison. But clearly the incentive for each prisoner individually is to maximize his or her "good" by implicating the other, especially as neither is allowed to talk with the other.

Many business situations resemble prisoner's dilemmas. For example, the airline industry constantly finds itself engaging in price wars in which no company wins. The best outcome for the industry (the system) would be to avoid the price war. Individual companies, however, at least in the short term, find it hard to resist the potential gains in market share and revenue that come from starting to reduce prices. But once one company has reduced prices, others find it necessary to follow in order to be competitive, thereby reducing overall industry revenues (and possibly benefiting consumers at least in the short run).

Companies that are proactive in incurring costs that others do not incur at the same time may also find themselves in a form of prisoner's dilemma. Going back to our pollution example, then, we can see that the company that installs the pollution equipment proactively may place itself at a competitive disadvantage relative to others who may not choose to take such actions voluntarily, despite the environmental public goods that result.

Avoiding prisoner's dilemma situations is difficult unless there are rules of society in place that create the same standards, policies, and regulations for all companies in an industry, providing some justification for creating the rules of society in the first place. Another way of dealing with prisoner's dilemmas involves creating a set of shared values that establish the same expectations for all players in a situation. Shared values and expectations can help corporate citizens avoid both the tragedy of the commons and free ridership, discussed below, because they establish a higher ground—or a common good—on which those involved in a situation agree.

The Tragedy of the Commons

Similar to the prisoner's dilemma in its implications is what biologist Garret Hardin called the tragedy of the commons.[33] Such situations arise when there are public goods available to all, but that can be consumed or destroyed if overused. Whatever the attractiveness of the commons, there are incentives for each individual to overuse the common in an effort to gain individual advantage, thereby destroying the resource for all.

For example, many people enjoy the serenity and beauty of a lake and, as a result, build houses with docks at the edge of the lake, then put motorboats into the water so that they can enjoy the lake's beauty. Soon, there are too many houses, the lake becomes polluted, and the noise of constant motorboating has destroyed the very serenity that people sought out.

The environment, the planet, is a global commons, as is notable in the discussion above about the ecological underpinning for human civilization. Because of the tendency that biological systems of all sorts have to overuse commons, protecting them is an imperative for the future of human civilization as well as the natural environment. Thus, there is a critical role for laws and regulations to protect the "commons" that we all share, such as the natural environment.

Free Riders

When there is a common good to be gained or when an externality can be avoided through the actions of some, there is a tendency toward free ridership.[34] Free riding occurs when it is difficult or impractical to exclude people or organizations from a benefit or public good. When such goods are available, there is little incentive for any one individual or organization to pay for them, which gives rise to a tendency to "free ride" to gain the benefits without paying the costs.

Trade or industry associations, for example, can give rise to free ridership when they seek out benefits for the industry as a whole. Members in the association pay dues that support the seeking of benefits, but all members of the industry, whether they join the association or not, will benefit from the association's efforts. Thus, there is a tendency to let others join and pay dues, while avoiding membership in the association. The costs of membership are imposed on members, while free riders gain the benefits without incurring associated costs.

As with protecting the commons, avoiding free ridership means leveling the playing field for all by creating rules and regulations that all must follow. Another way to deal with free ridership is through associations that establish industry, trade, or market standards that pressure both companies and individuals to live up to expectations and standards of what one observer called a civil market.[35]

Laws, Regulations, and Court Rulings

Laws, regulations, and court rulings help governments create a system that attempts to balance public goods and externalities, avoid the tragedy of the commons, and reduce free ridership, making the so-called playing field level for all. Thus, in the example of public goods, the company that installs pollution equipment may incur higher costs than competitors, placing itself at a competitive disadvantage. In the case of externalities, companies have incentives, particularly given their values of economizing, to externalize as many costs as possible, placing themselves at an advantage relative to companies that internalize more of their costs by behaving more responsibly. The role of laws, regulations, and court rulings under such circumstances is to attempt to provide an equitable outcome or demand equitable inputs. For example, all companies following a court decision or regulatory decree need to internalize similar costs or incur the same costs to avoid the externalities, placing none of them at a competitive disadvantage relative to others following the same guidelines.

Over time, the rules of societies shift. Shifts occur in part because of technological changes, such as those that made it necessary to break down regulatory barriers among financial institutions. They also occur because societies recognize formerly unmet needs (e.g., for public or worker safety, or consumer or environmental protection), which were some of the arenas that generated activism during the 1960s that resulted in the passing of protective laws and regulations in the United States. Finally, they occur because information availability raises consciousness about issues that are of public concern and need to be addressed.

The Shifting Public Policy Agenda

What shapes the public policy agenda with which governmental officials contend? Here we speak largely of democratic societies, because in more authoritarian societies those groups and individuals in power typically determine the public policy agenda, rather than a more broad-based constituency. In democratic societies, public policy is shaped by a number of forces that are often competing or contesting with each other to gain dominance and voice and to have their positions represented in whatever rules of the game are created.

Among the factors that shape the public policy agenda are public opinion. *Public opinion* includes what is thought about by "opinion leaders," that is, key leaders whose voice is listened to by others, and also by what is reported in the media about surveys, case studies, and other research undertaken by various polling groups and various social researchers. Public opinion is shaped by the experiences that people have within their communities and at work, as well as by what is reported in the media. For example, the experiences of the community in Woburn, Massachusetts, where children were dying of leukemia ostensibly from toxic waste pollution generated by the W. R. Grace Company, became a public issue when community members became aware of how many children were ill and dying. The events that followed were chronicled in the book and movie *A Civil Action.*

Political and social activists also help to shape public policy through interest and pressure groups that bring public attention to an issue. Activists use events, including boycotts and protests, publicity, and media relations to try to frame issues in ways that meet their needs and interests, while those groups opposing the activists attempt to frame the issues differently. One such issue is smoking, which health activists have framed as an issue about health and addiction, while cigarette company officials have framed the issue around smokers' rights. Policy makers are frequently caught in the middle of competing interests such as tobacco because states and the federal government rely upon the jobs and taxes generated by the issue, while paying the health-related costs of smoking. Sorting out what is actually in the public interest in such a contested situation is fundamentally what the job of the public policy maker is all about.

Leadership in social organizations of all sorts, including businesses, also helps to shape public issues by framing the debate, testifying before Congress in the United States, making speeches, and issuing reports that garner media and public attention. Elected officials can use the "bully pulpit" created by their elective office to frame issues, as can legislators, governors, and local elected officials. Many business organizations attempting to shape the public policy agenda send leaders to testify before the U.S. Congress. They also hire lobbyists to represent the company's perspective to legislatures at the national and state levels, and create PACs (political action committees) or other political action organizations to supply information and expertise about the company's industry to elected officials who may be deciding upon a law that will affect the company.

One of the problems associated with such corporate political activism relates to the significant economic resources and therefore power that companies possess to have their positions represented. This power becomes especially apparent when companies create PACs to lobby on behalf of the corporation, hire lobbyists, or provide public officials with industry-biased information. Communities, activists, and individuals may have significantly fewer resources at their disposal. Some people raise questions about whether sufficient public "voice" is available to less powerful or resource-rich parties in the public policy arena to assure equitable outcomes that really do represent a level playing field for all in society.

Shifting Public Issues

Attention and activity in the public policy arena changes over time with the shifting of competing interests, as well as with the relative amount of power and voice different contesting parties have. Social problems exist in any society, but they become public issues when sufficient public attention is devoted to them.[36]

A *public issue* has a number of elements.[36] First public issues are in the public arena, possibly subject to public policy or nonpublic resolution. An issue develops for a stakeholder when something is or becomes problematic for at least one stakeholder and when it is controversial; that is, when something is contested in the public arena. The "contest" arises particularly when there are multiple opinions (often of people or groups of equal goodwill) on what the best resolution of that issue should be. Further, issues develop when there is a gap between at least one stakeholder's perception of what "is" and what the stakeholder thinks "ought to be." Further, unless that gap creates some significant perceived present or future impact on the organization, society, or stakeholder, it is unlikely to become an issue. Frequently, issues arise when there is a question of legitimacy about the issue or when there is controversy about what the costs and benefits of issue resolution are.

Issue Life Cycle

Public issues tend to go through a generalized (although not always exactly the same) life cycle as they emerge from obscurity, indifference, or simple inattention of the public and its policy makers onto the public policy agenda. Not all issues are resolved through the public policy process. Many companies have established issue management, public relations, and public affairs units in the hope that they can work cooperatively with governmental and community stakeholders or forestall actions before issues are resolved legislatively or in the court system. But those issues that do gain public attention and concern become public issues, which frequently are dealt with through the public policy process.

Public issues generally begin in *unmet expectation,* that is, in the gap between what is and what "ought" to be in the minds of at least one or more stakeholder.[37] This gap draws attention to the issue from stakeholders, who begin to—or at least try to—shape or "frame" the issue in ways that meet their interests and perceptions. Often this gap develops when society is changing with resulting changes in public expectations.

For example, the use of DDT as a pesticide was largely uncontroversial until the 1963 publication of Rachael Carson's *Silent Spring,* which galvanized environmentalists into action.[38] Similar triggering events include the publication of the Surgeon General's Report on smoking and health in the 1960s, which generated a great deal of antismoking activism. More recently, sweatshop conditions in developing countries from which clothing and shoes are sourced have drawn outrage from the general public when publicized by activists such as the International Labor Organization (ILO). During the first or gap stage, only a few people or groups, typically activists or opinion leaders, may be interested in the issue, but once their activities begin to draw concern and attention, the issue enters the second stage of its life cycle.

The second or political stage of the issue life cycle occurs when the issue, as framed by one or more of the interested stakeholders, begins to draw public attention and concern typically through the media or through various forms of activism. In this stage, the new expectations have become more widely known and accepted and the issue itself may become politicized.[39] As Figure 3.3 suggests, public awareness of the issue increases rather dramatically during this stage and more stakeholders are likely to become involved in the effort to frame the issue in ways that benefits their particular point of view. In this stage, the contest of different values is in full swing.

Government or political actors become involved as the issue progresses to the third stage or legislative stage of the life cycle, as they begin to try to figure out how and where the issue should be dealt with legislatively, if that is to be the actual outcome. Once legislators begin to consider an issue and it has entered the legislative phase of its life cycle, public debate of and contested framings of the issue are likely.

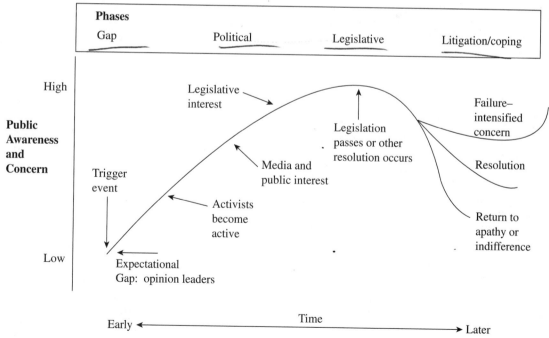

FIGURE 3.3. Issue Life Cycle
Source: Adapted from Preston and Post, 1975; and Mahon and Waddock, 1992.

During this phase, business leaders and others may be called to testify before the relevant legislative body. In this stage, lobbyists also become proactive in getting information to legislators or other decision makers in the hope of influencing the outcome in favor of a company or industry stakeholder group.

Assuming legislation is passed, the issue enters a fourth stage, called litigation or coping, in which stakeholders are expected to comply with the new legislation. If they continue to disagree with the outcome, they might fight it through the court system by means of litigation. If legislation does not pass or is unsatisfactory to some powerful stakeholders, the issue can take on new life. This is what happened in the 1980s when it became clear to the environmental movement that existing regulations were insufficient to cope with newly recognized ecological problems like acid rain, rain forest depletion, and the shrinking of the ozone layer. Renewed environmental activism ensued in an effort to pass stricter laws protecting the environment; in 1992 the United Nations sponsored the first global conference to deal with the increasingly global nature of environmental problems generated by population growth and processes of industrialization.

Generally speaking, the government is one of at least three primary stakeholders in any public issue that affects business (not all public issues impact businesses). The other two are corporations or the economic community, and the particular activist or issues group interested in pursuing the issue to resolution.[40] Gaining a rich and comprehensive understanding of any issue therefore requires a capacity to hold the multiple perspectives of at least these stakeholders simultaneously and to see where their interests diverge and where they converge. This, generally, is the task of public policy makers, as they attempt to determine what outcome, at that point in time, would be in the public interest. In their quest to determine the public interest, public policy makers' ideas and perceived solutions are shaped, along with those of all members of a culture, by the national or community ideology of that country.

Economic Development and the Political Sphere

There are many people who hold that developing countries need to progress through the same stages of industrialization today that Western industrialized nations passed through in their own development. For many Western and Eastern European nations, these stages meant that little regard was given to respecting people or their needs and rights; they were viewed as tools to be used and discarded when used up, rather than as full human beings. Additionally, respect for the environment and its resources was generally lacking as corporations aimed at economizing by externalizing as many costs and problems as possible. As one can see in many parts of the world today, the costs of such externalizing and disregard for the human spirit are manifold. Evidence can be seen in the burning of rain forests in South America with the consequent problems for the ozone layer and presence of carbon dioxide in the atmosphere. It exists in the prevalence of sweatshop conditions and child labor in less developed countries to which much business is "outsourced." And, among other places, it exists in the general disregard for human rights in some developing nations.

Such lack of respect for people and ecology, which is permitted in some parts of the world even today, encourages companies to act, in the interests of economizing and power aggrandizing, with disregard for the impacts of their actions. Many corporate actions affect not only nature but also civil society, where the relations generating civility and community are developed. Because governments in less developed countries do not always have the resources or indeed the incentives to create appropriate infrastructures or regulations to protect their people, abuses do occur. The result is people working in sweatshop conditions, where they are allowed little freedom of movement, even to go to the bathroom. In some places, pay is less than a living wage even for local conditions; workers make mere pennies an hour. Some workers in such situations are punished physically for not meeting production schedules. And they are not permitted to "associate" or attempt to form unions to gain some power and voice so that efforts can be made to improve conditions.

Some developing countries desperately need economic development, so governments are willing to permit companies to engage in practices that they might otherwise wish to avoid. Too frequently in less developed nations, many of the factory workers are young children, who by international standards should be in school, or young women, whose only other employment opportunities may be even worse than the sweatshop conditions in which they work. For example, when Bangladesh forbade the employment of children in factories, many of these young workers seeking alternative work found themselves in prostitution or doing the burdensome manual labor of "breaking bricks."[41]

Companies wishing to become leading corporate citizens in the global arena need to be aware of the pressures that exist in countries to trade human lives and ecological protection for economic development. Leading corporate citizens know that balance is necessary to sustain human civilization over the long term, and that consumers increasingly recognize that value is best added through good citizenship practices. Leading corporate citizens therefore work interactively with governmental bodies to create conditions of employment, jobs, and economic opportunities that maintain a healthy environment and society wherever they operate.

The Political, Economic, and Civil Society Spheres

Notwithstanding the importance of the economic sphere in generating the goods and services needed in societies, business as we know it would not be possible without the infrastructure of rules and regulations created by the public policy process in another important sphere, the political sphere or sector. In effect, these rules and regulations, which we have called the rules of societies, establish the infrastructure by which businesses operate so that there can be a degree of predictability to markets and a general trust in the underlying system.

Just as sustaining a healthy body requires a balanced diet and a life balanced among work, play, exercise, and family/friends, so a healthy social system—at the most macro of levels, the planet—also demands *balance.* For companies to succeed in the long term, corporate power must be balanced with that of governments, which establish the *rules of the game* by which economies exist and businesses compete.

And, as will be discussed in the next section, corporate power must also be balanced with human needs for the civilizing relationships, meaningful work and life, and community that are found in civil society.

THE CIVIL SOCIETY SPHERE

Civil society is fundamentally associational society. *Civil society* is comprised of those entities and organizations in society that develop civility and coherence through the long-term building of civilized community and what can be called social capital, the capital of relationships. Basically, civil society is comprised of organizations and associations that constitute community at whatever level of analysis is being considered. Civil society includes families, religious institutions, nonprofit organizations and other nongovernmental organizations (NGOs), educational institutions, health care institutions, voluntary organizations, civic and political organizations, and associations of all types.

In one sense, civil society is everything outside the economic and political spheres of activity, or as political scientist Alan Wolfe expressed it, "those forms of communal and associational life which are organized neither by the self-interest of the market nor by the coercive potential of the state."[42] In its positive and constructive sense, civil society is comprised of those enterprises and associations that promote what is thought to be the common or collective good in societies; that is, we would like to be able to exclude negative associational entities, such as terrorist or-

---

E-Commerce Raises New Regulatory Issues

The advent of e-commerce has raised a whole series of regulatory and legal issues that governments have never had to face before. For example, does a document that you "sign" online have a legally useful signature? How is such a document to be notarized? What do Internet companies do with the "cookies," or markers, that visitors to their websites leave behind? What happens to an e-commerce company's electronic customer list when that company goes belly-up, as ToySmart.com did in 2000? Should e-commerce companies keep information about visitors to their websites private? How much about their policies regarding the use of the information obtained do they need to reveal to visitors to websites?

Other questions remain. Should companies selling goods bought online pay state taxes? What are the implications for states, who rely on sales taxes, if the answer is no? What about the implications for the companies' competitiveness if the answer is yes? What about new technological developments, like Napster, which permit individuals to download music from other individuals, avoiding having to pay for the music. The Napster situation has the music industry, particularly recording companies, and consumers incensed. The music industry wanted to limit the use of Napster and in late 1999 sued in an effort to put the company out of business, outraging millions of Napster users. This situation represents only one of many similar situations that e-commerce companies will face as governments begin to tackle some of the public policy and public interest issues raised by this new medium for commerce.

ganizations or radica
"civil" society, since
uncivil in their intent

The fundamental
tween social instituti
community. Hence, th
civility, and communi
the basic values of an
cussed above. These
love, and personal v
power-aggrandizing
the "X-values"[44] that
they are also deeply
They are, in short, th
deeply intertwined w

At one level, civ
spheres. Just as there
tion, so there is a ne
capital to support e
that governments co
of trust and civility
provides a foundatio
munity. Civil society
litical and governm
the humanizing ele

The humanizati

One reason that a decline in civic, eng
civic engagement and social capital bolste
symptoms of decreased association are
volved in public life and discourse,
school affairs, and fewer attend
tional activity include fewer
falling union membership,
duced membership and

Putnam entitled hi
comfiting" data sou
decreasing has to
tion with each
United Stat
leagues
count
ati

within a given community create a network of reciprocal relation
ligations among individual members of that community. Community members also
exchange information, which helps them build a shared sense of identity and common
set of values. In turn, these values generate norms of behavior and appropriate practices that provide sanctions where appropriate and rewards where feasible.[45]

Bowling Alone

In research spanning some 20 years, scholar Robert D. Putnam found that Italian
provinces having the strongest associational ties—civil society—were also the most
prosperous and politically successful.[46] Those regions where associational ties were
fewer and people were generally less engaged in society were substantially less
healthy and productive.

After completing his long-term study of Italy, Putnam turned his attention to the
United States, where he uncovered significant evidence that civic engagement and
association—social capital—may be decreasing in America. In a widely cited article titled "Bowling Alone" and in later work, Putnam identified a number of factors
that he believes could be related to the possible decline in affiliational activity in the
United States.[47]

...agement would be problematic is that ... democratic institutions and norms. Some ... that fewer people vote or become actively in- ... fewer participate in public meetings on town or ... political events. Other symptoms of less associa- ... people reporting themselves as religiously affiliated, ... less involvement in parent-teacher associations, and re- ... volunteering in civic and fraternal organizations.

... article "Bowling Alone" because one of the "whimsical yet dis- ... rces for his conclusion that civic engagement in America may be ... do with the number of people bowling in leagues, that is, in associa- ... other. While he found that the total number of people bowling in the ... es increased by 10 percent between 1980 and 1993, the number of bowling ... decreased by 40 percent, perhaps evidence of individualistic orientation in this ... ry. As Putnam pointed out, it is not so much the bowling alone that is problem- ... c; rather, the "broader social significance . . . lies in the social interaction and even occasionally civic conversations over beer and pizza that solo bowlers forgo."[48]

Putnam attributed the declines in civic engagement and consequent social capital to a number of possible factors.[49] One is the pressure of time and money. A second is the changing role of women, which brought many women into the workforce, reducing the amount of time available for associational and volunteer activities. A third factor is the breakdown of the family, resulting from higher divorce rates and increases in single-parent families and one-person households. Putnam also noted that there is circumstantial evidence that the rise of the welfare state may have crowded out private initiative, decreasing social capital in its wake. One other factor is the generational effect that older people tend to be more civically engaged than younger people.

But none of these possible explanations fully satisfied Putnam, who came up with another likely culprit: television. For a number of reasons television might be a disruptive force for civil society. The timing is right. TV viewing is associated with low social capital because it takes the place of other activities in which people might be with others generating social capital. TV affects viewers' outlooks, particularly with respect to the benevolence of others, and it takes the place of hobbies, clubs, and outdoor activities, visiting, and just hanging out for children.

Putnam's work has generated a great deal of controversy and debate. Not everyone agrees that social capital in the United States is diminishing, while some scholars believe there is significant evidence that high social capital is indeed an important element of a healthy society. Maria Poarch, for example, found that many people in America today form their associational ties through work rather than within their communities as was more common in the past.[50] Of course, this finding has significant implications for corporate citizens and those who lead them because to the extent that people find association and develop civility in the workplace, the workplace will need to generate meaning and purpose that is both uplifting and inspiring. Further, more closely linking the association of community and civil society into the economic sphere brings together these spheres and the values that underpin them in wholly new ways. These issues will be explored in more depth in Chapters 4 and 5.

Civility and Society

Overall, when social capital diminishes there is less sense of community, less "common" good because people have less in common, and less of a sense of shared identity. Clearly, healthy societies need to be comprised of healthy social institutions that build strong and vibrant communities. The institutions that comprise civil society—family, civic and nonprofit organizations, religious and educational institutions, and membership organizations of all sorts—bring people into contact with each other to develop a sense of what it means to be part of that particular community.

Strong families (however we define family) are at the base of healthy communities, along with many types of associational activities that help people to become actively involved with their communities. Among these activities are voluntary and nonprofit organizations that meet needs that political and economic enterprises cannot. These needs might be spiritual or affiliative (i.e., having to do with loving, trusting, and caring relationships) and health-related, intellectual as with educational enterprises, or physical and structural as with meeting the needs of disadvantaged people.

Through their development of trust, shared identity, and sense of community, healthy civil societies develop proactive and capable citizens. In democracies, an active citizenry is capable of solving its own political and economic problems. Active citizens are also capable of placing restraints they believe appropriate on enterprises and activities in the other two spheres of activity and in civil society itself. These restraints occur through political action as well as through the activism associated with a range of causes of concern to different citizen groups when they share a common set of values and goals. Active citizens are capable of mobilizing themselves and the other spheres to deal with problems as they arise, while passive citizens, who feel little connectedness to or shared interest with their communities, may remain passive, and the problems go unresolved.

Jihad and McWorld

Today we face further ambiguities, particularly with respect to the impact of economic sphere activities, especially the forces and power of multinational corporations, on civil society. These forces have probably been best articulated by Benjamin Barber in his book *Jihad versus McWorld.*[52] Barber tells us of a world torn between what Barber terms jihad, or the forces of tribalism and parochial ethnicity, which foster what he termed a tyrannical paternalism, and those of globalizing market forces or what he calls McWorld. McWorld has a corporate-centric focus on consumption, markets, and profits that encourages companies to satisfy what seems to be unmitigated self-interest in a world without boundaries. Neither Jihad nor McWorld in its extreme form is conducive, Barber suggested, to democracy, responsibility, or civil society.

Strong civil ties (i.e., larger amounts of social capital) generally enable citizens to challenge governments and locally unacceptable corporate practices when there are problems so that communities' needs, aspirations, and ideas of the common good can be met.[53] In its more negative connotations, however, and when taken to extremes as in Barber's notion of jihad, too much social capital can be exclusionary and negative. Jihad too often takes social ties to an extreme. Once again, we see the need to balance society's interests because even the ties of identity can be destructive when they are too strong and create too much of an "us versus them" attitude among communities.

In some respects, social capital (in its positive and less extreme forms) is a necessary countervailing force to the homogenizing influence and power of McWorld as well as to extreme forms of jihad. Communities with healthy amounts of social capital do not necessarily wish to see their distinctiveness and identity eroded by uncontrollable forces of globalization; they value their sense of community. Unless leading corporate citizens understand this reality, they are likely to face resistance to their presence. Corporate citizens, like people, need to be rooted in the identity of the localities in which they operate if they hope to be successful in the long run because that is where values and norms develop and where meaning is generated.

Additionally, a strong civil sphere provides a necessary counterpoint to the otherwise dominating power of the multinational corporation with its values focused on material goods, consumerism, and other more individualistically oriented values. In a sense, having a strong civil society creates numerous public goods that can then be shared by all members of the relevant communities. While the forces of globalization are likely to continue, smart corporate citizens will recognize the need to construct their business operations carefully to reflect the interests and needs of local communities, rather than simply believing that the same products or services can be delivered in the same way throughout different societies.

Respecting Cultural Differences

Social capital, ideology, and cultures derived from differing religious and social traditions, histories, and worldviews make for remarkable differences in human societies around the world. Leading corporate citizens recognize and honor these differences, even when operating on a global scale. They can do this because they operate, as the next two chapters will suggest, with integrity and deep respect for the traditions of the multiple cultures and peoples of the world.

ORGANIZING ENTERPRISE IN THE THREE SPHERES

Earlier we explored the differences among the three spheres of activity and influence in human civilization: economic, political, and civil society. Each of these spheres of activity is generally associated not only with a distinct values basis, but also with different organizational types and different primary purposes.

Business Organization in the Economic Sphere

In the economic sphere, organizations are businesses and are usually "private" in that they are privately owned, either by a sole proprietor or family, through a partnership arrangement, or through legal incorporation, which grants them certain rights and responsibilities. In some nations, of course, businesses have been nationalized and are government owned, and, increasingly, many businesses are employee owned, at least in part.

These complications aside, if the organization in question is a company that is driven by economizing, its purposes should revolve around production of goods and services truly needed by customers. Generally, all companies will have as *primary stakeholders* owners, employees, customers, and, to the extent that the company is a virtual company relying on specific providers of services and goods that have been "outsourced," suppliers as well as allies and partners (see Table 3.2).

Governmental Organization in the Political Sphere

Governmental organizations (GOs), in contrast to business enterprises, are formed to serve the public interest or the public good within the political sphere, and their major underlying value is power aggrandizing, particularly emphasizing the use of political capital. GOs thus have as their primary stakeholders a set of quite different stakeholders than companies.

The stakeholders of GOs include the political or governmental body that established them (in the United States, this might be the legislative, executive, or judicial branch of government). Stakeholders also include the general public for their franchise and, because public opinion sways governmental bodies to act (at least in democratic societies), employees, the clients, or customers served. In addition, "society" or the local community is a primary stakeholder for governmental organizations because their fundamental purpose is serving the public interest and because the operating expenses of GOs are paid by taxes garnered from the public. Some of the key differences in the organizations found within each sphere of activity are noted in Table 3.2.

Nongovernmental Organizations in the Civil Society Sphere

Another common type of organization, particularly in the United States, is the nonprofit or not-for-profit organization, which is the most popular organizational form in the civil society sphere. In most countries, such entities are called nongovernmental organizations (NGOs). The primary form of capital in NGOs is social capital; NGOs tend to be helping or service organizations that accomplish humanizing-oriented goals rather than being money-making or for-profit enterprises.

There are many types of organizations in this sphere, including religious institutions, educational institutions, and political organizing bodies, as well as families and associations. Although families are part of civil society, for purposes of this discussion, we will consider only formally organized entities, rather than the less formally structured relationships among families.

Many if not most NGOs are not-for-profit organizations in that they attempt to break even rather than having profitability as a goal. This not-for-profit status does not mean that NGOs lose money or even that they do not seek profits (or at least break even). Rather, the financial bottom line is not their most important bottom line. Instead, NGOs tend to focus on other bottom lines such as ecology, health, associational, spiritual, social, and others, which we can summarize as social capital in its broadest sense. Unlike companies, NGOs have no "owner," but tend to be funded by individuals, governments, or foundations to pursue particular purposes, typically related to the social or common good.

Lack of owners makes the primary stakeholders of NGOs different from those of private firms. NGO stakeholders include employees, clients (instead of customers), and funders, as well as those interest groups or activists in society that have a stake in the particular domain and activities of the NGO. Funders can be individuals, foundations, or government-funded bodies. In some cases, we may want to include suppliers as NGO stakeholders, although those suppliers may be other agen-

TABLE 3.2. Primary Stakeholders of Organizations in Different Spheres

Dominant Type of Organization	Sphere of Influence	Primary Purpose	Dominant Values	Key Stakeholders
Business (private sector) Proprietorship Partnership Corporation	Economic	Produce goods and services	Economizing	*Primary* Owners Customers Employees Suppliers Allies/partners *Critical Secondary* Community Governments
Governmental Organization (GO) Executive officers (elected officials, regulatory agencies) Legislative officials Judiciary	Political	Serve public good/interest	Power aggrandizing	Government General public Employees Clients/customers "Society"
Nongovernmental Organization (NGO) Nonprofit Religious organizations Health care organizations Educational institutions Civil and civic organizations Political, trade, and industry associations	Civil society	Build/maintain society and community	Civilizing Building and maintaining relationships	Funder(s) Clients Employees Suppliers "Society"

cies that make a necessary link between clients needing services and the nonprofit organization hoping to provide the service or product.

Blurring Boundaries

Although we have described activities within each of the spheres of activity as if they were easily separable, it is clear today that some of the boundaries between these different types of enterprises are blurry at best. For example, there has been a considerable rise in the number, focus, and extent of intersector collaborations or partnerships since the early 1980s when they first became popular. Among these are school-business partnerships and multisector partnerships that integrate all three sectors.[54] Strategic alliances of all sorts have become commonplace among and between businesses, as well as between businesses and other social institutions such as schools and job training programs.

Additionally, many companies are blurring the relationships among stakeholders through, for example, employee stock ownership plans (ESOPs). ESOPs typically offer stock and some degree of participation as owners in the company to employees, thereby converting them into owner-employees. Further blurring occurs as a result of the huge proportion of retirement monies invested in equity funds, which give many employees an often unrecognized ownership stake in long-term corporate performance.

In many places, nonprofit organizations are undertaking profit-making activities as a way of funding their social causes, rather than relying solely on donations from individuals, foundations, or governments. In similar fashion, governmental agencies, particularly regulatory agencies like the Environmental Protection Agency in the United States, have increasingly turned to market mechanisms, such as selling pollution rights, as means of improving government efficiency and creating incentives for others to act in the public interest. And large business organizations, especially in the United States, have increasingly turned to marketing tools, such as cause-related marketing, which link making a profit with some aspect of financial and social benefit when some of the proceeds are then donated to the social cause.

Further, the pace of change and the linkages created by the electronic revolution, which permit people and organizations to be connected at all times wherever they are, have created what authors Stan Davis and Christopher Meyer have called the "blur" of a connected economy.[55] Combine the blurring of boundaries with the need to build and maintain ongoing positive relationships with the many stakeholders that both comprise and connect the business enterprise today and you get a need to construct business (and other) enterprises as *networks* rather than as traditional hierarchical organizations.

Network organizing does not mean that hierarchy disappears because hierarchy is still necessary within many business functions, particularly as part of the control system. The roles of hierarchy and dominance, however, diminish in the network enterprise, as companies attempt to treat key stakeholders with respect and dignity and work in the collaborative mode more appropriate to the network form. In networks, collaboration and cooperation assume, as they do in biological systems, greater importance than or at least as much importance as competition. Solutions in networks tend to converge toward win-win solutions rather than win-lose competition because network members recognize their interdependence with others for their own success.

Such approaches to stakeholders elevate the role of what are called boundary-spanning functions within the firm to serious relationships that need to be managed effectively if the organization is to be successful, which will be discussed at length in Chapter 7. Of course, all of this necessitates new leadership and management skills for individuals running any modern enterprise in whatever sphere or spheres of activity it exists, as the case of Amanz'abantu illustrates (see box below).

Amanz'abantu: Providing Water through Multisector Collaboration

The village of Mgwangqa is high in the barren hills facing the East Indian Ocean in the Eastern Cape province of South Africa. It has approximately 90 households totaling about 500 inhabitants. Most of the residents have moved there from other areas, such as nearby farms. The vast majority of the population is unemployed and pension benefits are the major income source. A two-kilometer dirt road leads to the main road and the nearest town called Peddie Town is eight kilometers away.

Traditionally the villagers depended upon collecting rainwater and a dam shared with animals for their water supply. Given that the region has about 600 mm of rain a year, the villagers were better off than many rural South African communities. However, the rainfall does not fall evenly throughout the year and health problems arise from the use of these traditional water sources, including scabies among children, running stomachs among all ages, and food poisoning.

The villagers' water options changed in April 1999 with completion of a R42 million (about $6 million) water project that brought water to standpipes to within 200 meters of the households. The project was completed as part of the first phase of a much larger scheme called the Peddie Regional Water Supply Scheme through the collaboration of five signatories to a contract called Amanz'abantu (AA). The signa-

tories represent all three spheres of human activity and include the following:

WATER & SANITATION SERVICES SOUTH AFRICA LTD. (WSSA)

This is a 50-50 joint venture between the French multinational, Suez Lyonnaise des Eaux, and a large South African construction company, Group Five. Formed in 1995, it functions as Operations and Maintenance service provider and is lead partner in the consortium. Suez Lyonnaise is a major French multinational company.

GROUP FIVE CIVILS LTD. (GROUP FIVE)

This is a joint venture between two Group Five companies, one (45 percent) that focuses upon roads and earthworks and another called Civils (55 percent) that focuses upon construction of large structures such as dams. Group Five is a major South African construction company operating internationally.

NINHAM SHAND EAST LTD. (NS) IN ASSOCIATION WITH FONGOQA SKADE TOYI & ASSOCIATES CLOSE CORPORATION (FST)

Under NS's initiative, these two companies jointly responded to the design portion of the contract. They have divided their responsibilities between work dealing with untreated and treated water.

NS does raw water, dams, and water treatment facilities; FST does pipelines, reservoirs, internal reticulation, and communal standpipes. NS is a long-established national company. FST was established in 1995 to provide design excellence with a staff that reflects the racial makeup of South Africa.

THE MVULA TRUST (MVULA)

This is a nongovernmental organization established in 1993 to improve WS services to increase access of marginalized peoples to safe and sustainable water and sanitation services. It has an international reputation for pioneering the development of good practice in the sector by testing and advocating sustainable models for cost-effective delivery and management.

SEIT POINT INDUSTRIAL TECHNOLOGY LTD (VSA) IN ASSOCIATION WITH KHULANI GROUND WATER CONSULTANTS LTD. (KGC)

Seit Point is a public South African company traded under the name VSA Geoconsultants; together the companies provide services to analyze the availability of water and the optional ways to obtain it for use.

In addition to these original signatories, Amanz'abantu now includes:

AMANZ'ABANTU TRUST

This Trust was established to promote the role of historically disadvantaged communities and individuals.

Phase 1 of the scheme serves 25,000 people and Phase 2 will bring water to another 21,000. The first phase was completed a year and a half after approval was given to develop the site. The challenge to the project's success is amply demonstrated by a series of false starts over the previous decade, and the fact that over the first months of operation consumption averaged only 2.5 liters a day. This water use is far below the national standard, which ensures the system can provide 25 litres a day, and the 10 litres needed to provide sufficient revenue to maintain the project.

Amanz'abantu took the lead in developing the Peddie project. AA represents a new approach to providing sustainable water and sanitation systems for the poorest and most remote of South African rural communities by combining the resources and competencies of government, business, and civil society organizations. It is one of four similar companies that grew out of a national initiative in South Africa to speed implementation of self-sustaining water systems on a grand scale.

Source: Steve Waddell, Senior Researcher and Consultant, Organizational Futures, http://www.thecollaborationworks.com.

LEADING CHALLENGES:
ECOLOGY, COMPETITION, AND COLLABORATION

The implications of the more ecological and integrated perspective we have been developing in these three chapters on management thinking are profound. Fundamentally, such a perspective means that interdependence, collaboration, cooperation, and partnership are ironically enough at the heart of competitive success, as many companies are now discovering through their numerous alliances. Just as such a vision of a more collaborative approach to management changes our perspective on what is important to foster in organizations, so does it influence our view of society.

Partnership and collaborative approaches in the midst of intense competition are necessary elements of leading corporate citizenship today. The paradox implied by the tension of opposites—competition and collaboration—operating simultaneously places many demands on leaders and their corporate citizens. Because leading corporate citizens increasingly intersect with individuals and organizations operating in spheres other than their own, they have to learn to work with them productively, understand the values and imperatives that drive organizations in other spheres, and learn how to work with people very different than themselves.

New leadership skills are needed to work in a wide range of global contexts with differing ideologies and consequently differing cultures, as well as in different spheres. These include the capacity to work with people different than ourselves. Not only do leading corporate citizens need to understand how to operate responsibly and with integrity within the context of their own company and industry, but increasingly they need to understand how their work fits in the network of relationships that constitutes the broader system. The ability to understand where others are "coming from" and to value differences, a capacity to "hold" multiple perspectives in one's own head simultaneously, and to understand values that go well beyond economic values will hold leading corporate citizens in good stead as they attempt to accomplish their own work. Just what is necessary to begin these important tasks will be the subject of the next chapter.

NOTES TO CHAPTER 3

1. George C. Lodge and Ezra F. Vogel, *Ideology and National Competitiveness: An Analysis of Nine Countries* (Boston; Harvard Business School Press, 1987).
2. Ibid., p. 2–3. Much of this discussion of ideology is based on Lodge and Vogel's book.
3. See Lodge and Vogel, p. 12–23, for these definitions. This section is derived from Lodge and Vogel's work.
4. For a good illustration of this tension, see Robert N. Bellah, Richard Madsen, William M. Sullivan, Ann Swidler, and Steven M. Tipton, *Habits of the Heart: Individualism and Commitment in American Life.* (New York: Harper & Row, 1985).
5. Thanks to Jerry Calton, University of Hawaii, Hilo, for suggesting the ideas in this paragraph.
6. The following discussion is based on George Cabot Lodge, *Comparative Business-Government Relations* (Englewood Cliffs, NJ: Prentice Hall, 1990).
7. Ibid., p. 4.
8. See, for example, Robert C. Solomon, "The Moral Psychology of Business: Care and Compassion in the Corporation," *Business Ethics Quarterly,* 8, no. 3 (July 1998), pp. 515–33.
9. William C. Frederick, *Values, Nature, and Culture in the American Corporation* (New York: Oxford University Press, 1995), p. 28.
10. The negative side of this development will be explored later in the book.
11. Rosabeth Moss Kanter, *World Class: Thriving Locally in the Global Economy* (New York: Simon & Schuster, 1995), p. 37.
12. Ibid., pp. 41–48.
13. Stan Davis and Christopher Meyer, *Blur: The Speed of Change in the Connected Economy,* (Reading, MA: Addison-Wesley, 1998).

14. This paragraph links Kanter's three ideas—concepts, competence, and connections—to the stakeholder concepts being used throughout this book to show how these ideas can be applied proactively and constructively.

15. Charles Derber, *Corporation Nation: How Corporations Are Taking Over Our Lives and What We Can Do About It* (New York: St. Martin's Press, 1998), p. 122; Derber's ideas are used in this paragraph.

16. Cogent and articulate explanations of free market capitalism and critiques of neoclassical assumptions can be found in a number of sources, including Derber, 1998; David Korten's two books: *When Corporations Rule the World* (San Francisco: Berrett-Koehler, 1995) and *The Post-Corporate World Life After Capitalism* (San Francisco: Berrett-Koehler, 1999); and Lee E. Preston and James E. Post, *Private Management and Public Policy* (New York: Prentice-Hall, 1975). This section is consolidated from these texts and general understanding.

17. See Korten, pp. 37–63; and Derber, pp. 118–136.

18. Robert Leaver, President, Organizational Futures, personal communication.

19. Korten, pp. 51–59.

20. Preston and Post, op. cit.

21. Ibid., p. 95.

22. Ibid., p. 96.

23. One very interesting perspective on this is James Moore's *The Death of Competition: Leadership and Strategy in the Age of Business Ecosystems* (New York: HarperBusiness, 1996).

24. For an insightful and stimulating set of insights into the history of General Electric during Welch's tenure see Thomas F. Boyle's *At Any Cost: Jack Welch, General Electric, and the Pursuit of Profits* (New York: Random House, 1998).

25. For example, see Hazel Henderson, *Building a Win-Win World: Life Beyond Global Economic Warfare* (San Francisco: Berrett-Koehler, 1996); and William Greider, *One World, Ready or Not: The Manic Logic of Global Capitalism* (New York: Touchstone Books, 1998).

26. Issues of sweatshops are explored in detail in Pamela Varley, ed., *The Sweatshop Quandary: Corporate Responsibility on the Global Frontier* (Washington, DC: Investor Responsibility Research Center, 1998).

27. See, for example, James E. Post, "Meeting the Challenge of Global Corporate Citizenship." Boston College Carroll School of Management, Center for Corporate Community Relations, Series on Corporate Citizenship, 2000; see also James E. Post, "Moving from Geographic to Virtual Communities: Corporate Citizenship in a Dot.Com World." *Business and Society Review* 105, no. 1 (2000), pp. 27–46.

28. Preston and Post, p. 56.

29. Much of the thinking in this paragraph is derived from Preston and Post, p. 56.

30. Preston and Post, op. cit.

31. Deborah Tannen, *The Argument Culture: Stopping America's War of Words* (New York: Ballentine Books, 1999).

32. Richard Zeckhauser and Elmer Schaefer, "Public Policy and Normative Economic Theory," in *The Study of Policy Formation,* ed. by Raymond A. Bauer and Kenneth J. Gergen (New York: Free Press, 1968, pp. 27–101).

33. Garrett Hardin, "The Tragedy of the Commons," *Science* 162 (1969) pp. 1243–1248.

34. Mancur Olsen, Jr., developed the concept of free riders in *The Logic of Collective Action* (Cambridge: Harvard University Press, 1965).

35. Bruyn, Severyn. *A Cerynivil Economy* (Ann Arbor: University of Michigan Press, 1999).
36. This definition is adapted from Steven L. Wartick and John F. Mahon, "Toward a Substantive Definition of the Corporate Issue Construct: A Review and Synthesis of the Literature," *Business and Society* 33, no. 3 (December 1994), pp. 293–311. Wartick and Mahon discuss a corporate issue, while the discussion here focuses on public issues more generally and a broad range of stakeholder interests.
37. The public issue life cycle as outlined here is discussed in James E. Post, *Corporate Behavior and Social Change* (Reston, VA: Reston Publishing, 1978), and John F. Mahon and Sandra A. Waddock, "Strategic Issues Management: An Integration of Issue Life Cycle Perspectives" 31, no. 1 (Spring 1992), pp. 19–32. See also H. A. Tombari, *Business and Society: Strategies for the Environment and Public Policy* (New York: Dryden Press, 1984), for an original discussion of the public issue life cycle used in Mahon and Waddock's article.
38. This example is used in Post, *Corporate Behavior and Social Change.*
39. Ibid., p. 23.
40. See Mahon and Waddock, .
41. Sandra Rahman, The Global Stakeholder's Message, The Firm's Response, and an Interpretation of the Ensuing International Dilemma: Moving Children from Tin Sheds to Brick Houses. Ph.D. Dissertation, Nova Southeastern University, 2000.
42. Alan Wolfe, "Is Civil Society Obsolete? Revisiting Predications of the Decline of Civil Society in *Whose Keeper?*" *The Brookings Review* 15, no. 4 (Fall 1997), pp. 9–12.
43. Alan Wolfe, *Whose Keeper? Social Science and Moral Obligation* (Berkeley: University of California Press, 1989).
44. Frederick, op. cit.
45. This paragraph is based in part on Karen Penner, "The Ties that Lead to Prosperity," *Business Week,* December 15, 1997, pp. 153–155.
46. Robert D. Putnam, *Making Democracy Work: Civic Traditions in Modern Italy* (Princeton, NJ: Princeton University Press, 1993).
47. See Robert D. Putnam, "Bowling Alone: America's Declining Social Capital," *Journal of Democracy* 6, no.1 (January 1995), pp. 65–78, and "The Strange Disappearance of Civic America," *The American Prospect* 24 (Winter 1996 [http://epn.org/prospect/24/24putn.html)]. The discussion that follows is derived from these two articles.
48. Putnam, "Bowling Alone," p. 69.
49. Putnam, "The Strange Disappearance of Civic America."
50. Maria Poarch, "Civic Life and Work: A Qualitative Study of Changing Patterns of Sociability and Civic Engagement in Everyday Life" (Ph.D. dissertation, Boston University, 1997).
51. Jean Bethke Elshtain, "Not a Cure-All," *The Brookings Review* 15, no. 4 (Fall 1997), pp. 13–15.
52. Benjamin Barber, *Jihad vs. McWorld* (New York: Times Books, Random House, 1995).
53. See Michael W. Foley and Bob Edwards, "The Paradox of Civil Society," *Journal of Democracy* 7, no.3 (1996), pp. 38–52.
54. See, for example my book on business involvement in schools, Sandra A. Waddock, *Not By Schools Alone: Sharing Responsibility for America's Education Reform* (Greenwich, CT: Praeger, 1995); and Steve Waddell, "Market-Civil Society Partnership Formation: A Status Report on Activity, Strategies, and Tools," *IDR Report* 13, no. 5 (1998); and Steve Waddell and L. David Brown, "Fostering Intersectoral Partnering: A Guide to Promoting Cooperation among Government, Business, and Civil Society Actors," *IDR Report* 13, no. 5 (1997).
55. Davis and Meyer, op.cit.

Leading Corporate Citizens with Vision, Values, and Value Added

CHAPTER 4

Personal and Organizational Vision

The organizing tendency of life is always a creative act. We reach out to others to create a new being. We reach out to grow the world into new possibilities.

Every self is visionary. It wants to create a world where it can thrive. So it is with organizations. Every organization calls itself into being as a belief that something more can be accomplished by joining with others. At the heart of every organization is a self reaching out to new possibilities.

This does not mean that all intents to organize are good or healthy. . . . But every act of organizing is the expression of a self that has realized it cannot succeed alone. We organize to make our lives more purposeful. We organize always to affirm and enrich our identity.

It is strange perhaps to realize that most people have a desire to love their organizations. They love the purpose of their school, their community agency, their business. They fall in love with the identity that is trying to be expressed. They connect to the founding vision. They organize to create a different world. . . .

Identity is the source of organization. Every organization is an identity in motion, moving through the world, trying to make a difference. Therefore, the most important work we can do at the beginning of an organizing effort is to engage one another in exploring our purpose. We need to explore why we have come together. How does the purpose of this effort connect with the organization? Does it connect to our individual hopes and desires? Is the purpose big enough to welcome the contributions of all of us?

—MARGARET J. WHEATLEY AND MYRON KELLNER-ROBERTS, *A Simpler Way*

VISION, VALUES, VALUE ADDED

The example of Royal Dutch/Shell's recent activities in the corporate citizenship arena, particularly in developing and implementing its principles (see Chapter 1) highlight a key linkage we need to make: A company's vision and values guide its economic success and the way it approaches citizenship. Successful companies achieve value added—or profitability for shareholders—through a sustained effort to develop excellent products and services to meet the needs and interests of their customers, that is, to achieve a vision.

What Is Vision?

The term "vision" has connotations that provide helpful insights in understanding the linkages that we must make among the three spheres of society (and the ecology) described in the previous chapter. Of course, vision means to see with the eye, but it means more than that: A *vision* is also a power to perceive what is not actually present, a form of imaging the possibilities and potentials, of anticipating what could be. Used constructively and positively, visions provide a "picture," quite literally an image that taps into the imagination and allows it to soar.

In *The Fifth Discipline,* his seminal work on the learning organization, Peter Senge defined vision as a picture of the future that you seek to create.[1] To the extent that a vision is a "picture," it helps us to "see" where we want to go and make choices about how to get there.

Visions of course can be negative, oppressive, or autocratic, as were those of Hitler or Stalin. Thus, as we will discuss at length in the next chapter, it is important to corporate citizenship that the *values* that underpin and support a company's vision be positive and inspiring—that is, constructive. Values that are constructive aim toward enhancing human spirit and building a better world, in contrast to being destructive of the human spirit and the ecology that sustains us. But first we must have a clearer understanding of the role of vision at both the individual and organizational levels.

Visions are created by visionary individuals or in organizations by managers or groups working together collaboratively to achieve some higher purpose. In the past, visionaries were considered to be impractical dreamers out of touch with reality. Today, however, it is well recognized that successful organizations need visionaries who can help them dream about higher purposes that inspire action, commitment, and connection, especially among key primary stakeholders like employees. In this positive sense, *visionaries* are first of all those who see what is clearly and unrelentingly. They are realists, willing to grapple with the hard facts, figures, and relationships that constitute organizational life. But second and equally important, visionaries are those who are able to imagine a possible or hoped-for future—and to represent that future to others in ways that capture their imagination and help guide them toward the realization of the vision.

Visions Create Meaning and Foster Purpose

Visions and the visionaries that inspire them help create *meaning* within corporate citizens and help others to make the connections between actions, values, and the purposes of the enterprises in which they are involved. *Visions become organizationally real when they are widely held and widely shared,* not when they are housed solely in one individual's mind. Visions tap the spirit and souls of people, they draw out feelings and emotions; in short, visions inspire. Shared visions, when not foisted on people, draw out the individual's own personal visions (or what R. Edward Freeman and Daniel R. Gilbert, Jr., called personal projects). Shared visions provide opportunities for each individual to live out a dream through productive organizational work that calls for personal commitment and engagement and allows the individual to see that she or he is really making a difference or contribution.[2] As Senge commented:

> A shared vision is not an idea. It is not even an important idea such as freedom. It is, rather, a force in people's hearts, a force of impressive power. It may be inspired by an idea, but once it goes further—if it is compelling enough to acquire the support of more than one person—then it is no longer an abstraction. It is palpable. People begin to see it as if it exists. Few, if any, forces in human affairs are as powerful as shared vision.[3]

Clear visions in organizations are created by developing, implementing, and sustaining what scholars James Collins and Jerry Porras term *core ideology,* which consists of the vision or company purpose and a set of core values that sustain so-called visionary companies even through bad times.[4] And all companies face bad times. The key to vision and values guiding action or practice is to hold true to the underlying core ideology and to make sure that the vision is positive and inspiring and helps create sustained meaning for everyone involved with the firm. Simultaneously, companies need to make the changes that are necessary to sustain the company strategically and competitively and work on those elements of strategy that need to change as the internal and external context changes. The same dynamic holds true for individuals.

Visions are necessarily implemented through practices that "operationalize" core values in day-to-day initiatives that corporate citizens undertake to get the work done. Values are demonstrated in how relationships are developed with stakeholders, including employees, customers, community, owners, natural environment, and local authorities. In other words, visions are implemented through processes, policies, and procedures that constitute the practices organizations develop.

By creating visions that inspire commitment, loyalty, meaning, and a sense of community among primary stakeholders and implementing practices that sustain positive interaction with key stakeholders, corporate citizens arguably can achieve high levels of performance over time. Developing shared visions that embody what we will call end values (see Chapter 5) is not necessarily easy. *End values* are deeply felt core values that inspire the human spirit. Such visions can inspire at the individual, group or unit, and organizational levels, particularly as successful organizations interact with stakeholders. What vision is, how it inspires individuals and organizations, and what its implications are for society will be the focus of this chapter.

Why Vision?

Clearly articulated visions serve as guides to action and decisions. Because the vision serves as a guide, it delineates for individuals and organizations just what actions and decisions make sense. Further, clear and constructive visions help determine what kinds of actions should *not* be taken because those actions are unnecessary, deter achievement of the vision, or are inconsistent with the vision or its associated values. When they are positive and constructive, visions guide participants in a common enterprise toward the achievement of shared goals and toward productive ways of interacting with each other. Visions are "enacted" through organizational norms and cultures—that is, the shared set of practices and beliefs that tell "how things are done here"—as well as what the company stands for. Visions provide, both figuratively and literally, a picture of where the company is going and how it is going to get there.

Vision inspires in multiple ways, not least of which is getting people to commit to doing something together that they believe makes a (positive) difference in the world. It is this sense of making a difference that creates meaningfulness. Vision can create aspirations; it can enhance the pursuit of a larger purpose, something outside and bigger than oneself or one's own purposes. Constructive and positive visions can exhilarate, encourage, and connect people in their pursuit of common purpose. Visions help to create a sense of "we" rather than "us versus them" in an organization, as well as a sense of belonging to a community doing important work together. Shared visions can also foster creative risk taking and experimentation, which are necessary for innovation and entrepreneurship even within large corporations. And vision helps overcome the notorious short-term orientation of some managers by focusing their attention on the long-term achievement of that vision.[5] These outcomes of vision are critical to companies becoming leading corporate citizens.

Both individuals and organizations can have visions, as will be discussed in the next sections. At the individual level, we frequently see entrepreneurs, founders of organizations, and individuals who lead change in difficult situations as the desirable leaders, particularly when they can help others visualize new ways of doing things. At the organizational level, creating a vision about the purpose of the enterprise that is shared by organizational members and their external stakeholders is one way of gaining commitment and moving the organization toward success.

In some respects, most corporations operating today are neither visionary in the sense that we have been describing, nor is their citizenship exemplary. And even if they were, vision alone is insufficient to guide corporate citizenship, especially as we have defined it in the context of developing positive stakeholder *relationships*. Relationships inherently require a capacity to see into another's position and perspective, to understand others' perspectives, and, even when one doesn't agree, to work toward solutions to issues that take all relevant perspectives into account. This capacity is at the heart of building successful stakeholder relationships and it makes significant demands on leaders of corporate citizens.

This chapter argues that in addition to vision, mindfulness is one of the foundations of citizenship, along with integrity, which will be the subject of the next chapter. Being mindful means that corporate leaders, increasingly, will need to think through the consequences of their actions, a capacity that management scholar Russell Ackoff has called wisdom.[6] Wisdom in turn demands that leaders achieve relatively high cognitive, moral, and emotional levels of development so that they can take the perspectives of different stakeholders into account simultaneously and think about decisions and actions systemically rather than only linearly. Thus, one emphasis in this chapter is to determine what kinds of individual and organizational vision combined with other capabilities need to be developed in leaders and organizations. Ultimately, the goal is to transform both individuals and business enterprises into leading corporate citizens, so they can act mindfully with respect to the impacts they necessarily have on their stakeholders.

VISIONARY LEADERS

Some individuals are considered visionaries. They can see what others cannot. They make linkages that others do not necessarily make. They are aware of their surroundings and are systems thinkers who understand the relationships among different facts, events, and opportunities. They see underneath the chaos of daily life to discern possibilities, potentials, and meaning and can articulate those possibilities in ways that make sense to others. It is the awareness of those possibilities, potentials, and meanings that inspires others to join in efforts that link people in common efforts, whether those are community efforts, businesses, or social change agendas. We all know some of these people. We call them visionary leaders.

Leadership, even visionary leadership, is not some arcane undertaking available only to the select few. Arguably, with work and personal exploration of what is important in one's life, each person (and, as we will see later in this chapter, each organization) can develop an awareness of self and others, awareness of his or her impacts, and awareness of the profound values that underpin actions and decisions. That awareness helps an individual understand his or her impact on the context, know where significant changes can be made internally or with others, and can result in a personal vision that can in turn inspire organizational vision. Personal and organizational visions inspire work, life, and play. Visions that inspire organizations and even whole societies create an internal sense of meaning and purposefulness in the people who belong to them. Inspirational organizational visions embed responsibility, higher purpose, and significant meaning in the enterprise to provide a basis for working together on something.

Crafting a positive and inspirational vision, whether personal or organizational, therefore involves determining what is meaningful, what provides purpose, and what goals will inspire self or others to action. Abraham Zaleznik pointed out in his important article "Managers and Leaders: Are They Different?" that leaders

> are active instead of reactive, shaping ideas instead of responding to them. Leaders adopt a personal and active attitude toward goals. The influence a leader exerts can alter moods, evoke images and expectations, and establish specific objectives that determine the direction an enterprise takes. The net result of this influence changes the way people think about what is desirable, possible, and necessary.[7]

Zaleznik pointed out further that modern organizations, operating in the chaos of change and ever-increasing competition, need real—visionary—leadership more than ever. "Vision," he wrote in his retrospective commentary, "the hallmark of leadership, is less a derivative of spreadsheets and more a product of the mind called imagination." Zaleznik urged business leaders to learn to cope with the chaos of uncertain change, rapid technological evolution, and rapid evolution by using their imaginations. He further suggested that opportunities for vision can potentially be found in anomalies such as customer complaints, necessary process improvements, or new applications of technology as much as in smooth operations.[8]

Developing that visionary imagination and awareness, and translating it to the organization, is a critical part of developing leading as opposed to ordinary or non-mindful corporate citizens. The next sections will focus on three domains of human development in which we will argue that higher rather than lower levels of cognitive (consciousness and intellectual), moral, and emotional development are necessary for the leaders of corporate citizens today if they are to lead mindfully and operate with consciousness of the impacts of their actions on stakeholders. Indeed, a stakeholder-based approach to leading corporate citizens requires that not only are leaders self- and other-aware in these domains, but also that they imbue their organizations with a set of values and operating principles that guide actions toward mindfulness at all levels of the enterprise.

INDIVIDUAL AWARENESS AND REFLECTION: DEVELOPMENT IN MULTIPLE DOMAINS

Consciousness or awareness, particularly self-consciousness, is what distinguishes human beings from other sentient beings. Humans are the only beings that are truly conscious of their own existence.[9] This awareness results in a capacity to reflect. Reflection provides the significant capacity for humans to continue to learn and develop cognitively.[10] But there is more. The capacity to reflect also provides for growth and maturing processes in other domains. In organizational life, moral and emotional learning and development are also essential for good citizenship. Such development is, in particular, a necessary condition for working effectively with stakeholders, the key ingredient of corporate citizenship.

Consciousness—self- and other-awareness—is intricately tied to language, as the biologists Humberto Maturana and Francisco Varela pointed out.[11] The close linkage of the development of consciousness and awareness of language suggests that human beings are inherently social creatures, creating through their interactions not only individual meaning and purposes, but also communities. Communities are shaped by cultural, spiritual, and economic bonds that result from human interactions. Because humans are social creatures necessarily embedded in communities and because "self-awareness is at the core of being human,"[12] creating shared meanings through awareness, vision, and reflection are part of the human experience and, when generatively embedded in organizations, a core of citizenship.

The communal nature of human society, which Frans de Waal has documented among our primate progenitors, gives rise not only to language and meaning, common purpose and shared identity, but also to notions of right and wrong—that is, ethics.[13] Organizations in the economic and other spheres are a part of this communal nature, hence the way that they operate and the shared meanings that their purposes allow them to fulfill are also inherently and fundamentally premised on ethics and values. Individuals in key decision-making capacities within organizations—leaders and managers—need to understand how to create purpose and shared meaning through the visions they engender. Only then can leaders develop organizations that embody positive visions that contribute constructively to society in ways that enhance work in the other spheres and treat the natural environment respectfully.

Creating shared purpose, or meaning, with its inherent values basis is the primary function of leaders. Creating meaning is not limited in time or space and in modern "networked" organization can be found throughout any enterprise. Meaning exists wherever a leader works with others to create it and not only in the top echelons of the enterprise.

Transformation: From Managers into Leaders

There is a long-standing debate about whether leaders are born or made. Here we take the perspective that leadership capacity can be developed and nurtured as an individual matures, particularly as cognitive, moral, and emotional capacities develop. Higher development in these three critical arenas means that leaders are more aware of their impacts and can think through and develop better relationships, all skills critical to corporate citizenship.

Wisdom, Ackoff wrote, "is the ability to perceive and evaluate the long-run consequences of behavior." This capacity of what we shall call mindfulness is "associated with a willingness to make short-run sacrifices for long-term gains."[14] The notorious shortsightedness, not to mention the sorry state of relationships that many companies have with some of their stakeholders, suggests that mindfulness may be in woefully short supply among corporate leaders.

Certainly, mindfulness—wisdom—requires a degree of maturity and insight that not every leader finds easy to attain. Being mindful demands that individual decision makers who are acting on a company's behalf function at relatively high developmental levels, not only cognitively but also morally and emotionally. It also demands, particularly if corporate citizenship requires building relationships with stakeholders, insightful understanding of these stakeholders' perspectives—and doing that requires a fairly high cognitive capacity as a starting point.

Seeing the consequences and implications of actions, one of the requisites of integrity as described above, marries cognitive with moral development, also at a relatively high level. Not only does thinking through consequences demand systemic thinking, but it also means leaders have to be well aware of the ways that other stakeholders will perceive and understand their actions and practices. Additionally, they have to be willing to reflect honestly about their understanding, about their relationship with other stakeholders, and about their own roles within the company.

Developing this level of understanding and reflection means that leaders not only need the cognitive capacity to perspective-take, but also the moral capacity to understand how their decisions affect others (which is the essence, after all, of ethics). Further, because sound relationships are key to the stakeholder-based definition of corporate citizenship, leaders also need emotional maturity sufficient to build lasting relationships with critical stakeholders. Emotional maturity means that leaders can engage in "good conversations" or dialogue with stakeholders, and take actions that respect and are sensitive to stakeholders interests while still achieving their own interests.

While it might be ideal if an individual were as mature morally and emotionally as she or he is cognitively, there is ample evidence that some individuals who achieve very high levels of one type of development may be significantly less or more developed in other areas. For example, a scientist may have a highly developed cognitive capacity. At the same time, it is entirely conceivable that she or he is emotionally immature or morally undeveloped, which can result in an inability to get along well with others or think through the ethical consequences of developing a new technology. Cognitive development appears to be a necessary (but not sufficient) precondition for other types of development, such as moral and emotional development, all of which we view as essential to leading corporate citizens today.[15]

Highly developed cognitive, moral, and emotional capacities allow people to understand issues that stakeholders raise from the perspectives of these other stakeholders as well as their own. The way issues are raised has to do with the way an individual or institution "frames" it. Frames are the underlying structure of beliefs and perceptions used.[16] All issues, policies, and perceptions are necessarily viewed through some sort of lens or frame. Understanding this reality means that one has acquired the ability to understand others' points of view. In contentious arenas, such as those involving stakeholder relationships studded with controversial issues, it is particularly important to understand where others are coming from. Having the reflective capacity to understand that most of the frames that people use are tacit—that is, unarticulated—rather than explicit, can help in analyzing a situation more incisively and coming to a reasonable and agreeable resolution among all parties when multiple frames are at play.

The consequences of lack of maturity in an important domain (e.g., cognitive, moral, or emotional) may be significant harm to an organization's relationship with key stakeholders and to its capacity to develop a shared sense of meaning and responsibility for its own actions. Thus, the definition of leadership used here relates to both vision and a capacity to take varying perspectives into account, while taking responsible action: *Leaders* are individuals who achieve personal vision, work effectively in organizations to create shared meaning and constructive vision/values, and are able to reflect on and understand the perspectives of a range of stakeholders and the implications of their actions and do the right thing in the circumstance.

Development and Leading Corporate Citizens

Understanding the frames that others bring to a situation and developing strategies for dealing with the civil society, political, and ecological spheres that intersect with the economic sphere requires significant *cognitive development*. Leading corporate citizenship also means carefully reflecting on policy and strategic decisions and their long- and short-term implications for the company, the industry, and the broader set of stakeholders who are affected. Since these decisions necessarily affect others, and hence have inherent ethical content, leading corporate citizenship also demands a high level of *moral development.* Finally, working with others to actually develop and implement effective policies and make good decisions necessitates high levels of *emotional development.*

Fundamentally, we will argue in this chapter that awareness of and the capacity to reflect upon the systemic impacts of leaders' decisions comes from greater cognitive, moral, and emotional development and is, ultimately, a key to long-term organizational success. To fully understand these arenas of development requires a brief foray into developmental theory.

Developmental Theories

Research on personality, cognitive, moral, emotional, and even spiritual development suggests that individuals go through a variety of stages as they mature. Developmental theorists now believe that there are numerous different domains of development[17] and that individuals generally move through these stages in order, progressing from the least to the more developed—and typically more encompassing—stage, without regressing backwards. Individuals may, of course, be only partially "in" the next stage at any given time. Although the stages of these different types of development are associated with physical maturing that comes with the aging process, they are not invariably concurrent with each other or necessarily associated with any given age.

Developmental theorists believe that development has certain characteristics. Stages are considered to be invariant (at least by some researchers) in that all individuals go through them in the same progression as they mature. Howard Gardner (who researched multiple "intelligences"), Lawrence Kohlberg (who studied moral development), and Jean Piaget (who studied child development) all claimed, among others, that there are three waves or stages—preconventional, conventional, and post conventional—that constitute a generic stage framework.[18] Ken Wilber suggested that there are further stages of development, the *post-postconventional,* that are relevant to spiritual growth, but the three generic stages will serve as our guiding framework below.[19] Many developmental theorists agree on these three general stages of development, which have analogues in multiple arenas.

Preconventional reasoning generally means that a person does not yet understand society's expectations and rules, but operates instead from a fear of punishment if rules are broken or when there is self-interest to do something.

Conventional reasoning means "conforming to and upholding the rules and expectations and conventions of society or authority just because they are society's rules, expectations or conventions."

Postconventional reasoning individuals understand and accept that society has rules but realize that there are general principles that underlie those rules and can apply those principles in different situations.[20] To the extent that these generic stages apply to many forms of development, they represent a useful framework for understanding cognitive, moral, and emotional development below.

Further, many developmental theorists argue that stages are, in a sense, nested. In effect, they consider each stage a holon—that is, a whole/part—that is subsumed within and surpassed by the next stage or holon, as we have discussed earlier. With each stage comes a greater degree of capacity and depth of understanding in that earlier understandings are nested within or encompassed by the greater capacity exhibited in the later stage. Thus, many of these developmental theorists believe that once an individual has moved from one stage to the next, it is unlikely that he or she will regress. The new ways of understanding (i.e., a capacity to take another's point of view as opposed to believing that there is only one's own point of view) become incorporated into the new stage.

With these basic tenets of developmental theory in mind, we can begin our exploration of the three specific arenas of development especially critical to the development of reflective and aware leaders who are able to interact responsibly with stakeholders. These are cognitive development (which is linked to social and personality development), moral development, and emotional development.

Cognitive Development

PHYSICAL-COGNITIVE DEVELOPMENT IN CHILDREN. The psychologist Jean Piaget was the first to document the developmental stages through which a child progresses.[21] Studying his own child, Piaget determined that individuals pass through several stages of social maturing and reasoning processes, that is, personality development. He termed these stages (which follow learning to speak): the intuitive (about ages 2–5), the concrete operational (about ages 6–10), and the formal operations stage (age 11–adulthood). Although these stages are associated with physical maturity, they are not inevitably linked to any given age.[22]

In the *intuitive stage* a child makes inferences through symbols and images in a sort of "magical thinking." Children at this stage may confuse real and imagined events and objects or be unable to understand the difference between perception and reality.

The *concrete operational stage* is characterized by an ability to make logical inferences and classifications, and to recognize that things can stay the same in terms of number, class membership, length, and mass when they appear to change. A classic example is that children in the intuitive stage will persist in the view that there is more water in a tall, thin glass than in a short, wide one even when they see it poured from one container into the other. In contrast, children in the concrete operational stage recognize that there is the same amount in either glass. Most adolescents and almost all adults will have passed through the concrete operational stage into the next stage, at least partially.

Piaget's highest stage, *formal operational thinking* is characterized by abstract reasoning—that is, a capacity to consider multiple possibilities, the relationships between elements in a system, and to make hypotheses and inferences that can be tested against reality. This stage of development permits formal and logical reasoning, or what is typically termed rational thought.

COGNITIVE DEVELOPMENT IN ADULTS. Robert Kegan and William Torbert have pursued adult developmental theory.[23] Kegan built on the work of Piaget by considering the frames that an individual is capable of using at any given developmental stage.[24] Kegan's work is helpful in generating understanding of the ways in which individuals develop a capacity to take the position of the "other," that is, to view things from another's (or stakeholder's) perspective. Children at the preconventional stage are cognitively capable of perceiving only their own point of view. From their perspective, there *is* only self. Actions result from fantasy (magic) or impulses. As they enter the stage of concrete reasoning, children begin to appreciate that others are "out there," and can begin to make cause and effect inferences, typically based on roles in a tit-for-tat or reciprocity kind of reasoning. Kegan showed these dispositions using simple figures that illustrate clearly the perceptual and cognitive capacity of the individual at each stage (see Table 4.1).

In Kegan's third stage—*traditionalism*—individuals can make inferences, generalizations, hypotheses, and propositions because they are able to reason abstractly. (Note that this stage is Piaget's formal operational stage.) In this stage, individuals become conscious of the roles they take and interact with expectations of reciprocity from others. They are aware of their own subjectivity and are self-conscious; they can realize that others also have these capabilities. Many adults stay in this stage for most of their adult lives.

Kegan called the fourth stage *modernism.* Here individuals have the capacity to do systems thinking and begin to understand that there are relationships among the abstractions they make. They also understand that institutions have roles, and they can see themselves within a number of such institutions. Individuals begin to understand that they can be self-regulating or self-forming in the application of ideas and principles.

Kegan's final stage is *postmodernism,* which few individuals actually reach. Kegan's research determined that the complexity of modern life increasingly requires more people to reach this stage of development if they are to cope effectively with the competing demands imposed upon them. This assessment seems particularly relevant to leaders of corporate citizens, who by necessity must contend with the demands, pressures, and perspectives of many different types of stakeholders.

In the postmodern stage, individuals are capable of understanding and holding multiple *systems* or paradigms in their heads simultaneously. Individuals at the postmodern stage understand that systems interact, just as individuals in the traditionalism stage understand that people have different perspectives that can interact.

Individuals at the postmodern stage of development are comfortable with paradox and contradiction. Further, they are probably not tied in with any particular ideology because they can understand and "hold" (in their heads) multiple ways of viewing the world at once. Thus, postmodern-stage people can grasp multiple perspectives simultaneously. They tend to view other institutions and individuals as self-regulating, self-forming, and self-authoring.

Note that if leaders are to work well with multiple stakeholders in developing their companies' corporate citizenship, they will very likely need to have achieved at least the systems capacities of modernism and, better, will have advanced to the postmodern level of understanding. As Kegan pointed out, it takes time (the maturity that comes with age) as well as real work to develop these capacities. Not many

TABLE 4.1   Kegan's Developmental Stages

	Subject	Object
Stage 1 Intuitive		Single point/
Perceptions: Fantasy	Movement	immediate/
Social Perceptions		atomistic
Impulses	Sensation	
Stage 2 Concrete Operational	Perceptions	
Concrete: Actuality, cause-effect, data		
Point of view: Role-concept	Social perceptions	
Simple reciprocity		
Enduring Dispositions	Impulses	
Needs, preferences self-concept		Durable category
Stage 3: Traditionalism	Concrete	
Abstractions		
Ideality, inference, generalization hypothesis, proposition, ideals, values		
Mutuality/interpersonalism	Point of view	
Role consciousness		Cross-categorical
Mutual reciprocity		Transcategorical
Inner States	Enduring dispositions	
Subjectivity, self-consciousness	Needs, preferences	
Stage 4: Modernism	Abstractopoms	
Abstract systems		
Ideology		
Formulation, authorization		
relations between abstractions		
Institution	Mutuality	
Relationship-regulating forms	Interpersonalism	
Multiple-Role Consciousness		
Self-authorship	Interstates	System/complex
Self-regulation, self-formation	Subjectivity	
identity, autonomy, individuation	Self-consciousness	
Stage 5: Postmodernism	Abstract system	
Dialectical	Ideology	
Trans-ideological/post-ideological		
Testing formulation, paradox		
contradiction, oppositeness	Institution	
Interinstitutional	Relationship	
Relationship between forms	regulating forms	
Interpenetration of self and other	Self-authorship, self-	Trans-system
Interpenetration of selves	regulation, self-formation	Trans-complex
Inter-individuation		

individuals reach the fifth stage, but that level of development is what the modern world demands of us cognitively. Dealing with complex problems, testing assumptions, inquiring about rationales behind decisions, and engaging in dialogue with others, including stakeholders who are very different from corporate leaders, can be helpful ways of developing these capacities, as will be briefly discussed below.

ADVANCING COGNITIVE CAPACITY IN CORPORATE CITIZENS. If leading corporate citizenship is based on developing stakeholder relationships, then understanding the stakeholders' perspective cognitively is a key to success. Arguably, one way to advance cognitive development is through techniques that involve various forms of conversation and dialogue—that is, the type of conversation in which different parties to an argument or issue express their point of view. Of course, dialogue is a core feature of developing constructive relationships between corporate citizens and their stakeholders. Individuals studying leadership, organizational behavior, and corporate responsibility in business schools frequently study by means of case analysis, experiential exercises in class, field-based projects, and, when feasible, work-based learning as other methods of advancing cognitive development, particularly in applied subjects.

Cognitive development can also potentially be advanced, as Chris Argyris argued, by having individuals explore the reasoning behind behaviors and decisions, both one's own and that of others. Other scholars, such as William Torbert and Dalmar Fisher, suggested that individuals should undertake personal experiments involving new behaviors focused in inquiry (i.e., seeking out the perspectives of others) in order to move from one stage of development to another.[25] Torbert developed a framework of action inquiry, in which managers enter into difficult conversations or conversations where perspective taking is needed. Action inquiry can be undertaken by first framing the situation, next illustrating his/her own point of view, then advocating a position, and finally and perhaps most importantly, openly inquiring about the perspective, position, and rationale of the other person.[26]

Action inquiry, as well as the dialogue processes recommended by William Isaacs, can be helpful in developing good corporate citizenship.[27] Companies can help their leaders develop these cognitive capacities through appropriate training and development programs, not just for top managers but also for individuals throughout the organization.

Moral Development

The second developmental arena that is critical to corporate citizenship is moral development because, after all, citizenship is about responsible practice. To operate responsibly and with integrity, corporate citizens need leaders who understand how to reason from principles rather than simply assuming that "everything goes" because "it all depends."

Lawrence Kohlberg, who studied moral reasoning in males, found a clear link between the development of the capacity to reason abstractly at the level Piaget termed formal operational thinking and the capacity to think in moral terms. Moral development is dependent upon the development of sufficient cognitive capacity to

TABLE 4.2.   Stages of Cognitive/Social and Moral Development

Stage	Social Perspective	Moral Perspective
1	Concrete individual perspective	Preconventional
2	Member of society perspective	Conventional
3	Prior-to-society perspective	Postconventional or principled

reason in more advanced ways—that is, at least at the third stage of Kegan's framework. According to Kohlberg, an individual who is at any given stage of cognitive development cannot reason morally at a higher stage of development.[28]

Kohlberg identified six stages of moral development, two within each of the generic developmental levels (see Table 4.2). Individuals in the preconventional level reason through what Kohlberg calls heteronomous morality at stage 1 and individualism, instrumental purpose, and exchange at stage 2 (see Table 4.3).

1. *Stage 1 (preconventional, heteronomous) individuals focus on obedience and punishment.* They reason that it is wrong to break rules because one is likely to be punished and therefore should avoid damaging others or their possessions. The motivation for doing the right thing from this stage is to avoid being punished or because higher authorities say you should. The general perspective is egocentric, in that the people at stage 1 quite literally do not recognize that other people may have a different perspective from their own.

2. *Stage 2 (preconventional, instrumental purpose and exchange) individuals act morally to further their own interest.* Stage 2 individuals focus on individualism, instrumental purpose, and exchange, following rules because it is in their self-interest to do so. They view what is right as what is fair and emphasize agreements, deals, and exchanges as ways of determining what is fair. The rationale for being ethical from the person's point of view at stage 2 is that it will be in one's self-interest to do so, especially since there is some recognition that others also have self-interests that they will want to have met. The reasoning in this stage is based on concrete individualism, which means that the person is aware that others have a point of view and set of interests and may, therefore, have a different sense of what they need.

3. *Stage 3 (conventional, interpersonal concordance) individuals act to meet the expectations of their immediate peers and close groups.* Many (most) teenagers, who conform to peer group norms and expectations, are at this stage. Individuals in stage 3 believe that what is right is what some important reference group expects. Individuals at this stage also understand the need to develop ongoing relationships through trust, loyalty, respect, and gratitude. Stereotypes of what is expected and reference to the golden rule dominate this type of reasoning (i.e., "Do unto others as you would have them do unto you"). The perspective is one of the individual in relationship to other individuals with some capacity to take the other's point of view emerging at this stage.

4. *Stage 4 (conventional, social concordance, and system maintenance) individuals act to meet the social expectations articulated in the laws and rules*

TABLE 4.3.   Kohlberg's Stages of Moral Reasoning

What Is Right	Reasons for Doing Right	Social Perspective of Stage
Level 1: Preconventional		

STAGE 1: HETERONOMOUS MORALITY

Obedience and punishment. Avoid breaking rules, fear of punishment, obedience, avoid physical property/personal damage.	*Act to avoid punishment or painful consequences to oneself.* Superior power of authorities.	*Egocentric point of view.* Doesn't consider the interests of others or recognize differences in points of view. Actions based in physical reality, not psychological interests. Confusion of authority and own perspective.

STAGE 2: INDIVIDUALISM, INSTRUMENTAL PURPOSE AND EXCHANGE

Instrumental purpose and exchange. Follow rules when in immediate interest, act in one's own interest and needs (others do the same). Right is "fair," equal exchange, a deal, an agreement.	*Act to further one's interests.* Serve one's needs or interests in a world where you recognize that others have interests too.	*Concrete individualistic perspective.* Aware that everyone has his or her own interests to pursue and conflicts exist among these. "Right" is relative (in concrete individualistic sense).

Level 2: Conventional

STAGE 3: MUTUAL INTERPERSONAL EXPECTATIONS, RELATIONSHIPS, AND INTERPERSONAL CONFORMITY (INTERPERSONAL CONCORDANCE)

Interpersonal accord, conformity to group norms. Live up to others' expectations within your role(s). "Being good" is important: means having good motives, showing concern for others, keeping mutual relationships like trust, loyalty, respect, and gratitude.	*Act to meet expectations of immediate peers.* Need to be a good person in your own and others' eyes. Caring for others, believe in "golden rule," desire to maintain rules and authority that support "good" behavior.	*Perspective of the individual in relationships with other individuals.* Aware of shared feelings, agreements, expectations that take primacy over individual interest. Concrete golden rule relates points of view, puts self in other person's shoes. No generalized systems perspective.

TABLE 4.3. Continued

STAGE 4: SOCIAL SYSTEM AND CONSCIENCE

Social accord and system maintenance. Fulfill actual duties you agree to. Laws to be upheld except when they conflict with other social duties. Right means contributing to society, the group, or institution.	*Act to meet societal expectations stated in law.* Keep the institution going as a whole, avoid breakdown "if everyone did it." Imperative of conscience to meet defined obligations.	*Differentiates societal point of view from interpersonal agreement or motives.* Takes point of view of system that defines the roles and the rules. Considers individual in relationship to the system.

Level 3: Postconventional or Principled

STAGE 5: SOCIAL CONTRACT OR UTILITY AND INDIVIDUAL RIGHTS

Social contract. Aware that people hold variety of values and opinions, most of which are relative to group and should usually be upheld in interest of impartiality because they are the social contract. Some nonrelative values and rights exist that should be upheld regardless of majority opinion.	*Act to achieve social consensus and tolerance on conflicting issues.* Sense of obligation to law because of social contract to make and abide by laws for the welfare of all. Contractual commitment, freely entered upon, to family, friendship, trust, work duties. Laws, duties based on rational calculation of overall utility, "greatest good for the greatest number."	*Prior-to-society perspective.* Perspective of rational individual aware of values and rights prior to social attachments and contracts. Integrates perspectives by formal mechanisms of agreement, contract, objective impartiality, and due process. Considers moral and legal points of view (sometimes conflict).

STAGE 6: UNIVERSAL ETHICAL PRINCIPLES

Universal ethical principles. Follows self-chosen ethical principles. Particular laws or social agreements usually valid because they rest on principles. When laws violate principles, act in accordance with the principles, which are universal: justice, equality of human rights, and respect for dignity of human beings as individual persons.	*Act consistently with self-selected moral principles.* Belief as rational person in validity of universal moral principles and sense of personal commitment to them.	*Perspective of a moral point of view.* Understands principles from which social arrangements derive. Any rational individual recognizes the nature of morality fact that persons are ends in themselves and must be treated as such.

Source: Adapted from Lawrence Kohlberg, "Moral Stages and Moralization: The Cognitive-Developmental Approach," in *Moral Development and Behavior* (New York: Holt, Rinehart and Winston, 1976), pp. 34–35; and Jeanne Logsdon and Kristi Yuthas, "Corporate Social Performance, Stakeholder Orientation, and Organization Moral Development," *Journal of Business Ethics* 16 (1997), p. 1214.

of society. At this stage individuals begin to understand the system as a whole. They believe in doing what is right by fulfilling the duties that society (or an institution) has imposed, but can see that there are times when doing so conflicts with other duties. They recognize the importance of the system as a whole and the need for rules and obligations to keep the system healthy. They can differentiate their own point of view from that of society as a whole and can place themselves within the larger context. Most adults are at this stage of development.

Postconventional stages (5 and 6, discussed below) emphasize principled reasoning, which may well be the type of reasoning that will be most useful in a global economy where corporate citizens have to contend with multiple cultures and varying moral frameworks. At lower stages of development, however, managers are likely to engage in what is called ethical relativism, which can get them into trouble if they believe that the practices that may occur in a culture are indeed acceptable. A prime example is bribery, which is against the law in virtually every country in the world. Reasoning from relativism (the conventional stage), a leader might suggest that because bribery happens in a culture, it is acceptable. Reasoning from principles (the postconventional stage), however, makes it much harder to justify paying bribes, because principles of fairness, rights, or care can be used to show the problems associated with bribery for the whole system.

5. *Stage 5 (postconventional, social contract) individuals act to achieve social consensus and tolerance on conflicting issues with the integrity of the system in mind.* Individuals at this stage are aware that people hold numerous values and opinions relevant to one's own group. But they also begin to recognize that there may be some nonrelative values or principles, like life and liberty, that should be upheld under any circumstances. Doing right in this stage means respecting the law because the social contract exists for the benefit of all. The dominant form of ethical reasoning (see Chapter 5) in this stage is utilitarian analysis or "the greatest good for the greatest number."

6. *Stage 6 (postconventional, universal ethical principles) individuals act consistently with self-selected moral principles.* They emphasize universal ethical principles, following self-chosen guidelines. They recognize that the social contract may be valid because it generally rests on valid principles, such as justice, equality of human rights, and human dignity. Doing right at this stage means living up to one's own principles. The moral point of view in this stage recognizes that all persons should be treated not as means to some end but as ends in themselves (see Chapter 5 for a further discussion of ethical principles).

As with the psychosocial and cognitive development discussed in the previous section, moral development brings with it an increasing capacity to take the perspective of others and to think through decisions and their implications systemically, which we have argued is essential for developing good stakeholder relationships and ultimately leading corporate citizenship. The later stages of development, because they encompass earlier stages, represent more advanced ways of reasoning that take increasing amounts of information and complexity into consideration and allow people to think more systemically and in a longer time frame.

TABLE 4.4. Gilligan's Stages of Moral Development in an Ethic of Care.

Developmental Stage	Focus	Implications
Preconventional	Caring for self	Good is ensuring survival.
Transition stage		Caring for self is considered "selfish." Perspective of "other" is considered.
Conventional	Self and other	Connection between self and other is developed by concept of responsibility to ensure care for the dependent and unequal. Good equals caring for others. Conform to expectations of others, self-sacrifice.
Transition stage		Illogic of inequality between self and other results in reconsideration of relationships.
Postconventional	Dynamics of relationship	New understanding of interconnectedness between other and self. Care is self-chosen principle of judgment about relationships, universal in condemning hurt and exploitation.

Source: Carol Gilligan, *In a Different Voice: Psychological Theory and Women's Development* (Cambridge: Harvard University Press, 1982).

RELATIONSHIPS, CARE, AND MORAL DEVELOPMENT. Kohlberg's research has been criticized because it was done entirely on men. Carol Gilligan studied moral development in women (unfortunately for the scientific validity of her work, only in women) to see if they reasoned morally using the same principles that men do at later developmental stages. Gilligan found that in contrast to men, who reason (at the higher levels) from principles, women perceive themselves and their moral obligations as embedded within a *network* of relationships, which Gilligan called an *ethic of care.*[29] Interestingly, Gilligan's work also suggests that individuals move through the same generic developmental stages of preconventional, conventional, and postconventional thinking identified above (see Table 4.4).

Gilligan's stages of moral development indicate that the women she studied based their reasoning on the impact of decisions on the relationships in which they were embedded. Strikingly, however (and not always well recognized), the women went through similar developmental phases in their capacity to role-take as the men in Kohlberg's studies. During the preconventional stage, women reason from caring about self, thinking about survival; that is, they do not take the perspective of others. They begin questioning their self-emphasis when they begin to develop a capacity to role-take, or see the perspective of others, which translates into the conventional stage as caring for others, regardless of concern for the self. The transition stage into postconventional reasoning is characterized by a recognition that it is illogical to care only for others without regard for self, thus precipitating a need for reconciling these competing views for the good of the system as a whole.

The postconventional stage is one in which multiple perspectives are held simultaneously, in this case from an understanding of the interconnectedness of those embedded in the relevant relationship web. Note that Gilligan suggested that principled reasoning is going on at this stage. Even though the set of principles tends to focus on condemnation of exploitation and hurt compared to the principles of justice and rights used with the men in Kohlberg's studies, the capacity to role-take provides a basis for thinking in more universal, complex, and generalizable terms than in earlier stages.

In looking at the studies of the moral development of women and men, it is important to note that they represent norms, not absolutes. Such studies suggest that men *tend* to reason from principles at the higher stages of development, while women *tend* to reason from an ethic of care or relationships. But these tendencies do not mean that men never reason from care nor that women never reason from principles, merely that the genders have tendencies in these directions.

Kohlberg suggested that one important means of enhancing moral development is through social interaction, the opportunity for dialogue and exchange, which helps an individual to gain insight into the perspective of others. Such role-taking is essential to moral development at the higher levels.[30] Role-taking is particularly important for understanding corporate citizenship in the multiplicity of contexts and issues that stakeholders bring to the attention of managers for action. But, as we shall see next, a third set of developmental capacities, those based on emotional maturity, is also necessary for effective leaders of corporate citizens.

Emotional Development

Writer Daniel Goleman highlighted the third arena of critical importance to leaders who need to work interactively with stakeholders: emotional intelligence or development.[31] Goleman documented that individuals mature emotionally as they age, although he did not use the same kind of developmental theory we have been discussing. Nonetheless, emotional development is essential in the process of working with others, as well as in gaining a realistic perspective on the self.

Emotional intelligence (or development) encompasses five critical skills.

1. *Knowing one's emotions:* self-awareness or the capacity to recognize feelings as they happen—the cornerstone of emotional intelligence.
2. *Managing emotions:* handling feelings appropriately, which builds on self-awareness.
3. *Motivating oneself:* marshaling emotions in the service of a goal, which is essential to paying attention.
4. *Empathy, or recognizing emotions in others:* attunement to the subtle social signals that indicate what others need or want.
5. *Handling relationships:* managing emotions in others.

Clearly, all of the skills of emotional development are crucial to successful leaders and, ultimately, to the success of the enterprises they manage. We have already discussed the importance of self-awareness. *Knowing one's emotions* or *awareness* is the key to developing a vision that is personally meaningful and, when tied with the other skills of emotional intelligence, can result in visionary organizations whose purpose and meaning are widely shared. When meaning is not developed and shared (or is trivial), people can get stuck in meaningless jobs doing work that they feel is of little or no value to anyone and makes no contribution to their lives other then putting bread on the table and shelter overhead. (In some circumstances this is enough, but for individuals and organizations operating at higher levels of development, it is probably not sufficient nor, as we shall see in the chapter on stakeholders, does such treatment embody the necessary respect for human dignity.)

Managing emotions successfully provides a sense of self-mastery or what Senge called personal mastery. As Senge expressed it, personal mastery involves "approaching one's life as a creative work, living life from a creative as opposed to a reactive viewpoint."[32] Individuals who can manage their own emotions are in balance and harmony with themselves and the rest of the world, able to express their feelings appropriately to the circumstances.

Motivating oneself means taking the initiative when appropriate opportunities arise and working toward goals. Obviously, leaders need this capacity to energize themselves before they will be able to help energize others toward pursuit of common goals. Research in cognitive psychology suggests that *optimism*—setting high but achievable goals—and thinking positively (i.e., visioning) can be powerful tools of motivation, not only to oneself, but also to others. A feeling of *self-efficacy,* or the belief that one can control events in one's own life, is another key to self-motivation.

Although one would never know it from many headlines and cover stories in the business press, which glamorize the "tough" boss, truly successful leaders have a great capacity to empathize with others. *Empathy* means putting oneself in the place of others and understanding what they are feeling. As we noted above, the cognitive capacity to role-take is obviously essential to developing this emotional capacity.

Corporate citizenship means developing positive relationships with the many stakeholders who influence or are influenced by a company's activities. *Handling relationships* well means developing a capacity to be effective in managing interpersonal relationships. Goleman noted that four distinct abilities that add up to the capacity to manage relationships effectively. These competencies are organizing groups, negotiating solutions, personal connection, and social analysis. Table 4.5 summarizes the competencies and capabilities needed in emotional development.

If we think about what is really needed to humanize and make modern organizations stakeholder friendly, it is the capacity to "manage with heart," as Goleman wrote.[33] Managing with heart means taking a positive—and visionary—approach to managing and leading, not putting others down through unwarranted criticism or a reactionary posture. Managing with heart makes sense, particularly when dealing with touchy issues or stakeholders who are sensitive to corporate activities.

Goleman offered advice, derived from the work of Harry Levinson,[34] about how to manage difficult interactions in an emotionally mature way. Although intended for giving criticism, the advice applies equally well to developing positive relationships with stakeholders. First, *be specific.* Pick a significant situation or incident that needs changing. Second, *offer a solution.* Criticisms without suggestions about what can be changed and how to do so are likely to leave the other parties feeling frustrated and unsatisfied. In developing stakeholder relationships, it is important to offer a solution,

TABLE 4.5. Emotional Development: Competencies

Emotional development entails:
1. Knowing one's emotions.
2. Managing one's emotions.
3. Motivating oneself.
4. Empathy, or recognizing emotions in others.
5. Managing interpersonal relationships.

Capabilities needed:
1. Organizing groups.
2. Negotiating solutions.
3. Personal connections.
4. Social analysis.

Source: Daniel Goleman, *Emotional Intelligence.*

but also to be truly open to solutions that may come from the stakeholder in an open dialogue. Third, *be present.* Face-to-face interactions make a lot more sense than distanced ones, where misinterpretations are far more likely and where misunderstandings can fester because they cannot be immediately addressed as they can in person. Finally, *be sensitive.* When difficult issues arise, being attuned to the point of view and feelings of others in the situation can be far more effective than insensitivity.

Developing Personal Vision

The keys to emotional health are confidence, curiosity, intentionality (wishing and having the capacity to have an impact), self-control, relatedness (ability to engage with others), communication skills, and being cooperative.[35] These are capacities possessed by very young children who are treated well. Such attributes are also critical in organizational life today. They can be enhanced by the development of personal vision.

Developing a personal vision—and translating it to a shared organizational vision—is one way to begin to understand what is really important in life. It is also important for building collaborative relationships with stakeholders that are based on a sense of common purpose or meaning in the enterprise. Having a sense of purpose, understanding what is meaningful, is one of Steven Covey's "Seven Habits of Highly Effective People."[36] It is also an essential element of personal mastery. How, after all, can individuals effectively lead an organization or group, or build effective relationships with stakeholders whose perspectives are very different, if they are unaware of themselves and what they stand for? We will see in the next chapter how important self-knowledge is to the types of constructive values that underpin successful corporate citizens and generate a sense of shared meaning in an organization.

In *The Fifth Discipline Fieldbook,* the authors suggested writing a personal vision statement, one that has been seriously considered, as a good starting point for developing personal mastery, personal vision, and ultimately organizational vision.

As they wrote in the fieldbook, "Wherever you are, start here."[37] It is self-aware individuals who have achieved personal mastery that enable corporations to become the visionary corporate citizens needed to lead in the economic sphere of tomorrow. (See the box on the vision of Cisco Systems' CEO.) Only through working on developing maturity in all of the domains discussed above can individuals avoid becoming what one of my former students called "instruments of the corporation."

Cisco Systems: An Unabashed Visionary Leader and Company

Called by *Business Week* an "unabashed evangelist for radical changes in management," Cisco Systems CEO John T. Chambers has put his vision of a new, progressive business model into practice in the company. Taking the perspective that "click-and-mortar will become the only means of survival," Chambers has built Cisco Systems into the world's most Internet-centric big company, according to *Fast Company* magazine. Here is one company in which personal and organizational vision are unified.

Cisco's vision is that the Internet will transform the way people work, live, play, and learn. Today change is happening faster than ever before, and Cisco helps companies turn that change into a competitive advantage, by helping them become agile. How? With expertise, a strong network of partners, and superior technology including intelligent network services and scalable architectures. Cisco is the worldwide leader in networking for the Internet.

With a will to put jobs wherever the right infrastructure, educated workforce, and supportive government exist, Chambers bills the company as the business network solution. Aiming to provide network resources enterprise-wide, Cisco Systems provides a comprehensive line of networking products. The company's mission is nothing less than to "shape the future of the Internet by creating unprecedented value and opportunity for our customers, employees, investors, and ecosystem partners."

Cisco has sales offices in about 115 countries, using direct sales, distributors, value-added resellers, and system integrators to reach its customers, who are large complex "enterprises" (large corporations, governments, and institutions where networking capability is needed), service providers, and small and medium sized businesses. Founded in 1986, the company has grown dramatically and is now the market leader in most of the market segments in which it is active. With annual revenues over $12 billion, the company has become one of the largest companies in the world.

Cisco's unique strategy is built on establishing excellent—and online—relationships with its primary stakeholders. It has built an internal network structure that allows its stakeholders instant access to the company and its resources from anywhere around the world. For customers, Cisco has the IPC, Internetworking Product Center, which allows customers to order online and have access to technical support, speeding processing of orders and deliveries. Potential customers can log onto the CCO, Cisco Connection Online, to get instant access to detailed corporate information, products, and services.

Suppliers are networked through the CSC, Cisco Supplier Connection, which allows direct access to Cisco's materials resource planning system and enables suppliers to monitor orders and ship automatically. Partners are linked through the PICA, the Partner-Initiated Customer Access, which provides resources for sales initiatives, and employees are connected via the CEC, Cisco's Employee Connection, an intranet that is intended to improve productivity.[38]

But it isn't just size or its 80 percent market share that makes Cisco a visionary company. Chambers is clear about the type of organization his vision implies. "The reason people stay at a company is that it's a great place to work. It's like playing on a great sports team. Really good players want to be around other really good players. Secondly, people like to work for good leadership. So creating a culture of leaders that people like is key. And the third is, are you working for a higher purpose than an IPO [initial public offering] or a paycheck? Our higher purpose is to change the way the world works, lives, and plays."[39]

To live up to these standards, Cisco applies its corporate citizenship very broadly to its customer and ally relationships, and has also implemented a number of strategically important community- and education-oriented programs. For example Cisco deploys employee volunteers in local communities into many local projects with corporate support. More important to its mission as a network services provider, the company has established The Cisco Community and Educational Technical Advocates (CETA) program, which integrates technical expertise and assistance into Cisco technology grants given to educational institutions.

Most important of all, Cisco has established a program that will ensure a trained base of employees in the future, while providing much needed help to many school systems, in its Networking Academy Program. The Academies teach high school and college students how to design, build, and maintain computer networks, with a curriculum that ranges from basic networking skills to advanced troubleshooting tools.

Organized as an innovative public-private partnership, the Academies provide 280 hours of web-based, hands-on curriculum in all 50 of the United States and 84 countries. Some 81,000 students are estimated to be enrolled in the 5,040 Academies, with more than 10,000 already having graduated by the summer of 2000. Cisco's Chambers has clearly discovered a way to "do well and do good." Cisco's initial $20 million investment in the Academies promises to yield long-term benefits not only to graduates of the program, who will have useful and needed skills, but also to the company itself and to the schools that benefit from getting resources essential to educating tomorrow's workforce.

Sources: Various parts of the Cisco website were sources for this case; http://www.cisco.com/warp/public/779/largeent/why_cisco/vision.html; John A. Byrne, "Visionary vs. Visionary," in *Business Week,* August 21/28, 2000, p. 210 ff; Anna Muoio, "Cisco's Quick Study," *Fast Company,* October 2000, pp. 30, 286 ff; http://www.cisco.com/warp/public/779/edu/academy/overview/curriculum/; http://www.cisco.com/warp/public/779/edu/academy/overview/fast_facts.html; also Michael I. Eizengerg, Donna M. Gallo, Irene Hagenbuch, and Alan N. Hoffman, "Cisco Systems, Inc.," in Michael A. Hitt, R. Duane Ireland, and Robert E. Hoskisson, *Strategic Management: Competitiveness and Globalization,* 4th ed. (Cincinnati, OH: Southwestern Publishing, 2001).

VISIONARY CORPORATE CITIZENS

Developing mutually beneficial relationships with stakeholders is underpinned by corporate vision and values in leading corporate citizens, as the work of James Collins and Jerry Porras in their important book *Built to Last* clearly shows.[40] Collins and Porras demonstrated that what makes companies great is a well-conceived and shared vision. Vision consists of articulated core values and core purposes that guide the corporation through its many hurdles. Vision and values, which Collins and Porras called "core ideology," are combined with clear descriptions of how to achieve the vision or strategies, which these authors termed envisioned future and BHAGs (big, hairy audacious goals). Core ideology remains relatively immutable and stable over time in the visionary companies, while the strategies underpinning BHAGs change as conditions warrant.

Collins and Porras's work is particularly rigorous in identifying the factors that have resulted in dramatically successful results for their visionary companies. Visionary companies, it seems, have successfully made the link between rhetoric and reality, closing the gap between what they say they are going to do and what they actually do in day-to-day practice. In other words, they like individuals who are cognitively, morally, and emotionally mature, are self-aware and self-reflective, who acknowledge their faults and work to improve themselves.

In their study, Collins and Porras compared the visionary companies to a second group of companies in similar industries about the same age. By most measures these comparison companies were also highly successful but nonetheless dramatically underachieved the visionary companies in terms of long-term financial and stock market performance. Despite the success of the less visionary companies, many if not most companies fail dramatically to create and implement visions and may be hard-pressed to live up to their potential for financial, market, and other measures of success. Most companies, it would appear, have a long way to go to create alignment between vision and values and their day-to-day operating practices, particularly with respect to treating stakeholders well.

Additionally, even when companies are classified as "excellent," such as those studied in the early 1980s by T. J. Peters and R. H. Waterman,[41] it is clear from the many problems those companies faced as time went by that *sustaining excellence is no easy task* and requires constant managerial attention and leadership.[42] Thus, not only do gaps exist between rhetoric and reality with respect to making vision real, but also even when they are brought into alignment, sustaining that alignment clearly requires constant attention.

Like individuals, then, leading corporate citizens need to develop shared vision through a capacity for self-awareness and reflection on the implications and impacts of their actions and decisions. They need to be conscious of the decisions they make and the impacts that those decisions will have on other stakeholders. This consciousness comes about through dialogue and interaction, through sharing of assumptions and rationales, and through efforts to work collaboratively toward common goals—all of which can be termed *mindfulness*. Such development in organizations is a constant process, but unlike the development of individuals it may not be a "staged" process in quite the same way, as we shall explore in the next section.

Vision and Change: Transforming Organizations

Organizations do develop, much as people do. One important aspect of that development is structural, where corporations tend to be shaped by four key dimensions: age, size, industry growth rate, and its stage of "evolution or revolution,"[43] as Larry Greiner discussed in his classic *Harvard Business Review* article. Unlike people, organizations can and do regress from more "advanced" stages to less advanced stages, depending on their circumstances. Organizational structures represent one form of organizational (corporate) development. For example, downsizing, acquisitions, and other forms of restructuring can quickly change an organization's structure and associated developmental stage backward or forward with significant implications for the company's interactions with key stakeholders.

Greiner argued that organizations become increasingly institutionalized as they age and grow in size, and that the rapidity of their growth depends on industry dynamics. Organizations go through both evolutionary periods, or relatively

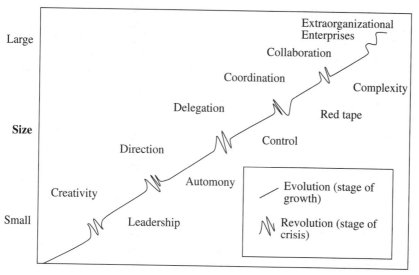

FIGURE 4.1. Greiner's Five Phases of Organizational Growth
Source: Larry E. Greiner, "Evolution and Revolution as Organizations Grow," *Harvard Business Review,* July–August 1972, pp. 37–46.

stable periods of development, and revolutionary periods when change and turbulence is constant. With each developmental phase comes a crisis with which the organization must cope if it hopes to continue to be successful in the future (see Figure 4.1).

Greiner's five phases of evolutionary organizational development are creativity, direction, delegation, coordination, collaboration, and we can add a new one of complexity. These relatively stable phases are punctuated by periods of crisis, a particular type of which is associated with each phase of growth. Thus, as the young and entrepreneurial organization in its *creativity* phase matures, it enters a crisis of leadership. Sometimes founders leave or are replaced during this crisis, as the organization requires more formalized management systems than are typically found in small creative enterprises. The crisis of leadership involves determining who will lead the organization out of its crisis.

The second evolutionary phase is one of *direction*. During this period the organization typically has hired a manager to establish a formalized organizational structure (frequently a functional structure) and generally systems, such as accounting, budgets, rewards, and communications, are formalized and installed. At the end of this phase, the company enters a second revolution; it is facing the crisis of autonomy. People lower in the organization feel too controlled and become ineffective because things have become overly centralized; they desire more autonomy.

The next evolutionary phase is one of *delegation,* to deal with the crisis of autonomy. Responsibility tends to be decentralized through structures such as profit centers, and divisionalization of the organization may occur to create new incentives for innovation and entrepreneurial activities. However, the seeds of the crisis of control are planted in this decentralization as communication within the organization falters because managers are running their own units autonomously. This creates a need for more coordination and integration across units.

Faced with the need to reintegrate the organization, the next evolutionary phase the organization enters is that of *coordination*. In coordination, units tend to be merged into new groupings, formal communication and review procedures are established across units, and the headquarters begins to exert more control to bring all units into line with each other. Of course, this coordinating activity generates the next crisis: the crisis of red tape.

Hamstrung by all the bureaucratic coordinating mechanisms, the organization now begins to emphasize *collaboration* in its fifth stage. This stage is built around becoming more flexible through teamwork and collaborative problem-solving measures, the creation of flexible organizational arrangements, and the encouragement of experimentation. Greiner now posited that the crisis after this stage, the one in which organizations have become weblike structures, will be one of recognizing that the solution to the problem is not internal, but may be external.

Indeed, Greiner suggested that a sixth phase, *extraorganizational enterprise,* may now be evolving in which growth depends on the design of external solutions (e.g., alliances, networks, and stakeholder relationships), rather than internal solutions. The crisis facing organizations at this highly developed stage is likely to be one of coping with change and complexity.[44]

At each stage of structural development, companies are faced with the need to explain their actions and decisions to their stakeholders. Primary stakeholders, such as employees, customers, and allies, are clearly affected by the organizational structure and practices that a company has generated to cope with the changes. In addition, as companies change shape by acquiring and divesting other companies (moving toward or away from centralized, decentralized, or network structures), not only can employees be retained or let go, but also communities and supplier networks are impacted. Leading corporate citizens at whatever stage of structural development need to have leaders who maintain awareness of these stakeholder impacts and relationships so that companies' reputations, which are increasingly critical to their success, are maintained positive and intact. Only by pushing the company to maintain a relatively high level of moral development, no matter what its stage of structural development, can leaders rest assured that stakeholders will be well treated.

Organizations and Moral Development

At the same time as its structure represents one type of development, a company's level of awareness or consciousness represents a wholly different domain of development, one that can generally be characterized as how progressive a company is. Like structure, the level of "progressiveness" or consciousness about how a company's decisions impact stakeholders can quickly change (either more or less progressive), depending on a number of factors related to leadership, corporate culture, competitive circumstances, and internal dynamics. At the same time, it is clear that leading corporate citizens strive toward more aware cultures built on constructive values where all stakeholders are respected and valued, where dialogue is possible, and where assumptions and actions can be questioned and, if need be, reversed. Thus, one goal of a leading corporate citizen must be to maintain the progressive awareness of stakeholders no matter what is happening to the company structurally.

In a very interesting application of moral development theory to organizations, Jeanne Logsdon and Kristi Yuthas proposed that the approaches of organizations to guiding values and stakeholders relationships can be compared (though they are obviously not completely parallel) to individual development.[45] Unlike people, however, organizations *can* (and frequently do) regress from more complex and advanced stages of development to less developed stages as structure, leadership and the management team, the reward system, industry dynamics, competition, performance, or internal culture change. Stages of organization development are neither necessarily invariant (same-sequenced) nor are they necessarily always moving in a positive direction. Nonetheless, organizations do exhibit differences in what we can term their moral climate, which suggests that some companies are more or less progressive than others.

Logsdon and Yuthas compared the motivations and rationales for organizational actions to the moral reasoning stages of individual development, which we suggest are not exactly stages (as organizations need not progress through them), but rather *states* of being or cultural frames (see Table 4.6). Organizations in an obedience and punishment cultural frame, similar to the preconventional reasoning stage of individual development, act only to avoid painful consequences to the organization. Thus, leaders of organizations operating in this state will obey the law to avoid being punished, but will not really think about whether that is the right thing to do nor will they think about it from any other perspective. They are reactive in their posture toward stakeholders and largely unresponsive to stakeholder interests other than perhaps those of owners to whom they are financially accountable. Sunbeam Corporation under Al Dunlap, known popularly as Chainsaw Al, may well have been in this state. Dunlap aggressively restructured Sunbeam, shutting down factories and outsourcing jobs with little regard for stakeholders other than owners. Ultimately, the harshness backfired and Dunlap was fired by the board of directors when the company consistently failed to meet its financial targets.

In a slightly more progressive state, instrumental purpose and exchange, leaders of companies act more proactively to further their own interests, which is to achieve benefits from acting responsibly, or at least appearing to do so.

In the conventional stages, companies are acting for reasons of interpersonal concordance. Such companies conform (as do teenagers) to the interests of their peer group, in this case to meet the expectations of industry competitors, trade associations, or business community norms. In the social accord and system maintenance state, they recognize the need to meet societal expectations as articulated in the law and therefore begin to act with a compliance mentality. Most U.S. companies today are likely to be operating from this type of cultural frame.

Leaders of companies can also operate from a principled set of reasoning when they achieve a postconventional stage cultural frame. In this state, they focus proactively on

TABLE 4.6.   Organizational Cultural Frames

Developmental State Kohlberg	Rationale and Motivation Applied	Operating Posture with Stakeholders
Preconventional		
1. Obedience and punishment	Act to avoid painful organizational consequences.	Reactive
2. Instrumental purpose and exchange	Act to further one's interests.	Reactive
Conventional		
3. Interpersonal accord, conformity to group norms	Act to meet expectations of peer companies, industry, or local business community norms.	Proactive
4. Social accord and system maintenance and regulations	Act to comply with current laws and regulations.	Proactive
Postconventional		
5. Social contract	Act to achieve social consensus on issues not fully addressed by legal standards.	Interactive
6. Universal ethical principles	Act to identify, communicate, and apply universal moral principles in organizational decision making.	Interactive

Sources: Adapted from Jeanne M. Logsdon and Kristi Yuthas, "Corporate Social Performance, Stakeholder Orientation, and Organizational Moral Development," *Journal of Business Ethics* 16 (1997), pp. 1213–26; operating modes are based on Lee E. Preston and James E. Post, *Private management and Public Policy* (New York: Prentice Hall, 1975).

their corporate citizenship so they can achieve social consensus and tolerance on conflicting issues. From this state, companies leaders may act to achieve social consensus on issues that go beyond mere legal standards and constraints. Such companies recognize that some things need to be done because they are simply the right thing to do. We have already seen that leading citizens like Johnson & Johnson seem to have achieved and consistently maintain at least this stage of development, as was evidenced many years ago by their response to the Tylenol crisis discussed in Chapter 5.

The most progressive state is when self-defined universal principles come fully into operation. Companies operating from universal principles act to identify, communicate, and apply universal moral principles in their organizational decision making, and are likely to do so in collaboration with their stakeholders, taking multiple perspectives into account.[46] These are the companies that achieve the status of visionary companies as defined by Collins and Porras and may be exemplified by the type of dialogic process that the Shell Group (see Chapter 1) is attempting to achieve. It is highly developed, progressive companies that have the possibility to begin to treat their stakeholders well through the practices they develop and particularly, to move into the interactive mode of dialogue needed to truly engage with stakeholders, as will be discussed below.

Note that Table 4.6 also highlights the "posture" that an organization is likely to take given its state of development. Using a preconventional cultural frame, companies are acting primarily to avoid punishment or further their own interests; they are likely to be fairly reactive in their posture toward stakeholders, acceding to demands and pressures only when necessary to avoid punishment.[47] Because their perspective is primarily one of self and self-interest (as with people), the best they can do is act to avoid the consequences their actions might generate.

More progressive firms using conventional reasoning are more proactive with their stakeholders. Such companies would likely be active in trade and industry associations that attempt to establish and work with recognized standards; they recognize the importance of sustaining the peer group's identity and the social system more generally. From conventional reasoning, a company can go outside itself enough to recognize that some stakeholder-related actions are needed to maintain the structure and well-being of the industry. They can thus move beyond mere reaction to proaction.

From postconventional reasoning, a company's leaders recognize inherently the need for doing the right thing as a part of their position in society. They act from principles that help to build and sustain the necessary relationships they have with stakeholders (as Gilligan's work would suggest[48]) and they also clearly articulate the values on which their enterprise is built.

As noted, such clarity helps to guide decision-making processes and also helps a company build ways of engaging interactively in dialogue and conversation with stakeholders to determine their needs and interests, rather than assuming that they already know what those needs and interests are. In this interactive mode of engagement, mutual learning and mutual change and accommodation can take place, bringing about the type of balance of interests demonstrated as necessary among the three spheres of activity in human societies.

LEADING CHALLENGES: DEVELOPMENT AND THE VISION THING

Leading corporate citizens with vision is no easy task, particularly in a world that places such complex demands on both the company and its organization. Yet thinking about the role of vision, individual and corporate, in creating the type of world in which we can all live may be essential to building a better future. In this chapter, we have looked at three types of development upon which leaders need to work if they hope to create corporate visions that enhance, rather than harm, societies. By consciously choosing visions that create common and inspirational purposes that focus on building a better world, leaders can begin the long-term process of working productively and interactively with stakeholders. This interaction is necessary to building the successful stakeholder relationships required in our complex world.

And to do it well, leaders need to work on knowing themselves and their own purposes—visions—well, and building in learning opportunities for themselves and others in their organizations. Only by constantly working to enhance individual *and* corporate awareness of the implications of action can the necessary grounding of mindfulness and wisdom, necessary not only for corporate success but also for the well-being of society and nature, be built. Developing higher levels of awareness and mindfulness means taking time for *reflection* on the implications of decisions for the company's many stakeholders. It also means making time for engaging *dialogue* with those stakeholders to assure their points of view are understood and incorporated into the company's plans, an emerging corporate posture called *stakeholder engagement.* These activities can heighten and advance development in the leaders of corporate citizens so that they will be able to avoid getting "in over their heads," to use Robert Kegan's term. Such development is also needed for leaders to think systemically about their own and their companies' actions, understanding the implications of those actions on communities, employees, customers, and others who rely on and trust the company to act in good faith.

The argument made above suggests that it is better for a company to be interactively engaged with stakeholders in a dialogue than in mere compliance—that is, more rather than less progressive in its attitudes and posture toward stakeholders. Such interaction helps to determine the best ways to meet their *mutual* needs and interests rather than for a company to merely be complying with the laws at the conventional stage of development or assuming that it is the only actor that matters.

Progressive companies—leading corporate citizens—understand the visions and values on which their activities are built, and work toward these higher stage ways of interacting. In this way they are not only adding value for relevant stakeholders, but also are upholding the values that they have articulated and, thereby, doing the right thing with respect to all stakeholders. The link between vision and values—and the necessary link to value added—will be the topics of the next two chapters.

NOTES TO CHAPTER 4

1. The seminal book is Peter M. Senge, *The Fifth Discipline: The Art and Practice of the Learning Organization,* (New York: Doubleday, 1991). Further definition and multiple exercises to help develop vision can be found in Peter M. Senge, Charlotte Roberts, Richard B. Ross, Bryan J. Smith, and Art Kleiner, *The Fifth Discipline Fieldbook: Strategies and Tools for Building a Learning Organization* (New York: Currency Doubleday, 1994).
2. Senge, p. 207; see also R. Edward Freeman and Daniel R. Gilbert, Jr., *Corporate Strategy and the Search for Ethics* (Englewood Cliffs, NJ: Prentice Hall, 1988) for a discussion of personal projects; and Sandra A. Waddock, "Linking Community and Spirit: A Commentary and Some Propositions," *Journal of Organizational Change Management,* special issue on Spirituality and Work, 1999, 12(4): 332–344.
3. Senge, *Fifth Discipline,* p. 207.
4. See James C. Collins and Jerry I. Porras, *Built to Last: Successful Habits of Visionary Companies* (New York: HarperBusiness, 1994); see also Collins and Porras, "Building Your Company's Vision," *Harvard Business Review,* September–October 1996, pp. 65–77.
5. These outcomes of vision are derived from Senge, pp. 207–11.

6. See Russell L. Ackoff, "On Learning and the Systems That Facilitate It," *Reflections* 1, no. 1 (1999), pp. 14–24.

7. Abraham Zaleznik, "Managers and Leaders: Are They Different?" *Harvard Business Review,* March–April 1992, p. 4.

8. Ibid., p. 7.

9. See Ken Wilber's *Sex, Ecology, Spirituality: The Spirit of Evolution* (Boston: Shambala Publications, 1995); Edward O. Wilson, *Consilience: The Unity of Knowledge* (New York: Knopf, 1998; Humberto R. Maturana and Francisco J. Varelo, *The Tree of Knowledge: The Biological Roots of Human Understanding* (Boston: Shambala Press, 1998, and Frans de Waal, *Good Natured: The Origins of Right and Wrong in Humans and Other Animals* (Cambridge: Harvard University Press, 1996); de Waal does present some evidence that some members of the primate group other than humans may have a degree of self-consciousness.

10. See, for example, Edward O. Wilson, *Consilience:* and de Waal, *Good Natured.*

11. Humberto R. Maturana and Francisco J. Varela, *The Tree of Knowledge: The Biological Roots of Human Understanding,* rev. ed. (Boston: Shambala Press, 1998).

12. de Waal, p. 67.

13. de Wall; see also William C. Frederick, *Values, Nature, and Culture in the American Corporation* (New York: Oxford University Press, 1995).

14. Ackoff, p. 14.

15. Lawrence Kohlberg, "Moral Stages and Moralization: The Cognitive-Developmental Approach," in Thomas Lickona, ed., Gilbert Geis and Lawrence Kohlberg, consulting eds., *Moral Development and Behavior: Theory, Research, and Social Issues* (New York: Holt, Rinehart and Winston, 1976).

16. Frame analysis is elaborated by Donald A. Schön and Martin Rein in *Frame Reflection: Toward the Resolution of Intractable Policy Controversies* (New York: Basic Books, 1994).

17. We will focus here mainly on the three domains of cognitive (personality and social), moral, and emotional development.

18. Some people criticize developmental theories because they appear to be elitist in that the later stages are "better" than earlier stages. In the sense that later stages supercede and encompass the earlier stages in the nesting fashion described in the text, this criticism appears to be founded on reality. Without engaging in a debate about developmental theory, there is significant evidence that such nesting occurs. Each developmental stage incorporates a richer and more complex understanding than the previous stages, with the ability to consider more perspectives simultaneously. In that sense there is a higher state of consciousness among human beings than among animals. This is one reason that humans are considered to be morally superior to animals. There is, as Wilber pointed out, more "depth" of understanding (or complexity) at later stages of development, while there is more "span" or breadth in lower stages.

19. Howard Gardner, *Frames of Mind* (New York: Basic Books, 1983); and Ken Wilber, *The Eye of Spirit: An Integral Vision for a World Gone Slightly Mad* (Boston: Shambala Press, 1998).

20. Kohlberg, p. 34.

21. One source among many is Jean Piaget, *The Psychology of the Child* (New York: John Wiley, 1969). Piaget's work is nicely summarized in Robert Kegan's *The Evolving Self: Problem and Process in Human Development* (Cambridge: Harvard University Press, 1982).

22. These stages are summarized nicely in Kohlberg's "Moral Stages and Moralization"; see also Kegan, *The Evolving Self.*

23. See Dalmar Fisher and William R. Torbert, *Personal and Organizational Transformations: The True Challenge of Continual Quality Improvement* (London: McGraw-Hill, 1995).

24. See, for example, Robert Kegan's *The Evolving Self* and *In Over Our Heads: The Mental Demands of Modern Life*. (Cambridge: Harvard University Press, 1994).

25. Fisher and Torbert, see also Chris Argyris, *Knowledge for Action: A Guide to Overcoming Barriers to Organizational* (*Change* San Francisco: Jossey-Bass, 1993).

26. William R. Torbert, *The Power of Balance: Transforming Self, Society, and Scientific Inquiry* (Newbury Park, CA: Sage Publications, 1991); see also Fisher and Torbert.

27. William Isaacs, *Dialogue and the Art of Thinking Together* (New York: Doubleday Currency, 1999).

28. Kohlberg, Much of this section is derived from this article.

29. Carol Gilligan *In a Different Voice: Psychological Theory and Women's Development* (Cambridge: Harvard University Press, 1982).

30. Kohlberg, pp. 48–50.

31. Daniel Goleman, *Emotional Intelligence* (New York: Bantam Books, 1995); see also Goleman's *Working with Emotional Intelligence* (New York: Bantam Books, 1998). This section is drawn largely from Goleman's writings.

32. Senge, 1991, pp. 139–141.

33. Goleman, *Emotional Intelligence*, chap. 10.

34. Harry Levinson, "Feedback to Subordinates," *Addendum to the Levinson Letter* (Waltham, MA: Levinson Institute, 1992); cited in Goleman, *Emotional Intelligence*, pp. 153–54.

35. Goleman, *Emotional Intelligence*, p. 194.

36. Steven Covey,

37. Senge et al., *The Fifth Discipline Fieldbook*.

38. Michael I. Eizenerg, Donna M. Gallo, Irene Hagenbuch, and Alan N. Hoffman, "Cisco Systems, Inc.," in Michael A. Hitt, R. Duane Ireland, and Robert E. Hoskisson, *Strategic Management: Competitiveness and Globalization*, 4th ed. (Cincinnati, OH: Southwestern Publishing, 2001).

39. John A. Byrne, "Visionary vs. Visionary," in The 21st Century Corporation, *Business Week,* August 21/28, 2000, pp. 210 ff.

40. Collins and Porras.

41. T. J. Peters and R. H. Waterman, *In Search of Excellence: Lessons from America's Best Run Companies* (New York: Harper & Row, 1982).

42. For example, see James O'Toole, *Leading Change: The Argument for Values-Based Leadership* (New York: Ballantine Books, 1996).

43. See Larry E. Greiner, "Evolution and Revolution as Organizations Grow," *Harvard Business Review,* July–August 1972, pp. 37–46; reprinted with comments from the author, as HBR Classic, May–June 1998. Greiner's model is developed in this section.

44. This latter point is the author's.

45. Jeanne M. Logsdon and Kristi Yuthas, "Corporate Social Performance, Stakeholder Orientation, and Organizational Moral Development," *Journal of Business Ethics 16* (1997), pp. 1213–26.

46. Logsdon and Yuthas provide much of this framework.

47. The reactive, proactive, and interactive framework can be found in Lee E. Preston and James E. Post, *Private Management and Public Policy* (New York: Prentice Hall, 1975); however, the application to states or cultural frames relative to moral development is the author's.

48. Gilligan, *In a Different Voice: Psychological Theory and Women's Development* (Cambridge: Harvard University Press, 1982).

Values in Management Practice:

OPERATING WITH INTEGRITY

The social imperative is to think anew rather than retreat inward. Like it or not, this will require people to reimagine themselves as social beings on a larger stage, not helpless cogs in an awesome market system, and to glimpse the all-encompassing possibilities that the global revolution has put before them. The challenge is not to abandon old identities and deeply held values, but to enlarge them. If capitalism is now truly global, what are the global social obligations that accompany it? The wrenching economic changes will be understood in time as a great new opening in history—an invitation to social invention and human advancement—but only when people learn how to think expansively again about their own ideals . . .

A revolutionary principle is embedded in the global economic system, awaiting broader recognition: Human dignity is indivisible. Across the distances of culture and nations, across vast gulfs of wealth and poverty, even the least among us are entitled to their dignity and no justification exists for brutalizing them in the pursuit of commerce. Anyone who claims to hold human values cannot escape these new connections.

—WILLIAM GREIDER, One World Ready or Not

INTEGRITY: HONESTY AND WHOLENESS

We have all known people we admire because they have great integrity. We also know companies that we admire for their integrity as corporate citizens. Companies that are leading corporate citizens know that the key to their citizenship is operating with integrity. Integrity means that they know who and what they are; that is, such people know what they stand for, and act consistent with that knowledge. IBM, for example, was recently listed as number one in a *Business Ethics* magazine rating of "100 Best Corporate Citizens," but many readers complained that the company had recently changed its pension policies, hurting some employees and retirees.[1] Although the company reversed that problematic decision, these readers were concerned about the company's integrity, which had previously been little questioned.

Leading corporate citizens have values that are clear and compelling enough to influence their decisions and actions. IBM, which had been through troubled times in the 1990s, clearly made a mistake with its decision to change its pension policies in ways that harmed some employees. Those employees had a different expectation: that a company known for its integrity would continue to act with integrity.[2] Companies, especially those that are most successful over the long run, do indeed act with integrity in both good and bad times. This chapter will explore the meaning of operating with integrity, particularly in organizations, but also in individual terms, in the belief that such integrity is at the core of long-term success and leading corporate citizenship.

The Meanings of Integrity

It is important to be clear about the meanings of *integrity,* of which there are two primary definitions. First is soundness of moral principle or character: *honesty.* People and organizations have integrity when they are honest. They mean what they say and their behavior reflects that intent. Companies with integrity work hard to live up to the principles and values that they articulate (assuming they do this at all), they are trustworthy, and they respect others.

The second meaning of integrity is *wholeness* or completeness. People and organizations, by this definition, have integrity when they are whole, rather than when they are fragmented or atomized. Companies operating with this second meaning of integrity in mind recognize that they represent a system within society, or a "holon"; that is, they are both whole within themselves and also a part of something larger and more developed than themselves—or whole/parts.[3]

As wholes, companies are complete *systems.* In a system, what happens in one arena impacts what happens in other arenas within that system. By implication, the way that one stakeholder is treated affects not only the way that stakeholder perceives and interacts with the companies, but also the way ripple effects influence other stakeholders within the system. As "parts," companies recognize their interdependence with society, that they are an embedded element of the larger structure. Therefore, they recognize that what they do has numerous impacts, both expected and unexpected. Thus, they are careful in developing the practices that constitute their day-to-day activities, recognizing that whatever they do and however they treat their stakeholders will have long-term ripple effects on the company and on society.

Companies who recognize this second definition of integrity also know that they exist in the multiple domains of individual and collective, subjective and objective—and they find ways to bring these domains into all that they do. Organizations with integrity find ways to treat their stakeholders according to the principles they have established, so that they too can remain successful and healthy. They engage not only the traditional bottom line, but also the "softer" bottom lines associated with

117

*CHAPTER 5
Values in
Management
Practice: Operating
with Integrity*

the relationships a company develops with other stakeholders. Additionally, they inspire meaningful relationships that tap not only the "hard" or quantitative aspects of performance, but also the softer aspects of emotion, meaning making (or developing meaning in an organization), belonging, and commitment.[4] Leaders of such companies act mindfully, aware of the impacts their decisions have on many constituencies. They take the time to step back and reflect upon their values and about the ways that their actions reflect—or do not reflect—those values.

The definition of integrity as wholeness also speaks to the inclusion of all four of the domains that Ken Wilber has identified; that is, it is not enough for an enterprise to be successful only in the material or objective sense, or only for an individual or specific group. The subjective—meaning making, even inspirational and spiritual—aspects of life for individuals and communities must also be satisfied if an organization is to operate with integrity, that is, as a principled whole. Integrity also speaks to the recognition of the need for the whole/partness of society—that is, the integration (integrity) of companies into the three-sphere system with its ecological underpinning described in Chapters 2 and 3.

Values and Integrity

Values are the basis of any organization's ability to operate with integrity. It is important that companies that wish to operate with integrity articulate a set of positive and constructive values to guide their behavior. The best vision and mission statements embody what leadership theorist James MacGregor Burns termed *end values,* while simultaneously establishing a series of modal values to guide practice. End values describe desirable "end states," or collective goals or explicit purposes, establishing standards for making choices among a set of alternatives. Thus, end values combine two meanings: goals and the standards by which those goals will be met.[5]

Modal values, in contrast, define modes of conduct or, in the corporate context we are describing, managerial *practice.* Burns described modes as the means by which human enterprise should be conducted, although they are sometimes goals in themselves. Modal values include such things as honor, courage, civility, honesty, and fairness. Some modal values are *intrinsic* in that they are ends in themselves (i.e., worth achieving simply because they are worth something), thus serving as both ends and means. Others are *extrinsic* or *instrumental,* in that they help us achieve a goal or end value.[6]

Operating with integrity means consistently operating with constructive and positive end values clearly in mind, and it requires leaders who are highly developed cognitively, emotionally, and morally as the previous chapter suggests, so that they can serve this transformational leadership role, inspiring others to join in the enterprise's worthy goals.[7] Achieving such end values helps all stakeholders involved in the enterprise to develop their own meaning about the purposes of and involvement in their work and is essential to what we called meaning making above. If implemented properly, core values provide a means for identification with the broader and higher purposes articulated by the company, thus sustaining individual growth and development as well as enhancing development of a collective spirit among stakeholders, particularly employees, who see themselves as a part of the firm.

118

PART TWO
Leading Corporate
Citizens with Vision,
Values, and Value
Added

Organizations with positive core values that guide their decision making can succeed by operating with integrity, even when tough decisions have to be made—or perhaps especially when tough decisions have to be made. While sometimes such enterprises may suffer negative short-term consequences (e.g., by turning away from doing business in countries where corruption is rampant), there is mounting evidence that they achieve lasting long-term success.

The downside risk of having inspiring and meaningful end values with their associated visions, which generate commitment and loyalty from employees, is the risk of creating cults, with all of their attendant dangers. Indeed, researchers James Collins and Jerry Porras have pointed out that the visionary companies they studied do indeed have "cult-like" cultures, where one either belongs or does not.[8] In addition, cults or organizations with too powerful cultures can override individuals in their effort to have everyone conform to the organization's vision. Thus, in creating the core values by which an enterprise is to be guided, it is critically important that leaders consider the *nature* of the values they are articulating and what the implications of those values are for behavior. Such end values are likely to influence people's behavior within the system that constitutes the company in significant ways. Looking specifically at the kinds of values that good corporate citizenship inspires, as we will do below, will help companies avoid this problem and empower their stakeholders while sustaining their own profitability.

CITIZENSHIP: VISION AND PROCESS

Leading corporate citizenship fundamentally involves developing a constructive, positive vision that inspires people, as the previous chapter has suggested. But the vision needs to be thoroughly underpinned by a set of positive end values that guide policy development and implementation, as well as the ways in which stakeholders are treated every day (i.e., the stakeholder relationships on which a company is built).[9] Being a good citizen is not about becoming a paragon of virtue, as some proponents of corporate social responsibility might argue. All companies, as human systems, get into trouble at times. For example, The Body Shop has pursued an overtly socially responsible strategy linked to its business purposes, which generates some considerable controversy when there are problems. IBM's pension decision noted at the beginning of this chapter clearly illustrates the tension facing corporations trying to act as leading corporate citizens.

Rather than aiming to be a paragon of virtue, becoming a good organizational citizen is about honestly committing to and engaging in the ongoing *struggle* to live up to a set of core values. This struggle is both a process and an end in itself, just as modal values can be both means and ends.

The end values embedded in core ideology are typically articulated in a mission or vision statement. The "living up to" is done through the development and implementation of operating policies, procedures, and programs—that is, the *practices* that define "the way business is done here." Implementing values through managerial, employee, and other stakeholder-related practices, such as customer relations,

119

CHAPTER 5
Values in
Management
Practice: Operating
with Integrity

supplier relations, or governmental relations, is ongoing in that new developments and conflicts will inevitably arise as the external context changes, new decisions are made internally, new competitors arise, and technology continues to advance.

All of this suggests that one key to leading corporate citizenship, particularly at the global level, is to find a set of core values that are both constructive and truly meaningful within the internal and external context of the firm. Additionally, this meaningfulness must be expressed alongside and in some degree of congruence with the dominant value set of business—economizing—as discussed in Chapter 3. Corporations are in the business of doing something well for someone and making a profit as a result. Their natural and rightful tendencies toward economizing need to be balanced by constructive values that place weight on other important aspects of citizenship in society.

The function of this chapter will be to focus on the positive and proactive ways that values result in economizing that is helpful to society through the living out of corporate values. Such values are typically expressed in a mission or vision statement. Far too many corporate mission or vision statements are left to molder in drawers or hung on walls where few people ever see them. Perhaps they go unnoticed— and not lived up to—because they have been developed without significant thought given to whether the values they embody are actually "lived" within the corporation.

A second key to leading corporate citizenship at the global level is having managers, leaders, and employees who are highly developed personally in all three of the domains discussed in the previous chapter: intellectually or cognitively, emotionally, and morally. This type of individual development, when shared across an organization, creates a climate or culture (combined with appropriate structure and reward systems) in which ongoing learning can take place. Learning is essential to an organization that has any hope of succeeding in today's rapidly changing competitive environment, because it is through the learning context that people can develop to the point where they can make sense of the many conflicting demands of different stakeholders, not to mention in the pressure cooker of the changing dynamics within the three intersecting spheres that influence business health and activity.

ENTERPRISE STRATEGY: WHAT DO WE STAND FOR?

Leading corporate citizens, in articulating their values and their fundamental purposes in society, make a clear determination about what they stand for. In contrast to the situation where a company's code of conduct, business principles, or vision statement finds itself buried unnoticed in someone's drawer, when values are "lived," everyone in the company knows what they are and how well they are implemented. Such values become an essential part of what authors R. Edward Freeman and Dan Gilbert called "enterprise strategy," in which the organization and the individuals within it ask the fundamental question, "What do we stand for?"[10] Freeman and Gilbert suggested that this question should be asked along with the fundamental strategic question, "What business are we in?"

In this questioning process, values become an integral part of the practice of daily management, that is, rather than merely being "added on" to practices that already exist, they *become* the practices: They are the system that the company develops to put its vision into operation and implement its values. They become the means by which the company acts with integrity.

Organizations operating with integrity as corporate citizens adopt a systemic approach to developing and implementing their vision, mission, and values, as well as what purposes they serve in society. They are clear in their values, willing to question assumptions, and allow for both vulnerability and mistakes. And these corporate citizens stick with their philosophy over time, even when troubles arise, as they inevitably will. By asking both the strategic and enterprise strategy questions, particularly in the formulation of vision and values that need to be lived if the vision is to be achieved, leading corporate citizens build a values base right into the basics of how they do business, with whom, and for what purposes.

The strategic question creates direction and (business) purpose. The enterprise strategy question focuses on the ways the company and its participating stakeholders will operate and how they will treat each other in doing business. In articulating and implementing core values through their day-to-day operating practices, particularly those that support a systemic and well-integrated management approach, companies can help create a meaningful context for stakeholders participating in the enterprise.

As we shall see in Chapters 6 and 8, business success is built on constructive values that generate a sense of community within the corporation. Contrary to some people's beliefs, corporations are more than profit-generating machines: To succeed, they require community, integrity, and the trust of stakeholders. To think otherwise is simply shortsighted and ignores the fact that companies exist in societies which depend on them for jobs, taxes, and key elements of the social structure.[11]

Freeman and Gilbert also argued that one possible outcome of enterprise strategy would be to allow people to achieve their individual purposes through the pursuit of personal projects. Individuals could pursue these projects while simultaneously operating in the context of a community within a corporation, assuming that these projects do not interfere with the rights and dignity of others—and their ability to pursue their projects. It is relatively easy to see that if a company is generating an inspirational vision and corresponding set of values, then stakeholders, particularly employees, might find ways to achieve their own personal projects in the context of the company's goals.

An Ethic of Business Practice

What are the values that successful and progressive companies, companies with integrity, live up to in their effort to become good corporate citizens? Business scholars and managers alike have developed numerous approaches to thinking about what models of management are likely to help organizations succeed in the turbulent global arena. Starting with the participative management theories of the 1970s and including more recent corporate innovations, such as collaboration, strategic thinking, reengineering, total quality management (TQM), and the learning organization,

121

CHAPTER 5
Values in
Management
Practice: Operating
with Integrity

not to mention numerous others, corporations have adopted new approaches to managing in the hopes that one of them will improve performance.[12]

Sometimes, however, it seems as though companies rather thoughtlessly attempt to slap these models on top of the practices that already exist, as if an add-on could somehow change the direction, culture, and operating practices of the firm. Truly successful companies recognize that if any one of these models is to work for the company, it cannot be applied piecemeal or overlaid on existing systems. Instead, the entire corporate system and all of the relevant stakeholders need to become involved in making the transformation by fully implementing the approach and understanding the values that seem to underlie all of these approaches.

Management scholar Jeanne Liedtka has proposed that many of these management systems have a common set of values which, if fully implemented, would constitute a progressive and constructive "ethic of practice." These common values would still allow companies to develop their unique and individual strategies to fulfill the strategic elements needed to compete effectively.[13] The work by Collins and Porras on their "built-to-last" or visionary companies supports Liedtka's argument since it is the long-term success of these companies' capacity to sustain and implement their visions to which Collins and Porras attributed their success. Remember that Collins and Porras said that visionary companies had both sustaining and relatively immutable core ideologies, as discussed in the previous chapter, combined with the vivid descriptions that comprise strategies that change as the situation warrants.[14]

Liedtka, drawing upon the work of Alisdair MacIntyre,[15] defined the essential elements of what is meant by practice. A *practice* is (1) a cooperative human activity, with (2) intrinsic goods or outcomes related to the performance of the activity itself, and (3) a striving toward excellence both in the ends and the means, providing (4) a sense of ongoing extension and transformation of the goals of the practice.[16] As we think about leadership and management practice, particularly as our understanding of values-based management practice evolves, we should try to keep this understanding of the term "practice" in mind.

We are all familiar with the many management "fads," some noted above, in which corporations have been involved in recent years. For example, a company adopts one approach to improving performance, lays it on top of what exists, then abandons it when, because it was not fully implemented throughout the system, it fails to achieve results within the relatively short time frame management expects. Then the next approach comes along and the cycle begins again, with the same failure in achieving the expected results. The real problem, however, may lie not so much in the theories—any one of them could help the enterprise if fully and systemically implemented—but in their implementation. In reality, few of these programs are typically fully implemented in the way that their original authors proposed; hence, evaluating their effectiveness is extremely difficult.

The genius of Liedtka's approach is to uncover the common threads—the similarities in intent and values among these vastly different theories that serve as fads for managers unwilling to look deeply within and make serious transformational changes. For example, Liedtka covered Peter Senge's learning organization (to which we will return elsewhere in this book), W. Edwards Deming's total quality management, and Michael Hammer and James Champy's reengineering, to take three of the best known current approaches.[17] Each of these approaches, along with others including strategic thinking, collaboration, and participative management, is best applied systemically as a means of transforming the entire enterprise so that the goals of economizing can be achieved fruitfully and within the constraints of ecology.[18]

If only part of the approach is implemented or it is simply laid over existing approaches without any significant effort to really change the system, then elements like organizational structure, rewards, culture, and power relationships remain essentially unchanged and the organization itself is unlikely to change for the better. Liedtka's insight, however, is that all of these approaches are founded on a common values basis which, if taken seriously, would allow for transformational change that builds in the direction of fostering visionary companies or, in our terms, leading corporate citizens. Thus, one might argue that any one of these approaches, applied systemically by embedding it fully into the operating practices of the firm, might dramatically enhance performance. Table 5.1 illustrates the values identified as common to each of these approaches.

VISION CREATION. The first values-based element common to the management approaches is vision creation, which has been discussed at some length in the previous chapter. What is particularly important in thinking about creating shared meaning as a value is that the effort to do so links the individual to the organization. Thus, meaning and vision tap into what is typically considered to be the "soft" side of business. Meaning making focuses on the need of people to identify with an organization and to find personal meaning (or "projects") in the larger context of doing something to make the world a better place, which arguably all individuals desire.[19] Of course, as anyone who has ever been a manager knows, the so-called soft stuff is really the hard stuff; that is, bringing the systemic and meaning-making elements of management into reality is among the hardest—and arguably one of the most important—of managerial tasks.

SYSTEMS OR STRATEGIC THINKING. The second value common to all these approaches is that they attempt to develop in people within the enterprise an understanding of the system as a whole, and of the place within that system that any part (whether individual or group) has. This perspective, Liedtka pointed out, helps participants see the system as a whole and develop an ability to view it from the perspective of different stakeholders. This capacity to be what Henry Mintzberg termed a "strategic thinker" and Senge a "systems thinker" is a critical element of creating a stakeholder-friendly environment.[20]

PROCESS APPROACHES. The third commonality among all these management theories is their emphasis on processes rather than hierarchy or structure. These process approaches allow for continual learning, growth, and development, which is necessary because the situation itself in which companies find themselves continues to evolve.[21] Companies that value process as well as "product" or outcomes do not

123

CHAPTER 5
Values in
Management
Practice: Operating
with Integrity

TABLE 5.1. Values-Based Management Practices in Systems Approaches to Managing

Convergent Themes	Relevant Values-Based Practices
Create a shared sense of meaning, vision, and purpose that connects the personal to the organizational.	• Values community without subordinating the individual. • Sees community purpose as flowing from individuals.
Develop a systems perspective in all—a view held by each individual of him- or herself as embedded within a larger system.	• Seeks to serve other community members and ecosystem partners.
Emphasize business processes, rather than hierarchy or structure.	• Believes work itself has intrinsic value. • Belief in quality of both ends and means.
Localize decision making around work processes.	• Responsibility for actions. • Primacy of reach, with needed support.
Leverage information within the system.	• Truth telling (honesty, integrity). • Full access to accurate and complete information.
Focus on development at both personal and organizational levels.	• Value the individual as an end. • Focus on learning and growth at both individual and organizational levels.
Encourage dialogue.	• Freedom and responsibility to speak and to listen. • Commitment to find higher ground through exchange of diverse views.
Foster the capacity to take multiple perspectives simultaneously.	• Willingness to understand and work with the perspectives of others, rather than imposing own views.
Create a sense of commitment and ownership.	• Promise keeping. • Sense of urgency. • Engagement rather than detachment.

Source: Adapted from Jeanne Liedtka, "Constructing an Ethic for Business Practice," *Business and Society* 37, no. 3 (September 1998), pp. 254–280.

tend to get stuck on issues of power and politics and can move forward when circumstances warrant without being threatened by the process of change itself. As Liedtka noted, such a system requires—and develops—a sense of commitment and ownership among members of the organization and even of external stakeholders associated with the enterprise.

LOCALIZED DECISION MAKING. Localizing decision making around work processes, the next value common to systemic approaches to management, allows for participants in an organization to "own" their own work and its associated outcomes. Such ownership creates a pride in a job well done, as well as fostering organizational commitment, loyalty, and a sense of place or belonging, which is essential to fostering community and spirit.[22]

LEVERAGED INFORMATION. Leveraging information within the system is particularly important in today's knowledge-based enterprises, where knowledge is *a*—if not *the*—critical source of competitive advantage.[23] If organizations are to change on a continual basis and individuals are to grow within them, and if stakeholder relationships are to be developed positively, then sharing information honestly is needed.

PERSONAL AND ORGANIZATIONAL DEVELOPMENT. As must be obvious from the foregoing, constant attention to personal and organizational development is another value in the approaches Liedtka discussed. Only if people and their organizations can achieve higher levels of development will they be able to engage in the difficult struggle that implementing these values systemically entails—and only then can they continue to adapt and change as necessary in the complex environments within which they exist.

ENCOURAGEMENT OF DIALOGUE. Both external and internal stakeholders continually pressure companies to perform better for a variety of reasons, in part because organizations are human systems imbued with human failings. Thus, dialogue takes us back to the notion with which we began in Chapter 1. These systems encourage dialogue among stakeholders because through "good conversations" new solutions to intractable problems can be developed.[24]

UNDERSTANDING MULTIPLE PERSPECTIVES. Good conversations also permit the articulation of assumptions, the discussion of issues that might otherwise be "undiscussable,"[25] and help to move understanding toward what Buddhists call "third-way thinking,"—that is, new understandings that evolve in dialectical fashion from the preexisting understandings of participants in the conversation. The capacity to understand multiple perspectives, another common characteristic of the systems Liedtka discussed, is essential to generating such new understandings and innovative potential. Openness is the key to encouraging dialogue, so that one is free to speak one's mind and willing to challenge one's own thinking. With this openness comes the potential for new ideas, innovations, and new relationships that create entirely new possibilities for the organization that would otherwise be missed.

SENSE OF COMMITMENT AND OWNERSHIP. The combination of the factors noted above, along with a capacity to make decisions locally, especially those that affect one's own work, generates finally a sense of ownership and commitment to the enterprise. The combination of these factors creates a system with integrity in both meanings of the word. Such systemic approaches, properly implemented through values-based managerial practices (identified on the right-hand side of Table 5.1), provide a basis for what can be called enterprise strategy, which was discussed in the last section.

125

CHAPTER 5
Values in
Management
Practice: Operating
with Integrity

Stakeholder Relationships as Practice: Implementing Constructive Values

Corporate global (or local) citizenship integrates the needs and interests of a range of stakeholders into the core purposes of a company and engages their commitment through the ongoing practices involved in managing that enterprise (see Table 5.1). These practices influence not only the traditional objective bottom-line indicators of financial performance. They also engage the spirit and hearts of stakeholders in constructive ways that help to build a positive and proactive corporate culture and set of operating policies and procedures by which a company interacts with its numerous stakeholders—that is, they are integrative of the whole person.

Specific practice-related values underpin each of the themes common across the multiple managerial approaches that Liedtka discussed. Further, these values support both definitions of integrity identified above.[26] Developing shared meanings is supported by valuing community without subordinating the individual, developing community purposes from "individual purposes," much as the "individual projects" approach suggested by Freeman and Gilbert advocates.

Note that embedded within the implementation of practices associated with this theme, as well as in numerous others, is the type of "both/and" logic that Collins and Porras discovered in their visionary companies; that is, good corporate citizens value *both* individuals *and* communities internally, as well as the communities (stakeholder groups) they intersect with externally.[27] Similarly, individuals embedded in a system show strong evidence of reciprocity rather than one-sided self-interest.

The focus on business processes, rather than simply products or outcomes, suggests the need for companies and their managers to pay attention to the structuring of work itself so that individuals within the firm can see the inherent or intrinsic value of it. People in visionary companies or companies motivated by good citizenship tend to be motivated partially by the nature of the work and the achievement of the core purpose, as well as—very likely—by extrinsic factors such as money or other rewards.

Dignity and Respect

Key ethical practices associated with the common themes are respect and human dignity. These ideas can be operationalized as valuing the individual as an end, rather than as a means to an end, which the German philosopher Immanuel Kant (1724–1804) proposed as a foundation for ethical behavior.[28] One should always *value human beings as ends* in themselves, not as mere instruments for achieving other ends. If companies take this practice and the values that underpin it seriously, then companies will treat all of their "human resources,"—the people who interact with them in whatever capacity—with dignity and respect. This respect extends to customers, who deserve good products that serve useful and necessary purposes, and to employees, including laborers in less developed countries, where standards are not as high as they might be domestically, but who still deserve fair wages and adequate working conditions. We will return to this aspect of stakeholder relationships later in the book when we discuss corporate relationships with different stakeholder groups.

Foster Development

Other aspects of the practices involved in generating integrity within firms include fostering higher levels of human and organizational development. Highly developed firms can encourage freedom and responsibility because they know that engaged stakeholders are committed to the purposes of the firm and will work toward them. They also encourage freedom of speech and the responsibility to listen as well as to speak out when things go wrong—and when things go right, so that they are noted and appreciated! The capacity to take multiple perspectives, which is necessary to hold multiple viewpoints of different stakeholders simultaneously, demands a relatively high level of cognitive development as noted above.

Companies pursuing the path of integrity foster such development among employees, managers, and other stakeholders. They are not threatened by the questioning of assumptions and need to take full responsibility for actions, which develop when individuals achieve at such high levels, because such individual responsibility is the basis for solid long-term organizational performance.

Responsibility

Responsibility at all levels—the individual, the group, and the organization as a whole—is characteristic of the good corporate citizen. If companies are to expect that employees will be responsible for entrepreneurial and innovative efforts within their own domains, as many do these days, then they need to foster a supportive environment for doing so. Among supportive elements to create such an environment are the devolution of responsibility to the appropriate level where action can be taken, access to complete and accurate information, consistency of word and deed (honesty or promise keeping), and serious engagement in the work of the enterprise, rather than detachment from it. Further, and this is a critical point, the reward system must support the actual behaviors that are desired, because behaviors that are rewarded are the ones that happen!

Connection and Community

Note that such enterprises can foster an emotional commitment, a loyalty, and sense of connection and community among stakeholders engaged with the enterprise. Thus, one implication of fully implementing the type of system that generates corporate integrity and good citizenship is that such companies are willing to acknowledge the importance of the human or soft investments in companies, as well as the harder, more objectively measurable results. Ways of assessing these purportedly softer forms of capital and their performance will be addressed in Chapter 8.

Living Values

The combination of the enterprise strategy question, "What do we stand for?" with the articulation and implementation of values helps companies to step back from problematic situations and ask an important question. That question is not just "What can we do?"—which really asks what can feasibly be accomplished—but the more fundamental question: *What should we do?*

127

CHAPTER 5
Values in
Management
Practice: Operating
with Integrity

Not all situations facing companies are ethically easy to resolve. Many times managers face ethical dilemmas; that is, situations for which there is no clear or ready answer and where any decision presents a tension or a conflict. A *dilemma,* by its very nature, puts the decision maker into a quandary. How can individuals and organizations operate with integrity in the face of such difficulties? Unless the decision maker, as well as the organization, has some principles and values to guide it, decision making becomes even tougher. Johnson & Johnson (J&J) is one company that has a clear set of values, called the "Credo," which guide its actions (see the box below).

Defining Core Values: The J&J Example

The first step, whether individually or organizationally, is to define a clear set of values that set forth what you stand for. A clear set of values can help shape an appropriate—and ethically acceptable—response to a crisis or a dilemma, as Johnson & Johnson's McNeil Division found out during the Tylenol poisoning crisis of the early 1980s. During that crisis, the company withdrew its product from the market at an initial cost of more than $100 million. Such a response, although it sometimes involves significant costs, can ultimately help to win the trust of a critical primary stakeholder: the customer. The company withdrew the Tylenol product because it

---

Johnson & Johnson: Our Credo

We believe our first responsibility is to the doctors, nurses and patients, to mothers and fathers and all others who use our products and services. In meeting their needs everything we do must be of high quality. We must constantly strive to reduce our costs in order to maintain reasonable prices. Customers' orders must be serviced promptly and accurately. Our suppliers and distributors must have an opportunity to make a fair profit.

We are responsible to our employees, the men and women who work with us throughout the world. Everyone must be considered as an individual. We must respect their dignity and recognize their merit. They must have a sense of security in their jobs. Compensation must be fair and adequate, and working conditions clean, orderly and safe. We must be mindful of ways to help our employees fulfill their family responsibilities. Employees must feel free to make suggestions and complaints. There must be equal opportunity for employment, development and advancement for those qualified. We must provide

competent management, and their actions must be just and ethical.

We are responsible to the communities in which we live and work and to the world community as well. We must be good citizens—support good works and charities and bear our fair share of taxes. We must encourage civic improvements and better health and education. We must maintain in good order the property we are privileged to use, protecting the environment and natural resources.

Our final responsibility is to our stockholders. Business must make a sound profit. We must experiment with new ideas. Research must be carried on, innovative programs developed and mistakes paid for. New equipment must be purchased, new facilities provided and new products launched. Reserves must be created to provide for adverse times. When we operate according to these principles, the stockholders should realize a fair return.

Source: Johnson & Johnson, http://www.johnsonandjohnson.com.

was clear to management, following the Credo, that there was only one "right" or ethical choice, which was to take the product off the shelves. Although in hindsight we know this was a wise decision, at the time pundits predicted that J&J would never be able to bring Tylenol back and reclaim the high market share the product had previously enjoyed. But, because customers trusted the company to do the right thing, the pundits were proved wrong. Tylenol was reintroduced onto the market and continued to enjoy a very high market share. J&J earned plaudits for its forward-looking and progressive stance toward its stakeholders.

Now translated into more than 36 languages, the Credo is more than 50 years old and provides a framework to help J&J managers and employees make decisions. The Credo was initially written by Robert Wood Johnson, founder of the company. Johnson wanted to forward a "new industrial philosophy," one that we would now characterize as a stakeholder orientation (the box shows the Credo as of 1999), by articulating these values, which were first written down in 1943. Periodically updated and revised slightly as the external environment or internal situation changes, the Credo has served as the source of the company's core values and as a guiding document during many turbulent years since the first writing. The Credo is thus a living statement of J&J's core ideology.[29]

This document is important when we think about living up to a set of values from the perspective of stakeholders. First, note that J&J puts its customers first in priority among its stakeholders, because it is their health that will be affected by the products the company makes. In doing so, the Credo also notes that suppliers and distributors require fair treatment. Next in consideration are employees, who need to be treated with dignity and respect, as will be discussed in more detail below. Then come the communities and countries—and for J&J, which has more than 150 operating companies, these are numerous—and the ecological environment. Once these stakeholder interests have been satisfied, then owners will realize a fair (not "maximized") return. Although seemingly a pretty radical stakeholder approach, this philosophy and set of core values has served the company well throughout its history.

Finally, and critical to an understanding of the purpose of a values-based document like the Credo, is J&J's understanding of its purpose. Stated succinctly on its webpage, that understanding can be summarized as follows:

> When Robert Wood Johnson wrote and then institutionalized the Credo within Johnson & Johnson, he never suggested that it guaranteed perfection. But its principles have become a constant goal, as well as a source of inspiration, for all who are part of the Johnson & Johnson Family of Companies. About 50 years after it was first introduced, the Credo continues to guide the destiny of the world's largest and most diversified health care company.[30]

Note two things about this statement. The Credo provides a goal and an inspiration for members of the company, but it does not guarantee perfection. What it does is provide important *guidance* for decisions and helps the company get back on track when mistakes are made, as they inevitably will be, or when, as the next section discusses, decision makers face dilemmas.

Negotiating Dilemmas

Something more is needed than a vision or values statements when a dilemma arises. There is nothing quite as difficult to cope with as an *ethical dilemma*. By definition, a dilemma requires making a choice among undesirable alternatives, some of them equally so, or alternatives that have negative consequences for some stakeholder. Sometimes, despite the presence of clear vision and values, difficult choices have to be made. How do managers work through dilemmas and still feel good about their decisions?

One way is to reframe the dilemma so that it is not an either/or proposition with negative consequences, but to see whether a win-win proposition can be formulated using "third-way thinking." Sometimes win-win propositions can be developed by moving the analysis at least one level higher than where the problem seems to reside. At other times, the difficult decision must be made despite the dilemma.

Business ethicists Gerald F. Cavanagh, Manuel Valasquez, and Dennis Moberg have provided a helpful framework for just such situations based on four major philosophical traditions in ethics.[31] This framework helps guide the decision maker through the difficult situation toward the best possible answer, even when it is clear that no answer is perfect.

When one is confronted with an ethical dilemma, it is not enough to make a choice using only one type of reasoning. Although complexity remains in making the decision, the best decision can be made by using all four of the following bases for ethical decision making: the norms of rights and duties, justice, utilitarianism (or the greatest good for the greatest number), and caring (see Figure 5.1).

Rights and Duties

A *right* is an important, normative, justifiable claim or entitlement which, as we saw earlier, is one of the bases of becoming a stakeholder. Rights derive from the basic premise that each person is a unique individual deserving of human dignity. According to Cavanagh, *moral rights* have the following characteristics: individuals using them can pursue their own interests, and rights impose duties, obligations, requirements, or prohibitions on others. *Legal rights* are those written into specific laws, judicial decisions, or a constitution.[32]

In the United States, for example, the Bill of Rights to the U.S. Constitution spells out the essential rights of a U.S. citizen: life, liberty, and the pursuit of happiness. In the international arena, the International Labor Conference has spelled out rights and principles for individuals at work that include freedom of association (i.e., collective bargaining), freedom from forced labor, and the abolition of child labor and discrimination in labor, among others. We will explore such codes and their implications for global businesses more thoroughly in Chapter 10.

If we think of rights as one side of a coin, then we know that there is another side: *duties* or *obligations*. All rights come with a set of corresponding duties that need to be upheld if the right itself is to be sustained and societies are to be kept healthy. For example, individual freedom unfettered by obligations means that one person living out his or her rights could trample on the rights of others.

130

PART TWO
Leading Corporate
Citizens with Vision,
Values, and Value
Added

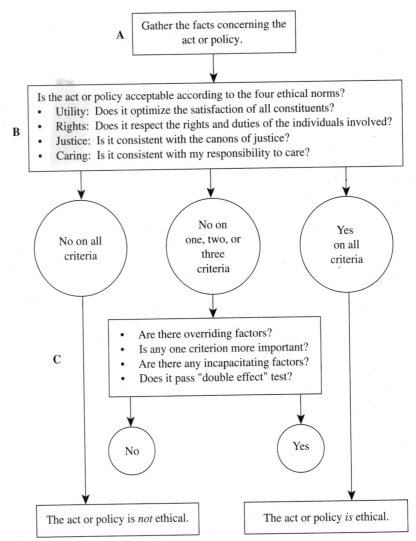

A — Gather the facts concerning the act or policy.

B — Is the act or policy acceptable according to the four ethical norms?
- Utility: Does it optimize the satisfaction of all constituents?
- Rights: Does it respect the rights and duties of the individuals involved?
- Justice: Is it consistent with the canons of justice?
- Caring: Is it consistent with my responsibility to care?

No on all criteria

No on one, two, or three criteria

Yes on all criteria

C —
- Are there overriding factors?
- Is any one criterion more important?
- Are there any incapacitating factors?
- Does it pass "double effect" test?

No

Yes

The act or policy is *not* ethical.

The act or policy *is* ethical.

FIGURE 5.1.   Flow Diagram of Ethical Decision Making
Source: Gerald F. Cavanagh, *American Business Values with International Perspectives,* 4th ed. (Upper Saddle River, NJ: Prentice Hall, 1998).

Examples of rights include the rights to life and safety, truthfulness, privacy, freedom of conscience, free speech, and private property. Some of these are written into the law or other codes, while others are fundamental moral rights that enable communities and organizations to be viable over time. One problem, however, is that too much emphasis on rights can result in selfish and overly individualistic behavior. On the other hand, attention to rights assures respect for individual freedom and property. In

131

CHAPTER 5
Values in
Management
Practice: Operating
with Integrity

using the framework illustrated in Figure 5.1, the first question to ask is, Does this act respect the rights and duties of the individuals involved?

Justice

In addition to considering whether rights are abrogated or supported in making a decision, the decision maker also has to consider the implications of the decision for justice. *Justice,* according to Cavanagh and his colleagues, requires that people be guided by fairness, equity, and impartiality, emphasizing in particular a fair distribution of societal benefits and burdens, fairness in the administration of laws and regulations, and fairness in sanctioning wrongdoing or compensating for wrongs suffered.[33]

Standards of justice, for example, prohibit discrimination and enormous inequalities in the distribution of goods and services within a society. In doing this, justice speaks to the issue of what philosopher John Rawls called "distributive justice," which has as its fundamental principle that "equals should be treated equally and that unequals should be treated in accord with their inequality."[34] Rawls also suggested that societies—and the distribution of goods and services within them—should be constructed using a "veil of ignorance"; that is, decision makers should make their decision as if they did not know where it would end up in the system impacted by the decision. By doing this, they will make a decision that is fairest to all. This approach allows them to overcome their own biases, based on their current position within the system.

One way to identify the constraints on justice was emphasized by Kant in what he called the *categorical imperative.* One formulation of the categorical imperative is: I ought never to act except in such a way that my principle should become a universal law. The second formulation of the categorical imperative states: An action is morally right for a person in a certain situation if and only if the person's reason for carrying out the action is a reason that he or she would be willing to have every person act on, in any similar situation.[35]

In using the analytical framework in Figure 5.1 for ethical decision making, Cavanagh and his colleagues have suggested that we need to know about justice as well as rights: Is this decision consistent with the canons of justice? Would I make the same decision if I could end up anywhere in the system after its impact has been felt?

Utilitarianism

The third basis for making ethical decisions is called utilitarianism, which is generally expressed as "the greatest good for the greatest number." Utilitarianism, which is the reasoning used in systems of *cost-benefit analysis,* is the most common kind of managerial reasoning. It does not necessarily mean that the "majority rules," but rather that the harms and benefits of an action need to be considered from all perspectives. Some kind of calculation as to the degree of harm and benefit is needed when using utilitarian analysis. As noted above, however, utilitarian outcomes need to be considered with both justice and rights as well as their benefits and harms kept firmly in mind.

The concept of the greatest good for the greatest number, while difficult to operationalize quantitatively, proposes that the best action is the one that results in the best overall good (i.e., for the most people affected by that decision). Thus, when weighing a decision that has both positive consequences for some groups and negative ones for others, it is important to consider where the most good is to be accomplished and where the most harm will be done. Decision makers need to weigh such considerations as how many people will be affected either positively or negatively, and the extent of the good or the harm done to each group (assuming these can be known in advance and quantified, which are two of the problems with utilitarian analysis). For example, a decision that would kill one person should never be made simply because, say, a large group will benefit financially.

Further, as Cavanagh et al. pointed out, utilitarian norms emphasize the good of the group—the common good or the collectivity—over and above the good of any given individual, particularly the decision maker. Such a norm avoids the problems of self-interest that might otherwise arise in utilitarian analysis.[36] And, as noted above, to enhance utilitarian analysis, it is necessary to incorporate consideration of rights, justice, and, as will be discussed below, implications for the ethic of "care."

Caring

As noted in the previous chapter, some research suggests that women's moral development may proceed somewhat differently than that of men and that women (as well as many men) may use a different basis for making ethical judgments than the principles of rights, justice, or utility. According to Carol Gilligan, Mary Field Belenky and colleagues, and Nell Noddings, among others, women are focused more explicitly on what has been termed an *ethic of care*.[37] In business situations as well as in life situations, according to this ethic, emphasis on principles can be balanced effectively by consideration of "how this decision affects people and the relationships among people"—that is, by relationships and care.

The ethic of care proposes that we exist *embedded within a network of relationships* that are affected by the implications of ethical decisions. In making decisions according to an ethic of care, we take into account how this decision will affect those relationships and the people in the network. As Cavanagh pointed out, "care" is left somewhat vague in feminist ethicists writings, but it can be delineated by noting that the obligation to care varies according to the closeness of the relationship and the particular roles embedded in the relationship. For example, a mother has a clear and strong obligation to care for her child while she has less of an obligation to care for an acquaintance. The obligation to care also exists only in accordance with one's capacity to give it.

It is interesting that such an ethic of care seems to be more common in countries with a more collectivist—or communitarian—orientation than in the more individualistic countries like the United States. Thus, in business situations in Japan and Korea, for example, this ethic seems to be the basis for extended networks of companies, known as Keiretsu in Japan and Chaebol in Korea, that share mutual obligations to support each other before doing business with "outsiders." Indeed, in some Asian countries the concepts of rights, justice, and utiliarianism as the basis of ethical thinking might seem strange indeed, as the far more important consideration would be the ethic of care: the impact of any given decision on important relationships.

133

*CHAPTER 5
Values in
Management
Practice: Operating
with Integrity*

Thus, an ethic of care suggests that when weighing a decision, one needs to ask how will this affect the people that I care about? And in addition, as the next section suggests, what does this decision say about me as a person—or as an organization?

Virtue and Character for Leading Corporate Citizens

Robert Solomon, a consultant, ethicist, and scholar, argued passionately that there is a "better way to think about business" than the typical "greed is good" way promulgated by the media and by Wall Street financiers like Ivan Boesky, who got in trouble for insider trading during the 1980s. He wrote that good companies not only provide profits to shareholders, but also develop a morally rewarding climate where good people can develop their skills and their virtue.

Solomon argued that companies need to develop a culture that promotes integrity and virtue—or good character—among manager and employees. Companies are themselves communities, social entities.[38] To be successful and enhance the commitment and personal integrity of their own employees, they need to build trust, a sense of community, and other "civilizing influences" (see the values articulated in Table 5.1) that help the business rise above pure self-interest. The box below illustrates one company's efforts to live up to its values.

"Pull on Your Boots and Make a Difference" at The Timberland Company

"Pull on your boots and make a difference." With a motto like that, the Timberland Company, a New Hampshire–based manufacturer of hiking boots sets a high standard for companies attempting to express and live up to their values. The family-run company has revenues of nearly $1 billion and a brand that has sometimes been considered "magic." Part of that magic resides in the values-based relationships that the company has developed with its core stakeholders: employees, customers, distributors, and retailers.

Jeffrey Swartz, CEO and President of Timberland, acknowledged the critical role that the company's values play in promoting the company's brand and identity as not only a producer of top quality rugged, outdoor footwear, but also a company that lives up to its values and gives back to its communities. Core beliefs at Timberland revolve around the capacity of all people in the company to make a difference in the world and are articulated on the company's website:

Human history is the experience of individuals confronting the world around them. Timberland participates in this process, not just through our products or though our brand, but through our belief that each individual can and must make a difference in the way we experience life on this planet. As a team of diverse people motivated and strengthened by this belief, we can and will deliver world-class products and services to our customers and create value for shareholders around the world.

The Timberland boot stands for much more than the finest waterproof leather. It represents a call to action. Pull on your boots and make a difference. With your boots and your beliefs, you will be able to interact responsibly and comfortably within the natural and social environments that all human beings share.[39]

For Swartz, being successful in this business means developing relationships with customers and with the local entrepreneurs who run Timberland local retail outlets, which the company calls community stores. The ripple effects of a successful store in otherwise underserved areas go well into the community and the lives of employees'. For example, the company recently established a store in Washington, D.C., in a location that, Swartz pointed out, is

... in an environment that is underserved from a retail perspective, so it's a good business opportunity. It's also a good community opportunity because we hire locally, and part of the proceeds from the store are turned into scholarships for young people from the neighborhood where the store is located. It's good for the community in that sense. It's also good for the shareholder because we are serving the consumers otherwise not served with proper respect. We developed a terrific relationship with a local entrepreneur who's got a community/wealth/profit motivation . . . It's good for the consumer, and the shareholder, and the employee. That's community wealth. It's not about charity, it's about social wealth. That's a different concept.[40]

It is this integration of the needs of multiple stakeholders that creates the kind of business culture and environment that Swartz and other employees at Timberland value. The company lives out its philosophy in numerous other ways as well, for example, by serving as the founding sponsor of the City Year Program with a $1 million investment. City Year allows individuals to devote a full year of time to community service in one of ten cities across the United States, as well as sponsoring one-day "serv-a-thons" nationally. Timberland also supports numerous other community-based activities, such as Share Our Strength, a program aimed at alleviating world poverty and hunger, AmeriCorps, which provides thousands of service opportunities annually, and City Cares of America programs, in which professionals are encouraged to volunteer their services.

For Swartz, Timberland's involvement in service and environmental activities, its encouragement of its employees to become involved, and its many commitments are a part of doing business well, and building the type of company culture that will attract the talented employees needed for future growth. As he stated,

Moments of greatness occur when we do things as a genuine community. Our greatest strength is that we have seen the potential to be a great and genuine community of caring, committed, passionate, professional people. If we perform at our highest level as a community, then we will make Mountain Athletics [a new venture] a better brand and we will make Timberland Pro a better brand and service our retailers better and we will have better results for our shareholders on a more consistent basis. We have goals, we have high purpose, and we have really talented people, and every once in a while, because we are deeply committed to this connection, we have these moments where we really are a community. We speak honestly. We take risks. We transcend our limitations. We aren't employees, we are passionately committed to the same high purpose. And I think in those moments is our greatness.[41]

Sources: Judy Leand, "Jeffrey Swartz, President & CEO, The Timberland Co., The SGB Interview," *Sporting Goods Business,* August 4, 2000, pp. 34–37; and http://timberland.com.

MANAGING: ETHICAL AT THE CORE

All managing and leading is ethical at the core because leadership inherently involves making decisions that affect stakeholders. Acting on the basis of principles, with care, and with the virtues associated with developing successful communities constantly kept in mind is what it means to operate with integrity. The flow diagram in Figure 5.1 can help when there is a difficult decision to be made, although it is critical that decisions be made from a position that honors personal integrity as well as common sense and the ethic of care. By their nature, dilemmas are difficult to resolve. The first step is to gather data and make a determination about the decision according to the four norms of ethics discussed above. Cavanagh and his colleagues then suggested that four additional questions need to be addressed before the ethics of the decision can be determined.

135

*CHAPTER 5
Values in
Management
Practice: Operating
with Integrity*

First, are there any overriding factors? Overriding factors are issues that justify, in a given case, one of the types of ethics. For example, commission of a heinous crime may justify a decision to use the death penalty on a criminal. Second, is one criterion more important than others? Third, are there any incapacitating factors, such as physical force or violence, that overrule other considerations?

Finally, we need to determine where a "double effect" might be present in the decision, that is, where different principles suggest different decisions. When such a double effect is present, the act is considered ethical under three circumstances: (1) when there is no direct intent to produce a bad effect; (2) when the bad effect is simply a side effect of the decision and not a means to the end; and (3) when the good effect sufficiently outweighs the bad one that it becomes an overriding factor.[42]

Note that the analysis of principles and effects using this model allows for conflicts among the principles and for making the inherently difficult determination about the extent to which they should affect the decision and in what direction. And that decision becomes even more complex when one also needs to consider how others will be affected by it in terms of care, and how one's own character—or that of the organization—will be affected by the decision. The Johnson & Johnson case is one in which all of these factors were clearly taken into consideration and handled well.

Cultural Difference: Leading Citizens around the World

Cultural differences, like the differences in national ideology discussed in Chapter 3, also make a difference in terms of how companies can and do operate with integrity in different nations around the world. All of this of course complicates the difficulty of making an analysis of the ethics of a given situation; however, understanding the bases of some of these differences can make life a lot easier. Many of the models of corporate responsibility have been developed in the United States, although concepts of corporate citizenship and the triple bottom line (or economic, social, and ecological bottom lines) are now current in the United Kingdom and the rest of the European Union. Businesses in Japan tend to view their citizenship less in the "social" sense and often fragmented ways that are popular in the United States, and more holistically as we are advocating with the stakeholder lens developed in this book. In other words, Japanese companies tend to view their citizenship as part and parcel of the way they do business day-to-day, the way they treat customers and employees, and how they relate to their government and the public interest defined by government.[43] Table 5.2 indicates five major sources of cultural differences.

Language

Operating with integrity in different cultures certainly means that the leading corporate citizens must understand the important differences that exist among cultures. Readily recognizable, of course, are differences in language, including different structures, vocabularies, and word meaning.[44]

Other important differences are those in context, perceptions of time, equality, and what is termed power distance, and information flow (see Table 5.2). Misunderstandings can easily arise in global settings where individuals from two

136

PART TWO
Leading Corporate
Citizens with Vision,
Values, and Value
Added

TABLE 5.2.   Five Important Sources of Cultural Differences

Cultural variables that impact leading corporate citizenship

- **Language.** The agreed upon structure, vocabulary and meanings of written or oral communications, and the specialized dialects or jargons adopted by subcultures (including professions).
- **Context.** The elements that surround and give meaning to a communication event. On a scale of high to low, low-context messages themselves hold information. In the single message or event, high-context communications are more subjective and distribute the information in the person. The meaning of the event in the high-context culture is deeply colored by elements including relationships, history, and status as opposed to only the information in the message.
- **Time.** Cultural attitudes toward time are generally *monochronic* (one event at a time) or *polychronic* (many events at once). Polychronic time is a state of being; monochronic time is a resource to be measured and managed. Concepts of time differ in interrelationships between past, present, and future.
- **Power Distance.** The distance and types of relationships between people and groups with respect to degree of equality, status, and authority.
- **Information Flow.** How messages flow between people and levels in organizations, and how action chains move toward communication and task completion. The general flow patterns can be sequenced or looped.

companies, both of whom view themselves as operating with integrity, have deeply seated cultural differences (e.g., language, context, power distance, time, or information flow) that the other party does not understand.

Context

One key type of difference involves what sociologists call context. *Context* involves the elements that surround and give meaning to communication. Cultures, such as the United States, Germany, and the Scandinavian nations, are low-context cultures that focus on objective communication—that is, the word, gesture, or physical gestures give meaning to it. In contrast, high-context cultures, such as Japan, China, and Mexico, take their cues about the meaning of a communication as much from the situation and the relationships of all the people involved as from the words themselves; that is, words have little meaning without understanding the context in which they were said.

Relationships are significantly more important in high-context cultures than in low-context cultures, which helps to explain why it takes longer to develop business opportunities in Japan, for example, than in the United States, where relationships among the players do not matter as much. For U.S. executives, having a written contract may be enough to establish an alliance that can be successful and operate in a way that pleases both partners. In Japan, however, establishing longer-term relationships is essential to building trust, connection, and a shared sense of what is needed to make the alliance work. Anyone trying to establish a contract in a first meeting would be likely to be viewed as untrustworthy—that is, operating without the necessary context of relationships—and therefore without integrity.

137

*CHAPTER 5
Values in
Management
Practice: Operating
with Integrity*

Time

Another cultural difference can be found in the perception of time. Some cultures are essentially monochronic, where people pursue one event, action, or activity at a time, while others are polychronic, where people may be simultaneously pursuing multiple activities. For people in polychronic cultures (such as many Latin American countries), time is a state of being and things are viewed as cyclical and iterative, while in monochronic cultures, time is considered a scarce resource to be measured and managed carefully. Thus, for a monochronic U.S. manager, dealing with one customer at a time means treating him or her respectfully and with integrity. A polychronic Mexican manager or employee, on the other hand, dealing with customer from the same culture would be surprised if the customer were insulted because she or he was answering the phone, writing out one customer's order, and simultaneously waiting on a third customer. Handling multiple activities at once is what is expected in that nation.

Power Distance

Cultures also differ in the ways people handle power and equality across organizational and social levels. For example, countries like the United States and those in Northern Europe have lower power distance and are relatively accepting of the idea that all people are created equal (at least in principle). Most nations of the world, however, have more hierarchical power relationships and accept inequalities and hierarchical arrangements more readily, including uneven application of rules, as a way of life. Clearly, if these differences in the way power is handled and people are treated are not understood, there can be conflicts and concerns about whether corporations with operations in different cultures are actually living up to their values or operating with integrity.

Information Flow

The final variable that has been identified as creating important cultural differences has to do with information flow and whether information is sequenced (i.e., linear) in organizations or looped in more cyclical fashion. Generally speaking, low-context cultures like the United States tend to get "straight to the point" concerning issues of information flow. Information flow involves both the path and speed of communication, and U.S. managers like to be both direct and speedy. In contrast, managers from many other cultures, especially high-context cultures where relationships matter and polychronic cultures where time is viewed more cyclically and less linearly, tend to see information as looped and connected with other processes not immediately involved in any given situation.

LEADING CHALLENGES: OPERATING WITH INTEGRITY

We have seen the importance of companies (and individuals) having a clear and inspiring vision embedded with positive values if they hope to operate with integrity and provide for integration of the subjective and the objective. The challenges of operating with integrity are many and leaders clearly need to develop personal awareness and mindfulness of the impacts of their decisions on other stakeholders.

Mindfulness demands personal presence and integrity, and leaders who recognize that the same person who makes business decisions is the one they must face in the mirror in the morning. There can be no disconnection between business judgments and personal integrity if managers are aware, conscientious, and ethical. And, of course, common sense is paramount, especially in applying the simple rule of "what would I do if I knew this decision were going to be broadcast on TV tomorrow?" At the same time, while it is important to base decisions impacting stakeholders on principles, it is also clear that leading corporate citizens need to take into account fundamental cultural differences in attitudes toward time, relationships, and information or problems will multiply needlessly.

Because of the very complexity of making corporate decisions with integrity, particularly in the complex global arena, the capacity to take other stakeholders' perspectives into account becomes the key to success. So too is the ability to think critically—and systemically—about the implications of a decision about to be made. Leading corporate citizens know this and provide plenty of "safe spaces" in the company for reflection, for questioning of actions, for critical thinking, and for stakeholder input before and not after major decisions are made.

In the next chapter, we will explore the ways in which operating practices can be assessed for companies operating both domestically and globally in an ecological sustainable way.

NOTES TO CHAPTER 5

1. See Sandra Waddock, Samuel Graves, and Marjorie Kelly, "On the Trail of the Best Corporate Citizens: The Methodology and Theory Behind This New Listing," *Business Ethics,* March-April 2000, pp. 15–17; see also, Tom Klusman, Marjorie Kelly, Sandra Waddock, and Samuel Graves, "The 100 Best Corporate Citizens: Celebrating Those Companies That Excel at Serving Multiple Stakeholders Well," *Business Ethics,* March-April 2000, pp. 12–14.
2. See Marjorie Kelly and Tom Klusmann, "Is IBM Still Socially Responsible? *Business Ethics,* July-August 2000, pp. 4–5.
3. See, for example, Ken Wilber, *A Brief History of Everything* (Boston: Shambala Publications, 1996).
4. Ibid.
5. James McGregor Burns discussed end and modal values extensively as the key to transformational leadership in *Leadership* (New York: Harper Torchbooks, 1978), pp. 74–76.
6. Ibid., p. 75.
7. The "downside risk," of course, is that such inspiration can create cults.
8. James C. Collins and Jerry I. Porras, *Built to Last: Successful Habits of Visionary Companies* (New York: HarperBusiness, 1997).
9. See Burns.
10. See R. Edward Freeman and Daniel R. Gilbert, Jr., *Corporate Strategy and the Search for Ethics* (Englewood Cliffs, NJ: Prentice Hall, 1988).

139

CHAPTER 5
Values in
Management
Practice: Operating
with Integrity

11. See, for example, Robert C. Solomon, *A Better Way to Think about Business: How Personal Integrity Leads to Corporate Success* (New York: Oxford University Press, 1999).

12. The thinking in this section is largely derived from Jeanne Liedtka, "Constructing an Ethic for Business Practice: Competing Effectively and Doing Good," *Business and Society* 37, no. 3 (September 1998), pp. 254–80.

13. Ibid.

14. See Collins and Porras.

15. Alisdair MacIntyre, *After Virtue* (South Bend, IN: University of Notre Dame Press, 1981).

16. Liedtka, p. 260.

17. The learning organization concept was popularized by Peter M. Senge in *The Fifth Discipline: The Art and Practice of the Learning Organization* (New York: Doubleday, 1991); for the seminal book on quality, see W. Edwards Deming, *Out of the Crisis* (Cambridge, MA: MIT Center for Advanced Engineering Study, 1982). Numerous books exist on total quality management; the popular book on reengineering is Michael Hammer and James Champy, *Re-Engineering the Corporation: A Manifesto for Business Revolution* (New York: HarperBusiness, 1993).

18. William C. Frederick, *Values, Nature, and Culture in the American Corporation* (New York: Oxford University Press, 1995).

19. See Freeman and Gilbert; see also Sandra A. Waddock, "Linking Community and Spirit: A Commentary and Some Propositions," *Journal of Organizational Change Management,* 1999, 12 (4), pp. 332–44.

20. See Henry Mintzberg's book *The Rise and Fall of Strategic Planning* (New York: Free Press, 1994) or his article, "The Fall and Rise of Strategic Planning," *Harvard Business Review,* January-February 1994, pp. 107–14; see also Senge.

21. For a discussion of "continual" as opposed to continuous improvement in the context of quality management and personal growth, see Dalmar Fisher and William R. Torbert, *Personal and Organizational Transformations: The True Challenge of Continual Quality Improvement* (New York: McGraw Hill, 1995).

22. See my paper "Linking Community and Spirit."

23. Stan Davis and Christopher Meyer discuss this at some length in *Blur: The Speed of Change in the Connected Economy* (Reading, MA: Addison-Wesley, 1998).

24. The term "good conversation" was developed by James A. Waters and published in Frederic R. Bird and James A. Waters, "The Moral Muteness of Managers," *California Management Review,* Fall 1989, pp. 73–88.

25. Chris Argyris focuses on "undiscussability" in *Knowledge for Action: A Guide to Overcoming Barriers to Organizational Change* (San Francisco: Jossey-Bass, 1993); see also Bird and Waters, pp. 73–88.

26. Liedtka, pp. 254–80; the practices discussed in this section are from Liedkta's article.

27. Collins and Porras.

28. Immanual Kant, *Groundwork of the Metaphysics of Morals,* trans. H. J. Paton (New York: Harper & Row, 1964).

29. Collins and Porras.

30. http://www.johnsonandjohnson.com/who_is_jnj/cr_index.html.

31. The decision-making framework is summarized in Gerald F. Cavanagh, *American Business Values with International Perspectives,* 4th ed. (Upper Saddle River, NJ: Prentice Hall, 1998). Much of the discussion in this section is adapted from either that book or one of the following versions of the framework, published in the following

140

PART TWO
Leading Corporate
Citizens with Vision,
Values, and Value
Added

articles: Manuel Velasquez, Dennis J. Moberg, and Gerald F. Cavanagh, "Organizational Statesmanship and Dirty Politics: Ethical Guidelines for the Organizational Politician," *Organizational Dynamics,* Autumn 1983, pp. 65–80; Cavanagh, Moberg, and Velasquez, "The Ethics of Organizational Politics," *Academy of Management Review* 6, no. 3 (1981), pp. 363–74; and Cavanagh, Moberg, and Velasquez, "Making Business Ethics Practical," *Business Ethics Quarterly* 5, no. 3 (July 1995), pp. 399–418.

32. Cavanagh, *American Business Values,* p. 75.

33. Ibid., pp. 78–79.

34. Ibid., p. 79, citing John Rawls, *A Theory of Justice* (Cambridge: Harvard University Press, 1971).

35. Immanual Kant, *Groundwork of the Metaphysics of Morals,* trans. H. J. Paton (New York: Harper & Row, 1964), cited in Cavanagh, *American Business Values,* p. 78. Much of this discussion is adapted from Cavanagh.

36. Cavanagh, *American Business Values,* p. 81.

37. See Carol Gilligan, *In a Different Voice: Psychological Theory and Women's Development* (Cambridge: Harvard University Press, 1982). For an extension of this work into cognitive domains, see also Mary Field Belenky, Blythe McVicker Clinchy, Nancy Rule Goldberg, and Jill Mattuck Tarule, *Women's Ways of Knowing: The Development of Self, Voice, and Mind* (New York: Basic Books, 1986). Nell Noddings, *Caring: A Feminine Approach to Ethics and Moral Education.* (Berkeley: University of California Press, 1984).

38. Solomon, op. cit

39. See http://timberland.com.

40. Quoted in Judy Leand, "Jeffrey Swartz, President & CEO, The Timberland Co., The SGB Interview," *Sporting Goods Business* 33, no. 12 (August 4, 2000), p 35.

41. Ibid. p. 37.

42. Cavanagh, *American Business Values,* pp. 83–87.

43. This difference became clear on a visit in September 2000 to the Boston College Center for Corporate Citizenship by a contingent of Japanese businessmen representing the Kaneiren, the Kansai Economic Federation of Japan.

44. The five cultural differences discussed here are based on Mary O'Hara-Devereaux and Robert Johansen, *GlobalWork: Bridging Distance, Culture and Time* (San Francisco: Jossey-Bass, 1994), who in turn drew from the work of Edward T. Hall and Mildred Reed Hall, *Understanding Cultural Differences: Germans, French, and Americans* (Yarmouth, ME: Intercultural Press, 1990) and Geert Hofstede, *Cultures and Organizations: Software of the Mind* (New York: McGraw-Hill, 1991).

CHAPTER 6

Value Added:

THE IMPACT OF VISION AND VALUES

Something strange and wonderful is taking place in business.

Slowly, but ever so surely, companies of all sizes and sectors are discovering that they function best when they merge their business interests with the interests of customers, employees, suppliers, neighbors, investors, and other groups affected, directly or indirectly, by their companies' operations. Some of these companies are led by forward-thinking leaders who have come to recognize that the dangers threatening society—the breakup of families, inadequate schools, unaffordable health care and housing, escalating crime, a deteriorating environment, inner-city turmoil, apathetic citizens, and all the rest—also threaten productivity and profits. The effects that some business leaders' corporate reputation and their workplace, environmental, and community policies can have on financial performance include increased sales and stock prices, reduced turnover and retraining costs, increased efficiencies, and reduced waste and energy costs. Others have built their companies' operating principles around a business philosophy or moral vision that views employee well-being, environmental stewardship, or community welfare as critical to success. These leaders are developing bottom-line strategies based on the belief that long-term profitable performance and corporate . . . responsibility are not only compatible but are inevitably linked.

—JOEL MAKOWER
Beyond the Bottom Line: Putting Social Responsibility
to Work for Your Business and the World

VALUE ADDED

The previous chapters have discussed the importance of corporate operating practices in developing appropriate and positive stakeholder relationships, and, ultimately, in achieving value added for the company. In the last chapter, we explored the values basis of constructive corporate practices.

What does it mean to practice something? At a very simple level, to *practice*, as in a sport, musical instrument, or meditation, is to repeat something over and over with the intent of developing expertise, or improving. In the sense we are exploring, practicing also involves careful *reflection* about what worked and what didn't work so the practice can continue improving. The final and most important step is to move toward the betterment implied by having a vision in mind for the practice. That gets us to the value added by having positive stakeholder relationships, which we will discuss in this and the next chapter.

Practice in the sense we are using it never ends. Companies attempting to achieve value added through their stakeholder practices and the associated processes, such as quality improvement or customer, employee, or community relations, quickly discover this reality. There are always improvements that can be made, especially in the turbulence and dynamism of the modern economic and social landscapes. A critical question remains, however. Do practices that treat stakeholders well actually result in higher levels of performance as assessed by traditional financial measures?

In thinking about this question, we are exploring whether or not operating with principles and standards—that is, operating with integrity and respect for stakeholders and the environment—actually matters to organizational performance. While operating with integrity is important in its own right, there is emerging evidence that it also has positive performance implications. There are other, more fundamental, reasons for treating stakeholders well that have to do with the more foundational reality that treating people—stakeholders—as ends rather than means, with integrity and respect, is inherently the right thing to do. This perspective can also apply to a respect for the integrity and health of the natural environment as the foundation of human civilization. Still, some case examples of companies that have conducted social audits with an eye toward improving profitability while still operating with integrity help to illustrate the close relationship between stakeholder-related practices and value added to be explored in this chapter.[1]

Value Added and Stakeholder-Related Practices

Employee Relations and Profitability

A leading regional insurer wanted a strategy to reduce its high employee turnover in dead-end positions. An intensive study of employee policies resulted in improvements in job satisfaction with the potential to raise net profits by 7 percent, increased worker employability by offering a placement service for other area companies seeking qualified employees, which in turn provided a new revenue stream to offset replacement costs.

Employees, Quality Improvement, and Profits

A Fortune 500 firm in the throes of downsizing helped adversely affected employees, reduced operational inefficiencies associated with making critical decisions under pressure, and avoided potential legal action and employee violence by implementing policies and procedures recommended after an intensive assessment of its operations. The assessment also resulted in a strategy for a 10 percent reduction in medical costs and absenteeism totaling more than $450,000. Implementation of a quality management system was simultaneously estimated to increase productivity and effective manufacturing capacity, reduce production cycle time, and decrease operating costs by two to three times over a three- to five-year period.

Environmental Management and Profits

A leading multinational manufacturing company had won numerous environmental awards. Nonetheless, the company found that after an analysis of its environmental policies it could reduce the high costs of regulatory compliance by teaming research and development, production, and the sales department to improve production efficiencies and eliminate waste at the source. The strategy was estimated to save nearly $200,000, excluding the reduction of up to 50 percent in disposal costs and water use, and increase production capacity by 25 percent.

MAKING A *DECISION* TO OPERATE WITH INTEGRITY

There is a long-standing debate among scholars about whether it "pays" to be responsible; that is, is there a positive relationship between responsibility and financial performance? While we will go over in this chapter some of the mounting evidence that this relationship is a positive one, it is clear from the beginning that leading corporate citizens—and their leaders—have a fundamental choice to make. They can choose to operate with only the interests of economizing and power aggrandizing in mind. Or they can articulate their own values, understand what they stand for in a positive and constructive way, and operate with integrity with respect to their many stakeholders, sometimes even when there is a short-term cost to doing so.

The choice is thus fundamentally a moral one that involves an important distinction between the concepts of *effectiveness* and *efficiency*. In the words of management theorist Russell Ackoff, quoting Peter Drucker:

> Peter Drucker once made *a distinction between doing things right and doing the right thing. This distinction is the same as that between efficiency and effectiveness.* Information, knowledge, and understanding contribute primarily to efficiency but provide little assurance of effectiveness. For effectiveness, wisdom is required.[2]

Leading corporate citizens seek wisdom in their choices and the impacts of those choices; thus, they have to do both: Be efficient *and* effective, do things right, economizing appropriately so little is wasted and their activities and the communities that support them are sustainable. And they need to do the right thing so that they can operate with integrity and respect for the dignity of their stakeholders as well as the health of the natural environment. Once again we are faced with implementing decisions using the logic of both/and rather than the less progressive logic of either/or.

Companies that understand what they stand for and operate within their stated values will—and do—*choose* to operate with integrity and treat stakeholders well. We have seen this earlier, for example, in the successes of the Shell Group and

Johnson & Johnson. Sometimes operating with integrity and respect means internalizing costs that might otherwise be externalized. Sometimes it means putting a code of conduct or set of operating principles in place—and sticking to them even when there is temptation to lapse. Sometimes, as the examples above suggest, it simply means thinking through the consequences of operating practices and choosing those that do the least harm or help stakeholders the most, using the type of decision framework presented in Chapter 5.

For example, companies can develop hurtful employee policies that make recruitment difficult and turnover high, that essentially treat employees as "cogs in the machine" of business rather than as people, discarding them through layoffs when the going gets rough. Or they can choose policies that retain highly skilled and knowledgeable workers to improve productivity in the longterm, even when times are tight. They can be careless about product and packaging design, generating waste and harmful by-products, or they can carefully design products to minimize packaging and waste and move toward sustainability. They can develop shoddy products that may sell quickly but ultimately create ill will among customers and hence fewer repeat sales, or they can pay attention to quality and value added for the customer, leaving customers satisfied and willing to purchase again. They can seek the lowest possible cost materials from suppliers, stretching the resources of suppliers to the maximum and inhibiting their survival. Or companies can work in alliance with their suppliers to build a healthy network of relationships and sufficient profits that the supplier can make appropriate and adequate investments in R&D, infrastructure, human resources, and equipment to meet long-term demand.

Further, companies can treat their local communities and the natural environment as temporary stopping (or, more accurately, stomping) grounds, grabbing tax breaks and infrastructure development from the community, or externalizing pollution, without recognizing the long-term costs to the community. Or they can recognize the mutuality of the corporate-community relationship and become a neighbor of choice, instilling goodwill and positive long-term commitment that enhances the well-being of community and natural environment.[3]

Fortunately (at least for those who believe that doing the right thing whatever the consequences is what companies need to do), there is significant and growing evidence that the both/and of effectiveness and efficiency, integrity and economizing, doing things right and doing the right thing brings about long-term success. Minimally, there seem to be few negative by-products of operating responsibly, at least when many companies are studied together. More importantly, much of the research suggests that there may be positive benefits to acting responsibly. The rest of the chapter will explore some of the evidence for the link between effectiveness and efficiency, doing the right thing and doing things right—or, ultimately, operating with integrity.

RESPONSIBILITY AND PERFORMANCE

There is a long tradition of research on the relationship between financial performance and what has been called corporate social responsibility, which we have simply termed responsibility or responsible practice. This research takes many forms and has actually looked at many different relationships, including those between vision and performance, social and financial performance, social screening of investments and portfolio performance, employee treatment and performance, and environmental management and performance, to name but a few. The rest of this chapter will explore a few of the findings from the numerous studies that have been undertaken but that begin to show consistent patterns linking responsible practice and strong performance.

Vision and Value Added

One of the more striking studies of impact of vision can be found in the work of James Collins and Jerry Porras (see Chapter 4). In their book *Built to Last*, Collins and Porras reported on studies of 36 companies, 18 classified as visionary and 18 as runners-up, which were not necessarily "unvisionary" companies but had exhibited fewer of the qualities of visionary companies cited in Chapter 4. Although the comparison companies are good companies, matched in size, industry, and longevity to the visionary companies, Collins and Porras thought of them as silver or bronze medal winners compared with the gold medal winners classified as visionary.

The critical element of Collins and Porras's study, however, is determining the impact of vision on long-term performance. And that impact is dramatic! Despite the visionary companies' exhibit of elements of their human (and therefore fallible) origins in some of the strategic and performance bumps and hurdles they have passed through over their years (and they are all long-lived companies), the visionary companies markedly outperform the comparison companies. In doing so, the visionary companies, guided by their core ideology and meaningful sense of purpose, display what Collins and Porras termed remarkable resiliency, the ability to bounce back from adversity.[4] Let Collins and Porras's findings speak for themselves:

> Visionary companies attain extraordinary *long-term* performance. Suppose you made equal $1 investments in a general-market stock fund, a comparison company stock fund, and a visionary company stock fund on January 1, 1926. If you reinvested all dividends and made appropriate adjustments for when the companies became available on the Stock Exchange, your $1 in the general market fund would have grown to $415 on December 31, 1990—not bad. But your $1 in the visionary companies' stock fund would have grown to $6,356—over six times the comparison fund and over fifteen times the general market.[5]

See Figure 6.1 for Collins and Porras's results.

One of the counterintuitive conclusions (to many people, but by now perhaps very intuitive to readers of this book) that Collins and Porras reached from their work on visionary companies was to debunk several management myths. One important conclusion they reached is that:

> Contrary to business school doctrine, "maximizing shareholder wealth" or "profit maximization" has not been the dominant driving force or primary objective through the history of the visionary companies. Visionary companies pursue a cluster of

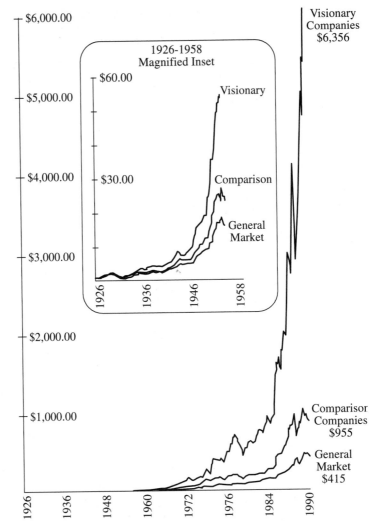

FIGURE 6.1. Cumulative Stock Returns of $1 Invested
January 1, 1926—December 31, 1990
*Source: James C. Collins and Jerry I. Porras, Built to Last: Successful
Habits of Highly Effective Companies (NY: HarperBusiness, 1994).*

objectives, of which making money is only one—and not necessarily the primary
one. Yes, they seek profits, but they're equally guided by a core ideology—core values and sense of purpose beyond just making money. Yet, paradoxically, the visionary companies make more money than the more purely profit-driven comparison companies.[6]

The key to understanding Collins and Porras's findings is to understand that *profitability is a by-product of doing something well, not the end in itself*. Unlike Collins

and Porras, however, we have argued here that the most successful visions are those driven by end values that add meaning and meaningfulness to the sets of relationships embedded in a company or any organization.

If constructive values that treat stakeholders with respect really underpin effective visions, then it would make sense that visionary companies outperform nonvisionary companies in practices they have evolved in their relationships with their stakeholders. Research with my colleague Sam Graves on this very topic, using the same companies that Collins and Porras studied, indicated that visionary companies do treat their primary stakeholders better than the nonvisionary companies do.

Visionary companies outperform the nonvisionary companies in the way that they treat owners, through financial performance, which Collins and Porras addressed, but also customers, employees, and communities. Although our study showed no statistically significant difference in the treatment of the environment between the two groups of companies, the difference was nearly statistically significant and positive. When treatment of stakeholders was combined into a single measure, the difference between the gold medal visionary companies and silver medal comparison group was significant in each year we studied.[7] Figure 6.2 shows the overall social performance of the built-to-last or visionary companies against the comparison group in our study.

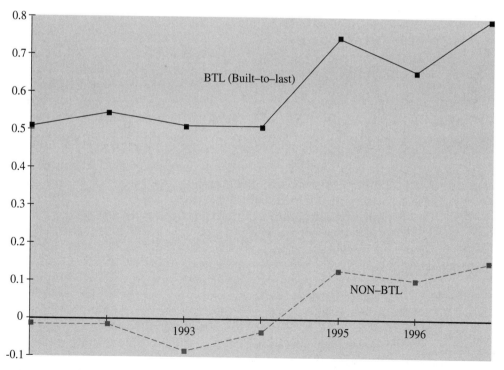

FIGURE 6.2.   CSP-Overall Average Comparison of Built-to-Last and Non-BTL companies.

This research strongly supports the idea that by living out values through constructive operating practices and positive stakeholder relations, companies also "do well" for their owners financially over the long term. But, as we shall see, there is much more evidence that this relationship holds.

Social and Financial Performance

As noted in the introduction to this section, there is a long history of research on the relationship between financial and social performance in large corporations. The results of this research have been quite mixed; however, it was not until quite recently that ways of assessing social performance—or stakeholder relationships—have begun to be developed that adequately reflect the complexity of corporate responsibility and stakeholder relationships.

The typical assumption, particularly in financial circles, is that there is a necessary trade-off between social and financial performance. This assumption means that if a company is to be environmentally responsible, for example, it might invest in costly pollution control equipment or internalize costs that others are externalizing, putting it at a competitive disadvantage. But, as we have seen in exploring both/and logic rather than either/or logic, it is entirely possible that a commitment to sustainability might actually provide a competitive advantage or financial benefits, as the three mini-case examples at the beginning of the chapter highlight.

Three major studies of the rather extensive array of research on the social-financial performance link have recently been undertaken, which provide interesting insights. When taken as a body of work, the weight of these studies shows clearly that there is at minimum no apparent "cost" to responsible practice, and very likely there is a positive relationship between social and financial performance.[8]

Here is one example of recent research on this relationship between social and financial performance. In a 1997 paper, my colleague Sam Graves and I showed that there is a positive relationship between social and financial performance, when we studied the Standard & Poor's 500 largest U.S. corporations, using data from Kinder, Lydenberg, Domini (KLD), the social research firm. In this study we created an index for corporate social performance comprised of a weighted average of the social performance/stakeholder indicators in the KLD database and compared the financial performance of companies to that index.

Our study showed that social and financial performance are positively related, whether we assume that good financial performance results in better social performance (what we called the "slack resources" hypothesis) or that better social performance provides a base for improved financial performance (what we termed the "good management" hypothesis). Because the way we measured social performance included stakeholder practices, we then developed the concept that forms one of the foundations for this book: that the quality of management is integrally related to the quality of relationships that a company has with its stakeholders, thereby extending the good management hypothesis.[9] This relationship will be further explored in the next section.

Stakeholder Relationships and Performance

One thesis of this book is that the better an organization's relationships with its stakeholders are, the better its long-term performance will be. If this thesis is correct, then there ought to be some additional evidence that treating stakeholders respectfully through constructive stakeholder-related practices enhances performance. The following paragraphs will briefly explore some of the existing evidence.

Responsibility Investing

We have already seen that companies with better overall social performance also seem to do better financially. One question that investors, considered as owners, seek answers to (in the old either/or logic) is whether there is a penalty for investing in more responsible businesses. Several studies suggest that, as with financial (accounting-based) performance, there seems to be no penalty with respect to stock performance for investing in responsible firms compared to investing in those with less responsible practices. For example, one study compared the performance of socially screened and traditional unscreened stock and found no performance differences.[10]

Another study used the Council on Economic Priorities' screens to evaluate the effect of ethical screening on portfolio performance and found that "ethical screening of portfolios neither helps nor hinders portfolio performance."[11] Similarly, a prize-winning study by John Guerard found no significant differences and "no meaningful cost" to socially screened funds compared to unscreened funds, a finding corroborated by another study by Sam Graves, Renee Gorski, and me.[12] The last study found no significant performance differences between the screened and unscreened companies (albeit not in a particular fund). Although the screened companies tended to be smaller, they also tended to produce better returns on shareholder investment when considered in financial terms alone.

Another way that social and traditional performance can be evaluated is through comparison of indexes of socially screened companies with those of nonscreened or traditional indexes like the Dow Jones Industrial Average or Standard & Poor's 500. The Domini Social Index (DSI) is one such index, comprised of 400 companies that have been screened on social criteria by the social research firm KLD. About half of the companies in the DSI are traditional S&P 500 firms, while the rest are selected companies that meet the social criteria but have somewhat smaller market capitalization or are known to have strong social performance. These additions provide broad industry representation in the Domini Social Index, which excludes some categories of companies, such as alcohol, tobacco, and military contractors simply on the basis of the screens.

The Domini Social Index, which is weighted by market capitalization, was begun in 1990 as a tracking index against the S&P 500. In the years since its initiation, the DSI has outperformed the S&P 500 consistently on the basis of total returns, as well as on a risk-adjusted basis, providing further evidence that doing well and doing good may go hand in hand. Figure 6.3 shows the results of the first nine years' performance of the Domini Social Index compared to the S&P 500.

Another striking bit of evidence that responsibility and financial performance go hand in hand in a both/and way has been the performance of social investment funds. In 1999, for example, socially screened equity funds were twice as likely as traditional nonscreened funds to earn the top rating from the mutual fund research firm Morningstar, Inc.[13] Morningstar's analysis found that about 20 percent of social funds earned the highest five-star rating compared to only 10 percent of all mutual funds. In a press release, Morningstar's Jon Hale commented, "We see from the numbers that socially responsible mutual funds are clearly competitive with nonscreened funds. And, from a risk-adjusted performance standpoint, screened funds have generally performed better than unscreened funds. This is the kind of evidence that should put to rest the old canard that socially responsible funds are incapable of delivering competitive performance."[14]

Further, when the Social Investment Forum, a group of socially responsible investors, analyzed the performance of social funds using a broader array of data, they found that roughly three-quarters of the largest social funds receive top ratings (those with more than $100 million by mid-1999). More than half of all social funds were top rated. Finally, such funds could be found in every asset class, providing a basis for portfolio diversification for investors interested in investing in responsible firms.

Overall, the research on whether investors earn as much on their investments in responsible as compared to less responsible companies is promising. It suggests that

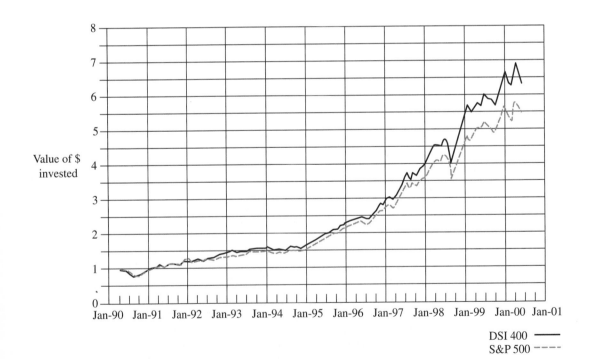

FIGURE 6.3. Domini Social Index Compared to the Standard & Poor's 500 Index

there need not be trade-offs for investors who make such investments and that, indeed, they may actually benefit from the better management practices and stakeholder relationships associated with greater levels of responsibility. Financially and in market terms, it appears that responsible companies do as well as, if not better than, less responsible firms. Minimally, it appears, the relationship is a neutral one and since there is a choice to be made—and the choice is fundamentally, as we pointed out above, a moral one—then it makes sense to invest in more responsible companies.

Employee Relations and Performance

The impact of treating employees well is far from trivial. Jeffrey Pfeffer and John Veiga summarized a good deal of research on the relationship between firm economic performance and employee relations.[15] Quoting from two major studies, they noted:

> According to an award-winning study of the high performance work practices of 968 firms representing all major industries, "a one standard deviation increase in use of such practices is associated with a . . . 7.05 percent decrease in turnover and, on a per employee basis, $27,044 more in sales and $18,641 and $3814 more in market value and profits, respectively." Yes, you read those results correctly. That's an $18,000 increase in stock market value *per employee*! A subsequent study conducted on 702 firms in 1996 found even larger economic benefits: "A one standard deviation improvement in the human resources system was associated with an increase in shareholder wealth of $41,000 per employee"—about a 14 percent market value premium.[16]

Given this strong relationship between the ways employees are treated and organizational performance, it makes sense to ask, What kinds of company practices produce such results? In some respects, the policies are easily determined and might be identified by anyone using common sense about the way he or she would like to be treated. Going back to our discussion of values in Chapter 5, we can argue that developing such policies really means operating with integrity and implementing constructive practices with respect to employees.

Implementation is difficult in part because of the basic values driving the economic sector, which were discussed in Chapter 2: economizing, which emphasizes efficiency as a first priority, and power aggrandizing, which drives managers to want to accumulate ever-increasing amounts of power for themselves. Perhaps by recognizing these driving values underlying some of the more negative practices of corporate life, leaders can overcome their short-term tendencies to want to acquire more power or cut costs in the near term and develop better practices that help the company achieve longer-term success. Doing so and implementing positive employee policies can result in significant performance improvement, as many companies with excellent employee policies (e.g., Starbucks and Patagonia) and the research cited above demonstrate.

In an exciting book, Pfeffer also showed the value of "putting people first" in terms of company profitability as well as in terms of other ways of assessing organizational performance.[17] After looking at the five-year survival rates of initial public offerings, studies of profitability and stock price in numerous industries, and research on specific industries, Pfeffer concluded that gains on the order of 40 percent can be achieved when high-performance management practices like those discussed in Chapter 7 are implemented. The analysis showed that survival rates were associated with the real value placed on people, as well as the reward system in the company. For example, policies such as employee stock ownership plans and profit sharing significantly improved survival rates.

In their summary of research on employee policies and organizational performance, Pfeffer and Viega concluded that progressive employee practices help companies improve their performance because:

> Simply put, people work harder because of the increased involvement and commitment that comes from having more control and say in their work; people work smarter because they are encouraged to build skills and competence; and people work more responsibly because more responsibility is placed in hands of employees farther down in the organization.[18]

Diversity Management, Work/Family Policies, and Performance

Another approach to assessing the relationship between the way that companies treat employees and financial performance is to assess their approach to diversity management and the work-family relationship. There is considerable belief among management scholars that greater levels of diversity will result in better performance because more and different points of view will be represented in decisions, which should improve performance. This assumption rests on the resource-based view of the firm, which says that the more and better resources are used, the better the firm will perform strategically and in other ways.[19]

A recent study attempted to study whether companies that had more women in its management ranks, as well as on the board of directors, outperformed those with less diversity in management. Although the study found no relationship between the number of women on the board and performance, the researchers did find a significant positive relationship between the percentage of managers who were women and financial performance.[20]

Similarly, in a series of studies published in *The Wall Street Journal*, the reporter concluded that "a growing number of employers suspect improving employee satisfaction will have an indirect but important effect on profit."[21] Because intellectual and human capital are becoming increasingly important sources of competitive advantage, and because there are structural changes in the economy that have caused a scarcity of skilled and knowledgeable employees, many companies have really begun to find new ways to treat their employees with respect and integrity. For example, Sears Roebuck found that employee attitudes impacted not only revenues, but also customer satisfaction. "If employee attitudes on 10 essential counts improve by 5 percent, Sears found, customer satisfaction will jump 1.3 percent, driving a one-half percentage point rise in revenue."[22]

Northern Telecom of Toronto found similar relationships among employee attitudes and satisfaction, customer loyalty, and profitability. MCI Communications found links between employee attitudes and turnover. In part, this relationship exists because experienced employees are more efficient and knowledgeable than newer employees, and because retention reduces turnover and recruitment costs.[23]

As must be obvious, a company's treatment of one group of primary stakeholders is critically related to the way it is perceived—and the way it treats—other stakeholders. We will continue to explore these important interrelationships in the next sections.

Customers and Responsibility

In addition to investors and employees, many customers too are seeking responsible practices from the companies from which they purchase goods and services. In Chapter 7 we will discuss in detail the impact of quality programs on customer relationships, as well as the costs of losing existing customers and having to replace them with new customers. Customer loyalty, gained through responsible and high-quality products and services is increasingly important to gaining status as a leading corporate citizen. Also, the reputation of the firm with customers is critical, as the work of Charles Fombrun and his colleagues indicates. One other aspect of developing positive relationships with customers has to do with their perception of a company's overall level of responsibility, which increasingly is being seen as influencing their propensity to purchase from that company.

Research by Susan Mohrman, Edwin Lawler, and Gerald Ledford, Jr., showed that linkages between employee involvement and total quality management programs appear to work together in an integrated way to contribute to overall corporate performance measured in financial terms. Generally speaking, these researchers found that these two types of systems-oriented programs, which provide a meaningful relationship between the employees and the work in ways that improve the product (so customers are better served), also are significantly related to better financial performance. In this study, financial performance was measured by return on sales, return on assets, return on investment, and return on equity.[24]

A study by Rob Duboff and Carla Heaton linked employee satisfaction to ensuring customer loyalty and long-term growth. Because customers typically relate to a company through a specific employee, the loss of that employee tends to reduce the customer's loyalty and commitment to the company, thereby reducing growth potential. The authors of the study suggested straightforwardly that "engendering loyalty among valuable employees is imperative" because "to develop effective, long-term relationships with profitable customers, [. . .] firms must also develop effective, long-term relationships with valuable employees who are able and willing to serve those customers."[25]

In another approach to looking at customer relationships, Cone/Roper, an innovative marketing research firm, studied consumer attitudes about cause-related marketing. Businesses that engage in cause-related marketing associate the use or purchase of their goods and services with philanthropic contributions to a worthy cause. When customers make a purchase, part of the proceeds goes to the cause.

A survey by Cone/Roper found that 78 percent of adults surveyed would be more likely to purchase products associated with causes that concern them. Some 66 percent of those surveyed indicated they would change brands and 62 percent said they would change retailers to support a cause they cared about. About a third of respondents even said they would pay 5 percent more (and about a quarter said 10 percent more) for products associated with causes that concern them.

Interestingly, in the same study these consumers were asked what were the most important factors in their purchasing decisions. About one-third of this U.S.-based sample took a company's responsibility into consideration in determining whether to make a purchase, after considering price and quality.

Research from the United Kingdom substantiated these trends with actual purchasing behavior. For example, in a sample of 30,000 people, the British Cooperative Wholesale Society found that 35 percent said they had boycotted products because they were concerned about animal rights, the environment, or human rights. Some 60 percent said they would do so in the future.[26]

It is becoming increasingly clear to marketers, as well as to corporate citizens interested in establishing good customer relationships through relationship marketing, that they need to pay attention to many factors, especially those associated with product quality and corporate reputation, not to mention employee policies that impact attitudes, to maintain customer loyalty.

Overall Stakeholder Relations and Performance

Throughout this book we have defined corporate responsibility as the way that a company treats its stakeholders through its operating practices day to day. Using this definition of corporate responsibility, my colleague Sam Graves and I performed another study that assessed the link between the overall quality of management in firms and their stakeholder relations (including their relationship to owners, measured in terms of financial performance).[27]

In this study we used the *Fortune* reputational rating for quality of management (and the overall reputational rating as well) to assess the perceived quality of management of companies. We compared that rating to the ratings companies received for specific primary stakeholder categories which included the owners (financial performance), employee relations, and customer relations (a product and quality measure), as well as the ratings for society through a community relations measure and for environmental management through a measure related to the environment.

We found that a higher quality of management was strongly associated with better treatment of owners through financial performance, employee relations, and customers (through the product variable), and that it was significantly associated with treatment of "society" through the community relations variable. In this particular study, treatment of the environment had no apparent relationship to improved perception of quality of management by outside observers, such as the CEOs and analysts who contributed to the *Fortune* quality of management and overall reputational ratings.

Overall, however, the findings indicate that quality of management and quality of stakeholder relationships are highly interrelated, providing further support for the idea that good management is the same thing as good stakeholder relationships. Since positive financial and social performance are also related to each other, it would appear that there is mounting evidence that treating stakeholders respectfully and from a basis of integrity can contribute to corporate success.

This argument is somewhat problematic, according to social auditor Simon Zadek, because "it often is not right in practice in the short run, and the short run (as John Maynard Keynes pointed out) can last a hell of a long time."[28] Instead, as

Zadek argued, this relationship really matters when stakeholders gain sufficient "voice" over corporate affairs that they are "heard" by management and can influence practice. As we have seen from the studies and data cited above, such stakeholder voice is an increasingly important part of the corporate landscape.

The box below contains a case study of how Hewlett-Packard, the giant computer and electronic products manufacturer, and its new CEO ensure the company's continued adherence to its core values.

Hewlett-Packard:
Any Process, Any Asset Vision Sustained by Core Values and Company "Soul"

On July 19, 1999, Hewlett Packard (H-P) Company stunned the high-tech world by announcing that it was appointing the first woman chief executive officer of a Dow 30 company. Carly Fiorina, who was also the first outsider to head H-P, took the reins at the computer giant, after a successful stint at AT&T's spin-off, Lucent Technologies (becoming CEO in 1999 and assuming the additional duties of Chairman in 2000), with a difficult charge. As *Business Week* put it, Fiorina had to "strike a delicate balance between propelling H-P's stodgy culture out of its moribund ways while not losing the elements that have made the company an American icon—its deep engineering roots and its good, old-fashioned dependability."[29] She was also clear that in spite of the needed turnaround, H-P needed to retain the core values, known widely as "The H-P Way," instilled by founders which had built and sustained the company's greatness over the years: an egalitarian work culture, progressive attention to employee needs, and commitment to its communities.[30]

Although Fiorina's priority is to ensure that "the H-P Way" is sustained and that the company's well-respected core values of integrity, teamwork, and innovation remain core values, she also knows that these values need to be reinterpreted to provide inspiration for necessary innovations that helped H-P gain competitive advantages. H-P is well known for its corporate culture and particularly for the set of values that guide its operations, the H-P Way (see "Organizational Values: The H-P Way," below). Cited in the 1982 book by Peters and Waterman, *In Search*

of Excellence, as one of the excellent companies, H-P also found its way into the later and equally seminal *Built to Last* category of visionary companies by Collins and Porras. The H-P Way plays no small role in the company's consistency of performance over the years, despite some troubling times that Fiorina was brought in to reverse.

In a world that Fiorina calls the "new business landscape," H-P needs to be ready for what Fiorina believes are three shifts that will cause a digital revolution that will change organizations and other institutions permanently.[31] First is a shift in information system appliances and technology. The technology is migrating from an electronics base to a more biologically and organic platform that will permit microscopic computer devices to be installed in just about everything. Computer devices will become smaller and virtually ubiquitous, making the second shift toward "always-on computing" and the need for supporting infrastructure essential. Infrastructure needs to be pervasive, dependable, and invisible because of the third shift that Fiorina foresees. Accompanying the dramatic shifts in computer appliances and connective infrastructure will be a radical change in the products and services that most companies produce. Indeed, Fiorina sees a shift away from products toward digitally delivered services or e-services. Digitally delivered services will encompass "any process, any asset," so that products increasingly will be viewed and turned into services that can be delivered over the World Wide Web rather than simply being viewed as "finished" in their material forms. Her goal is to put H-P at the core of helping companies deliver these e-services. In Fiorina's own words:

With e-services you think of your business as a set of independent services—e-mail, accounting, inventory management, or human resources (HR)—that you enlist and pay for when you need them . . . not as business functions with expensive application infrastructures that you must support and maintain. With e-services, you can reach your customers wherever they are—even when they're on the move—because anything with a chip in it becomes a platform for the delivery of services. In an e-services world, all things become revenue opportunities. Capital assets. Material assets. A key competency. Know-how. Experience. A world-class process. They all can be delivered as a service over the Net to generate new revenue. H-P's mission is to invent useful customer solutions at the intersection of e-services, information appliances, and an always-on Internet infrastructure. We believe the real promise of transformation for this era lies in understanding the linkages . . . the connections . . . the intersection . . . of these three forces.[32]

Recognizing H-P's need to change to meet the demands of the revolutionary changes she describes, Fiorina nonetheless knows that it is necessary to preserve what has worked at Hewlett-Packard for so many years since the company's founding in 1939 by Bill Hewlett and Dave Packard. Fiorina knows that it is necessary to "preserve the best and reinvent the rest" to maintain what she terms the "soul" of Hewlett-Packard, which she views as "mission critical." Strategy must be ennobling so that the "company is built to last, not to flip," and it must truly serve the greater good with empowered people, developing leadership at all levels and all places. In this way, Fiorina believes, the company will be well on its way not only to a healthy organization that can cope with the new business landscape she has outlined, but also can produce the necessary returns for employees, customers, and shareholders. Fiorina's first year on the job showed the value of this approach, as H-P posted 15 percent gains in revenue over 1999 and projects similar growth in the foreseeable future.

Source: http://www.hp.com/abouthp/hpway.html#organizational. Sources: Peter Burrows and Peter Elstrom, "The Boss," and Peter Burrows, "Lew Platt on HP's Ups and Downs—and the HP Way," "Why Fiorina Convinced 'an Icon' to Become Chairman," *Business Week* cover stories, August 2, 1999, p. 76 ff. Also, http://www.hp.com/hpinfo/ceo/speeches/ceo_network0_00.htm; http://www.hp.com/abouthp/hpway.html#organizational; and http://www.hp.com/.

ORGANIZATIONAL VALUES: THE H-P WAY

We have trust and respect for individuals. We approach each situation with the belief that people want to do a good job and will do so, given the proper tools and support. We attract highly capable, diverse, innovative people and recognize their efforts and contributions to the company. H-P people contribute enthusiastically and share in the success that they make possible.

We focus on a high level of achievement and contribution. Our customers expect H-P products and services to be of the highest quality and to provide lasting value. To achieve this, all H-P people, especially managers, must be leaders who generate enthusiasm and respond with extra effort to meet customer needs. Techniques and management practices which are effective may be outdated in the future. For us to remain at the forefront in all our activities, people should always be looking for new and better ways to do their work.

We conduct our business with uncompromising integrity. We expect H-P people to be open and honest in their dealings to earn the trust and loyalty of others. People at every level are expected to adhere to the highest standards of business ethics and must understand that anything less is unacceptable. As a practical matter, ethical conduct cannot be assured by written H-P policies and codes; it must be an integral part of the organization, a deeply ingrained tradition that is passed from one generation of employees to another.

We achieve our common objectives through teamwork. We recognize that it is only through effective cooperation within and among organizations that we can achieve our goals. Our commitment is to work as a worldwide team to fulfill expectations of our customers, shareholders and others who depend upon us. The benefits and obligations of doing business are shared among all H-P people.

We encourage flexibility and innovation. We create an inclusive work environment which supports the diversity of our people and stimulates innovation. We strive for overall objectives which are clearly stated and agreed upon, and allow people flexibility in working toward goals in ways that they help determine are best for the organization. H-P people should personally accept responsibility and be encouraged to upgrade their skills and capabilities through ongoing training and development. This is especially important in a technical business where the rate of progress is rapid and where people are expected to adapt to change.[33]

ENVIRONMENTAL MANAGEMENT, SUSTAINABILITY, AND PERFORMANCE

Environmental management and the increasingly apparent need to move toward sustainable development poses another set of questions for leading corporate citizens. This question focuses on whether incorporating good environmental practice can result in better profits. We have already seen that value can be added through improved relationships with investors (owners), customers, employees, and, through overall responsible practice, society in general. What about environmental management? Does it too result in better profitability?

Let us start with an example of a forward-thinking company whose environmental practices have not only enhanced its reputation, but also have saved it a lot of money. That company, known for its overall innovation, is 3M Corporation, as seen in the box, "Pollution Prevention Pays at 3M."

Pollution Prevention Pays at 3M

3M Corporation has saved nearly $810 million dollars since 1975 by implementing a progressive environmental management program it calls "Pollution Prevention Pays" (3P). 3M's approach is to use techniques of source reduction in products and manufacturing processes, rather than attempting to reduce waste once a product has been created and its approach is now applied companywide. Table 6.1 lists the savings that 3P generated for the company between 1976 and 1996.

The 3P approach works by focusing on reducing pollution at the source through product reformulation, process modification, equipment redesign, and recycling and reuse of waste materials. By encouraging all of 3M's employees to participate in the program, 3M has generated close to 5,000 approved projects over the years, each of which meet four criteria:

- Eliminate or reduce a pollutant.
- Benefit the environment through reduced energy use or more efficient use of manufacturing materials and resources.
- Demonstrate technical innovation.
- Save money through avoidance or deferral of pollution control equipment costs, reduced operating and material expenses, or increased sales of an existing or new product.

TABLE 6.1. 3M's Pollution Prevention Record 1975–1996

Pollutants/Projects	Quantity
Air pollutants	246,000 tons
Water pollutants	31,000 tons
Sludge/solid waste	494,000 tons
Waste water	3.7 billion gallons
Approved 3P projects	4,651
Savings	$810 million

Source: http://www.mmm.com/profile/envt/3p.htm.

Furthermore, recent research on the links between environmental management and stock price suggests that, like other constructive practices for building positive stakeholder relationships discussed above, better environmental policies actually improve financial performance for owners in terms of share prices. Companies not only can achieve direct cost reductions through programs like 3M's, but such programs also have "a significant and favorable impact on the firm's perceived riskiness to investors and, accordingly, its cost of equity capital and value in the marketplace."[34] Indeed, the authors of this study showed that improved environmental performance and management systems contribute as much as 5 percent to stock price.

SOCIAL CAPITAL AND PERFORMANCE

Leading corporate citizens know that relationships with primary and secondary stakeholders matter now more than ever. The research on social capital cited in Chapter 8 bolsters this argument and enhances our understanding of why these relationships matter. *Social capital* can be viewed as the trust and alliances generated by the relationships people in a given system have developed over time. The emergence of strategic alliances and networked or virtual organizations, the connectedness imposed by electronic technology, and global awareness of company performance are only a few of the many factors that have enhanced the value of relationships in recent years.

We have argued that integrity is critical to corporate responsibility. Integrity is also essential to building trusting relationships with stakeholders with whom a company is increasingly interdependent. This interdependence, a characteristic of social capital, is increasingly recognized by companies as critical to their long-term success. Companies that build positive and lasting relationships with their stakeholders, in whatever sphere of activity they operate, can cope better with the connectedness imposed by globalism and technology. Such companies may also better understand the dynamics and forces operating in the political and civil society spheres of activity than companies with less well developed relationships.

Further, companies that operate with integrity and have developed trusting relationships with all of their stakeholders may also enhance their social and intellectual capital, potentially creating a new source of competitive advantage. An emerging theory of the firm argues, as we have argued here, that firms need to be understood as complex sets of relationships—a web of relationship—in which companies can be seen as comprised largely of relationships with primary stakeholders.[35]

Given this definition of the firm, social capital clearly plays an important role in fostering interaction and efficiency or economizing in the firm. Scholars Janine Nahapiet and Sumantra Ghoshal have argued that social capital provides two distinct kinds of benefits to companies. First, social capital increases efficiency, particularly information diffusion, and may also diminish opportunism, thereby decreasing monitoring costs. Second, social capital aids efficiency because it is based on trust and relationships by encouraging cooperation and therefore innovation.[36]

These same scholars made a link between social and intellectual capital, a link that is increasingly important in the knowledge-based economy facing corporate citizens in the 21st century. Defining *intellectual capital* as "the knowledge and knowing capability of a social collectivity," they argued that it is a valuable organizational resource created by the presence of a lot of social capital. The combination of social and intellectual capital contributes to organizational advantage, in part because—based on relationships as it is—social and intellectual capital represents a resource or core competency that is difficult for competitors to imitate.

So, we begin to see a system of relationships and interlinkages among the elements we have been addressing as we developed the concept of the enterprise based on stakeholder relationships. Starting with operational integrity—wholeness and honesty—we see that companies build trusting relationships and therefore social capital both internally and externally by creating constructive and positive operating practices that impact stakeholders. Because they are inextricably embedded in a web of relationships inside and outside the company, corporate citizens will increasingly need to pay attention to the quality of those relationships—to their social capital—and they must do this because building social capital and its associated intellectual capital results in a system that works for all stakeholders.

Even when there are short-term trade-offs, the company that understands the inherent value of its relationships will act respectfully toward its stakeholders, continuing to build social and intellectual capital. As we shall see in the next two chapters, the future is likely to bring about more connectedness and a greater than ever need for transparency in all actions. Transparency is demanded because of the increased public capacity to know what is happening within and to companies because of the connections made available by the Internet. It is also clear that the world poses ever more change and complexity. In such a world, leading corporations will need all of the social and intellectual capital with their stakeholders that they can muster.

LEADING CHALLENGES: MAKING THE VALUE ADDED CONNECTION

In a world where the narrow maxim of "maximizing shareholder wealth" is still held in many quarters to be the dominant or only purpose of the corporation, leading corporate citizens to treat all stakeholders respectfully can be a significant challenge. Yet it is clear that either/or thinking is more limiting to managerial leadership than the both/and approach that values all stakeholders (and the environment) as ends to be respected and treated with dignity.

Value can be added in many ways that empower and involve key stakeholders (e.g., employees, customers, and suppliers), making them partners and collaborators in the enterprise of doing business. In this chapter we have explored what can be called the "business case" for corporate responsibility in a number of important stakeholder domains, as well as with respect to the environment.

For leaders of corporate citizens, it is important to be able to explain that doing well and doing "good" with respect to key stakeholders does not necessitate a trade-off as much as it is an investment in good relationships. In this web of good

160

*PART TWO
Leading Corporate
Citizens with Vision,
Values, and Value
Added*

relationships, leading corporate citizens will find significant sources of competitive advantage. In the next chapter, we will explore some of the specific practices that leading corporate citizens have evolved to develop the web of relationships with their stakeholders on whom they depend.

NOTES TO CHAPTER 6

1. The following three examples are from my paper with Neil Smith called "Corporate Responsibility Audits: Doing Well by Doing Good," *Sloan Management Review*, 2000, based on the work of management consulting and research firm SmithOBrien in Cambridge, MA. Winter, 41(2), pp. 75–83.
2. Russell L. Ackoff, "On Learning and the Systems that Facilitate It," *Reflections* 1, no. 1 (1999), pp. 14–24, (reprinted from The Center for Quality of Management, Cambridge, MA, 1996).
3. These two paragraphs are derived from Waddock and Smith, "Corporate Responsibility Audits: Doing Well by Doing Good".
4 James C. Collins and Jerry I. Porras, *Built to Last: Successful Habits of Visionary Companies* (New York: HarperBusiness, 1997), p. 4.
5. Ibid.
6. Ibid., p. 8.
7. See Samuel B. Graves and Sandra A. Waddock, "Beyond Built to Last . . . Stakeholder Relations in 'Built-to-Last' Companies" *Business and Society Review*, 2000, 105, no. 4, pp. 323–345.
8. For comprehensive reviews of this literature, see Jennifer J. Griffin and John F. Mahon, "The Corporate Social Performance and Corporate Financial Performance Debate: Twenty-five years of Incomparable Research," *Business and Society* 36, no. 1 (March 1997) pp. 5–3; Moses L. Pava and Joshua Krausz, "The Association between Corporate Social-Responsibility and Financial Performance: The Paradox of Social Cost," *Journal of Business Ethics* 15 (1996), pp. 321–57; and Donna J. Wood and Raymond E. Jones, "Stakeholder Mismatching: A Theoretical Problem in Empirical Research on Corporate Social Performance," *International Journal of Organizational Analysis* 3, no. 3 (July 1995), pp. 229–67.
9. This research is reported in Sandra A. Waddock and Samuel B. Graves, "The Corporate Social Performance-Financial Performance Link," *Strategic Management Journal* 18, no. 4 (1997), pp. 303–19.
10. Sally Hamilton, Hoje Jo, and Meir Statman, "Doing Well While Doing Good? The Investment Performance of Socially Responsible Mutual Funds," *Financial Analysts Journal*, November-December 1993, pp. 62–66.
11. David Diltz, "The Private Cost of Socially Responsible Investing." *Applied Financial Economics* 5, no. 2 (April 1995), p. 76.
12. John B. Guerard, Jr., "Is There a Cost to Being Socially Responsible in Investing?" *The Journal of Investing* 6, no. 2 (Summer 1997), pp. 11–18; and Sandra Waddock, Samuel B. Graves, and Renee Gorski, "Performance Characteristics of Social and Traditional Investments," *Journal of Investing* 9, no. 2, Summer 2000, 27–38.
13. See http://socialinvest.org/
14. From http://www.socialinvest.org/areas/news/1999-Q2performance.htm.
15. Jeffrey Pfeffer and John F. Veiga, "Putting People First for Organizational Success," *Academy of Management Executive* 13, no. 2 (May 1999), pp. 37–48; for a similar set

of ideas, see Gary Dessler, "How to Earn Your Employees' Commitment," *Academy of Management Executive* 13, no. 2 (May 1999) pp. 58–67.

16. Pfeffer and Veiga, "Putting People First," pp. 37 and 39. The first study cited is B. Gates, "Compete, Don't Delete," *The Economist*, June 13, 1998, pp. 19–21; the second study cited is Jeffrey Pfeffer *Competitive Advantage through People: Unleashing the Power of the Workforce* (Boston: Harvard Business School Press, 1995), p. 9.

17. Jeffrey Pfeffer, *The Human Equation: Building Profits by Putting People First* (Boston: Harvard Business School Press, 1998).

18. Pfeffer and Veiga, "Putting People First," pp. 37–48.

19. Jay Barney, *Gaining and Sustaining Competitive Advantage* (Reading, MA: Addison-Wesley, 1997).

20. Charles B. Shrader, Virginia Blackburn, and Paul Iles, "Women in Management and Firm Financial Performance: An Exploratory *Study," Journal of Managerial Issues* 9, no. 3 (Fall 1997), pp. 355–72.

21. Sue Shellenbarger, "Companies Are Finding It Really Pays to Be Nice to Employees," *The Wall Street Journal*, July 22, 1998.

22. Ibid.

23. Examples from Shellenbarger, "Companies Are Finding It Really Pays to Be Nice to Employees."

24. Susan A. Mohrman, Edward E. Lawler, III., and Gerald E. Ledford, Jr., "Do Employee Involvement and TQM Programs Work?" *Journal for Quality & Participation* 19, no. 1 (January-February 1996), pp. 6–10.

25. Rob Duboff and Carla Heaton, "Employee Loyalty: The Key Link to Value Growth," *Planning Review* 27, no. 1 (January-February 1999) pp. 8–13

26. Reported in Simon Zadek, "Balancing, Performance, Ethics, and Accountability." *Journal of Business Ethics* 17, no. 13 (October 1998), pp. 1421–41

27. See Sandra A. Waddock and Samuel B. Graves, "Quality of Management and Quality of Stakeholder Relations: Are They Synonymous?" *Business and Society* 36, no. 3 (September 1997), pp. 250–79.

28. Zadek, p. 1423.

29. Peter Burrows and Peter Elstrom, "The Boss," *Business Week*, August 2, 1999, p. 76 ff.

30. Peter Burrows and Peter Elstrom, "Lew Platt on H-P's Ups and Downs—and the H-P Way," *BusinessWeek*, August 2, 1999, p. 76 ff.

31. Speech delivered by Carly Fiorina to the Boston College Chief Executives Club, Boston, September 27, 2000.

32. From a speech by Carly Fiorina, "New Realities: At the Heart of a Radical New World," delivered to Networld + Interop, Atlanta, GA, September 26000; http://www.hp.com/hpinfo/ceo/speeches/ceo_networld_00.htm.

33. Burrows and Elstrom, "The Boss," pp. 76 ff; Burrows, "Lew Platt on H-Ps Ups and Downs," and Burrows, "Why Fiorina Convinced 'an Icon' to Become Chairman," *Business Week*, August 2, 1999, pp. 76; Also, http://www.hp.com/hpinfo/ceo/speeches/ceo_networld_00.htm; http://www.hp.com/abouthp/hpway.html#organizontal; and http://www.hp.com/.

34. Stanley J. Feldman, Peter A. Soyka, and Paul G. Ameer, "Does Improving a Firm's Environmental Management System and Environmental Performance Result in a Higher Stock Price? *Journal of Investing* 6, no. 4 (Winter 1997), p. 88.

35. See Janine Nahapiet and Sumantra Ghoshal, "Social Capital, Intellectual Capital, and the Organizational Advantage," *Academy of Management Review* 23, no. 2 (April 1998), pp. 242–66.

36. Ibid.

PART THREE

Leading Corporate Citizens and Their Stakeholders

CHAPTER 7

Stakeholders:

THE RELATIONSHIP KEY

Contrary to widespread impressions, Adam Smith, the inventor of economics, celebrated the individual not solely as an end in himself, but as the member of a community, one whose purpose was a better society. He hailed the power of "connections and dependencies" in promoting the greater good. He spoke of the entrepreneur as "a single cell in a larger organism." He said technological progress came from "combining together the powers of the most distant and dissimilar objects." In the very paragraph of The Wealth of Nations *containing his oft-quoted axiom of self-interest, Smith also makes the following claim: "in civilized societies [human beings] stands at all times in need of the cooperation and assistance of great multitudes." One telling fact: When Smith died, his estate was negligible. He had given it all away.*

After a century of hiding, Smith's values are reemerging through the pressures of a complex and interdependent world. Until recently, most business owners saw themselves as lone battlers eking out their claim in a hostile environment; many, perhaps most, still do. But the kind of spectacular success possible in today's economy is accessible not at arm's length but through a full embrace. As the economy splinters into ever-smaller pieces, those very individuals prosper principally through expressions of solidarity. Where business is concerned, the personal and the social are two halves of the identical dynamic, no different, as it happens, than elsewhere in nature.

—THOMAS PETZINGER, JR., The New Pioneers.

BUILDING SUSTAINABLE STAKEHOLDER LINKAGES

Business organizations, we have argued, are constituted of their network of *primary stakeholders:* owners, customers, employees, and, at least in the case of "virtual" or network organizations, suppliers, and of course partners and allies with whom a company is affiliated. Relationships with these primary stakeholders are therefore essential to the long-term health and success of any business enterprise. Depending on their sphere of activity, all business enterprises also have *critical secondary stakeholders* on whom they are dependent or who depend on their success. Critical secondary stakeholders include communities in which operations are located and, for most companies, governmental agencies that interact with the enterprise (if the organization itself is not a governmental agency) in setting the relevant rules of society(ies) where the company operates. Companies depend upon the infrastructure and supports provided by local communities for their well-being, and they depend upon governments for setting the rules of society necessary to make the business system feasible, as discussed in Chapter 3.

Critical secondary stakeholders depend to some extent upon the company's success for their own well-being; that is, for taxes and with communities, for the community outreach and philanthropic activities that help support the development of healthy communities. For highly regulated companies, of course, government might well be a primary stakeholder, and for companies like utilities that are necessarily community based, community might be a primary stakeholder. Society as a whole might in some cases be considered a critical secondary stakeholder because of companies' long- and short-term impacts.

Further, all business enterprises have an array of particular secondary stakeholder relationships that arise because of the specialized interests, business activities, and purposes of the enterprise itself. These *particular secondary stakeholder relationships* can include various activists, the media, relevant citizen groups, (nongovernmental organizations (NGOs, also called nonprofit organizations), as well as relevant trade, industry, and civic associations, intergovernmental organizations (IGOs), and partnership enterprises with which the company is engaged.

Finally, there are parties in society that fall outside the realm of primary and secondary activities for a company. These parties are nonstakeholders for any firm at a point in time. But society is dynamic, as are companies, so one of the important roles of leadership is to scan the external environment constantly and consistently for emerging issues and concerns that may convert nonstakeholders into stakeholders. This scanning process is one of the primary responsibilities of units and managers, who are charged with boundary spanning or boundary scanning, which we will discuss throughout the rest of this chapter. Increasingly, the responsibility for boundary-spanning activities rests with employees and leaders at all levels of an organization, especially in companies where electronic communications and commerce are central to the firm's existence. In many modern companies, it is individuals and groups throughout the company who actually implement the practices that evolve into the stakeholder relationships on which the company depends.

Organizing for Relationship: Boundary-Spanning Functions

To cope with the complexity and dynamism associated with dealing with multiple stakeholders and their associated bottom lines simultaneously, many companies have established a range of internal functions that cross organizational boundaries, either internally as with employee relations or, more frequently, externally.[1] Such functions are called boundary-spanning functions. In general, *boundary spanning functions* are responsible for developing, maintaining, and assuring the quality of a company's relationship with a particular stakeholder group and aspects of the broader social environment for which they are responsible. For the rest of this chapter, we will consider the ways that companies can organize these boundary-spanning functions to be effective (i.e., do the right thing) and efficient (economize) to make the business enterprise a success. Simultaneously, we need to recognize that the responsibility for developing good stakeholder relationships is inherent in the job of all managers. Of course, in smaller companies that have fewer management layers and departments than larger companies, these responsibilities may be inherent to all of the managerial positions in the firm.

Figure 7.1 illustrates a generic mapping of the major stakeholder relationships, with their related boundary-spanning functions for a typical firm. The focal organization shown in Figure 7.1 operates within the business sphere but, as can readily be seen, has linkages to entities operating in all of the other spheres. One primary stakeholder is the owners or shareholders, who are represented in the figure by the shareholder relations function. A second is employees, who are represented by various employee relations and human resource functions, designated in Figure 7.1 by the generic term employee relations. A third primary stakeholder includes the customers, who are represented through marketing efforts, product quality and service, and designated boundary spanning functions generically termed customer relations. The fourth group of primary stakeholders for many modern companies—which have outsourced many functions, created numerous alliances and partnerships, and depend on knowledge and expertise from outside suppliers—consists of suppliers, allies, and partners. Ally, partner, and supplier relations are typically handled through strategic alliances, contracts, and even joint ventures, some of which may well be with organizations that are otherwise considered to be competitors.

Critical secondary stakeholder relationships are also designated in the figure for a typical company. In the typical large corporation, the community stakeholder is handled by the community relations function. Governmental relationships are managed by the public affairs office, which may also include the firm's lobbying activities and political activity. The public affairs umbrella can also include particular stakeholder relationships such as public relations, issues management, crisis management, media relations, and community relations.

Finally, many modern corporations have also established environmental management programs and offices to cope with the need for sustainability and better stewardship of natural resources, and to handle relationships with environmental activists.

PRIMARY STAKEHOLDER RELATIONSHIPS

Coping with boundary-spanning relationships is complex but nonetheless critical to the success of the modern firm, particularly when we consider that the firm, literally and figuratively, is comprised of its primary stakeholders. Because the firm's

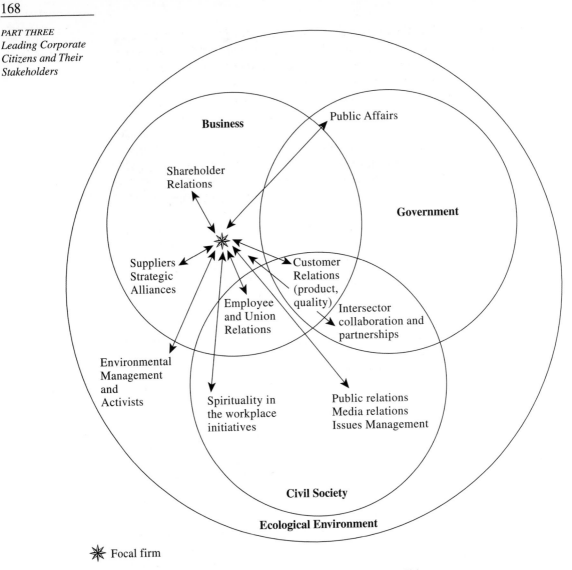

✳ Focal firm

FIGURE 7.1   Boundary Spanning Functions for Leading Corporate Citizens

long-term success is intimately related to the way it treats its stakeholders in these essential relationships over time, every manager is thus ultimately involved in some or most of these relationships. The next sections will detail the current state of the art in the particular boundary-spanning functions that deal with specific stakeholder groups.

Owners

The primary interest of owners in a company, according to the neoclassical economic model which still dominates thinking about the modern corporation, is maximizing profits or wealth. The investment made in a company by the owner stakeholder is of course a financial one, hence the relevant bottom line for stockholders or owners is the traditional financial bottom line. Shareholder relations thus encompass the many ways that companies communicate with and receive feedback from their shareholders, including governance and annual meetings.

Investor Relations

Many companies have investor relations departments whose role involves helping financial analysts correctly determine the company's value so that investors can make the proper decision regarding investing in a given firm. Of course, communicating with existing investors, as well as potential investors, is a critical element of this unit's job as well.

The investor relations department is also typically responsible for producing a company's annual report, which relays both financial and strategic information to existing investors or shareholders. Sometimes the investor relations function is encompassed under the broader umbrella of public relations or public affairs, functions also responsible for managing external perceptions of the firm.

Fiduciary Responsibilities

Appropriate and proper "treatment" of owners has to do with respecting owners' rights to have input into the governance of the company, as discussed in Chapter 6. Treatment of owners most importantly includes the owners' right to a fair return on the financial capital that owners have put at risk in making their investment in the firm in the first place. Such treatment is called the *fiduciary responsibility* of the company's directors, who oversee the hiring of top management and the general strategic direction of the firm for shareholders. The top management team is responsible for developing and implementing the company's vision, values, and strategy. Responsibility to owners or stockholders is typically measured in financial terms.[2] The fiduciary responsibility of corporate directors and their agents, the management team, requires that the management team operate with due care, loyalty, and honesty with respect to the stockholders' financial investment or interest in the firm.[3]

To be profitable, companies need to be productive and economize as much as possible. Profits are a by-product of doing something well for someone (e.g., a customer or many customers) rather than an end in and of themselves.[4] Indeed, how companies treat their owners financially is a legitimate concern among investors of all sorts, who have put their financial capital at risk on behalf of the firm with the expectation of good financial returns in the future. Still, the U.S. courts generally intend that the fiduciary responsibility of corporate directors is to give corporate directors the authority to prevent self-dealing, opportunistic behavior, and too much power-aggrandizing behavior on the part of managers.[5]

The primary relationship between the company and its shareholders is therefore one of safeguarding the investment made by stockholders, and ensuring that the owners, as investors, receive a fair return for the risk they have taken. The relationship is actually not that of agency, nor is it necessarily a contractual obligation among individual people. Rather, the fiduciary responsibility is intended to "protect legal owners who were not in a position to manage their own affairs from the unscrupulous self-dealing of those administrators the incompetent were forced to rely upon."[6]

Additionally, while shareholders have a right to expect honesty, candor, and care (i.e., integrity) from management, this right is similar to the rights that other stakeholders (e.g., creditors, suppliers and allies, employees, customers) also expect from companies. Second, courts are now starting to impose fiduciary responsibilities on corporate directors and managers for stakeholders other than owners.[7] Thus, shareholders need to be considered in some respects on a par with other stakeholders, rather than elevated into a unique status as the only important stakeholder. Particularly in the framing of what it means to be a corporation as discussed in this book, companies need to give due respect to all of the primary stakeholders that actually constitute the company, well beyond shareholders.

The key to success is balance. The interests of the primary stakeholders and some critical secondary stakeholders have to be assessed and balanced with each other to achieve the desired outcome: a company that operates with integrity and adds value for owners *and* other stakeholders. We will address how other stakeholders can be treated well in the sections that follow.

Employees

The primary interests of employees are earning a good wage for their efforts and making their personal contributions to the organization's achievement of its vision and values. The major investments of employees used to be their physical labor; in modern enterprises, however, particularly Web-based e-commerce and technologically sophisticated companies, it tends to be the employees' knowledge, known as *intellectual capital*. Also, employees put at risk their work lives, their capacity to contribute, and their earning power into making a commitment to an enterprise. As a result, they have a right to expect that their work contributes to a meaningful enterprise and that they can know and be valued for the meaning of their own contributions.

Employees and the contributions they make are central to any organization's success. Many companies, recognizing the importance of good relationships with employees, claim to put people first. Despite the rhetoric, the modern corporate landscape is fraught with corporate restructurings, layoffs, outsourcing of work to low-wage countries with low workforce standards, buildup of contingent or part-time workforces (to whom benefits do not need to be paid), and other cost-cutting measures that affect employees negatively. Such actions bear testimony to a different "reality" about the value of workers to many corporate leaders and have significantly eroded the loyalty that used to characterize the relationships of many companies with employees.

People—and their loyalty, commitment, and productive energy—*do* matter to the success and health of the firm. Treating employees well is essential for generating high levels of productivity over a long period of time. Treating employees well generates commitment to the organization's purpose, particularly if that purpose is shared with employees and they understand their role in accomplishing it.

Translating the organization's vision and values into employee policies that actually work is not rocket science. Yet despite their claims to value employees, many companies still operate their employee relationships on failed assumptions. Their practice, then, differs greatly from their rhetoric.

Failed Assumptions

In the employee arena, failed assumptions include viewing employees as costs rather than investments, focusing on the short rather than the longer term, dehumanizing employees (or infantilizing them), and not delegating enough.[8] Leaders tend also to be subject to two "perverse" norms about what good management is: The idea that good managers are "tough" or mean, and that good analysis is the same as good management,[9] a problem sometimes termed the "paralysis of analysis."[10] Further, because of embedded cultures and long-term policies that devalue people and their contributions, many companies need to transform their employee policies to bring the rhetoric and the reality of their cultures and operating practices more into line with the claims of their vision and values statements.

Successful Employee Practices

Highly successful organizations engage in a number of employee-related practices that provide employees with the sense of meaningfulness and contribution that are important to productivity (see Table 7.1). Some of these practices are directly counter to current management practices that result in erosion of employee loyalty (and correspondingly community health as well) and capacity. All of them are consistent with the works of Collins and Porras and Jeanne Liedtka, discussed in Chapter 5.

Employees, like other stakeholders, need and want to feel a part of something bigger than they are; that is, they seek meaning in their work and work setting.[11] High-performing companies provide security for employees who are carefully selected to accord with the vision and values of the company and are well rewarded through compensation plans that tie rewards not only to individual but also to group and companywide performance. They value their employees really, not just rhetorically, and demonstrate that valuation by providing extensive training, reducing status differences among levels, and sharing information about the company, its performance, and its policies broadly with employees. Such companies thereby provide a basis on which employees, as stakeholders, know that they are being valued and treated fairly, rather than being subjected to the short-term winds of profitability or the whims of power-aggrandizing management.

Employee Commitment/Company Commitment

Gaining commitment and loyalty from employee stakeholders to capture their productive capability to its fullest means creating, internally, almost cultlike cultures.[12] Commitment derives from a set of practices internally developed that inspire people to believe in the work of the enterprise, as we discussed in Chapter 4, generating a clear vision with well articulated underlying values that clearly demonstrate the contribution that is being made to something bigger than oneself. Commitment also

TABLE 7.1. Employee Practices of Successful Organizations

Employment security	Provides job security even when productivity improves. Retains knowledgeable, productive workers, builds commitment and retention, decreases costs associated with layoffs (including training and recruitment).
Selective hiring	Creates "cultlike" cultures built on common values. Requires large applicant pool, clarity about critical skills and needed attributes, clear sense of job requirements, and screening on attributes difficult to change through training.
Self-managed teams and decentralization	Teams substitute peer-based control for hierarchical control. Increases shared responsibility for outcomes, stimulating initiative and effort. Removes levels of management (cost). Ideas are shared and creative solutions found.
Comparatively high compensation contingent organization performance	High pay produces organizational success. Retains expertise and experience, and rewards and reinforces high performance. Rewards the whole as well as individual effort. Requires employee training to understand links between ownership and rewards.
Extensive training	Values knowledge and skills (generalist, not specialist). Relies on frontline employee skill and initiative for problem solving and innovation, responsibility for quality. Can be source of competitive advantage.
Reduction of status differences	Premised on belief that high performance is achieved when ideas, skills, and efforts of all are fully tapped. To do this requires reducing differences among levels, symbolically (language and labels, physical space, dress), and substantively (reduction of wage inequality across levels).
Sharing information	To create a high trust organization requires shared information across levels on issues like financial performance, strategy, and organizational measures. Helps everyone know where contributions come from, where they stand.

Source: Adapted from Jeffrey Pfeffer and John F. Veiga, "Putting People First for Organizational Success," *Academy of Management Executive* 13, no. 2 (May 1999), pp. 37–48.

means that the company is willing to commit itself with integrity to the well-being of employees over the long term.

Sustaining employee commitment and building loyalty is not easy in an era, such as the present, when loyalty both from and to employees seems a thing of the past. Many younger employees have essentially been "taught" by corporate downsizings or "rightsizings" that their first objective is to be an individual contributor, almost an entrepreneur within the company, looking out for self rather than others. Others lack loyalty to companies because they are employed as so-called contingent workers, hired temporarily or part-time to avoid the cost of benefits.

But companies with successful employee practices know that there are significant benefits to be gained by treating employees in the ways that Table 7.1 details.

For example, companies and employees benefit from employment security and from the creation of cultlike cultures built on selective hiring practices that screen out applicants for whom the company's culture is a mismatch. Once hired, employees find value in decentralized systems where they can be part of self-managed teams and be well compensated according to their actual contributions and performance. To accomplish this, highly successful companies provide extensive employee training, reduce status differences, and share relevant information with employees so they can perform their jobs well.[13]

In addition to the practices of successful organizations detailed in Table 7.1, organizations can do a number of things to build employee loyalty. They can, for example, stress their clear values throughout the orientation and training programs, implement the values in ways that build an organizational tradition through symbols and culture, and guarantee fairness or justice throughout the system, particularly through comprehensive grievance procedures. They also should provide for extensive two-way communications at all levels, create a sense of community through elaborating the common purpose, and hire people sympathetic to the company's vision and values. Such companies not only distribute rewards equitably and emphasize teamwork in many ways, but also they celebrate achievement and employee development in multiple ways.[14]

Intellectual or Knowledge Capital

In one sense, building positive relationships with employees at its most fundamental is about treating all people with the same dignity and respect with which we would treat family, peers, or organizational superiors. It is not extremely difficult, but it does require sustained effort to overcome the tendency toward viewing people as means rather than ends that is inherent in business's dominant value of economizing. Similarly, the premises of fairness and respect implicit in the practices described in Table 7.1 need to be constantly held up in light of the tendency in many types of organizations to value power aggrandizement. In the end, however, the performance results of using a respectful approach toward the critical employee stakeholder make the effort well worthwhile.

The rationale for building respectful relationships with employees, especially for the modern corporation, is that the intellectual or knowledge capital housed in the minds of employees, and the social capital that can be developed by winning their hearts, is a great aid to productivity. Knowledge or intellectual capital in many organizations today is a key, if not the only, source of competitive advantage. Companies that recognize this reality and develop practices that treat their employees with dignity and respect, rather than exploitation, and that develop cultures where employees can fulfill personal needs and dreams while also working on the corporate vision, will succeed where others fail.

Customers

Customer relationships have come to the fore in recent years with the emergence of new ways of thinking about what is generically called *relationship marketing*. What marketers and business leaders have recognized is that customers purchase goods and services from one company as opposed to another because they have reason to trust that those goods or services will meet expectations and therefore make a commitment to a company's goods or services. Thus, the relevant capital associated with gaining a customer's franchise is trust in the quality and nature of the product, which permits the commitment to be made.

The relationship marketing theory of marketing and customer relations operates alongside the traditional marketing mix of product, price, place, and promotion. Relationship marketing is especially important in service and knowledge industries such as retailing and financial services, where the relationships themselves may be what matter most to customers, although relationships are increasingly important for all types of companies because of electronic connectivity which can turn many "products" into "services" delivered electronically.[15] Terms such as relational contracting, relational marketing, working partnerships, symbiotic marketing, strategic alliances, comarketing alliances, and internal marketing have been used to describe aspects of what is meant by relationship marketing: developing a network of sustained exchange relationships between customers and companies.[16]

Like other emerging cooperative forms of relationships among Web-connected and allied companies and their stakeholders, customer relationships are emerging into importance because of the recognition that companies are embedded in networks where cooperative relationships matter at least as much as competitive ones.[17] Equally deeply embedded in this emerging relational perspective on customers is recognition of the need for high-quality products and services, as well as high-quality relationships that will sustain the necessary trust and commitment on which relationship marketing relies.[18] For example, the term *quality* is associated with, among other factors, customer satisfaction, business effectiveness and cost leadership, and cooperative relationships, even partnerships, with customers throughout the company's value chain.[19]

Mutual trust in customer relationships (and other relationships as well) exists when both of the parties have confidence in each other's reliability and integrity. Commitment exists when both parties consider the relationship important or valued over time; that is, the relationship is enduring. Among the factors that result in trust and commitment between companies and their customers are the potential costs of customers ending the relationship, shared values, and timely communication that helps the parties cope with and solve problems when they arise. Opportunistic and self-serving behavior on the part of one partner will very likely reduce trust and commitment.[20]

Customer Loyalty

The goal of enhancing customer relationships is to build loyalty among customers, who then make a long-term commitment to the company to continue purchasing goods and services. Companies that produce shoddy or harmful products will find it increasingly difficult to maintain customer trust and commitment in an era where sustained relationships and alliances of all sorts are increasingly central to producing sales and where information about problems spreads at the speed of electrons across the World Wide Web. Particularly as information about the nature and quality of products is made readily available electronically, working with customers collaboratively to ensure that they are actually getting what they need (as opposed to being sold what they may or many not need) becomes critical. Intel discovered this to its chagrin when it had problems with a Pentium chip that were broadcast to sophisticated users through a user group online, ultimately forcing the company to replace the chips.

There are many benefits of establishing ongoing relationships with customers rather than simply trying to sell them whatever product is made, a fact that many e-commerce companies have recognized and exploit with their technology. (See the box on Amazon.com's New Privacy Policy case for both the pros and cons of these policies and their implications for customer relationships.) First, customers' needs are really met in a relationship. As customer needs change over time, companies that communicate with their customers can shift accordingly, changing their offerings to better match those emerging needs. Costs of maintaining the relationship and selling, distributing, and delivering goods and services (called transaction costs) also decrease as trust and commitment increase and long-standing customers can provide excellent feedback that helps improve product and service quality. Customer relationships mean interacting regularly with customers to assure that value is being added, which can create additional ties through technology, shared knowledge or expertise, or social capital.[21]

Amazon.com's New Customer Privacy Policy

The year 2000 was a tough one for e-commerce giant Amazon.com. The company didn't make things any easier for itself—or its stakeholders—when it announced on August 31 that it was changing its privacy policy and notifying its 23 million customers of the shift by e-mail. The announcement set off a firestorm of controversy, raising the hackles of consumer advocates, such as Electronic Privacy Information Center, a Washington-based advocacy group, public policy makers concerned about uses of the data, and individual customers concerned about what would be done with the information.

Caught in the e-commerce sector's need to determine what to do with all of the information gathered when consumers purchase online, Amazon.com tried to make clear to its customers that it was changing the policy to build trust with them. The company hopes the new policy will provide customers with an under-standing of what information the company has—and what it is doing with that data. Of course, the new policy was created in the context of several class-action lawsuits against Amazon.com alleging that the company has secretly intercepted and transmitted personal information about customers to both Amazon and other companies through Amazon.com's Allegra software unit.

The privacy policy reads in part as follows:

INFORMATION YOU GIVE US

We receive and store any information you enter on our website or give us in any other way. Click here to see examples of what we collect. You can choose not to provide certain information, but then you might not be able to take advantage of many of our features. We use the information that you provide for such purposes as responding to your requests, customizing future shopping for you, improving our stores, and communicating with you.[22]

Clicking to see what data are collected reveals the following:

Examples of the information we collect and analyze include: the Internet protocol (IP) address used to connect your computer to the Internet; login; e-mail address; password; computer and connection information such as browser type and version, operating system, and platform; purchase history; the full Uniform Resource Locators (URL) clickstream to, through, and from our website, including date and time; cookie number; products you viewed or searched for; zShops you visited; your Auction history, and phone number used to call our 800 number.[23]

It was not immediately clear to what uses the world's biggest Internet retailer would put the extensive data gathered about customers, though clearly the company already uses customer information to competitive advantage. Customers logging on to Amazon.com's website find personalized recommendations on books or whatever types of products they have previously bought, based on the information Amazon.com gathers. But consumer advocate Mark Rotenberg, executive director of the Electronic Privacy Information Network, stated, "Consumers are demanding more protection for online transactions."[24]

At the same time, Amazon clearly considers the information an asset that can be sold. "As we continue to develop our business, we might sell or buy stores or assets. In such transactions, customer information generally is one of the transferred business assets." Further, the company's notice stated that "in the unlikely event that Amazon.com Inc., or substantially all of its assets are acquired, customer information will of course be one of the transferred assets."

Amazon.com, which began its life as the world's largest book e-tailer, has expanded its services to encompasses all types of music, toys, video games, electronics, software, tools and hardware, lawn and patio equipment, kitchen equipment, new cars, and multiple auction sites. Despite or perhaps because of the proliferation of products, the enormous warehousing facilities the company has constructed, and sales revenue of as much as $2.9 billion, the company was facing staggering debt loads of some $2.1 billion, reduced inventory turnover, and continued losses. In a year that saw the implosion of many dot-com companies' high-flying stock prices, Amazon.com also faced serious questions about its capacity to survive long term.

Early in the summer, Lehman Brothers analyst Ravi Suria published a scathing report about the dot-com retailer, focused on the company's negative cash flow and operating losses. According to Suria, such operating losses "would have caused any real-world retailer to fold in Internet time."[25] The report raised serious questions about the dot-com company's long-term viability and resulted in a *Business Week* cover story headlined "Can Amazon Make It?"

Coming right after two other Wall Street analysts predicted problems for the e-tailer in meeting its revenue estimates, Suria's report could hardly have been good news for CEO Jeff Bezos. Also in July 2000, the company's new president, Joseph Galli, announced that he was leaving to head up VerticalNet, a business-to-business company on the East Coast. Almost simultaneously, the company's website went down temporarily, a sign of vulnerability that was at best unwelcome.

CEO Jeff Bezos consistently argues that although Amazon is in the red, it is strategically attempting to build a dominant position in e-commerce, which requires significant up-front investment. While some analysts think the strategy of building warehouses, huge inventories, and an array of product lines still has merit, others, like Suria, are questioning the strategy. Some observers believe that the change in privacy policies can potentially give Amazon.com another source of revenue based in the power of the information that it has collected for years from its customers. Others, like some consumers, are questioning whether any company deserves the right to so much information about them. In any case, one thing is clear: Building trust with key stakeholders is far from easy.

Sources: Roberg Hof, Debra Sparks, Ellen Newborne, and Wendy Zellner, "Can Amazon Make It?" *Business Week,* July 10, 2000, pp. 38–41; Randall E. Stross, "E-biz Cliffhanger: Is Amazon's Jeff Bezos Running Out of Time?" *US News & World Report,* online, July 10, 2000, http://www.usnew.com/usnew/issue/0007/10/ 10domain. htm; Bloomberg, "Amazon.com Revises Privacy Policy," *USA Today,* August 31, 2000, http://www.usatoday.com/ life/cyber/tech/ cti473.htm; Manny Frishberg, "Amazon.com Shakeup Downplayed," *Wired News,* July 26, 2000, http:// www.wired.com/ news/print/0%2C1294%C37791%62C00.html; Associated Press, "Amazon to Share Customer Data," *USA Today,* September 1, 2000, UUNet.

Quality and Customers

For most companies, particularly those competing in the global arena, product and service quality today is a given. Along with the quality revolution, which occurred in the United States during the last 20 years of the 20th century and in the prior 30 years in Japan, came customer demands for nearly complete satisfaction with the quality and nature of products and services. Satisfied customers are a tremendous source of long-term business, as happy customers tell 6 others of their experience while unhappy customers tell 22, potentially costing significant business over a period of time.[26] Companies that operate with integrity want to assure that their customers are satisfied not only with the quality of products, but also that the product is useful and constructive rather than harmful. Cigarette manufacturers, for example, would have problems justifying their product given all of the research that links tobacco with disease, despite the profitability and presumed quality of their product and despite company protests that the link is not "proved."

Quality programs, following the advice of management guru W. Edwards Deming, typically focus on continual quality improvement through statistical process controls and quality management. The quality process, whether for product- or service-oriented companies, ensures that customer expectations are met and that trust is built. Table 7.2 lists the characteristics of companies in service and manufacturing companies considered to be world class and designed to develop excellent relationships with customers (and suppliers), along with employees.

It is interesting to note that many of these characteristics are similar to those needed to generate excellence in employee relationships as well. Both require that a company operate with integrity and a sound set of core values, ultimately with principled leadership. In addition, these practices associated with world-class companies highlight the need for integrity in all of the company's practices, including developing the goods and services that will be delivered to customers with whom the

TABLE 7.2. Characteristics of World Class Quality Operations

World-Class Plant	World-Class Service Organizations
1. Safety	1. Accessibility and follow-up by employees
2. Involved and committed workforce	2. Competence (required skills and knowledge, proactive)
3. Just-in-time manufacturing and deliveries to customers	3. Attitude (positive, flexible, continuous improvement)
4. Focus on product flow	4. Communication
5. Preventive/predictive maintenance	5. Credibility
6. Bottlenecks managed	6. Features/innovation in services
7. Total quality management program	7. Responsiveness
8. Fast setups	8. Tangible results
9. Extremely low inventories	
10. Supportive policies/procedures	

Source: Charles C. Poirier and William F. Houser, *Business Partnership for Continuous Improvement* (San Francisco: Berrett-Koehler, 1993).

company hopes to establish a long-term relationship for repeat purchases and all-important word-of-mouth marketing.

Some scholars link product and service quality with business effectiveness, making connections among customers, and partnering with suppliers as a source of competitive advantage. The quality movement has pushed many companies to benchmark their own operations and product/service quality against those of leading competitors to ensure that they stay abreast of new developments and meet changing customer needs.[27] Companies can enhance actual and perceived quality as well as the relationship with customers by providing technical service and user advice, installing just-in-time logistics systems in customer facilities, adapting invoicing to specific customer needs, and providing technical expertise, information, and social contact with customers, among other services.[28]

Establishing Customer Relationships

An important study explored the nature of relationship marketing, emphasizing its basis in trust and commitment. The study found that trust and commitment emerge when companies focus on relationships by (1) offering resources, opportunities, and benefits superior to those of competitors or alternative partners for the customer; (2) maintaining high integrity or high standards of conduct and values and associating with partners that have similar standards; (3) communicating important and valuable information that includes expectations, market intelligence, and evaluation of partner performance; and (4) avoiding opportunistic behavior with respect to the partner. One conclusion this study drew is that somewhat paradoxically, to be an effective competitor in today's global marketplace requires one to be an effective cooperator in some network of organizations.[29] Ironically, sometimes being cooperative means collaborating with companies that might in other circumstances be competitors so that they become allies under certain circumstances.

All of these and other benefits ensue when companies that are operating with integrity develop products and services that meet real customer needs and work closely to ensure that the quality of what they deliver meets customer expectations.

Suppliers, Allies, and Partners

Many companies organize themselves today in part through alliances with suppliers or other companies, including competitors, that can help them operate more efficiently. Alliances, joint ventures, partnership, and outsourcing are all ways of reducing nonessential activities and controlling costs, that is, economizing measures. When much of a company is organized through alliances and linkages to other companies, when major functions are outsourced, and when the companies are interconnected and share information through their computer systems, the company can be called a *virtual company*. The bottom line of supplier and ally relationships, as with employee relationships, can be found in the intellectual or knowledge capital inherent in the expertise for which the relationship is developed in the first place.

Alliances among companies, particularly suppliers, constitute the way that significant portions of the focal company's work is actually performed. Thus, for virtual companies, the network of relationships actually *becomes* the company in a very real way. Much the same can be said for knowledge-based and e-commerce companies, which rely on the expertise and knowledge in the heads of employees, who then become critical suppliers and simultaneously employees. The network of relationships created by moving toward virtuality can provide competitive advantage to the firm that manages it well because companies gain from the expertise provided by specialists in the function that is supplied, purchased, or received from the alliance.

Traditional Supplier Relationships

Traditionally and in many cases still today, companies formed relationships with suppliers to gain access to raw materials and services necessary to the company's business. Typical supplier-customer linkages are based on contracts that spell out the services or products to be delivered, the conditions under which they are to be delivered, and the relevant prices. The relationship under the contract can be arm's length, meaning that the two businesses have little interaction other than that necessary to exchange goods and services and receive payment.

Some companies, particularly in Asian countries where the ideology is more communitarian and where long-term relationships are considered essential to doing business with others, develop networks of long-standing intercompany relationships to get access to necessary goods and services. Some formed families of companies in similar and sometimes vastly different businesses, where linkages could be sustained over long periods of time. These networks, which derive from a communitarian ideology, are called *kereitsu* in Japan and *chaebol* in Korea. They establish a form of social capital or familylike relationships among the companies involved.

Traditional suppliers are interdependent with their customers in that each company in the relationship relies upon the other to deliver what has been promised. But when the relationships are solely contractual rather than based on trust and mutuality of interests, supplier-customer links can be established and dropped as prices or interests change without significant consequences to the purchasing company. Indeed, many companies, using a contractual mind-set, attempt to keep multiple suppliers "on the line" so that they are dependent on no single one.

Strategic Alliances and Long-Term Supplier Relationships

When companies form long-term customer-supplier relationships, joint ventures, or partnerships for receiving supply, they increase their mutual interdependence and therefore their mutual responsibility for the success of their joint endeavors. Of course, not all joint ventures are supplier-customer relationships, but all of them do demand more collaboration combined with integrity of intent if the relationship is to succeed.

The popularity of strategic alliances over the past two decades arose in part from recognition of the success of Japanese *kereitsu* during the 1970s and 1980s, when it was noted that cooperative alliances could provide strategic advantages that pure competition could not. The downside of such interlinked networks can of course be inbreeding and an inability to change, so linkages need to be balanced with innovation and the capacity to bring in new people and ideas when they are needed. In general, when companies commit to be responsible for their mutual success, they are more willing to invest in necessary equipment, employee development, and market development to assure that success than they would be if they thought the relationship could end with the next price increase. Such relationships help companies focus on the longer- rather than the shorter-term impacts of their decisions and help them through the bad times of the kind experienced by many Asian networks in the late 1990s.

Companies in supplier-customer or allied relationships, even traditional ones, do rely on each other for business. Because of this interdependence, they frequently make investments that align one company's resources with the other's needs—for example, by developing customer-specific equipment, standards, or products and services based on expectations that the relationship will continue. Because of this interdependence, suppliers and allies (and even some competitors) can be considered to be stakeholders that are essential to a company's operations, part of the primary stakeholder set that needs to be treated respectfully if both are to succeed. The tension between a company and its suppliers becomes even more intense when the customer firm is a virtual company engaged in numerous outsourcing relationships, as we shall discuss below.

Outsourcing

Many companies outsource formerly internal functions like production, human resource management, or the accounting function to experts in the particular specialized fields. *Outsourcing* is a practice whereby companies contract out functions that were previously handled in-house to other external suppliers. Thus a company like Nike is actually a marketing company, holding within its structure the marketing and distribution functions, while outsourcing all of its production activity. Many clothing companies like Liz Claiborne and some large retailers like Wal-Mart follow similar outsourcing strategies for most of what they sell.

As a means of economizing, some large companies outsource their production or even programming operations to smaller suppliers in less developed countries where wages and working standards are lower. The practice of outsourcing supply relationships creates potential downside risks for the company practicing this "virtuality." Boundaries between the firm and its suppliers, customers, or competitors tend to blur when the linkages are tight. Even more potentially problematic—although the boundaries are quite clear to both firms—these boundaries may be much less obvious to external observers, who view what happens in the supplying firm as integral to the integrity and responsibility of the supplied firm.

Outsourcing can create efficiencies and lowered costs because specialists are able to focus their efforts on particular areas of knowledge. Specialists gain not only the advantages of learning curves and scale economies, but also they develop significant intellectual or knowledge capital in that particular area of expertise, which makes them better at the particular task than generalists are.

If not managed with great integrity and consideration for the company's vision and values, however, outsourcing relationships can be a source of serious reputational difficulties. Wal-Mart and Nike, among others, have discovered this reality to their dismay, having been targeted by activists for allowing sweatshop conditions to exist in some of their suppliers' operations. Thus, although an outsourcing strategy can result in the benefits of economizing, it can also lead to problems if companies outsource functions or areas of expertise that are sources of competitive advantage or core competencies, or if they do not carefully monitor the conditions in their allies' operations.[30]

The Sweatshop Quandary[31]

When working with supplier, allies, and partners, companies are connected to any given firm only to the extent that they have developed an adequate working relationship and appropriate set of standards. Companies that have spent the time and energy to work through their vision and values need to assure that their suppliers are working up to the same set of standards and values. Otherwise, they can find themselves in the midst of controversies that arise when suppliers, closely linked to their customer firm, set lower standards.

Sometimes the lower wages and nonstandard working conditions of less developed countries come at a cost to corporations, particularly when activists become interested in the conditions of employment in supplier companies. Watchdog activists like "Sweatshop Watch" or the International Labor Organization pay close attention to working conditions in suppliers. When the customer firm purchases goods without sufficient attention to the conditions under which workers labor and when those conditions are significantly worse than would be allowed in the home country, companies can become the target of the activists.

Conditions and practices that draw attention include child labor, work weeks longer than 60 hours, mandatory overtime, and pay scales lower than the prevailing minimum wage. Workers treated like slaves, allowed to go to the bathroom only twice a day, regular pregnancy tests for female workers who are then fired if pregnant, and dismissal of union supporters have also incited the attention of activists.

Companies that permit (or ignore) such conditions to exist in their suppliers sometimes rightly indicate that it is difficult to monitor these long-distance relationships. These companies need to recognize that not only does sourcing from companies where such conditions prevail go against the vision and values they have articulated and applied to domestic operations, but also they denigrate the value of human life in other parts of the world. Treating workers as if they were mere cogs in a machine implies a distinct lack of respect for the human worth and dignity of each individual and for the communities these people come from.

Further, negative publicity seriously affects corporate reputations when companies are "caught" sourcing from substandard suppliers. U.S. firms have been subject to scrutiny by activists for many years and the scrutiny is now spreading to European firms as well.[32] German members of the activist group Clean Clothes Campaign focused attention on Adidas's sourcing of clothes from suppliers whose workers operated under sweatshop conditions. Toy, shoe, and clothing manufacturers alike have been subject to exposure by activists when their treatment of workers is considered unfair or abuse by external activist groups.

Codes of Conduct

To cope with supplier relationships and assure that workers are treated fairly, many companies adopt codes of conduct which they also apply to their suppliers.

Companies also develop internal codes of conduct that detail their relationships with their suppliers and recognize overtly their interdependence, as we saw earlier with Johnson & Johnson's Credo.

Chapter 10 will discuss in some detail emerging global standards and codes, as well as their implications and implementation. Here it is important to note that with supplier relationships so important strategically to many companies, it is essential that the conditions of work in those suppliers be carefully monitored if large companies hope to treat all of their stakeholders with the respect and dignity they deserve.

Operating with integrity demands nothing less. If integrity alone is insufficient, the growing numbers of activists who have access to information and can readily spread it through the World Wide Web will assure that companies pay attention to working conditions. When companies are once removed from the operations themselves, as in these supplier relationships, standards of operating with integrity especially need to be maintained to avoid reputational problems.

CRITICAL AND PARTICULAR SECONDARY STAKEHOLDERS

Governments and communities are critical stakeholders for all companies and sometimes become primary stakeholders—for example, when companies are highly regulated or are community based, such as utilities are. *Governments establish the rules of society by which companies must live, and communities provide essential infrastructure to support company operations.* The public affairs function, which is an umbrella for activities coping with numerous particular stakeholders, and the community relations function have evolved to provide venues for ongoing company interactions with these important stakeholder groups.

Public Affairs: Relationships with Government and "Publics"

Governments at all levels and in all branches wherever a company operates are critical secondary stakeholders for businesses. Business-government relationships are generally handled through the public affairs function, which can also be an umbrella for issues management, media relations, community relations (discussed below), public relations, and other external affairs activities. The goal of the public affairs office generally is to manage the legitimacy of the organization in its societies and attempt to influence or modify issues, legislation, regulations, and rulings so that they are favorable to corporate interests.[33]

To the extent that public affairs encompasses the other external relations functions noted, its goal is also to present the company in a favorable light to its many publics or external stakeholders. Thus, the public affairs function is also designed for generally managing external relations, including those with respect to public issues and the activists involved, the media, and occasionally agencies in civil society to whom the contributions function is linked. The business-government relations function of the public affairs office is directed toward helping companies under-stand, anticipate, manage, and ultimately cope with laws, regulations, and rulings generated by various governmental agencies.[34]

Public affairs developed originally as a fairly minor responsibility of the CEO. Not until the 1950s and 1960s did the function begin to become more formalized, while growth in the sophistication of public affairs occurred during the 1980s and 1990s.[35] By 1980 more than 80 percent of large corporations had a public affairs office.[36]

Managing Public Affairs

The underlying goal of the public affairs function is to productively develop and maintain a positive relationship between the company and the various branches and levels of government whose activities influence—or are influenced by—the firm's activities. On one level, the function helps present the company to key public offi-cials and opinion leaders in a positive light. The public affairs office also serves the reverse purpose of helping to explain the political environment to people within the corporation.[37] Public affairs is particularly focused on the political environment and political change as it is likely to affect the firm; its general charge is to establish and maintain relationships with public officials, whose bottom line is political capital and power.

In the global "village," these activities take place not only domestically for U.S. corporations, but also when companies operate in other parts of the world and need to work cooperatively with local governments. For example, many U.S. companies have divisions operating in the European Union that view themselves as European Companies of American Parentage (ECAPs) because they want to stress their European roots.[38]

Activities of public affairs officers involve lobbying public officials to ensure that they are well informed about a company's perspective on pending legislative or regulatory action. Political strategy for corporations can mean hiring lobbyists, whose job it is to work with and inform the public officials about a company's po-sition on issues and pending legislation and regulation. It might also mean having corporate officers testify on behalf of the company or industry before the relevant public body. Many companies develop political strategies and support specific can-didates for public office, frequently through political action committees or PACs.[39]

Political action could mean using corporate resources, often gathered through a political action committee, to generate a grassroots letter-writing, phone call-in, or e-mail campaign either protesting or supporting a proposed legislative or regulatory action. Lobbying also means providing information to public officials and their staffs, who might not otherwise be able to undertake the necessary analysis or find the relevant data. Or it can simply mean hiring lobbyists to represent the company's point of view before public bodies at the local, state, or national level, whichever is appropriate.

Companies clearly need to develop their political strategies carefully because, as is frequently noted, their resources give them great power. Responsible compa-nies will use this power wisely, not merely to serve the short-term and exclusively financial interests of the firm, but more broadly, to consider the important public responsibilities that leading corporate citizens bear simply because of the resources they command. Recognizing these responsibilities, they will work collaboratively and cooperatively with public officials in the public, not purely their private, interest. Working together collaboratively involves a give-and-take that allows governments and their officials to represent the public interest and the common good even, occasionally, when it would be in the short-term interest of the firm to do otherwise.

Issues Management

Issues in the public policy and social arenas can affect corporations and their stakeholders in a variety of ways. To cope with issues, many companies have established issues management units, sometimes independent of and sometimes within the public affairs function. *Issues managers* attempt to shape or frame public issues in ways that are helpful to the company. Corporate framings are frequently in conflict with framings that have been articulated by different activist groups that are interested in the issue at hand. Working productively with activists to settle on a mutual framing of the issue means engaging with them interactively in dialogue and ongoing conversation about the nature, scope, and implications of the issue. Relationships with activist groups may well be handled through the issues management function.

Issues managers have the responsibility of identifying emerging issues relevant to corporate concerns, analyzing the potential or actual impact of issues on the company, determining what kinds of responses the company should make, and then at least in some cases, implementing the response or ensuring that others implement it.[40] Issues managers are charged with identifying where gaps exist between stakeholder expectations and reality. In the international setting, the scanning process is more complex, in part because so many different cultures and contexts exist in each country, differing levels of development generate different types of issues, and stakeholders may have very different expectations of companies than they do domestically.

In the international environment, issues can cross national borders or can be located simply in one country. Experience with an issue in one nation, such as dealing with human rights abuses, can help a company cope with it the next time the issue arises. Experience can help companies avoid mistakes in developing relationships with appropriate stakeholders and managing issues locally, but only to the extent that cultural differences and political realities are taken into account in the next country.

ISSUE ANALYSIS AND MANAGEMENT. Issue analysis involves four major elements.[41] The first step is assessing the history of the issue. Next is forecasting how the issue might develop using the issue life cycle model presented in Chapter 3. Then companies can use forecasting techniques like scenario analysis to think about different possibilities and assign probabilities to each possibility. The final analytic phase is determining what the likely impact of the issue will be on the company. Following these steps allows a company to generate an internal issues agenda that will shape the company's strategic response to the issue based on the priorities given to the issues.

The final phase of issues management involves developing and implementing the company's strategy with respect to each of the high-priority issues.[42] Several alternatives are available to the company, including altering its own behavior to reduce or eliminate the issue in the minds and hearts of stakeholders. For example, Johnson & Johnson actively led the call for new packaging following the Tylenol crisis in which capsules were laced with cyanide and the company withdrew its product temporarily. J&J thereby put the company into a proactive, even interactive, mode that was positive with respect to government regulators, who might otherwise have imposed more burdensome regulations on all drug companies.

A company can also try to change stakeholder perceptions or expectations, possibly through educating politicians about the situation (i.e., the lobbying function) or doing a public relations campaign to educate key stakeholders. Advocacy advertising, in which companies state their position on an issue in paid advertisements, is a form of public education, as is the testimony given by company officials in the United States before congressional committees. Because companies have a great deal of power and access to significant financial resources, however, there is considerable controversy about corporate participation in U.S. political life.

Alternatively, a company can fight about an issue in the public policy arena, attempting to create its own framing of the issue, as the tobacco companies have done to create a debate about smokers' rights and to deflect attention from the negative health consequences of smoking. Sometimes the education process allows a company to move stakeholders' perceptions of what is happening closer to the reality of the situation.

When companies operate multinationally or transnationally, they face considerable complications in working with local governments and other stakeholders on relevant issues. Some countries, like the United States, readily permit pluralistic interest groups, including corporations, to "contest" public issues and provide varying sources of opinion and information to public policy makers. In other countries, however, where the ideology, public policy standards, and cultural norms are different, open lobbying on issues may be far less acceptable, particularly for foreign firms. In such circumstances, working through host country trade or industry associations, which represent the general interest of the companies in an industry, may be the only feasible way to try to influence public policy since direct intervention by corporations may be frowned upon.[43] This attitude may also explain why U.S.-based companies in Europe like to be viewed not as American firms, but as ECAPs, as noted above.[44]

Crisis Management

Organizational crises are highly ambiguous and low probability situations, where causes and effects are unknown, but pose a major threat to an organization's survival and at least some organizational stakeholders. Crises frequently surprise the organization and present a dilemma, the timely resolution of which will either help or hurt the enterprise.[45] Although there is controversy about whether crises can be prevented (since they are typically surprises), many organizations, particularly those where crisis is likely, have created crisis management units to help them cope when a crisis does arise. A crisis could result when an executive is kidnapped, a plane crash kills members of the top management team, a major fire or chemical spill happens, or in any number of circumstances. For example, the *Exxon Valdez* oil spill in Alaska severely damaged the environment and relationships with the state of Alaska. Union Carbide's chemical spill killed thousands of citizens near its plant in Bhopal, India. Neither company was fully prepared to deal with the consequences of these unexpected and humanly and ecologically disastrous events. Even a product can create a disaster as happened in 2000 when the alliance between Ford Motor and Bridgestone/Firestone was upset by reports that the Firestone tires were losing their treads and causing numerous deaths.

Companies may or may not be able to predict that such a crisis will occur, but they need to know what to do—and quickly—when it does. That includes public relations and the mobilization of a crisis team or crisis management unit, which is typically organized by existing employees rather than existing as a separate unit. Other types of organizations like hospitals use disaster planning in which a disaster is simulated to ensure that all parties understand what to do in the event of a real crisis. Crisis management efforts can be considered effective when the organization survives and can resume relatively normal operations, when losses to the organization and its stakeholders are minimized, and when enough is learned that it can be applied to the next crisis.[46] They can also be considered effective when a company's reputation as a good citizen is left undamaged by the actions taken during and following the crisis.

Sociologist Charles Perrow has studied high-risk technologies, such as those found in chemical and nuclear facilities and aircraft, and found that there is an inherently high risk of crisis in the functioning of these technologies. Such technologies have what Perrow termed "interactive complexity," which means they interact in complex ways, and "tight coupling," which means the functioning of each element is closely tied to that of its part of the technology. Time may be of the essence when a situation develops and the technology begins to fail. Slack may not be available, resulting in the quick escalation of the problem through a cascade of interdependent and generally unexpected effects. Perrow said that systems characterized by interactive complexity and tight coupling are prone to "normal accidents" because of the multiple unexpected interactions of failure.[47]

The Bhopal chemical spill, which killed more than 2,000 people and injured many others, is a "normal" accident in that it posed a considerable crisis for Union Carbide in part because the company was ill-prepared to handle it at the time. Diane Vaughan's comprehensive study of the *Challenger* explosion in 1988 detailed a similar perspective in which NASA and its partners were essentially unprepared for the crisis of a shuttle failure.[48]

CRISIS PREPAREDNESS. Scanning the potential for crises, especially in high-technology companies that risk normal accidents, is critical to preparedness and for breaking the boundaries of mental models that suggest "it won't happen here." Prepared companies put a crisis team, usually comprised of members of the executive team, in place that is ready to handle the psychological and sometimes physical trauma that frequently follows a crisis, particularly among employees.

Someone should be appointed to speak to the press and represent the company's perspective on the incident so that multiple messages can be avoided. The more quickly that accurate and thorough information is released, the better off the company will be. Although a crisis necessitates flexibility and improvisation with respect to the roles and responsibilities people assume, prior planning about who will do what, how, and when can reduce the uncertainty associated with the crisis. Planning can also provide a way for stakeholders to come together on behalf of the company facing the crisis and help out rather than getting in the way of efforts to resolve the situation.[49]

Media and Public Relations

The job of the media in a democracy is to report newsworthy information to the citizenry so that it can be publicly engaged and politically active, voting knowledgeably and actively influencing public policy makers when issues arise on the public policy agenda. When public issues arise and are reported by the print and broadcast media, it is generally because either the reporter or editor, or an opinion leader, has seen the gap between expectation and reality. Although the media is very influential in shaping and framing public perception about various issues, at one level, the media's real job is to direct public attention to the issues rather than to create the issues.[50] In the modern world, this principle may sometimes be violated.

Public and media relations generally involve efforts by companies to enhance their image in public opinion through positive representation in the media, typically through media reports for which the company does not pay (directly). The founder of the field of public relations, Edward Bernays, defined public relations as " 'the engineering of consent,' or the ability to get diverse individuals with varying perceptions and values to come to a 'consent to a program or goal.' "[51]

Some public relations practitioners see themselves as advocates for their companies (or when they are in public relations firms, for their clients). Others see their role as building consensus among stakeholders on various issues of relevance to the firm by creating carefully crafted messages that put the company's point of view in the public's eyes and ears.[52] Thus, modern public relations officers are responsible in part for helping to build local communities and in part for sustaining positive relationships with a company's many stakeholders.[53]

Public relations officers use many means of communicating the public image of the firm, including issuing press releases announcing the company's position on issues or positive developments within the firm (e.g., promotions, new product releases, special events, contributions made by the firm). Press releases can also attempt to fairly represent a company's point of view on an issue or situation. Thus, the public relations function is another means by which companies attempt to "frame" issues so that they reflect the company and its perspective positively.

Some companies generate advertisements, called advocacy ads, to state their position on specific issues. Oil and tobacco companies are particularly active in advocacy advertising; however, this technique tends to raise issues of credibility for the firm. Companies may sponsor events or particular causes as a means of gaining positive publicity without direct advertising, and they frequently work with community organizations on local causes. Another technique is to establish a speakers bureau or experts list that can be used by the press when questions about an issue, situation, or matter of interest arise.

Many public relations departments are also responsible for employee newsletters and other communications, as well as some of the communications with external audiences. The public relations department may work with the investor relations unit to produce the annual report for investors, as well as environmental reports, social audits, community newsletters, and other reports intended for external consumption.

Increasingly, companies use their websites to provide information to the computer-using public. The website offers not only product information and interactive services, but can be a rich source of official information about a company. Everything from a company's vision and values-statements, its mission, its annual report, new product developments and releases, financial information, and positive press coverage, not to mention means of obtaining the company's products and services, can be made readily available through the website.

WORKING WITH THE MEDIA. Many companies attempt to work collaboratively with the media in the interest of getting positive stories told. To do this well means developing an ongoing relationship with journalists, who can learn to trust the company as a reliable source. Here integrity is a critical matter!

Reporters, whether broadcast or print, seek certain things from company representatives. Among them are honesty, respect, and a mutually rewarding relationship built on trust—that is, the integrity expected of a leading corporate citizen. Reporters want to know not only that they can trust what a spokesperson says about the firm, but also that their queries will receive a quick response, as most reporters are working under tight deadlines. It is also important that company representatives are familiar with the editorial policies of the media outlets that might contact the firm so that they can generate a productive and collaborative, rather than an adversarial, relationship.[54]

The box provides an example of the way Ford Motor and Bridgestone/Firestone handled public relations and media reporting in the face of tragedies caused by faulty products.

Tire Deaths Hurt Allies Ford and Bridgestone/Firestone

The headlines tell it all: "A Company Under Fire," Ford Motor Company CEO "Jac Nasser's Biggest Test," "Lessons from the Tire Fiasco," "A Crisis of Confidence."[55] And these are only some of the public, reputational, image, and customer relations "hits" targeted at Ford Motor Company and its strategic partner and supplier, Bridgestone/Firestone, which supplied tires for the Ford Explorer sports utility vehicle (SUV).

The crisis was dramatic, testing the mettle of Ford's new CEO and Firestone's capacity to be forthright. As *Fortune* magazine expressed it, "It is every CEO's worst nightmare—the crisis that strikes from nowhere, jolts customers as well as suppliers and employees, sends the stock reeling, and threatens a company's good name." Under pressure of the crisis, Ford CEO Jacques Nasser vowed to demonstrate that Ford was "not just another car company."[56] But with the Bridgestone/Firestone tires on the Ford Explorers connected to more than 1,400 accidents and 88 deaths, with the U.S. federal government launching an investigation, and the need to recall some 6.5 million tires facing Ford and Firestone, both companies had their work cut out. At stake were Ford's hard-earned credibility as a trusted corporate citizen and Jacques Nasser's commitment to making Ford's highest goal that of pleasing the customer.[57]

It didn't help the situation that Ford's strategic ally and supplier of the problem tires was simultaneously in the spotlight for safety issues, labeled in 1994 as "offensive and unjustifiable" by then Labor Secretary Robert Reich, or that problems with other tires produced by the company began popping up. Some of the safety incidents at the company resulted in the deaths of employees, and in the same month that the tire recall devastated Firestone's reputation and public image, a worker was critically injured at a Firestone plant in Iowa. The series of incidents prompted Reich, now a professor at Brandeis University, to claim that Firestone plants have a "long, gruesome, dense history of injuries."[58]

Although Ford had been receiving complaints about the tire tread separation that was linked to the accidents since 1998 and had brought the problem to Firestone management, some questioned whether Firestone had stonewalled Ford in an effort to block a possible recall or lawsuit. Ford quietly began replacing the tires on some 50,000 vehicles in 16 non-U.S. countries in August 1999, but failed to mention the foreign tire recall to U.S. authorities until news reports on tire failures caused customer complaints to skyrocket—and drew regulatory attention to the problems.

There was plenty of blame to go around. As *Business Week* noted, "The biggest product recall since Tylenol is spiraling into a fiasco for all involved—Ford Motor Co., Firestone Corp., regulators, Congress, even the U.S. judiciary system. Everyone is blaming someone else, no one can yet explain the true cause of the tire problem, and the reported death toll keeps rising around the world."[59]

The U.S. regulatory system, in particular the National Highway Traffic Safety Administration (NHTSA), took its share of negative media attention for failing to gather information on foreign accidents and recalls. The U.S. Congress has "consistently starved auto-safety regulators for the past 20 years and has terrorized NHTSA into becoming cautious about launching recalls."[60] And, as *Business Week* reported:

Firestone, for its part, has resisted this recall every inch of the way. It first blamed Ford for the problem, saying the auto company told consumers to underinflate tires to make the ride on the Explorer softer. Then it denied knowing about the tread problem that showed up in the US, Venezuela, and elsewhere years ago. Bridgestone, Firestone's parent, has behaved much like . . . other Japanese corporations by publicly denying product problems and customer complaints while trying quietly to solve the trouble.[61]

At risk in this situation may be Ford's reputation and, ultimately, its brand, which was valued in a study reported in the *Financial Times* in 1999 at $33.197 billion, not to mention Firestone's, which some sources believed to be damaged beyond repair.[62] Because as much as 90 percent of Ford's profits come from its SUVs and pickup trucks, the slippage in orders following the tire debacle was a serious one for Ford. To complicate matters further, the tire recall attracted sufficient government attention that the safety record of SUVs, which have relatively high centers of gravity and a tendency to roll in accidents, was being seriously questioned. Even though the 2002 Ford Explorer model was expected to have enhanced stability features, including a lower center of gravity, the fury over the tire recall galvanized a recalcitrant Congress into action: By the end of 2000 a rating system for measuring the propensity of vehicles to roll over was finally, after years of delaying tactics by the auto industry, was expected to be in place.

Sources: In addition to the works consulted in notes 55 through 62 are the following: Alex Taylor, III, "Why Ford's Chairman Has Kept Mostly Mum," *Fortune,* October 2, 2000, pp. 43–48; Daniel Eisenberg, "Is This Vehicle Safe?" *Time,* October 2, 2000, p. 59; R. Tomkins, "Assessing a Name's Worth, *Financial Times,* June 22, 1999, p. 12, cited in Michael A. Hitt, R. Duane Ireland, and Robert E. Hoskisson, *Strategic Management: Competitiveness and Globalization* (Cincinnati, OH: Southwestern College Publishing, 2001), p. 94.

Community Relationships

Healthy communities are those in which citizens know and are connected with each other, share a common vision of the community's identity and culture, and are willing to work together for the common good. Corporations located in communities can—when they are "rooted" in and responsible to the community—play an important role in building and sustaining community health. Companies receive numerous supports from healthy communities, including infrastructure planning and development, an educated workforce, and a working environment that enhances competitiveness. Most companies work directly with their communities, enhancing what is known as social capital (or connections and relatedness) within the community, through their community relations functions.

Community relations programs in the United States, where they are most common, typically have encompassed a number of areas, including charitable contributions or philanthropy, volunteer programs, and community-based (public-private or social) partnerships. The relationships with communities embodied in these programs are handled through a number of functions that are frequently consolidated into a single office called Community Relations (CR). Generally speaking, the community relations function deals with community members and groups active in the civil society (and sometimes the political) sphere of influence.

The major investment by the community in a company comes in the forms of social capital generated by strong and healthy communities and the infrastructure generated by communities from taxes paid by individual and corporate citizens. Social capital, as has already been discussed, provides for healthy community-based relationships and positive civic and political action that help balance both economic and governmental sources of power. The infrastructure provided by communities includes the local educational system, which can provide an educated workforce for a company. Infrastructure also includes roads and highways, communications networks, local community-based services (e.g., garbage removal and sewage systems), and the local regulatory system, without which it would be impossible for firms to operate successfully.

Neighbor of Choice

Best practice companies in community relations operate on a principle that asks the company to become a "neighbor of choice."[63] A *neighbor of choice* means being a welcome, trusted neighbor with a positive relationship within the communities where the company has operations. According to Edmund Burke, who founded the corporate membership organization called Boston College Center for Corporate Community Relations (now the Center for Corporate Citizenship), neighbor of choice strategies derive from trusting relationships based on mutual respect and ongoing dialogue with communities and their representatives.[64] The key to becoming a successful corporate neighbor of choice is, as we have argued earlier for all stakeholders, to develop continuing and mutually interactive, power balanced relationships. Thus, one important consideration for companies wishing to attain balance between the interests of communities and those of the company is to assure that there is a significant place for the "voice" of community members on corporate activities.

Burke highlighted three specific program strategies essential to positive corporate-community relations, recognizing that strong community relations cannot be housed within a single department but are instead the responsibility of everyone in the company. Companies need first to build community relationships, then to identify issues and concerns within the community that are relevant to the company, and finally to design appropriate programs in the community to cope with those concerns.[65] A neighbor of choice community relations program begins with an internal assessment of company attitudes and practices toward the community, then moves outward to assess the situation and needs of those communities where the company has operations or where it hopes to develop a broad customer base.

To make the community relations programs strategic once needs and opportunities have been identified, companies need to map out the ways in which activities within the community can enhance their strategy. Additionally, companies can attempt to establish and live up to the "standards of excellence" outlined by the Boston College Center for Corporate Citizenship (see Table 7.3). These standards are supported by a diagnostic tool and emphasize specific practices that companies can develop to establish strong community relationships. One example is the use of strategic philanthropy (e.g., a chemical company donating lab facilities and materials that

TABLE 7.3. Standards of Excellence in Corporate Community Involvement

Standard I: Leadership
Senior executives demonstrate support, commitment, and participation in community
  involvement efforts.

Standard II: Issues Management
The company identifies and monitors issues important to its operations and reputation.

Standard III. Relationship Building
Company management recognizes that building and maintaining relationships of trust with
  the community is a critical component of company strategy and operations.

Standard IV: Strategy
Company management recognizes that building and maintaining relationships of trust with
  the community is a critical component of company strategy and operations.

Standard V: Accountability
All levels of the organization have specific roles and responsibilities for meeting
  community involvement objectives.

Standard VI: Infrastructure
The company incorporates systems and policies to support, communicate, and
  institutionalize community involvement objectives.

Standard VII: Measurement
The company establishes an ongoing process for evaluating community involvement
  strategies, activities and programs, and their impact on the company and the community.

Source: Boston College Center for Corporate Citizenship, 2000.

help train technicians to a local high school so that trained workers will later be available). Another is the use of volunteer programs to connect employees with local communities so that they not only can improve the community and the company's relationship with the community, but also improve employee morale and connectedness to the values and vision of the firm. Some companies engage in cause-related marketing in which they donate a percent of each sale or product use to a cause or charity with which local community members can identify. This technique, pioneered by the American Express Corporation, combines philanthropy and marketing.

Identifying Communities of Interest[66]

There are six generic types of communities, many of which are in the civil society sphere, to which most companies will need to pay attention if they wish to become a neighbor of choice. These types include the *site community,* which is geographically determined by the location of facilities. A second community is the *employee community,* which is not the internal employee group but the communities where employees live. A third type of community is the *fenceline community,* which includes the immediate neighbors surrounding company property.

Companies also need to pay attention to the *impact community,* which is comprised of the communities affected by company operations (particularly any externalities generated by the company). Impacts can derive from operations, political or social influence generated by a company's activities, or decisions to enter or exit a given community.

A new and evolving community to which many, if not most, companies need to pay attention, is the *cyber community.* Unlike traditional place-based communities, the cyber community has few boundaries and is not readily identifiable, yet it provides a ready market for a company's products or services, and may have substantial power to influence a company's success. Thus, the cyber community needs to be treated with the same respect as other communities.

Finally, there are *common interest communities* or functional communities. Common interest communities share a common interest or function, like the environment, education, religion or ethnicity.[67] These particular communities operate within other civil society institutions, like schools and universities or civic organizations, that may wish to develop ongoing collaboration with a company aimed at their mutual benefit.

Community Relations Strategies

Dealing with all of these different communities requires the development of specific community relations strategies and programs for each community. This process of relationship building cannot be left to chance and needs to be planned as carefully as any other corporate strategy if the company hopes to be able to work effectively with community constituencies.

There are a number of community practice programs that enable companies to develop ongoing dialogue within the context of a trusting relationship with community stakeholders.[68] Among the programs that companies use to invite community representatives into dialogue and relationship are plant tours and programs that expose people to what is actually going on within the facilities. Some companies also donate the use of their facilities to NGOs or nonprofits, including, when appropriate, allowing access of NGO leaders into corporate training programs. Others engage key leaders in mutual problem solving and planning activities related to a community's needs, interests, and quality of life.

Many companies identify key contacts within the company for specific kinds of community questions or needs, thereby creating a degree of needed transparency between the firm and its communities. Working in the reverse direction, some companies also develop their own list of key community contacts so they will know whom to contact when issues arise and to do so before the issue is framed in ways that go against the corporate interest.

A final way that progressive and visionary companies use to work interactively with community representatives is to create community advisory panels that provide a forum for dialogue about community-based issues of mutual concern. These panels enlist key community members to work with the community and the company on issues that are important to the community. Acting as a liaison between the community and the company, such panels can create a forum or a "space" for dialogue about what is important to both sides. An advisory panel can provide a common meeting ground and enhance not only the transparency of the company to the community but also the prospect of developing a shared view of what is in the long-term common good of the community and the company.

Social Vision and Social Capital[69]

The task of corporate leadership in the 21st century goes well beyond traditional community relations in dealing with the public responsibilities of the firm. As we have argued in earlier chapters, what is important in developing a corporate-community relations program that will be effective in the future is finding a way to balance the company's interests with those of its communities, many of which are found in the civil society sphere.

The presence of social capital—that is, connectedness among members of the communities of relevance—is the key measure of success in healthy and well-functioning communities. Companies have a choice: They can destroy social capital by economizing at all costs, laying off employees and devastating their communities when lower-cost options arise. Or they can develop lasting, trust-filled relationships with local communities and help strengthen those communities; in short, they can become "rooted" in communities rather than rootless. The result will enable companies to gain access to qualified, well-educated, and loyal workers; communities with adequate infrastructure to support company needs; and civil relationships with local leaders who believe that the presence of the company is a benefit to the community. By working toward the development of social capital through positive community-based programs, companies can indeed become neighbors of choice and help provide balance among the three spheres of influence.

LEADING CHALLENGES:
STAKEHOLDERS AND LEADERSHIP

Leading corporate citizens means dealing effectively—and efficiently (or economizingly)—with stakeholders. The double entendre of the phrase "leading corporate citizens" becomes clear in this chapter. Companies themselves need to lead others if they hope to gain a competitive advantage. Progressive stakeholder practices that treat stakeholders with respect and dignity, such as those described in this chapter, put companies on a path toward that competitive advantage.

There are many things that leading corporate citizens can do, as Tables 7.4 and 7.5 summarize, to become respected for their citizenship. Although best practices with respect to any given stakeholder group are always emerging and changing, the table summarizes what the current state of the art is for companies to develop positive and interactive stakeholder relationships with their wide range of constituencies. From the company's perspective, there are clearly structures that make sense to stakeholders through which the company can build effective relationships. But leading corporate citizens is not only a company matter.

Leading corporate citizens also applies to the individual leaders and managers within the firm, who are responsible for creating awareness within the firm of its impact on stakeholders and the natural environment. Leadership is particularly important in fostering environmental sensitivity and a positive attitude toward developing sustainable business practices, which will be further discussed in Chapter 9. Only with aware leaders can companies generate a culture that moves the firm toward constant questioning of its current practices. Such questioning can move the company toward accepting full responsibility for its impacts on the ecological sphere as well as its interactions with stakeholders in the political and civil society spheres. Leadership at this level of awareness demands systems thinking and the relatively high levels of cognitive development discussed in Chapter 4.

As this chapter has demonstrated, both individual and company leadership are critical. Companies need to develop the internal practices that show their true respect for the dignity and worth of each stakeholder, rather than trying to dominate or control them. Through this collaborative, interactive, and respectful approach to stakeholders and to the ecological environment on which they depend, companies can prosper over the long term and maintain the legitimacy they need to be accepted in society. Thus, leaders need to understand the relationships that their companies' activities have with communities, competitors, suppliers, employees, and whole societies in which they are embedded, not to mention the ecological surround on which they ultimately depend.

The key to developing respectful relationships is not "managing stakeholders," as is so often stated, but developing and managing productive, interactive, and positive *relationships* with the stakeholders on which the company depends for its existence. This chapter has focused on some of the practices that progressive and visionary companies use to develop and manage those critical relationships. In the next chapter, we will explore the ways in which corporate stakeholder practices can actually be measured.

TABLE 7.4.   Best Practices in Primary Stakeholder Relationships for Leading Corporate Citizens

Primary Stakeholders Bottom Line	Relevant Boundary-Spanning Functions	Best Practices of Leading Corporate Citizens
Owners/financial	Investor relations	Transparency and accountability with respect to fiduciary responsibilities, and achieving balance and a fair return for shareholders.
Employees/intellectual and human capital, commitment, and loyalty	Employee relations Human resource management Training and development	Employment security Selective hiring Self-managed teams and decentralization Comparatively high compensation Extensive training Reduction of status differences Sharing information Create meaningful, inspirational workplaces supported by vision, values, and implementation. Value employees as ends, not means to an end. Develop trust, commitment, and loyalty.
Customers/business franchise trust	Customer relations Relational marketing Marketing	Develop loyal customers, build trust through quality products and services that meet real customer needs and are delivered on time as advertised; interact with customers in an ongoing way. Commit to product quality, safety, continual process and product improvements, accessibility, positive attitude, and credibility to develop trust and communication with customers. Build trust and commitment by offering superior resources, opportunities, and benefits, maintaining high integrity and standards, communicating important information, and avoiding opportunism.
Suppliers, allies, and partners/infrastructure, relationship	Joint ventures, supplier and outsourcing contracts and partnerships, strategic alliances	Monitor suppliers, allies, and partners to assure that quality, employment, safety, and codes of conduct standards are met, and to build a lasting and trusting relationship with allies. Assure that the company's vision is communicated to and understood by allies and that they are willing to meet high standards and expectations.

TABLE 7.5. Best Practices for Secondary Stakeholder Relationships for Leading Corporate Citizens

Secondary Stakeholder	Relevant Boundary-Spanning Function	Best Practices of Leading Corporate Citizens
Government/public good, common good	Public affairs	Help public policy makers understand, anticipate, and cope with issues that arise from business practices in a way that serves the public interest/common good. Keep public policy makers informed about the company's perspectives, interests, and needs without exercising undue power or influence.
The general public or society/trust, development, growth	Issues management	Constantly scan and monitor the external environment for emerging issues. Assess history and development of issues, forecast possible futures using issue life cycle analysis, use forecasting techniques to develop scenarios, and determine possible impacts on company, then take necessary steps to contend with these implications.
	Crisis management	Anticipate and prepare for potential crises, have a crisis management team in place and trained to deal with physical and emotional trauma, but one that is adaptable to the situation and well prepared to deal with the media and general public as well as uncertainties of the situation.
Media/knowledge	Media relations Public relations	Advocate for the company's perspective and place the company in the best public light by working with community members and building positive relationships with many stakeholders through extensive and interactive communication means. Build trust and ongoing relationships with media representatives.
Community(ies)/ infrastructure	Community relations Stakeholder relations Corporate citizenship	Become a neighbor of choice by exerting leadership as a corporate citizenship, managing community-related issues effectively, building relationships with community members, developing a community relations strategy and relevant infrastructure that is assessed and measured regularly.

NOTES TO CHAPTER 7

1. Robert Leaver, president and CEO of Organizational Futures, developed one multiple bottom-line framework in *The Commonwealth Papers* (Providence, RI: Commonwealth Publications, 1995). I am also grateful to my colleagues in the Leadership for Change Program at Boston College for pushing this line of thinking over many years of collaborative work.

2. See Sandra A. Waddock and Samuel B. Graves, "Quality of Management and Quality of Stakeholder Relations: Are They Synonymous?" *Business and Society* 36, no. 3, (September 1997) pp. 250–79.

3. This argument is compellingly made by Richard Marens and Andrew Wicks, "Getting Real: Stakeholder Theory, Managerial Practice, and the General Irrelevance of Fiduciary Duties Owed to Shareholders," *Business Ethics Quarterly* 9, no. 2 (April 1999), pp. 273–93.

4. See James C. Collins and Jerry I. Porras, "Building Your Company's Vision," *Harvard Business Review,* September–October 1996, pp. 65–77.

5. See Marens and Wicks, pp. 273–93; and Oliver E. Williamson, *Markets and Hierarchies: Analysis and Antitrust Implications* (New York: Free Press, 1975).

6. Marens and Wicks, p. 277. The thoughts in this paragraph are derived from this article.

7. These two points are made in Marens and Wicks.

8. Jeffrey Pfeffer and John F. Veiga, "Putting People First for Organizational Success," *Academy of Management Executive* 13, no. 2 (May 1999), pp. 37–48; see also Gary Dessler," How to Earn Your Employees' Commitment, *Academy of Management Executive,* 13, no. 2 (May 1999), pp. 58–67, for a similar set of ideas. The framework in this section is developed from these two review articles.

9. Pfeffer and Veiga, p. 46.

10. R. H. Hayes and W. Abernathy, "Managing Our Way to Economic Decline," *Harvard Business Review,* July–August 1980, pp. 66–77.

11. See Dessler, citing Kanter, p. 59. Dessler's ideas are similar to those developed in Chapters 4 and 5 and are congruent with the practices of successful firms identified by Pfeffer and Veiga, pp. 37–48.

12. See Collins and Porras, pp. 65–77.

13. Summarized from Pfeffer and Viega, pp. 37–48.

14. See Dessler, p. 59.

15. See, for example, Christian Gronroos, "From Marketing Mix to Relationship Marketing: Towards a Paradigm Shift in Marketing," *Management Decision* 32, no. 2 (1994), pp. 4–20; and Robert M. Morgan and Shelby D. Hunt, "The Commitment-Trust Theory of Relationship Marketing," *Journal of Marketing* 58, no. 3 (July 1994), pp. 20–38.

16. Gronroos, pp. 4–20.

17. Morgan and Hunt, pp. 20–38.

18. See Kaj Storbacka, Tore Strandvik, and Christian Gronroos, "Managing Customer Relationships for Profit: The Dynamics of Relationship Quality," *International Journal of Service Industry Management* 5, no. 5 (1994), pp. 21–38.

19. Armand V. Feigenbaum, "Changing Concepts and Management of Quality Worldwide," *Quality Progress* 30, no. 12 (December 1997) pp. 45–48.

20. Morgan and Hunt, pp. 20–38, detail these determining factors.

21. Gronoos, pp. 4–20.

22. http://www.amazon.com/exec/obidos/subst/misc/policy/privacy.html/104-5258601-1634328.

23. http://www.amazon.com/exec/obidos/subst/misc/policy/privacy-automatic.html/104-5258601-1634328.

24. Quoted in Bloomberg, "Amazon.com Revises Privacy Policy," *USA Today,* August 31, 2000, http://www.usatoday.com/life/cyber/techn/cti473.htm.
25. Quoted in Randall E. Stross, "E-Biz Cliffhanger: Is Amazon's Jeff Bezos Running Out of Time?" *US News & World Report,* July 10, 2000, http://www.usnews.com/usnews/issue/000710/10domain.htm.
26. Feigenbaum, p. 46.
27. Ibid. pp. 45–48.
28. Gronroos, pp. 4–20.
29. Morgan and Hunt, pp. 19–20 of 26 online.
30. See C. K. Prahalad and Gary Hamel, "The Core Competence of the Corporation," *Harvard Business Review*, May–June 1990, pp. 79–91.
31. For a comprehensive study of the the "sweatshop quandary," see Pamela Varley, ed., *The Sweatshop Quandary: Corporate Responsibility on the Global Frontier* (Washington, DC: Investor Responsibility Research Center, 1998).
32. See William Echikson's commentary "It's Europe's Turn to Sweat about Sweatshops," *Business Week,* July 19, 1999, p. 96.
33. Martin Meznar and Douglas Nigh, "Managing Corporate Legitimacy: Public Affairs Activities, Strategies, and Effectiveness," *Business and Society* 32, no. 1 (Spring 1993), pp. 30–43; Peter Hannaford, "What Is Public Affairs?" *Public Relations Quarterly* 33, no. 3 (Fall 1988), pp. 11–14.
34. See, for example, James E. Post, Edwin A. Murray, Jr., Robert B. Dickie, and John F. Mahon, "The Public Affairs Function in American Corporations: Development and Relations with Corporate Planning," *Long Range Planning* 15, no. 2 (April 1982), pp. 12–21.
35. The history is given in Charles J. McMillan and Victor V. Murray, "Strategically Managing Public Affairs: Lessons from the Analysis of Business-Government Relations," *Business Quarterly* 48, no. 2 (Summer 1983), pp. 94–100.
36. The current state of the art is detailed in James E. Post and Jennifer J. Griffin, *The State of Corporate Public Affairs: Final Report 1996 Survey* (Boston: Boston University School of Management and Foundation for Public Affairs, 1996); and Alfred A. Marcus and Allen M. Kaufman, "The Continued Expansion of the Corporate Public-Affairs Function," *Business Horizons* 31, no. 2 (March–April 1988), pp. 58–62.
37. See Keith MacMillan, "Managing Public Affairs in British Industry," *Journal of General Management* 9, no. 2 (1983–1984), pp. 784–90.
38. See D. Jeffrey Lenn, Steven N. Brenner, Lee Burke, Diane Dodd-McCue, Craig S. Fleisher, Lawrence J. Lad, David R. Palmer, Kathryn S. Rogers, Sandra A. Waddock, and Richard E. Wokutch, "Managing Corporate Public Affairs and Government Relations: US Multinational Corporations in Europe," James E. Post, ed., in *Research in Corporate Social Performance and Policy* 15 (1993), pp. 103–38.
39. Post and Griffin.
40. See Douglas Nigh and Philip L. Cochran, "Issues Management and the Multinational Enterprise," *Management International Review* 34 (Special Issue 1994), pp. 51–59.
41. Adapted from Nigh and Cochran, pp. 51–59.
42. Responses are adapted from Nigh and Cochran, pp. 51–59.
43. Ibid.
44. Lenn et al., pp. 103–38.
45. Much of the information on crisis management in this section is derived from Christine M. Pearson and Judith A. Clair, "Reframing Crisis Management, " *Academy of*

Management Review 23, no. 1 (January 1998), pp. 59–76; see also Ian I. Mitroff and Robert H. Kilman, *Corporate Tragedies: Product Tampering, Sabotage, and Other Catastrophes* (New York: Praeger, 1984); Ian I. Mitroff, Christine M. Pearson, and L. Kathleen Harrigan, *The Essential Guide to Managing Corporate Crises* (New York: Oxford University Press, 1996); P. Shrivastava, I. Mitroff, D. Miller, and A. Migliani, "Understanding Industrial Crises," *Journal of Management Studies* 25 (1988), pp. 285–303; and Norman R. Augustine, "Managing the Crisis You Tried to Prevent," *Harvard Business Review,* November–December 1995, pp. 147–58.

46. Pearson and Clair, pp. 59–76.
47. Charles Perrow, *Normal Accidents: Living with High-Risk Technologies* (New York: Basic Books, 1984).
48. Diane Vaughan, *The Challenger Launch Decision: Risky Technology, Culture, and Deviance at NASA* (Chicago: University of Chicago Press, 1996).
49. Pearson and Clair.
50. Jennifer A. Kitto, "The Evolution of Public Issues Management," *Public Relations Quarterly* 43, no. 4 (Winter 1998–1999), pp. 34–38.
51. Edward L. Bernays, *Public Relations* (Norman: University of Oklahoma Press, 1952), quoted in Burton St. John III, "Public Relations as Community-Building Then and Now," *Public Relations Quarterly* 43, no. 1 (Spring 1998), pp. 34–40.
52. Jodi B. Katzman, "What's the Role of Public Relations?" *Public Relations Journal* 49, no. 4 (April 1993), pp. 11–16.
53. See St. John, pp. 34–40; and Augustine S. Ihator, "Effective Public Relations Techniques for the Small Business in a Competitive Market Environment," *Public Relations Quarterly* 43, no. 2 (Summer 1998), pp. 28–32.
54. Ihator, pp. 28–32.
55. Adam Bryant and Amy DiLuna, "A Company Under Fire," *Newsweek,* September 18, 2000, pp. 30 ff; Alex Taylor, III, "Jac Nasser's Biggest Test," *Fortune,* September 18, 2000, pp. 123–28; "Lessons from the Tire Fiasco," *Business Week,* September 18, 2000, pp. 178 ff; Joann Muller, David Welch, Jeff Green, Lorraine Woellert, and Nichole St. Pierre, "A Crisis of Confidence," *Business Week,* September 18, 2000, pp. 40–42.
56. Taylor, p. 123.
57. Muller et al., pp. 40–42.
58. Bryant and DiLuna, pp. 30 ff.
59. "Lessons from the Tire Fiasco," p. 178.
60. Ibid.
61. Ibid.
62. Muller et al., pp. 40–42.
63. The neighbor of choice principle is developed at length in Edmund M. Burke, *Corporate Community Relations: The Principle of the Neighbor of Choice* (Greenwich, CT: Praeger, 1999). Discussion of the community relations function within this section is based on Burke's book.
64. Burke, p. 24.
65. Ibid., pp. 47 ff. This section is based on Burke's chap. 4.
66. Burke, chap. 5.
67. Murray G. Ross, *Community Organization: Theory and Principles* (New York: Harper & Row, 1966), cited in Burke, pp. 65–66.
68. Burke, chap. 8.
69. The term appears in Burke, chap. 12; the framing of this section is the author's.

Measuring Multiple Bottom Lines:

GETTING TO VALUE ADDED

Measures have great power, almost like genetic code, to shape action and performance. Whether at the equivalent of the cell level, the organ level, or the systems level, measures become the directional device that influence or even dictates the shape of the enterprise. Change the measures, and you change the organism.

Measures have always had the power to shape a corporation's destiny, but the focus on financial figures alone limited their utility. Management accounting of the past forced managers to build world-class organizations with a truncated set of chromosomes. Today, though, with the help of revitalized cost accounting and nonfinancial measurement, managers can develop a full set of instructions—financial, operational, and social—for the enterprise. These instructions give them the capability to create accountability they never had before.

A balanced family of measures can evolve into a powerful system for executing strategy. The measures help to define the strategy, communicate it to the organization, and direct its implementation at every rung of the hierarchy, from the corporate level to the individual. They also keep everyone's efforts aligned, because they link strategy to budgets, to resource-allocation systems, and to pay programs. In the best of cases, they route such high-quality feedback through the organization that executives can make critical, mid-course adjustments in strategy.

—MARK J. EPSTEIN AND BILL BIRCHARD, Counting What Counts: Turning Corporate Accountability to Competitive Advantage

Corporate citizens, leading and otherwise, are increasingly being evaluated on social as well as financial performance criteria, whether they want to be or not. So much in-

201

CHAPTER 8
Measuring Multiple
Bottom Lines:
Getting to
Value Added

formation is available on company practices that its very availability in some cases may cause managers to "do the right thing" because otherwise their decisions are likely to garner unfavorable attention from one external source or another. The external attention to corporate citizenship has also focused the attention of some companies internally and caused them to audit their own practices to ensure that they are living up to their stated vision and values. All of this public attention to measuring progress in new ways has resulted in increased awareness of the need to take many factors now omitted from gross national and domestic product calculations into account for society as a whole.

Just one example. According to the Social Investment Forum (SIF), by 1999 more than $2 trillion was invested in equities in the United States that were in screened portfolios, shareholder advocacy and community investing—all forms of social investing according to SIF—or about 13 percent of investments under professional management in the United States.[1] Social investing was growing at twice the rate of all assets under investment in the country. Social investments are made by individuals and by funds concerned not only about financial performance, but also about the ways in which companies treat various stakeholders. And that is just one way in which corporate stakeholder and citizenship activities are now being evaluated.

Corporate citizens clearly need to be aware that their practices are under considerable scrutiny by social investors, who can readily communicate dissatisfaction globally through the World Wide Web. Demonstrations by labor, human rights, and environmental activists at meetings of the World Trade Organization to protest the continuing globalization of economies in 1999 and 2000 highlighted the speed with which information now travels around the world and raised hackles among those who perceive injustices. Leaders of corporate citizens today know that their actions are being measured in a whole range of new ways that begin to account for nonfinancial results and stakeholder relationships. Recognizing these new realities, many leaders are putting in place explicit social accounting methodologies and making the results transparent to external stakeholders—and also as a result making the companies themselves more accountable for their actions. Indeed, such measurement and its reporting may rapidly be becoming the sine qua non of corporate citizenship itself.

While many people believed for years that it was not possible to measure companies' stakeholder performance and citizenship except in financial terms, today it is clear that there are many ways to assess citizenship practices. This chapter will explore several ways that the multiple bottom lines associated with stakeholders and corporate citizenship are measured and evaluated, methods that progressive leaders are aware of and know how to implement for their unit as well as the whole enterprise. It is no longer enough to issue merely a financial report. As the emergence of triple (and multiple) bottom-line reporting indicates, new measures and methods of reporting to all-important stakeholders are increasingly a business imperative.

MEASURING RESPONSIBLE PRACTICE: EXTERNAL ASSESSMENT

As implied above, assessing the responsibility of corporate practices and citizenship requires a "multiple bottom-lines" approach, rather than the traditional single (financial) bottom line. A stakeholder approach to citizenship implies that corporate practices with respect to primary stakeholder groups, including owners, employees, customers, and suppliers (at a minimum for companies, others depending on the type of organization), and key secondary stakeholders of communities, governments, and other important relationships, need to be assessed. Ecological sustainability, as well as the quality of important stakeholder relationships—that is, the way the organization treats its primary stakeholders—are critical elements of this assessment. These interests represent multiple bottom lines related to the type of capital invested by each stakeholder. To simplify matters, we will consider mainly primary stakeholders, in the section below on social auditing, after we have discussed the growing importance of several types of social investing.

Measurement of multiple bottom lines is often thought to be the "soft stuff" in business. But assessing the quality and impact of company practices on key stakeholders is not really about the soft stuff. Rather, it is about the hard stuff of managing business activities and relationships well and simultaneously doing "good" for stakeholders with whom the business is interdependent for its success. Building responsible practices as we have seen in Chapter 6 does have positive productivity and bottom-line impacts. For now, however, it is important to look at how these purported soft areas of the multiple bottom lines can be and are being evaluated internally and by external observers.

Getting the numbers for the traditional bottom line—the balance sheet, income statement, and cash flow analyses of financial reporting—requires a good deal of judgment. Still, such reporting is a well-established and well-accepted practice in industrialized nations. Because there is a common currency—money—in which to assess the traditional bottom line, accountants and financiers have devised standardized auditing practices and common reporting systems that help accountants and financiers sort out the financial health of a firm. These accounting and finance measures track the traditional bottom line and all U.S.-based public companies (and those in many other nations) are required to report their financial results annually.

Such a "currency" is not as readily available for measuring a company's citizenship or stakeholder relations—that is, its multiple bottom-line activities. Hence many people assume that such measurement is impossible. But it can be and is being done every day in a variety of ways that are increasingly visible and important. It would be a tremendous mistake to think that, over the long term, a company's treatment of its primary stakeholders and its citizenship will go unnoticed, either in terms of its overall reputational impact or its effect on productivity.

FORMS OF SOCIAL INVESTMENT

External assessment of company citizenship in stakeholder arenas occurs in a number of different ways and is drawing increasing public attention. Much of this attention has focused on "social investment," which itself consists of multiple kinds of investment. Most social investment has some emphasis or purpose related either to (1) improving society or community or (2) putting pressure on companies to change various corporate practices so that specific stakeholders are treated better.

203

CHAPTER 8
Measuring Multiple
Bottom Lines:
Getting to
Value Added

One type of social investment includes social screens that have been created and implemented by investors or social research firms to be used by social investors to enhance and focus their investment decisions on companies. Related to the screens is the shareholder activism directed toward certain corporate practices through shareholder resolutions submitted for vote by corporate boards and shareholders. A third approach is actual social investment in socially desirable activities such as affordable housing or economic development of disadvantaged areas. The fourth approach is to provide venture capital to small capitalization firms or microenterprises, particularly in disadvantaged areas or to disadvantaged groups, to help them build their own economic base.

A second type of external assessment relates to the numerous and varied rankings now undertaken by researchers along a variety of dimensions of interest to different stakeholders and published in the popular and business press. A third way company performance is being evaluated externally occurs when external (typically, though not always, secondary) stakeholders use information about corporate activities released by various governmental or activists to put pressure on companies to change their practices. External stakeholders such as governments provide this information so that others (e.g., communities), can use it in the hope of influencing company behavior in socially constructive ways. By providing public information on various corporate practices (e.g., pollution), some agencies and researchers provide an opportunity for interested parties to "call" the company on activities that may cause social harm.

The wide scope of the electronic and broadcast media makes all sorts of corporate information increasingly available to all and, not by chance, brings continued public attention to both pro- and countersocial corporate activities. No company today can afford to ignore the fact that not only is this information available, but it can and will be used for investment purposes, to influence corporate activities, and in public policy making by governments and societies affected by corporate practices. Below we will investigate each of these forms of evaluation.

Social Screens/Social Investing

In recent years the movement variously called social, ethical, or values-based investing has begun to come of age. Started long ago by religious investors, the movement led by investor activists had focused attention by the mid-1980s on companies operating in South Africa under the now-disbanded apartheid system, which subjugated blacks to white dominance.[2] Investor protests caused some companies to disinvest from South Africa. Investors interested in this and other important political and social issues called upon large pension funds, universities, and other major institutional investors to pay attention to the ways in which they were investing their money.

By the mid- and late-1980s social screening was being done on companies' investment or presence in South Africa (and later in Myanmar and other countries with authoritarian regimes where human rights abuses are rampant) using what we can call *issue screens*. Issue screens now include numerous issues of concern to certain investors. For example, negative screens focus on corporate involvement with certain products or services, such as tobacco, alcohol, gaming, pornography, and military contracting, as well as involvement in nuclear power, child labor practices, and animal testing. *Negative screens,* which are generally issues-based, tend to focus on issues that certain investors actively wish to avoid because they pose what those investors perceive to be unacceptable and "incalculable risks" to certain stakeholder groups or to society in general.[3]

By the early 1990s, as investor interest in a range of corporate practices had grown, so had social screening for investment purposes. Several investment houses, led by Franklin Research and Development (now Trillium), Calvert Funds, and the Domini Fund, developed and expanded rating systems to encompass specific stakeholder arenas in addition to the issues screens. One U.S. firm, Kinder, Lydenberg, Domini, (KLD), formed a system for the explicit purpose of rating all of the Standard and Poors 500 largest companies annually along eight (later ten) dimensions of social performance and selling that information to interested investors and Wall Street financial houses. KLD also constructed an index, the Domini Index, consisting of equities that have "passed" KLD's screens (adding some smaller capitalization firms beyond the S&P 500 to balance the portfolio (see http://www. kld.com/). The Domini Index can be tracked in the same way that other indexes, such as the Dow Jones Industrial Average, are tracked.[4]

Spurred in part by pressures from social investors and the publication of the Council on Economic Priorities' *Rating America's Conscience,* which later became the *Shopping for a Better World* list of companies for consumers,[5] systematic rating of corporate performance along these "softer" stakeholder lines evolved quickly in the late 1980s. *Stakeholder screens,* which are positive and negative in their assessment of corporate practices (rather than only negative as the issue screens are), tend to focus on the types of risks associated with stakeholders. By the mid-1990s, new screens related to specific stakeholders had been developed with both negative and positive or constructive elements. Thus, for example, screens were developed for employee relations, community relations, diversity (or specific minority groups), product, environment, and related stakeholder arenas.

Stakeholder screens also provide for companies to be rewarded for proactive and progressive behaviors that can be viewed as strengths. The Council on Economic Priorities (CEP) also continued to develop its rating system (see the website http://www.cepnyc.org/), as did CoopAmerica, which rates the growing number of socially responsible mutual funds (see http://www.coopamerica.org/mfsc.htm). Other screens, used by managers of social choice funds, which tend to be for the sole use of investors in those funds, are built around similar ideas (e.g., Trillum Asset Management at http://www.frdc.com/pages/about/about_frame.html or Calvert Group Mutual Funds at http://www.calvertgroup.com/index4.stm).

The Triple Bottom Line

Many social investors are beginning to emphasize the "triple bottom line" in their investments and numerous companies are also starting to follow triple bottom line practices. The *triple bottom line* typically encompasses some combination of profitability, societal concerns, and ecological sustainability. This framing of the issue of long-term sustainability based on a more complex and holistic assessment of or-

205

CHAPTER 8
Measuring Multiple
Bottom Lines:
Getting to
Value Added

ganizational performance than that found in traditional financial assessment can be accomplished, as will be seen below, through social auditing practices and is regularly addressed by social investors.

Examples of enterprises following the triple bottom line are growing in number. For example, Trillium Asset Management (formerly Franklin Research and Development, see http://www.trilliuminvest.com/), one of the pioneers of social investment, focuses on the triple bottom line of ecology, equity, and economy. In Great Britain the organizational think tank called SustainAbility (see http:// www.sustain-ability.co.uk/sustainability.htm) emphasizes society, economy, and environment using a framing similar to that of Trillum. Another British organization called AccountAbility is pioneering certification standards and educational programs that will train auditors in these emerging techniques (see http://www.accountability. org.uk/).

It is important to note in terms of the spheres-of-influence framework around which this book is built that the triple bottom line encompasses the economic and civil society spheres, along with the ecological surround. As we have noted earlier, however, balancing human civilization also requires appropriate note of the values of power inherent in the political sphere. But, since these are not in direct control of business enterprises, they are typically not included in the triple bottom line measures.

The Screening Process

Various raters approach social ratings differently in terms of the specific things being measured. Most, however attempt to assess company performance systematically from year to year. The first task is to select the categories that will be rated. Typical categories are those used by KLD, where negative ratings are performed on issues that include involvement in alcohol, tobacco, gambling, military contracting, and nuclear power production. Positive and negative ratings or stakeholder screens are performed on a range of stakeholder categories. These categories include environment, community relations (philanthropy and volunteerism), diversity (women and minority groups), employee relations, product issues, non-U.S. operations, and an "other" category (which includes issues of CEO compensation, governance, and other issues that do not fit neatly into currently covered categories). KLD researches about 650 companies systematically each year. Less systematically, its research encompasses as many as 3,500 companies globally.

The Council on Economic Priorities has developed a similar rating system and issues a report called *Shopping for a Better World* to help consumers make purchases with social concerns kept in mind. CEP issues a "corporate report card" and gives annual awards, based on ratings in eight categories, each of which is given a letter grade similar to that used in universities: environment, women's advancement, minority advancement, charitable giving, community outreach, family benefits, workplace issues, and social disclosure. Financial performance, which is a measure of the way the owner stakeholder is treated, is of course available from multiple financial sources.

To cope with the issue of "softness," social researchers, including the social investment houses that have developed internal screening systems similar to the ones described above, try to use consistent and objective criteria that can be rigorously applied from year to year and compared from company to company. Such ratings, of course, are far from a perfect science. For the sake of an example, KLD's screening criteria and the reason codes for assigning a rating are listed for the stakeholder categories in Table 8.1. KLD rates companies overall from major concern to concern to neutral to strength to major strength for the stakeholder screens). A sample screening can be found at KLD's website (http://www.kld.com, click on "Socrates" and then "Sample").

Obviously, gathering all of this information annually, which is done from a range of publicly available data sources as well as company information, is a massive task. It is clear, however, that once researchers have gathered and made this information available to interested parties, it can readily be used by investors and other interested groups. Interested parties use such data to assess company practices in ways that go far beyond the traditional bottom line. Indeed, data like these begin to provide consistent means of evaluating and comparing companies on a range of practices and policies. Notably, such multiple bottom-line evaluation is taking place annually on many large companies, whether or not the companies themselves are undertaking social audits.

What is immediately obvious about Table 8.1 is the extent to which social researchers like KLD have tried to provide objective and bottom line oriented measures to assess practices within each of the categories. Thus, concerns tend to include fines paid for misbehavior, significant controversies reported in the press, notable positive or negative relationships with stakeholder interest groups, and similar assessments. Strengths tend to revolve around progressive policies that support the stakeholder group of interest in a variety of ways.

In addition to the Council on Economic Priorities and KLD, other corporate watchdogs that regularly assess corporate performance across multiple measures include the Ethical Investment Research Service, Trillium Asset Management, the Interfaith Center on Corporate Responsibility (ICCR), and the Investor Responsibility Research Center.[6] Such watchdogs pay close attention to the ways that companies treat stakeholders on an ongoing basis and their assessments influence investors interested in such treatment.

Issue and stakeholder screens, as must be clear, evaluate the performance of companies' along multiple bottom lines to enable investment managers to inform their investors about the performance of companies in these arenas. Since investment managers need to "screen in" companies with positive performance along dimensions in which investors are interested and "screen out" those companies with negative characteristics or performance, they tend to evaluate the full range of companies available in industries, size categories, market capitalization, or businesses of interest. As a result of investor interest these days, public companies in the United States and, increasingly, abroad find this type of scrutiny impossible to avoid as investment houses undertake this research on the range of available investment options for their clients. The box on page 210 discusses one company's efforts to reconcile its strict standards with the labor and human rights violations perpetrated by its suppliers abroad.

TABLE 8.1. Kinder, Lydenberg, Domini's Screening Criteria and Reason Codes in Stakeholder Arenas

Category: Community	
Areas of Concern	**Areas of Strength**
The company has paid fines, civil penalties, or is involved in major litigation relating to community.	The company has consistently given over 1.5% of pretax earnings to charity or otherwise demonstrated generous giving.
The company's relations with the community are strained due to plant closings or other breaches of agreements.	The company is known for innovative giving (e.g., support of self-sufficiency among the economically disadvantaged).
The company is a financial institution with community investment controversies.	The company is a prominent participant in public/private partnerships which support housing initiatives. The company supports education through long-term commitments to primary or secondary education.

Category: Diversity	
Areas of Concern	**Areas of Strength**
The company has paid substantial fines or civil penalties or been involved in major controversies relating to its affirmative action record.	The company's CEO is a woman or member or minority group.
The company has no women on the board of directors or among senior line managers.	The company has made notable progress in promotion of women and minorities. Women, minorities, and the physically challenged hold four seats on the board directors, or one-third of board seats if the board numbers less than 12. The company has outstanding employee benefits programs or programs addressing work/family concerns (e.g., child care, elder care, flextime). The company has a strong and consistent record of purchasing from or investing in women- and minority-owned businesses. The company has taken innovative hiring initiatives or other human resource programs directed at employment of the disabled. The company has adopted notably progressive policies toward gay, lesbian, and bisexual employees.

TABLE 8.1. continued

Category: Employee Relations

Areas of Concern	Areas of Strength
The company has poor union relations relative to others in the industry.	The company has strong union relations relative to others in its industry.
The company has recently paid significant fines or civil penalties over employee safety or been involved in major safety controversies.	The company has maintained a long-term policy of companywide cash profit sharing.
The company has had recent layoffs of more than 15% of its employees in one year or 25% in two years.	The company has a substantial sense of worker involvement/ownership through gainsharing, employee stock ownership, sharing of financial information with employees, or employee participation in management decision making.
The company has a substantially underfunded pension plan or an inadequate benefits plan.	The company offers its employees strong retirement benefits or other innovative or generous benefits relative to the industry.

Category: Environment

Areas of Concern	Areas of Strength
The company's liabilities for hazardous waste sites exceed $30 million or the company has significant involvement in more than 30 Federal Superfund sites.	The company derives substantial revenues from remediation products, services used in cleaning up the environment, or products that promote the efficient use of energy. Or it has developed innovative products with environmental benefits.
The company has recently paid significant fines or civil penalties, has a pattern of regulatory problems, or has been involved in major controversies involving environmental degradation.	The firm has made companywide changes in production processes to achieve reduced emission through elimination of toxic chemicals.
The company is among the top producers or legal emitters of chloroflurocarbons, hydrochloroflurocarbons, methyl chloroform, or other ozone-depleting chemicals.	The company is a substantial user of recycled materials as inputs in its manufacturing process, or is a major factor in the recycling industry.
The company's emissions of toxic chemicals are among the highest legal levels in the United States, or its emissions play a substantial role in the formation of acid rain.	The company derives substantial revenues from developing, using, or marketing fuels with environmental advantages, is a major factor in the cogeneration market, or has undertaken notable energy conservation projects.
The company is a substantial producer of agricultural chemicals.	The company's environmentally sensitive property, plant, and equipment is among the newest in the industry.

208

TABLE 8.1.   continued

Category: Product

Areas of Concern	Areas of Strength
The company faces major product safety controversies, product liability suits, or regulatory actions related to its products or services.	The company has a long-standing companywide quality program judged to be among the best in the industry.
The company faces a major marketing controversy, or has paid fines or civil penalties related to advertising practices, consumer fraud, or government contracting practices.	The company is a leader in its industry in R&D, evidenced by expenditures as a percentage of sales, effective new product development, or unusual inventiveness.
The company has paid fines or civil penalties relating to antitrust laws, including price-fixing, collusion, and predatory pricing.	The company's products or services particularly benefit the economically disadvantaged.

Source: Kinder, Lydenberg, Domini, 1998©.

Social Investing in Projects and Ventures

Another form of social investing occurs when investors desire to invest their assets in projects explicitly aimed at benefiting society or some disadvantaged groups in society. There are several emerging types of social investment projects: investments in projects to economically, academically, or socially develop otherwise disadvantaged communities or groups; using philanthropy strategically given to nonprofit and public agencies to meet the dual bottom line of social benefit and business gain; and using venture capital affirmatively to fund small or even "micro" businesses operating in disadvantaged areas or run by disadvantaged groups and individuals.

Social Investment Projects

For social reasons, investors sometimes wish to invest their assets in socially beneficial projects such as hotels or businesses that can help rebuild an economic base in disadvantaged communities. Some investors expect market returns from these investments, while others are more concerned with "making a difference" in society and therefore are willing to accept less than market rates of return. Some investment houses such as Calvert focus on issues such as affordable housing, microenterprise (see below), and community development (see http://www.calvertgroup. com/foundation/). Calvert has developed funds with the explicit goal of making such investments. In these funds, investors can sometimes choose the rate of return (less than market) that they desire. Their investment is then used to fund, for example, economic development activities in inner cities, such as a new hotel complex that has been constructed in Harlem in New York City.

Wal-Mart's Global Sourcing: The Search for Standards

As if doing business globally and dealing with communities that resent the negative impact on local retailers of the huge retail chain with all of its scale economies weren't difficult enough, Wal-Mart, the world's largest retailer, faces significant criticism from labor and human rights activists on its sourcing practices. To prove the difficulty of implementing self-monitoring and auditing of suppliers located in far-flung locations such as China, Wal-Mart faced damaging new allegations by the National Labor Committee (NLC) in a report issued in May 2000. The NLC is the same organization that exposed the company's labor violations with respect to products that carried Kathie Lee Gifford's name in Central America in 1997. The real issue highlighted by the NLC report, in some respects, is the difficulty that auditors face in uncovering even dramatic worker exploitation and mistreatment.

Indeed, it was the Kathie Lee Gifford fiasco in 1997 and all of the ensuing negative publicity that pushed Wal-Mart to implement stringent accountability standards and an extensive self-policing supplier auditing system in the first place. To monitor suppliers, Wal-Mart hired PricewaterhouseCoopers LLP and Cal Safety Compliance Corporation to inspect and audit its overseas suppliers. But the auditors themselves had a tough time figuring out that severe abuses were going on. It was not until *BusinessWeek* released the results of an intensive three-month investigation of a factory in China that significant ongoing abuses at the Chun Si Enterprise Handbag Factory in Zhongshan, a city in the Guangdong Province of southern China, were publicly exposed.

Workers, desperate for jobs and eager to take advantage of the living quarters supplied by the company, sign on at companies like Chun Si Enterprise despite rumors of long working hours and beatings by management. As *BusinessWeek* reported, the reality was even worse than the rumors. Not only did the company house workers in crowded dormitories, but it also charged workers $15 of the $22 they earned each month for food and took away their personal identification cards, issuing in their place expired cards. The latter action made the employees virtual prisoners, since only the local police knew of this practice. Further, workers were virtually kept in a prison, locked in a walled factory compound all day except for 60 minutes for meals. If they took too long in the bathroom, they were fined another $1 of the $22 earned weekly. One worker who joined about 60 other workers in a protest of working conditions in the local labor office had earned only $6 after three months of 90-hour weeks.

Even worse, the company had established a "front" to try to convince Wal-Mart's auditors that it was in compliance with the company's relatively stringent standards. Since 1997 Wal-Mart and numerous other U.S. companies have been trying to reassure customers that they have policies in place that prevent sweatshop conditions in their suppliers. For example, Wal-Mart has a code of basic labor standards that it has required all suppliers to sign since 1992 and the company has been hiring its own external auditors, such as PWC, since mid-1992 to ensure compliance with the standard by suppliers. *BusinessWeek*'s coverage of the abuses makes clear just how much attention companies today need to pay to their suppliers' practices if they are to avoid taking the "hit" of negative publicity to which customers are increasingly paying attention.

Assuring that suppliers live up to emerging global standards on labor is extremely difficult. To date, no one, not even the most progressive companies or even those who, like Wal-Mart, have been subject to intense activism and public scrutiny, can be completely assured of compliance. One response by companies like Nike, Inc., and Reebock International, Ltd., which have been perhaps the most intensely scrutinized companies of all, formed the Fair Labor Association (FLA) in 1998. The FLA now has about a dozen members and is setting up an independent monitoring system that includes labor and human rights activists, not just business people. Wal-Mart, however, refuses to join in the belief that it would have to share important proprietary information. Many critics argue that only through *independent* assessment that includes activists will such abuses finally be stopped.

Source: Dexter Roberts and Aaron Bernstein, "A Life of Fines and Beating," *BusinessWeek,* October 2, 2000, pp. 122–28; see also: http://www.nlcnet.org/.

211

CHAPTER 8
Measuring Multiple
Bottom Lines:
Getting to
Value Added

Additionally, lending institutions, particularly banks, in the United States are subject to the requirements of the Community Reinvestment Act (CRA) of 1977.[7] The CRA requires banks that benefit from and are subject to the regulatory oversight of the Federal Deposit Insurance Corporation (FDIC) to prove that they are acting to meet the credit needs of the entire community within their service areas.

The "entire service area" includes low- and moderate-income neighborhoods, particularly those in the inner city and rural areas that have been historically underserved by financial institutions. Many of these areas have been subject to "redlining" by banks in the past, a practice involving drawing (figuratively or literally) red lines on municipal maps to indicate where loans are discouraged or not made. The CRA was intended to stop this practice, opening up those neighborhoods to loans, credit, and other banking services that are readily accessible in more advantaged areas.

To ensure that banks meet their CRA obligations and invest in their communities appropriately, the FDIC rates banks' CRA performance on a scale from outstanding to substantial noncompliance. As with other data assessing corporate performance on significant stakeholder dimensions, CRA ratings are published by the government (see http://www2.fdic.gov/dcacra/cra_data.cfm, where you can search by individual financial institutions). This information, then, is part of the information that becomes available to activists, community members, and other parties interested in institutional performance.

To deal with the CRA, many U.S. banks have created community development banks to work locally with communities. For example, BankBoston (which has merged with Fleet Bank to become FleetBoston, New England's largest bank) created First Community Bank as a "bank within a bank." As with other community banks, the purpose of First Community Bank was to meet the financial needs of individuals and small businesses within the urban neighborhoods served by BankBoston. The community bank actively focuses its efforts on meeting the needs of minority- and women-owned enterprises, individuals, commercial real estate developers, and public/private partnerships focusing on economic development.

First Community Bank, like many similar community banks, discovered to its surprise that it could be quite successful, albeit the returns on its investment are somewhat reduced, by working closely with community-based organizations to tap the assets that they bring to enterprises and economic development. These community development activities of banks, initially established to meet CRA requirements, have proved useful mechanisms for building up the local community, and establishing new connections—new social capital—among different types of people and organizations within urban areas.[8]

Advantages of Disadvantaged Areas

Some people have come to believe in recent years that there can be great competitive advantage to investments in disadvantaged areas when an asset- and resource-based approach, rather than a deficit-based approach is used. Among these individuals are Jesse Jackson who started the Wall Street Project to end what he called the "multibillion dollar trade deficit" between corporations and minority vendors and consumers.[9] Jackson, a noted community and spiritual leader, mobilized minority

TABLE 8.2. Porter's Competitive Advantages of the Inner City

Strategic location
Local market demand
Integration with regional clusters
Human resources

consumers in the nation's 50 largest cities. Tactics involve informing these consumers about how minorities are treated by specific large corporations and organizing boycotts and other forms of activism. Publication of this information is meant to push companies toward equitable treatment of minorities when they fail to respond.

Another of the many creative initiatives was that undertaken by Harvard Business School professor Michael Porter through the Initiative for a Competitive Inner City (ICIC). Like the recent efforts of Jackson and others to view disadvantaged areas in a new light, Porter took an asset-based perspective on economic development of disadvantaged areas. ICIC is based on Porter's ideas about how cities can gain competitive advantage.[10] Porter recognized that a systemic approach to rebuilding deteriorated inner cities was necessary and that social and community health depends on access to jobs that pay a living wage—that is, a solid economic strategy. Using an asset-based approach to understanding the inner city, Porter developed a framework to determine what the competitive advantages of the inner city might be.

In his article, "The Competitive Advantage of the Inner City," Porter identified four main competitive advantages of the inner city, which displaced the mistaken common wisdom that the only advantages were low-cost real estate and lower labor costs (see Table 8.2). These advantages are strategic location in the downtown area (and, as it turns out, access to highways), local market demand, integration with regional clusters within and surrounding the city, and human resources. Competitive clusters, according to Porter, create advantages in terms of new business formation, particularly for business-to-business opportunities, and access to downstream products and services in local markets.

Both the Wall Street Project and the Initiative for a Competitive Inner City projects are focused particularly on inner cities within the United States; however, the asset-based perspective is applicable to any disadvantaged or less developed area, as Porter's framework suggests. These and similar projects illustrate the both/and logic of operating with an asset-based approach to community and economic development. They also suggest interesting new approaches that businesses and investors interested in making a positive difference in their communities can take.

The results indicate that Porter's theories have some validity. For example, research by the Initiative for a Competitive Inner City found that inner cities have many relatively untapped assets, including approximately eight million households, which represent about $85 billion in retail spending (or 7 percent of total retail spending) annually. Porter's work also found that there is significant unmet demand

213

CHAPTER 8
Measuring Multiple
Bottom Lines:
Getting to
Value Added

in inner cities, or about 25 percent of retail demand that either goes unfilled or is fulfilled elsewhere. Further, there is a large pool of talent available in inner cities to meet the increasing—and structural—need for employees that many businesses face. Interestingly, there is some evidence to suggest that inner-city residents spend more in absolute dollars on apparel than does the average U.S. household.

Couple these findings with the fact that some mainstream businesses that have already made investments in the inner city have succeeded beyond their dreams. For example, ICIC finds that the average inner-city grocery store in New York outperforms the regional average by 39 percent, and that business-to-business services are outpacing their regional counterparts in San Francisco. Additionally, the workforce in the inner city of Kansas City is reported to have lower than average turnover with 80 percent rated good to excellent.[11]

Through this research, Porter and his colleagues have demonstrated that there may indeed be competitive advantages—business opportunities—in troubled inner cities and that making "social" investments can simply be good business.[12] Indeed, ICIC started a new corporate ranking in 1999 called the Inner City 100, published in *Inc.* magazine, to highlight the fastest-growing and most successful enterprises in America's inner cities.

Social Venturing through Microenterprise

Globally, about three billion people live on less than $2 per day. Some remarkable new efforts to invest in disadvantaged areas in the United States are now being applied in less developed countries and rural areas for economic development. Done well, this form of development does not strip countries of their autonomy nor people of their traditional sources of livelihood, but instead allows them to improve their chances in life by using resources readily at their disposal: their own talents and energies, and local needs and interests.

Attempts to improve the lives of people living in such dire poverty historically have been done through grants, technical assistance, and other forms of philanthropy meant to help pull people, group by group, out of poverty. Poor people were typically viewed as having deficits that needed to be overcome through the help and assets that wealthier people could provide. Traditional approaches to poverty, including much corporate philanthropy and foundation giving, assumed that money needed to be given to help poor people because they could not help themselves. The problem with this approach is that only a few people can be helped through charitable donations; the problems of poverty are much more widespread and systemic globally.

In recent years, both in the United States and around the world, a different model—an asset-based model—has begun to take shape. This perspective assumes not that poor people have deficits and are in need of "fixing," but that they have many assets and strengths, and, given the right opportunities, will find a way to become more advantaged through their own resources. A similar philosophy to that now being used by social venture capitalists investing in U.S. inner cities, such as the ICIC and Wall Street Project initiatives described above, has emerged. This asset-based view of poor people says that given some resources, many poor people will be able to start, manage, and develop small businesses that will enable them to build better lives for themselves and their children. One key to making this approach work is the growing field of microenterprise development.

One individual credited with pioneering the microenterprise strategy is Mohammad Yunas, founder of the Grameen Bank in Bangladesh.[13] Recognizing that individuals, particularly women, living in dire poverty found it difficult to get even the minimal amount of capital needed to begin small businesses that could support them and their families, Yunas created a system in which small loans (usually well under US$1,000) could be granted to entrepreneurs through his bank. Each person then becomes accountable for paying back the loan to a peer group of other (about five or six) microentrepreneurs living in the same village. A bank employee meets with each group once a week to ensure that loans are on track toward repayment and that things are going well for the entrepreneurs, who still struggle with daily existence.

Grameen Bank's system (and other microenterprise systems) uses peer pressure and the social capital generated through weekly meetings of people who interact with each other regularly to create a system in which failure to repay the loan breaks trust with others. By creating a trust-based system, Grameen reversed traditional banking practice—and costs—and built in automatic accountability to known others. By tapping the individual energies of borrowers and their strengths, this grassroots-based initiative taps an emergent form of creative energy to generate both social and financial capital within very poor villages. Most borrowers have little or no collateral, except that they are known and respected by others within their village, who form with them a lending unit.

Today, Grameen Bank has more than 2.3 million borrowers, of whom 94 percent are women, because Yunas believes that women will use the fruits of their entrepreneurship to feed, clothe, and shelter their families more directly than men. The Bank's services cover some 38,950 villages in Bangladesh and the historical loan repayment rate, for loans averaging about $160, is more than 95 percent. To complement its microlending, Grameen has also started numerous other types of businesses as a means of building not only healthy communities, but also bigger enterprises that can at some point begin to operate in the world economy. For example, Grameen Uddog/Handloom represents an effort to revive the weaving industry in Bangladesh, while Grameen Krishi/Agriculture Foundation has a goal of building tube wells that provide safe drinking water. Other larger-scale initiatives involve fisheries, communications, and energy production.[14]

In the United States and Latin America, an organization called Accion International also has done pioneering work in providing microloans to entrepreneurs. With some loans as small as $75, Accion International helps U.S. entrepreneurs get off welfare, rebuild their communities through business activities, and create new jobs in places that large corporations have abandoned.[15] Using a similar peer-network system to use local social capital to ensure repayments and site visits to replace traditional bank paperwork (and reduce costs to make the loans feasible), Accion now serves as an umbrella organization for lending activities in eight U.S. cities and 13 Latin American countries.

215

CHAPTER 8
Measuring Multiple
Bottom Lines:
Getting to
Value Added

As with Grameen Bank, Accion and other microlenders' goal is to eradicate poverty by creating sustainable business enterprises at the microlevel and eventually more macrolevel. Accion's loans are intended to cover their own costs and return enough money through interest paid on the loans to help finance the cost of lending to the next borrower. Accion's average loan in the United States in 1997 was a little under $3,000, while in Latin America, where the cost of living is significantly less, loans averaged about $809. Accion had about 1,000 loans in the United States, compared with more than 340,000 in Latin America, and about 61 percent of its clients are women.[16] In its more than 25 years of history, Accion's historic loss rate is slightly over 2 percent.

The payback rates associated with both Grameen and Accion's microloans, and the general history of microloans using similar techniques, create revolving funds that can be used for additional loans once they are repaid, thereby fostering additional entrepreneurship among disadvantaged people. By emphasizing repayment of its loans and building in sustainability, Accion, for example, has been able to increase its loans from serving 3,051 people in 1988 to 340,000 in 1997. The use of social capital for Accion, as with Grameen Bank, has proved successful: Some 98 percent of loans are repaid, a rate that any traditional lending institution would envy.

Both Grameen and Accion, along with numerous other microenterprise lenders that have sprung up to attempt to cope with global poverty, assume their clients have numerous assets on which they will build their enterprises. For example, Grameen bases its loans on three C's of credit: character (integrity and past history of the borrower), capacity (debt capacity, income stream, and repayment history), and capital (current assets of the borrower as a form of collateral). Microenterprise activities have been so successful globally that in 1997 the United Nations issued a resolution promoting the use of microlending on a global scale.[17] Indeed, the activities of both Grameen and Accion have helped to spawn an industry of microlenders who believe that helping people to help themselves is a far better way for countries and individuals to pursue economic development than simply giving a helping handout.[18] And it can also be a profitable way to invest socially.

Social Venture Capital

Another type of social investment is providing venture capital to firms or individuals working to improve the lot of the disadvantaged through community and economic development enterprises. Businesses that can use this *social venture capital* are significantly larger than those that need microlending, usually requiring amounts over (and sometimes significantly over) $100,000. Sometimes social venture capital takes the form of loans for working capital, equipment purchases, debt refinancing, business acquisition, expansion, or credit lines, as do those of one of the pioneers of this type of lending, Chicago's South Shore Bank.[19] In other situations, social venture capital is supplied in return for an ownership interest in the firm, just as traditional venture capitalists expect.

The Initiative for a Competitive Inner City, for example, has formed a venture capital fund called American Securities, capitalized at over $1 billion. The specific purpose of American Securities, as a social venture capital fund, is to invest in companies operating in the inner cities of the United States at market rates of return. These investments provide capital for inner-city entrepreneurs, many of whom are people of color, to start and run new businesses. Social venture used wisely taps into the competitive strengths of the inner city that were identified in Porter's research, and provides significant potential for the development of much-needed employment opportunities in the inner city.

Social venture capitalists tend generally to focus either on underserved populations, otherwise unmet social needs, and ventures that attempt to improve the natural environment. They tend to use the same criteria regarding management strength, product or service concept, market opportunity, and expected financial return as traditional venture capitalists (though some are willing to accept less than market rates of return). In addition, however, they tend, as the Calvert Social Investment Fund does, to ask additional questions of the entrepreneur. Such questions might focus on whether the project meets an unmet social or ecological need, what the impact of the project on future generations is likely to be, and whether the project's results are likely to have a positive impact on society.[20]

For example, Calvert invested in a company called Earth's Best, which produces organic baby food so that concerned parents can avoid exposing their infants to pesticides found in traditionally grown foods. The fund purchased preferred stock at $3.33 per share. When the company had grown to $24 million in sales and established itself as a niche player in the baby-food industry, it accepted an acquisition offer from H. J. Heinz Company, in which the acquirer agreed to preserve the mission of Earth's Best as it mainstreams the product. The stock price at acquisition was $7.50 per share, providing a comfortable return to the venture capitalist and long-term sustainability for the company's mission and product.[21]

Corporate Social Investment and Strategic Philanthropy

Another type of social project investing occurs in *corporate social investing,* which is the dedication of corporate philanthropic donations to helping nonprofit and public institutions improve as a result of the investments made.[22] Companies using this approach seek at least dual bottom line benefits from their investments. This means that they hope to benefit their businesses in some way by what is frequently called "strategic philanthropy" and they hope to obtain a social benefit as well. Business benefits can accrue, for example, from having better-educated workers when a company devotes significant charitable resources to local schools.

Corporate social investing is related to *strategic philanthropy,* in which managers take a strategic approach to corporate contributions programs, hoping to see some benefit to their businesses over time. Corporate social investing allows companies to take credit for contributions that go beyond donations (e.g., volunteer programs, memberships and sponsorships for which no specific benefits are received back, and cause-related marketing). Because many companies are under considerable financial pressure to produce results, strategic use of philanthropic monies can benefit the company with respect to its community stakeholder, while also showing the owner-stakeholders what types of benefits are sought in making the contributions. When

217

CHAPTER 8
Measuring Multiple
Bottom Lines:
Getting to
Value Added

companies undertake this type of social investment program, they are encouraged to report on all of their social investments, not just financial contributions alone.

SHAREHOLDER ACTIVISM AND CORPORATE GOVERNANCE

Many people in the social investment community view shareholder activism as another from of social investment; hence it will be discussed here, in part because leading corporate citizens need to be aware of the impact of such activism on their decisions, and in part because activists are watching their citizenship practices. Managers can hardly make decisions in a vacuum when shareholders are affected— or when they wish to exert influence, as in the past 20 years they have found new ways of having their voices heard.

Shareholders—owners—are supposed to be the stakeholder to whom corporate managers pay the most attention according to the logic of the neoclassical economic model, which dominates the financial community in the United States and is gaining increased attention in Europe and Asia. Yet even within this logic, some shareholders have found it difficult to have a "voice" in corporate affairs, in part because most large companies have millions of shares held by numerous investors for whom day-to-day corporate practice is distantly removed. As a result, management dominates corporate decision making, leaving some shareholders wanting more influence. The issue of corporate governance, how well companies' boards of directors represent stockholder and other stakeholder interests, especially around financial performance, is therefore a major concern of activist shareholders.

Shareholder activists tend to operate through the votes that are accorded to them by means of their ownership interest in the firm, typically by submitting shareholder resolutions for shareholders to vote upon during the annual meeting. Such tactics, while they infrequently pass, draw attention to concerns about possible corporate abuse of power, weak governance structures, and poor managerial decision making. In some cases, the resolutions attempt to counterweight corporate tendencies to economize (e.g., through excessive layoffs or to improve "efficiency" by paying top managers inflated salaries and benefits). In other cases, activists shareholders work on the tendency of companies to power-aggrandize by making acquisitions simply for the sake of growth when there is little strategic reason to do so. To cope with such tendencies, some investors have been determined to influence corporate practice directly through submitting and calling for discussion on shareholder resolutions at company annual meetings. In this process of shareholder activism, they also gather publicity for the issues of concern to them.

Obstacles to Good Corporate Governance

Shareholder activists have identified multiple obstacles to good corporate governance that need to be addressed to help companies bring vision and values into alignment with practice.[23]

DIRECTORS' INTERESTS. Among these are issues of whether *directors' interests* are properly aligned with the interest of long-term shareholder value. Obstacles to good governance include the way directors are compensated and whether board members have conflicts of interest. *Cultural issues* also pose barriers to good governance within the board, for instance, when directors are overly aligned with the CEO, whether they are truly active in corporate decision making and sufficiently informed to make good decisions, and whether they sufficiently recognize their shareholder and fiduciary responsibilities.

STRUCTURE OF BOARD OF DIRECTORS. A second set of obstacles to good governance has to do with the way that boards are structured internally. Structural issues include the process used to appoint board members, member status as insiders (that is, members of the management team) or outsiders, the composition of board committees and their operations, the performance criteria for evaluating the board and the CEO, and the degree of independence from management that board members have and actually exercise. Generally, independent and outside board members, who can view corporate activities more objectively than individuals closely tied to management interests, are considered to offer better governance. Cultural issues include the adequacy of information provided to board members, the directors' degree of involvement in strategic decisions, and their capacity to ask good questions of management without micromanaging the company.

SHAREHOLDER RIGHTS AND ACTIVISM. The third set of barriers to good governance concerns the extent to which shareholders are—and are readily permitted to be—interested in corporate activities, or conversely, the extent to which they are disenfranchised. Concerns arise when management institutes self-protective measures, such as golden parachutes or greenmail, to further entrench themselves and consolidate their own power without due consideration to the good of the corporation.[24] Other structural issues have to do with the voting procedures instituted for shareholders and the extent to which these procedures are fair and equitable. Cultural issues have to do with communication between the company and its shareholders, which fosters the level of involvement by owners in corporate affairs.

Principles of Good Corporate Governance

Overcoming the obstacles to good corporate governance means adherence to principles of good governance, which leading corporate citizens well recognize. Although institutional investors, the large money managers that control equity funds, have basic fiduciary or financial obligations to meet, some also have become active in pressuring the management of companies to change their practices to conform to shareholder expectations and to govern themselves according to certain principles. Among these activists institutional investors is the California Public Employees' Retirement System (CalPERS), which recently issued a set of "corporate governance core principles and guidelines" that it believes well-governed companies should follow (see http://www.calpers-governance.org/).[25]

219

CHAPTER 8
Measuring Multiple
Bottom Lines:
Getting to
Value Added

TABLE 8.3. Global Principles of Good Governance

Accountability
Transparency
Equity
Voting methods
Codes of best practices
Long-term vision

Source: CalPERS, see http://www.calpers-governance.org/.

CalPERS' principles are based on six global principles that this influential pension fund believes are important to better overall corporate governance and ultimately company management. The first global principle is *accountability;* that is, companies need to assume responsibility for the impacts of their practices, policies, and processes and the decisions that stand behind those practices. Second is *transparency,* which means allowing corporate actions and decisions to be visible to interested stakeholders. Third is *equity,* which means fairness in the allocation and distribution of company resources to relevant stakeholders. Fourth is *voting methods,* which need to be open and accessible to all shareholders. Fifth is company adoption and implementation of *codes of best practices,* including ethical and values-based codes. Sixth is *long-term vision* for companies, the importance of which has been discussed extensively in Chapter 4. This six principles are shown in Table 8.3.

To make boards of directors more accountable to shareholders, CalPERS has proposed the following recommendations:

- Independent directors should comprise a substantial majority of seats on a board.
- Unless the board is led by an independent chairperson, an independent lead director should be designated.
- No director may also serve as a consultant or service provider to the company; competing time commitments of directors should be specifically addressed by each company.
- A mix of director characteristics, experience, and diverse perspectives should be reflected on each board.
- The board should consider director tenure and take steps to maintain an openness to new ideas and a willingness to critically reexamine the status quo.[26]

Many large institutional investors and business associations have become involved in the effort to make boards of directors and their corporations more accountable for performance, as well as for social impacts. Investor associations include the Council of Institutional Investors and the National Association of Corporate Directors in the United States. Major business associations include the Business Roundtable. In addition to CalPERS, other large institutional investors are the Teachers Insurance and Annuity Association/College Retirement Equities Fund (TIAA-CREF) and religious activists, including the Interfaith Center on Corporate Responsibility. All have efforts to build in guiding principles for corporate governance.

Similar policies about good governance have been developed by the Council of Institutional Investors (see http://www.ciicentral.com/ciicentral/core_policies.htm) and TIAA-CREF (http://www.tiaa-cref.org:80/set-search.html). Internationally, a great deal of work has been done to develop similar codes and principles for governing multinational corporations and making them accountable to their important stakeholders. Countries as far ranging as Australia, Belgium, Canada, Germany, Hong Kong, India, Italy, Japan, the Netherlands, South Africa, Span, Sweden, the United Kingdom, and the United States have experienced various efforts to reform or improve governance practices within corporations. For example, the European Corporate Governance Network provides a website (see either see http://www.ecgn.ulb.ac.be/ecgn/codes.htm or http://www.ecgn.ulb.ac.be/ecgn/codes.htm) that attempts to link efforts to reform corporate governance globally.

Although details differ and there are some conflicting viewpoints among these documents, particularly internationally, all aim at helping boards of directors become more effective at governing their enterprises and in the end more economically productive and responsive to shareholder—and societal—interests.

For all stakeholders, meeting these obligations means living up to the types of standards found in the principles articulated above. As must be clear, the principles tend to have clear and fair election rules for directors, director independence from management, disclosure of sufficient information that shareholders and directors can use to make effective strategic decisions (transparency), and board committee structures that are independent of undue management influence.

The reason for focusing shareholder activism on issues of governance was perhaps best stated by the great US Supreme Court Justice Louis Brandeis:

> There is no such thing to my mind . . . as an innocent stockholder. He may be innocent in fact, but socially but he cannot be held innocent. He accepts the benefits of the system. It is his business and his obligation to see that those who represent him carry out a policy which is consistent with the public welfare.[27]

What Happens When Governance Is Questionable

Companies that fail to implement practices associated with good governance can find themselves in significant trouble, looking more like poor corporate citizens than leading ones. One example of such problems, reported in *Business Week* magazine, is a case of sexual harassment charges against the CEO at Compuware.[28] In many cases such charges tend to be a case of "he said, she said," so having appropriate practices in place to deal with them is critically important. In this instance, in what proved to be "an intensely awkward moment for the board," the charges were brought directly to the board of directors, having been investigated only through an internal and what appeared to be relatively subjective process.

What happened next suggests the problem of having a board of directors that is too closely connected to management. As *Business Week* reported:

> Compuware's 11-member board—which is weighted heavily with insiders, the politically connected, Detroit area figures, and others whose companies have done

221

*CHAPTER 8
Measuring Multiple
Bottom Lines:
Getting to
Value Added*

business with the company—began to consider the report. But discussion quickly moved on to [the accuser's] job performance. Within 90 minutes, the board reached a consensus to terminate [the accuser's] employment. . . . But by basing their decision to fire [the accuser] on an investigation of the CEO overseen by his subordinates—and moving beyond the report into a review of her performance—Compuware's directors appear to have erred badly. Indeed, by failing to take on responsibility for the investigation themselves, the board may have increased the company's vulnerability to lawsuits.[29]

Compuware found itself in trouble largely because the board, comprised of insiders connected to management rather than more objective outsiders, failed in terms of the structure of the board and the processes through which the situation was handled. The question of guilt or innocence of the CEO, while critically important, might have been better handled had the board been able to investigate the charges more objectively (i.e., if it were not so closely tied to management). The outcome was a huge black mark on Compuware's reputation which might have been avoided had the company been following better governance practice as outlined above. And, as we shall discuss below, reputation proves to be a critical component of leading corporate citizenship.

"BEST COMPANIES FOR . . ." CORPORATE RANKINGS

Having a good reputation is essential to leading corporate citizenship and is another of the many visible factors that is constantly under public scrutiny today. Regular rankings identify the "best corporations" for a whole range of behaviors, including one by *Business Ethics* magazine that identifies the top 100 corporate citizens, using the KLD ratings discussed above.[30] Bradley K. Googins, director of the Boston College Center for Corporate Citizenship, claimed that a corporation's citizenship reputation will be a determining factor in gaining competitive advantage in the future. Rankings that measure one or another aspect of that citizenship are increasingly common.

The business—and interest group—press regularly investigates corporate practices and behaviors with respect to particular stakeholders. Following the lead of *Fortune* magazine with its annual Fortune 500 ratings and reputational (or "most admired" companies) ratings, which have been given annually since 1983, numerous other publications now develop lists of companies that are the "best" or "worst" in various categories. These best companies lists rank or name companies that are, for example, the best to work for, best for blacks and Hispanics, most family friendly, best and worst governed, best corporate citizens, best companies for gay men and lesbians, or best for working women, to name only a few.

Reputation is essentially the assessment of a company or any other organization held by external stakeholders. Reputation includes several dimensions, including an organization's perceived capacity to meet those stakeholder expectations, the rational attachments that a stakeholder forms with an organization, and the overall "net image" that stakeholders have of the organization.[31]

Many companies aspire to be on *Fortune's* annual corporate reputation index and list because of the prestige associated with being listed. One interesting analysis of Fortune 500 companies undertaken by New York University researcher Charles Fombrun highlighted the number of times various companies appeared on the reputation list. Fombrun found that during the 16 years in which *Fortune* issued its rankings, one company, Merck, was ranked 14 times, while Coca Cola was ranked 12 times, and two companies, 3M and Rubbermaid, made the rankings a total of 11 times.[32] Other most frequently cited companies include Procter & Gamble (10 times), Johnson & Johnson (8), Boeing (7), Hewlett-Packard, Liz Claiborne, and Wal-Mart Stores (6 each), and IBM, Dow Jones, and J. P. Morgan (5 each).

In addition to *Fortune,* annual company ratings are beginning to appear in other countries, including "Asia's Most Admired Companies" in *Asian Business,* "Review 200" in The *Far Eastern Economic Review,* "Britain's Most Admired Companies" and "Europe's Most Respected Companies" in *Management Today* and *The Financial Times.* Obviously, as an increasing number of such rating systems emerge, companies will have to pay greater attention to their stakeholder-related practices because they will be coming under intense external scrutiny.

Other work on corporate reputation by Fombrun and the New Economics Foundation in England (see below) assessed corporate reputation and performance from the perspective of stakeholders themselves.[33] Using this methodology, Fombrun was able to attach a dollar amount to the value of reputation in relation to a company's stock price. Such measures, it is likely, will gain increasing public attention in the future, further enhancing the critical importance of reputation to companies not only for sustaining customer goodwill and continued purchases, but also for being granted a "license to operate" by communities and governments. Fombrun also suggested that a growing body of research links corporate reputation to financial performance, making the link between reputation and corporate citizenship increasingly clear.

RESPONSIBILITY AUDITS: INTERNAL ASSESSMENT

Leading corporate citizens do not wait for external observers and stakeholders to make assessments of the responsibility of their stakeholder-related practices. Instead, they undertake internal assessments, typically called social or responsibility audits, to ensure that their citizenship activities—that is, the way they treat their stakeholders—are consistently excellent.

Social or responsibility auditing is a technique that a company can use for internal assessment of its stakeholder and related corporate practices with the goal of improving its own performance. Today, responsibility audits are increasingly used to link vision and values and to assess the multiple bottom lines associated with primary and some secondary stakeholders. As triple bottom line accounting and full-cost accounting become more widely practiced and expected by external stakeholders, we can expect that increasing numbers of companies will not only undertake such assessments, but also report them publicly, much as they do now with financial

223

CHAPTER 8
Measuring Multiple
Bottom Lines:
Getting to
Value Added

reports. Companies that begin to undertake such assessments voluntarily and proactively will be well ahead of those that are more reactive in linking vision and values with the practices that add value.

Assessing Internal Practice: Responsibility/Social Audits

Social auditing involves assessing internal corporate practices and/or stakeholder perceptions of corporate practices to determine how well a company is living up to its vision and values. Although social auditing has a long history, dating back as long ago as the 1940s, it did not actually begin as a field until the late 1970s and not until the late 1990s did social or responsibility auditing begin to gather much corporate attention.[34] There are two basic types of social audits today, those that tap external stakeholder perceptions of corporate practices and internal audits of the actual practices themselves to determine their impact on relevant stakeholders, as well as overall corporate performance.

Both types of audits are typically undertaken for purposes of improving internal practice. Frequently, the results are used internally as a means of determining where improvements need to be made to enhance practice. Occasionally, the results of the audit are published by the company in a social report, such as those issued by The Body Shop and Tradecraft, both of which are British companies.[35] Particularly when a company is following an overtly "socially responsible" strategy, as these two companies are, it is important that they are accountable and transparent to stakeholders concerning how well they are actually doing with respect to their stated values.

Because responsibility audits look at a range of practices and not simply the traditional bottom line, they tend to be more holistic and systemic than financial audits. One type of responsibility audit, for example, assesses company practices in four areas: employee practices, community relations practices, environmental practices, and quality practices. Practices in these arenas are then compared to the stated mission and values of the company to see where improvements could be made that would add to profitability.[36]

Such responsibility audits are based on simple premises related to different stakeholders, with the specific objective in mind that it pays to be responsible. For example companies that control their pollution will avoid fines and associated legal fees. Organizations that treat their employees with respect and develop proactive, family- and worker-friendly policies, find that their employees are more productive, loyal, and committed to company purposes. This loyalty not only results in higher productivity, but also lowers turnover, absenteeism, and tardiness, avoiding associated costs. Companies that develop policies that allow them to engage positively and interactively with communities, to help communities meet local needs, will find that communities are better able to meet the infrastructure needs of the firm because the community is healthier.

The New Economics Foundation in Great Britain has developed a somewhat different approach to social auditing.[37] By surveying external stakeholders and asking their opinions of company practices in various arenas, it seeks to determine what the outside perception of the company is so that internal practices can be changed where gaps between what is hoped for (i.e., the vision and values) and the way a company operates appear.

Two of the most prominent social audits undertaken by the New Economics Foundation are Ben & Jerry's (before it was acquired by Unilever Corporation in 2000) and The Body Shop (see http://www.neweconomics.org/asa.htm#Social Audits for a copy of The Body Shop's latest audit and some insight into how the audit can be used by the company to improve practice). Audits can also be used by values-driven organizations, such as NGOs, to determine how well they are meeting their basic values objectives and goals.

The Practice of Responsibility Auditing

Audits are typically undertaken with respect to specific stakeholder groups or domains against stated organizational values and mission with respect to that stakeholder. In the United States, responsibility auditing has been pioneered by SmithOBrien,[38] a firm located in Cambridge, Massachusetts, which emphasizes the holistic nature of the audit and, particularly, the ways that operating more responsibly can generate higher profitability. For example, an audit of employee relations would first look at a company's statements about employees in its mission or vision statement. Then auditors would assess the current state of employee retention and recruitment costs (both explicit and hidden, such as the costs of interviewing and training, and lower productivity associated with newer hires). They might also explore employee morale through interviews to determine the impact of morale on productivity, retention, and turnover.

In the environmental area, an audit might attempt to determine how much money could be saved through recycling programs (such as 3M's Pollution Prevention Pays Program) or through reduced use of paper through increased use of electronic communications. The technique of activity-based costing can be used in these stakeholder areas to develop an understanding of the real costs of these activities, as well as the ways in which the organization could benefit from improving their current practices.[39]

In addition to overall responsibility assessments, which evaluate the whole company, some companies issue periodic environmental reports. As part of the information that it makes increasingly available to interested stakeholders, the U.S. government annually releases a "toxic release inventory" that can be used by local communities and other parties interested in the pollution records of companies in their neighborhoods. Groups that are concerned about toxic releases can then put significant pressures on companies to change internal practices.

Clearly, evaluation of corporate policies with respect to a range of stakeholders can and is being done on a regular basis by a wide range of internal and external constituencies. Not all of these evaluations are in terms of dollars, but many of them are nonetheless getting increasing attention from the press, the public, activists, and corporate leaders. Well-managed companies truly attempting to live out their visions as leading corporate citizens recognize that they are and will continue to be under in-

225

CHAPTER 8
Measuring Multiple
Bottom Lines:
Getting to
Value Added

creasing public scrutiny with respect to their citizenship activities in our technologically connected age as Traidcraft does (see box below). Indeed, so important are these assessments of nontraditional financial and stakeholder arenas that measures of economic and social progress are being updated globally to include a range of social and stakeholder considerations formerly omitted.

Traidcraft's Transparency

Traidcraft is a £7.5 million for-profit trading company that imports and distributes fair trade foods, beverages, handicrafts, and fashion products from more than 100 producer groups in more than 30 countries around the world. Fair trade products are these that ensure that a reasonable portion of the proceeds goes directly to the producer. Traidcraft's mission is to "expand and establish trading systems which are more just and which express the principles of love and justice fundamental to the Christian faith. Its objectives arise from a commitment to practical service and partnership for change, which puts people before profit." Most of the producers who supply Traidcraft are small community-based groups, who rely on the opportunities provided by Traidcraft to begin working their way out of poverty and into economic stability.

Because its social mission is so explicit, Traidcraft has also pioneered in the area of social accounting, having published independently audited social reports since 1992. Indeed, so successful have these social audits been that Traidcraft has now entered the social auditing business itself. Traidcraft expects its suppliers to live up to high standards, and then it audits those suppliers annually to assure that the standards are met. For example, many of the producers focus on crafts and have to meet the following set of conditions. Each supplier group should:

- Be organized for the benefit of its members.
- Be concerned for the personal welfare of its members.
- Pay wages which are, or are above, the average in the locality.
- Make products that are, or may soon be, commercially viable.
- Pay no more than a reasonable service fee to agents (if they are involved).[40]

Similarly, Traidcraft hopes to alleviate some of the fluctuations in the commodity markets that its food and beverage producers face by:

- Paying people fair prices.
- Ensuring that smallholders and pickers who supply our tea and coffee receive a clear benefit from the purchase of their product.
- Giving the producers credit when they need it.
- Entering a long-term relationship of partnership.
- Cooperation—working together for a better future.[41]

Assuring that these standards are met in 30 different countries is far from easy. As a result, Traidcraft has put significant efforts into its assessment of stakeholder relationships. On its website, Traidcraft identifies key stakeholders as suppliers, strategic partners, customers and supporters (including, for example, fair traders, retailers, mail-order customers, wholesale customers, donors to Traidcraft Exchange, and shareholders), staff, funders, and networks and influences (including the UK government, the business community in general, the Fair Trade movement, and the media).

Traidcraft issues annual social audits so that the company can be held accountable for meeting its stated mission and goals, so that its practices are transparent and it communicates openly with its stakeholders, and to become a learning organization. Following a cycle of act→measure→report→learn, Traidcraft reports both the positive and negative results of its audits and then publishes them on its website: http://www.traidcraft.co.uk/. As one supplier comments, "Traidcraft is very, very open. Nothing is hidden in the costing system. We know where the end product is going. We know the mark up, the catalogue price and that we appreciate."[42]

Source: http://www.traidcraft.co.uk/.

MEASURING SOCIAL PROGRESS GLOBALLY

Many groups around the world are concerned that current measures of economic progress are inadequate. In part this concern arises because typical assessments of gross domestic product (GDP) includes extraction of resources from the environment as economic gains rather than the losses that they actually represent, and because many indicators of "progress" make people or societies worse off rather than better off. For example, GDP does not take into account increases in inequality between the rich and poor or damages to the environment, while it includes problematic social developments, such as higher divorce rates, as productivity gains because of increased legal fees, while ignoring the social costs of divorce.[43]

GDP, as currently constructed following the dictates of the Bretton Woods Conference after World War II, is a sum of products and services sold, developed purely on economic grounds. It makes few distinctions between activities that add to social health and well-being and those that detract from it. Thus, installing pollution equipment is considered an economic gain, rather than accounting for it as a loss because of the ecological destruction of the environment associated with the need for that equipment in the first place.

Even the creator of the GDP, Simon Kuznets, admitted in 1934 that its coverage is limited, stating, "The welfare of a nation can scarcely be inferred from a measurement of national income."[44] Furthering the conversation about what is meant by progress, the United Nations Human Development Program (UNDP) recently stated that all countries need to pay more attention to the quality of growth, not just the quantity, as assessed by GDP. Indeed, the UNDP identified five forms of growth that it actually considers damaging: (1) *jobless growth* or growth that does not translate into jobs; (2) *voiceless growth* or growth unmatched by the spread of democracy; (3) *rootless growth* or growth that snuffs out separate cultural identify of nations, regions, and other locales; (4) *futureless growth* or growth that despoils the environment; and (5) *ruthless growth* or growth in which most of the benefits are seized by the rich.[45]

Despite the problems of growth identified by the UNDP and their reality in the modern global economy, most business and governmental leaders unfortunately are still locked into thinking that the GDP is the best assessment of progress. One of the criticisms of measuring social progress more broadly is that it is difficult to obtain adequate measures of real social progress. Just as we saw with the assessment of corporate stakeholder and issues-related practices, however, significant attention is being paid these days to measuring progress more broadly and in ways that can be applied consistently over time to all types of situations. The concluding section of this chapter will explain one of the more important of these efforts.

Indicators of Development Progress[46]

A unique and important collaboration between global intergovernmental organizations (IGOs) and nongovernmental orgranizations (NGOs) is making substantial progress toward defining and implementing core indicators of social and development progress. Among the entities that have come together for this purpose are the

227

CHAPTER 8
Measuring Multiple
Bottom Lines:
Getting to
Value Added

World Bank, the United Nations (including the Statistics Division), United Nations Development Program (UNDP), United Nations Educational, Scientific, and Cultural Organization (UNESCO), United Nations Children's Educational Fund (UNICEF), The United Nations Population Fund (UNFPA), World Health Organization (WHO), Commission on Sustainable Development), and developing country statisticians, policy makers, and donors to the Development Assistance Committee of the Organization for Economic Corporation and Development (OECD). This Index of Sustainable Economic Welfare (ISEW) has received considerable attention in recent years.

This coalition has focused on economic goals like reducing extreme poverty by half, and social goals including universal primary education, eliminating gender disparity in education, reducing infant and child mortality by three-quarters, and universal access to reproductive health services. Further, they have specified goals of environmental sustainability and regeneration that include implementation of a national strategy for sustainable development in all countries by 2005 so that trends in the loss of environmental resources can be reversed by 2015. They have also identified important qualitative factors that these numerous groups believe will result in a better world: participatory development, democratization, good governance of organizations, and broad implementation of human rights.

To demonstrate that social progress is measurable, this group has developed a working set of core indicators that measure development progress (see Table 8.4) in much the same way that stakeholder assessments were demonstrated above. The set of indicators is not inclusive of all possible indicators and is generally still under development, but it is clear that it is feasible to measure progress not only in economic but also in human terms.

The indicators in Table 8.4 represent only one of a number of sets of indicators currently under development for assessing social progress in human and stakeholder terms, and particularly for assessing ecological sustainability. The United Nations Development Program, for example, is working with a Human Development Index (see http://www.undp.org/), while Calvert Group Mutual Funds and futurist Hazel Henderson are working together to develop a set of quality of life indicators. Another set of indicators called the "global reporting initiative" is being developed by a group of social investors under the auspices of the CERES (Coalition for Environmentally Responsible Economies) organization, which has developed the CERES principles for environmental sustainability (see the CERES case in Chapter 9).

The indexes cited represent only a few among many emerging sets of measures and indicators that attempt to reframe and broaden our understanding of what it means to live in human society. Life, obviously, goes well beyond economics, yet until these pioneering developments appeared, we confined much of our thinking about progress to the realm of economics. The developments in measuring stakeholder and ecological progress noted above, and many others not included, show that it is quite feasible to think broadly about what we mean by progress and the quality of life we are living.

Measures such as these, which account for benefits and drawbacks of various activities to society, can only help businesses that desire to operate responsibly with

TABLE 8.4. Working Set of Core Indicators for Measuring Development Progress

Goals	Indicators
ECONOMIC WELL-BEING	
The proportion of people living in extreme poverty in developing countries should be reduced by at least one-half by 2015.	1. Incidence of extreme poverty: population below $1 per day.
	2. Poverty gap ratio: incidence times depth of poverty.
	3. Inequality: poorest fifth's share of national consumption.
	4. Child malnutrition: prevalence of underweight under five years.
SOCIAL DEVELOPMENT	
Universal primary education There should be universal primary education in all countries by 2015.	5. Net enrollment in primary education.
	6. Completion of fourth grade of primary education.
	7. Literacy rate of children and young adults 14 to 24 years old.
Gender equality Progress toward gender equality and the empowerment of women should be demonstrated by eliminating gender disparity in primary and secondary education by 2005.	8. Ratio of girls to boys in primary and secondary education.
	9. Ratio of literate females to males (15 to 24 years old).
Infant and child mortality The death rates for infants and children under the age of five years should be reduced by two-thirds the 1990 level in each developing country by 2015.	10. Infant mortality rate.
	11. Mortality rate under five years old.
Maternal mortality The rate of maternal mortality should be reduced by three-fourths between 1990 and 2015.	12. Maternal mortality ratio.
	13. Births attended by skilled health personnel.
Reproductive health Access should be available through the primary health care system to reproductive health services for all individuals of appropriate ages, no later than the year 2015.	14. Contraceptive prevalence rate.
	15. HIV prevalence in 15- to 24-year-old pregnant women.

229

CHAPTER 8
Measuring Multiple
Bottom Lines:
Getting to
Value Added

ENVIRONMENTAL SUSTAINABILITY AND REGENERATION

Every country should have a current national strategy for sustainable development in the process of implementation by 2005, to ensure that current trends in the loss of environmental resources are effectively reversed at both global and national levels.

16. Countries with national sustainable development strategies.

17. Population with access to safe water.

18. Intensity of freshwater use.

19. Biodiversity: land area protected.

20. Energy efficiency: GDP per unit of energy use.

21. Carbon dioxide emissions.

GENERAL INDICATORS

Population.
Gross National Product.

GNP per capita.
Adult literacy rate.
Total fertility rate.
Life expectancy at birth.
Aid as a percent of GNP.
External debt as a percent of GNP.
Investment as a percent of GNP.
Trade as a percent of GNP.

Source: Development Indicators: http://www.oecd.org/dac/Indicators/index.htm.

respect to the many stakeholders with whom they are interdependent. Such measures are especially important when we begin to look, as we shall in the next chapter, at the ways in which value is added to stakeholders' lives by corporate activities.

LEADING CHALLENGES: THE MEASUREMENT OF RESPONSIBLE PRACTICE

You get what you measure. That slogan is the core of accounting practice and it is also at the heart of leading corporate citizenship. Leaders of companies that hope to meet the highest standards of corporate citizenship need to take the time to identify what those standards are and the best ways to assess the extent to which their companies are meeting them. Having a clear corporate vision with its attendant values is only the first step in an iterative process that involves determining next what kinds of measures are appropriate internally, as well as the ways in which the company will be evaluated externally.

What this chapter makes clear is that assessment of corporate citizenship is an ongoing proposition—and it goes on whether the company itself is involved or not. Social and traditional investors and, increasingly, customers seek information about companies from research services and from socially-conscious investment firms. Others, including major business publications as well as academics, produce reputational and other types of ratings that compare the performance of one company to another, publishing their results in highly visible places and gaining significant publicity from these rankings. Some observers, including the U.S. government and customers, are concerned about whether banks invest their business resources appropriately in local communities in the various forms of social investing described above. Others want to assure that corporate philanthropy is used to advance society's interests in a whole range of ways.

Companies that are truly on the leading edge of corporate citizenship take these external assessments seriously. Further, their leaders know that the best defense is a good offense: They take the initiative to understand how their external stakeholders view them, to engage in dialogue with stakeholders, and to assess their own internal practices long before they become visible to outsiders. Increasingly, these leaders of corporate citizens do such responsibility auditing preventatively, long before the company has problems. Ideally, they also make the results of their evaluations accessible to stakeholders. In addition, they try to learn from their evaluations how to improve their stakeholder-related performance, knowing that, in the end, it is their corporate practices that implement their visions and values, which in turn lead to both corporate effectiveness in carrying out their visions and to satisfying financial performance.

While the recognition of the importance of learning from such intensive self-assessments is only beginning to dawn on some corporate leaders, many already know that their company's performance on a whole range of dimensions related to primary and critical secondary stakeholders is visible to the investing community. If what gets measured is what you get, then companies that pay attention to measuring stakeholder performance will get better relationships with those who matter.

NOTES TO CHAPTER 8

1. See http://www.socialinvest.org.
2. See, for example, Eric M. Weigand, Kenneth R. Brown, and Eileen M. Wilhem, "Socially Principled Investing: Caring about Ethics and Profitability," *Trusts & Estates* 135, no. 9 (August 1996), pp. 36–42.
3. This view of incalculable risks was put forward by Steven R. Lydenberg and Karen Paul, "Stakeholder Theory and Socially Responsible Investing: Toward a Convergence of Theory and Practice," in *Proceedings of the International Association for Business and Society*, Jim Weber and Kathleen Rehbein, eds. (Destin, FL: 1997), pp. 208–213.
4. There is additionally a passive fund, called the Domini Social Fund, that is comprised of the companies in the Domini Index, which is separately managed, and should not be confused with the Index.
5. S. Lydenberg, A. T. Marlin, and S. Strub, *Rating America's Corporate Conscience* (Reading, MA: Addison-Wesley, 1986).
6. See http://www.reputations.org/sections/rank/rank_mn.sub.html.
7. The text of the Community Reinvestment Act can be found at http://www.fdic. gov/publish/12c30.html.
8. For a dissertation on this topic that emphasizes the ways social capital has been built between banks and community-based organizations, see Steven J. Waddell, "The Rise of a New Form of Enterprise: Social Capital Enterprise . . . A Study of the Relationships

231

CHAPTER 8
Measuring Multiple
Bottom Lines:
Getting to
Value Added

between American Bank–Community-Based Organizations," dissertation, Sociology Department, Boston College, 1997.

9. See http://www.rainbowpush.org/wallstreet/.

10. Published in Michael E. Porter, "The Competitive Advantage of the Inner City," *Harvard Business Review,* May–June 1995. Ideas in this and the following paragraphs are derived from Porter's article.

11. From Initiative for a Competitive Inner City (ICIC) website, http://www.icic.org/factoids.htm.

12. Ibid.

13. For the story of the history, development, and achievements of Grameen Bank see David Bornstein, *The Price of a Dream: The Story of the Grameen Bank* (Chicago: University of Chicago Press, 1996).

14. Ibid.; see also http://www.grameen-info.org/ for current data and information.

15. See http://www.accion.org/main.asp for more details of how Accion International operates.

16. From http://www.accion.org/about/main.asp.

17. See http://www.grameen-info.org/mcredit/ungar.html.

18. For a listing of other microenterprise organizations, see http://www.accion.org/world/main.asp.

19. See http://www.sbk.com/default.htm.

20. See http://csif.calvertgroup.com/diff/A5-2.htm.

21. Ibid.

22. This type of social investment is described at length in Curt Weeden, *Corporate Social Investing* (San Francisco: Berrett-Koehler, 1998), from which material in this section is derived. See also the associated website at http://www.bnsinc.com/csi/intro.html.

23. See CalPERS website, "Obstacles to Good Corporate Governance," http://www.calpers-governance.org/principles/other/barriers/page01.asp, for more details of the study reported in this section.

24. A *golden parachute* is a lavish severance package for an executive of a company who is either fired or made redundant by a corporate merger; *greenmail* is the buying of a large enough number of a company's shares to threaten a takeover and then reselling these shares at a much higher price than their market value.

25. See also the OECD's principles of corporate governance, at http://www.oecd.org/daf/governance/principles.htm.

26. From CalPERS, http://www.calpers.ca.gov/whatsnew/press/1998/0413b.htm. Complete copies of the principles for both U.S.-based and global companies can be found by entering http://www.calpers-governance.org/.

27. Quoted in Robert A. G. Monks and Nell Minnow, *Power and Accountability* in http://www.ragm.com/power/, chap. 1.

28. Joann Muller, "How Compuware Mishandled Its Explosive Sexual-Harassment Case," *Business Week,* July 5, 1999, pp. 74–84.

29. Ibid., p. 75.

30. See, for example, Sandra Waddock, Samuel B. Graves, and Marjorie Kelly, "On the Trail of the Best Corporate Citizens," and "The 100 Best Corporate Citizens" ranking in *Business Ethics* 14, no. 2 (March 2000), pp. 15–18.

31. See http://www.reputations.org/sections/rep/rep.html; see also http://www.business-ethics.com/the100.htm.

32. See Charles J. Fombrun, "Indices of Corporate Reputation: An Analysis of Rankings and Ratings by Social Monitors," *Corporate Reputation Review* 1, no. 4 (1998).

33. See http://www.reputations.org/ for some background on Fombrun's work on reputation, as well as that of other scholars.

34. See Kim Davenport, "Social Auditing: The Quest for Corporate Social Responsibility," in James Weber and Kathleen Rehbein, eds., *Proceedings of the International Association of Business and Society* (Destin, FL: 1997), pp. 208–213.

35. See http://www.the-body-shop.com/ and http://www.traidcraft.co.uk/sa/main.htm.

36. See Sandra Waddock and Neil Smith, "Corporate Responsibility Audits: Doing Well by Doing Good," *Sloan Management Review* 41, no. 2 (Winter 2000), pp. 75–83; and http://www.smithobrien.com/, which describes this company's approach to responsibility audits.

37. See http://www.neweconomics.org/index.htm.

38. See http://www.smithobrien.com/.

39. See Waddock and Smith for additional details.

40. See http://www.traidcraft.co.uk/ under social accounting.

41. Ibid.

42. See http://www.traidcraft.co.uk/sa/improve.htm.

43. A number of useful sources explore this issue of redefining what is meant by progress, including http://www.cyberus.ca/choose.sustain/well-being.shtml; http://www.foe.co.uk/progress/; and http://www.oecd.org/dac/Indicators/index.htm.

44. Quoted in http://www.foe.co.uk/progress/annex1.htm.

45. Ibid.

46. See http://www.oecd.org/dac/Indicators/index.htm for more information on this specific set of progress indicators. Much of this section is derived from this website.

CHAPTER 9

Ecological Thinking in the Global Village

Partnership is an essential characteristic of sustainable communities. The cyclical exchanges of energy and resources in an ecosystem are sustained by pervasive cooperation. . . . Partnership—the tendency to associate, establish links, live inside one another, and cooperate—is one of the hallmarks of life.

In human communities partnership means democracy and personal empowerment, because each member of the community plays an important role. Combining the principle of partnership with the dynamic of change and development, we may also use the term "coevolution" metaphorically in human communities. As a partnership proceeds, each partner better understands the needs of the other. In a true, committed partnership both partners learn and change—they coevolve. Here again we notice the basic tension between the challenge of ecological sustainability and the way in which our present societies are structured, between economics and ecology. Economics emphasizes competition, expansion, and domination; ecology emphasizes cooperation, conservation, and partnership.

The principles of ecology mentioned so far—interdependence, the cyclical flow of resources, cooperation, and partnership—are all different aspects of the same pattern of organization. This is how ecosystems organize themselves to maximize sustainability.

—FRITJOF CAPRA, The Web of Life

SUSTAINING A HEALTHY NATURAL ECOLOGY

During the last third of the 20th century, it became clear that the health of the natural environment that surrounds and underpins societies and the economies they produce is increasingly in peril. Environmental problems assumed a global rather than a local scope, necessitating that companies and communities alike develop significantly new approaches to the use and reuse of natural resources. Corporate programs of environmental management, especially those aimed at sustainability of both the natural and community environments, have assumed a great deal of importance in bringing more responsible practices to the use of environmental resources.

Environmental problems facing the planet include global warming and ozone depletion, water and air pollution, use of pesticides and disposal of toxic waste, and garbage and waste disposal in general. Add in the burning of tropical rain forests to clear land for short-term farming, and other processes leading to deforestation and even desertification, the resulting decimation of wildlife species, some of which have yet to be discovered, and coastal and wetlands erosion resulting from development. Further consider the scarcity of fresh water in some regions of the world, acid rain, and severe climate patterns that some attribute to changes in the ecology. Then recognize the continuing and growing pressures that population growth places on ecological resources, especially water. It quickly becomes clear that human civilization faces ecological crises the likes of which have never before been seen.

Many of these ecological problems are boundaryless in that they cannot be contained readily, if at all, within community, regional, or even national boundaries. The impacts of many of these problems affect communities far beyond their sources and require wholly new approaches to sustainable development.

Pressures on the Ecology

One interesting study shows that people in the developed world make significantly larger "ecological footprints" than do people in the less developed world. In an innovative study, Mathis Wackernagel and his colleagues estimated the available amount of biologically productive land mass per capita, and deducted about 12 percent of biological capacity that is considered politically feasible to allocate for the biodiversity that is essential according to the World Commission on Environment.[1] These researchers came to the conclusion that the earth can sustain human civilization at a rate of 1.7 hectares[2] per capita.

The researchers then estimated the ecological footprint—or rate at which ecological resources are actually used—in 52 different nations around the world. Given current population levels in different nations and different levels of industrialization and economic development, countries have larger or smaller ecological footprints. When countries' footprints are lower than 1.7 hectares, they are sustainable; when they are higher, that country's ecological capacity is being stretched beyond its sustainable limits. Table 9.1 gives a sampling of the results of this study for comparative purposes.

Note that in this selected listing the United States is the biggest consumer of environmental resources per capita, with an average ecological footprint of 10.3 hectares compared to those of less developed countries like Indonesia and Bangladesh, which are well under the 1.7 level for sustainability. Though there is a tremendous burgeoning of population in these less developed countries, the ecological footprints of individuals are much less, in part because poor people consume far fewer environmental resources to maintain their lifestyles. Given the lack of industrialization, developing nations do not consume nearly as much nor waste nearly as much as developed nations where lifestyles are much more encompassing of material goods.

TABLE 9.1.   Ecological Footprints of Selected Nations (1993 Data)

Country	Population (millions)	Footprint (hectares per capita)
Australia	18.6	9.0
Bangladesh	125.9	0.5
Canada	30.1	7.7
China	1,247.3	1.2
Czech Republic	10.3	4.5
Egypt	65.4	1.2
France	58.4	4.1
Germany	81.8	5.3
Hong Kong	5.9	6.1
India	970.2	0.8
Indonesia	203.6	1.4
Japan	125.7	4.3
Korea (Republic of)	45.9	3.4
Nigeria	118.4	1.5
Peru	24.7	1.6
Russian Federation	146.4	6.0
Singapore	2.9	7.2
Switzerland	7.3	5.0
United Kingdom	58.6	5.2
United States	268.2	10.3

Source: Mathis Wackernagel et al., "Ecological Footprints of Nations: How Much Nature Do They Use?—How Much Nature Do They Have?" 1999, in http://www.ecouncil.ac.cr/rio/focus/report/english/footprint/ranking.htm.

The study's authors concluded: "Humanity lives too heavily on the Earth."[3] On average, the ecological footprint of all the nations combined is 2.3 hectares, while there are only 1.7 hectares per capital available, for about a 35 percent overshoot. Indeed, they noted that "if everyone on earth lived like the average North American, it would require at least three earths to provide all the material and energy she or he currently uses."[4] What this means is that current approaches to economic and societal development are draining the earth's resources faster than nature can replace them even without the explosive growth in population that is expected over the next several decades. Clearly, the current approach to development and lifestyles is unsustainable in the long term.

ORGANIZING ENVIRONMENTAL MANAGEMENT

Sustainability of ecological resources and the so-called greening of business are fast becoming norms in leading corporate citizens with visions supported by values that respect both nature and human civilization, particularly when companies openly recognize their ecological impact. Progressive and visionary companies recognize that their own survival and well-being, along with that of their customers, employees, and other stakeholders, depends on a shift of perspective related to the impacts of business on the natural environment and the necessary changes in corporate practices to move toward sustainability. They know we all need a healthy ecological system to survive, as the four system constraints of The Natural Step outlined in Chapter 2 highlight.

To cope with the increased need to operate in long-term supportable ways with respect to the natural environment and local communities, many companies are adopting environmental management practices aimed at sustainability and better stewardship of environmental resources. This section focuses on ways that companies manage their relationship with "Mother Earth," or as ecologists say, "Gaia" (or the idea pioneered by James Lovelock that our earth is itself a living system).*

Change of Perspective

Truly "greening" business involves generating a new awareness of the importance of the natural environment among business leaders. This shift of consciousness moves thinking away from the dualism, fragmentation, and mechanistic view of nature found in traditional Western ways of viewing the world toward the more holistic, organic, and integrated perspective discussed in Chapter 2. The shift of consciousness and awareness depends in part upon the cognitive, emotional, and moral development processes discussed in Chapter 4. Making this shift, however, can help better align the interests of all three spheres of activity with those of nature or the ecological sphere that underpins human civilization. Where this shift of perspective takes hold, it becomes clear to observers that balance among all the spheres is essential to long-term sustainability and that corporate citizens, which are responsible for much of the consumption of earth's resources, have a significant role to play in the movement toward sustainability.[5]

Throughout the United States, the European Union, and Asia, corporations are adopting new environmental management practices because they are under significant pressures from a range of stakeholders to do so. Some researchers believe that this shift and the accompanying changes in awareness may even represent a "new industrial revolution," although that revolution is clearly in its early stages.[6] To manage this change of perspective, many companies are adopting proactive practices of environmental management, focused on waste reduction and cost cutting that have as their by-product satisfaction of customer demands for greener businesses and social investors' interest in environmental sustainability. Additionally, many companies are finding, to their surprise, that there is a "both/and" of enhanced profits and greening, which it turns out do go together.[7] Indeed, a recent study found that multinational corporations, rather than suffering from environmental regulations, are actually rewarded with higher stock market performance when they adopt strict global environmental standards such as those that will be discussed below.[8]

Companies that have been certified by the International Standards Organization as being in compliance with ISO 9000 quality standards are now beginning to adopt

*See James Lovelock, *Gaia: A New Look at Life on Earth.* Oxford University Press, 1995.

voluntary environmental quality management standards called ISO 14000 and ISO 14001 (see Chapter 10 for a more complete exposition), which bring their environmental policies in the direction of sustainability. These standards, however, are largely internal and oriented toward efficiency or economizing, rather than fully sustainable over the long-term. Imposition of voluntary standards, which can become a source of competitive advantage through waste reduction, quality improvements, and improved customer relations, comes after years of corporate resistance to such standards and efforts to avoid "command and control" regulation by governments.[9] The ISO standards are only one among many new environmental management practices that have emerged within the last two decades, as we will discuss in the next chapter.

Stages of Environmental Awareness

Ecologist and management theorist Stuart Hart has proposed a developmental framework along which firms and their leaders progress as they begin to shift their thinking toward sustainable practice.[10]

In the first stage, using prevention strategies, most companies focus on *pollution prevention* rather than cleanup and pollution control, which historically has been the focus for companies operating under the "command and control" regulations originally instituted by environmental specialists. Control strategies focus on cleanup, while prevention emphasizes waste minimization or even elimination (called source reduction). Hart pointed out that pollution prevention strategies resemble the quality movement because they emphasize continuous improvement in reducing energy use and waste.

Built on a logic resembling 3M's "Pollution Prevention Pays" program, pollution prevention is also aligned with the emerging global environmental standards embodied in ISO 14000 and 14001, which will be discussed in more detail in the next chapter. Importantly, Hart noted that "the emerging economies [and the environment itself] cannot afford to repeat all the mistakes of Western development."[11]

Companies operating at the second stage emphasize *product stewardship,* which attempts to minimize not only pollution related to manufacturing processes, but also all other sources of environmental impacts. Full-cost or life-cycle accounting for products can be used to reduce materials usage and really begin a process of fundamental change in product and process design, which is necessary in the shift toward sustainability. Full costing of production in both goods and services enhances the awareness of leaders about all of the ecological impacts the company has.

For developing nations, it makes sense to emulate not the plunder and pillage environmental strategies of earlier stages of development, but the best modern practices associated with sustainable development because this will help developing nations conserve their natural and human resources, providing long-term opportunities. Of course, this way of thinking represents a long-term view in which costs are internalized rather than externalized, and some developing nations find it difficult to think about ecological sustainability when they need to help their citizens put food on the table and shelter overhead. Hart's point, however, is that this long-term thinking is critical for world health, as well as for the ultimate health of developing nations.

The third stage in Hart's framework is called *clean technology*. In this stage, companies shift production and products toward altogether new technologies that use many fewer resources in their production and use and that last a long time. This shift, which is still rare, happens when leaders recognize that no matter how much they reduce wastes or conserve resources, many of today's technologies are simply not sustainable over the long term. Although few companies have reached this stage of development at this point in time, many ecologists, such as Hart, believe this is the necessary next step for the planet's ecological health. As Hart pointed out, significant new business opportunities exist for companies that can develop and sell new technologies. Even today, however, many companies have made significant strides toward sustainability through implementation of environmental management practices. See the box on Dow Chemical on the next page.

Environmental Management Practices

In recent years, significant gains have been made in environmental sensitivity and performance in developed nations, mostly resulting from the greening of business, tough environmental regulations, and outsourcing practices that have removed heavily polluting industries to less industrialized nations.[14] Of course, outsourcing creates potential problems in developing countries, which as they industrialize, generate additional pollution and extract more natural resources, shifting the ecological balance in a negative direction. This is why Hart argued that a different and more enlightened path must be followed today by developing nations. Already, quite a number of management practices are available to help move companies toward ecological sustainability.

Comprehensive environmental management systems include five major elements: "waste minimization and prevention, demand-side management, design for environment, product stewardship, and full-cost accounting."[15] Each of the elements of this comprehensive system is explained in Table 9.2. Michael Berry and Dennis Rondinelli, who developed this comprehensive approach to environmental management, noted that demand-side management can actually improve profitability. Procter and Gamble, for example, saved more than 152,000 tons of packaging material in 1995 through waste-minimization practices, simply by concentrating laundry detergents and using smaller packages.[16]

Demand-side management allows for better relationships with customers because they are being sold only and exactly what they need, rather than having salespeople simply fill their quotas and sell products and services the customer does not really need or want. Stewardship involves taking care of the resources and products developed by paying close attention to all aspects of their development and use; that is, by assuming full responsibility for the products and services and their impacts, whether they are direct or indirect. Full cost accounting (or life-cycle accounting) is necessary to take into account all of the costs of production, sales, distribution, and use, rather than externalizing them to society, just as is done in the responsibility audits described in Chapter 8.

Environmental Cost Accounting

One managerial tool being used with increasingly frequency is environmental cost accounting, the assessment of the overall ecological costs of producing goods and services. Traditional cost accounting is a tool used by managers to assess the full

---

Dow Chemical Emphasizes Sustainability

Founded in 1897, Dow Chemical has been in the chemical business for more than 100 years. One of the perennial "bad guys" of the environmental movement given its leadership role in producing chemicals, hydrocarbons, herbicides, and pesticides, Dow has nonetheless taken a leadership role in the effort to move the chemical industry toward more sustainable forms of development. With annual sales of more than $19 billion and a recent merger with the former Union Carbide Corporation, Dow has 123 plants operating in 32 companies in 162 countries.

Dow views corporate citizenship as core to its responsibility to society. According to Gerald Ring, director of Global Contributions and Community Programs, "Business success at Dow Chemical Company globally is meeting the expectation of four stakeholder groups: employees, shareholders, customers, and society/community." The second premise guiding Dow these days is a commitment to environmental sustainability, which the company views as a stool with three legs: social, environmental, and economic. According to Dow's Ring, the social side of sustainability represents "Dow's primary goal for being in business [which] is to improve the quality of life for people around the world with products and services we sell and the people we employee." Critical to achieving those goals is leaving a smaller ecological footprint on the world, while simultaneously maintaining economic viability and success.

To make its commitment to environmental sustainability both more real and more transparent, in 1999 Dow issued its first Public Report, consolidating formerly separate health and safety, and environmental reports into one (see http://dow.com/dow_news/feature/05_18_00/index.htm). According to *Investor Relations Business* magazine, "investors seem to be clamoring for more" of these types of reports.

Highlighting the ecologically sophisticated thinking necessary to take this position, Dow's CEO William S. Stavropoulous stated,

A powerful catalyst is driving Dow's triple bottom line business toward sustainable progress. It's our corporate integration—nothing less than the complete blending of the central elements of the Dow enterprise into a unified, truly interconnected whole. We are doing this by hardwiring financial, environmental and social responsibility and performance directly into our global businesses.[12]

Championing full-cost accounting for its environmental impacts since the early 1990s, Dow is a leader in the chemical industry's Responsible Care ® initiative, for which the company received Keystone Center's (an environmental education organization) "Leadership in Industry" award in 2000. Dow CEO Stavropoulos believes that the Keystone Center's award signals a shift in the industry. Chemical manufacturers, rather than always being targets of activists' negative attention on ecological issues, he believes, can begin to take the lead in " 'setting the standard' for product stewardship with the environment, health, and safety . . . practices mandated by Responsible Care."[13] The Responsible Care initiative encourages chemical manufacturers to be both proactive and interactive with stakeholders on issues related to environment, health, and safety. In addition, it helps to create a better public image for manufacturers in the chemical industry, which by the nature of the industry has tended to be extractive rather than sustainable in its approach to the environment.

Sources: Partially excerpted from a case by Jennifer Leigh, Boston College, and the Center for Corporate Citizenship at Boston College; see also Dow's Public Report 2000 Update, at http://dow.com/dow_news/feature/05_18_00/index.htm, and Bill Schmitt, "Responsible Care: Making New Connections," *Chemical Week*, July 5–12, 2000, pp. 38–40.

TABLE 9.2. Elements of Comprehensive Environmental Management Systems

Waste minimization and prevention	Prevent rather than control pollution by reducing, minimizing, or eliminating pollutants and wastes at their source. Includes materials substitution, process modification, materials reuse, recycling, and reuse within different processes.
Demand-side management	Understand customers needs and preferences so 1. Product is not wasted. 2. What is sold is exactly what is needed. 3. The customer becomes more efficient in using the product.
Design for environment	Produce for dissasembly, modular upgradeability, and recyclability initially, rather than facing product disposal, thereby reducing reprocessing costs and returning products to the market more quickly.
Product stewardship	Stewardship implies taking care in design, manufacturing, distribution, use, and disposal of products to reduce environmental risks and problems. Life-cycle analysis determines waste reduction at all stages. Seek less polluting or wasteful alternatives, reduce conformance and liability costs.
Full-cost accounting	Identify, quantify, and allocate direct and indirect environmental costs of operations. Four levels of costs: 1. Direct costs—like labor, capital, and raw materials. 2. Hidden costs, such as monitoring and reporting. 3. Contingent liability costs, such as fines and remedial action. 4. Less tangible costs, such as public relations and goodwill.

Source: Adapted from Michael A. Berry and Dennis A. Rondinelli, "Proactive Corporate Environment Management: A New Industrial Revolution," *Academy of Management Executive* 12, no. 2 (May 1998), pp. 38–50.

costs of producing something within the firm (i.e., including indirect as well as direct costs of production). Similarly, environmental cost accounting takes into account all of the ecological costs of production, such as energy consumed, waste produced, cleanup costs, and possible liabilities associated with production.[17]

In a sense, environmental cost accounting is similar to life-cycle accounting because it takes into account all of the costs of production, including dealing with any by-products and long-term societal impacts of production. Three categories of costs need to be considered in an environmental cost system: failure costs, prevention costs, and appraisal costs.[18] These costs need to be assigned to specific product/service lines so that each is fully costed out in terms of all direct costs and the environmental costs incurred, some of which may be hidden from traditional costing methods. Leading corporate citizens need to be aware of the impacts of these costs on society, both retrospectively and prospectively, which environmental cost accounting helps them do.[19]

Life-Cycle Accounting

Some companies are taking environmental cost accounting even further through the use of life-cycle accounting, which attempts to holistically assess the impacts of a product or service throughout its entire life cycle.[20] Based on the principle of ecological stewardship—or care taking—life-cycle accounting encompasses multiple disciplines in a holistic assessment of the planning for a product, its management during the product's useful life, industrial design associated with it, including engineering and design specifications, and costs associated with environmental and health protection.[21]

The Society of Environmental Toxicology and Chemistry has defined a complete life-cycle assessment as having three interrelated parts (see Table 9.3): life cycle inventory, impact analysis, and improvement analysis. These three elements combine to create a system through which costs can be calculated for all of the impacts of designing, developing, producing, delivering, and finally disposing of a product or service.

Environmental Audits

Because leading corporate citizens take responsibility for their ecological impacts, they frequently undertake and publish environmental audits along with audits associated with other stakeholder impacts, as noted in Chapter 8.

Environmental audits focus on ecological areas of concern to relevant stakeholders, including compliance officers who work with regulatory agencies and employees, whose training should include environmental stewardship issues. An environmental audit uses life-cycle, full, or environmental cost accounting techniques to assess the real and fully internalized costs of company production and distribution practices to the company and the customer (and, as a by-product, to society). Like other audits, environmental audits are published for the use of interested stakeholders.

TABLE 9.3.   Components of a Complete Life-Cycle Assessment

Life-cycle inventory	An objective, data-based process of quantifying energy and raw material requirements, air and water emissions, solid waste, and other environmental releases incurred throughout the life cycle of a product, process, or activity.
Life-cycle impact analysis	A technical, quantitative, and/or qualitative process to characterize and assess the environmental effects of energy, materials, and emissions identified in the life-cycle inventory. The assessment should include both environmental and human health considerations.
Life-cycle improvement analysis	A systematic evaluation of opportunities to reduce the environmental impact associated with energy and raw materials use and emissions throughout the entire life of a product, process or activity.

Source: Society of Environmental Toxicology and Chemistry, cited in William G. Russell, Steven L. Skalak, and Gail Miller, "Environmental Cost Accounting: The Bottom Line for Environmental Quality Management," *Total Quality Management* 3, no. 3 (Spring 1994), pp. 255–68.

The audit, once completed, highlights where potential problems and opportunities for waste or pollution reduction exist—and potential cost savings as well. The audit can also be used to help the company establish a cost basis for operations and set priorities for future initiatives.[22] Indeed, one scholar argued that investments in environmental sustainability make sense simply because they help companies gain a competitive advantage, achieve positive financial returns, reduce risks, and outpace competitors who may be using less progressive practices.[23]

Current Sustainability Practice

In recent years environmental regulatory agencies have begun to move away from their original command and control stance toward regulation and toward more market-based and less adversarial tactics intended to encourage sustainability. While the command and control legal frameworks still exist and indeed dominate most countries, there are instances of market incentives (e.g., the selling of pollution rights) and numerous public-private partnerships that foster a collaborative approach to the environment between business and government.

In the Netherlands, for instance, there has been a decided movement toward problem-solving techniques involving the establishment of covenants or voluntary agreements. Throughout Europe such agreements focus on specific environmental problems like waste management or energy efficiency, but in the Netherlands they have assumed a new character. Newer covenants emphasize reducing emissions from whole industry sectors over a long period of time and involve "institutionalized cooperation between industry and government."[24] Although these agreements have had numerous obstacles and stumbling blocks and have not reached their full potential, they do represent an important alternative to adversarial relationships on important environmental matters, particularly during certain phases of environmental policy development.[25]

In the United States, efforts to move corporate thinking toward sustainable practices have tended to focus on ways in which companies can build new businesses, save money, or gain a competitive advantage through more environmentally responsible practices. One approach, as articulated by Forest Reinhardt, is to use the problems of the environment strategically to gain advantage.[26] Reinhardt identified five approaches that companies can use to integrate an environmental perspective into business operations. Businesses can:

- *Differentiate* by using products or processes with great environmental benefits or that use fewer natural resources in their production, for which ecologically-sensitive consumers will pay higher prices (e.g., as Wal-Mart has done in identifying its "green" products for consumers).
- *Manage competitors* by working with industry groups to change society's rules or the rules of competition so that competitors need to incur higher costs to respond to environmental regulation. Because the company has been able to anticipate what will be needed, it can establish a "first mover" or pioneering advantage (e.g., as the chemical industry has done in establishing its Responsible Care® initiative).
- *Save costs* by improving environmental performance internally (e.g., as hotels have done in asking customers to reuse towels and linens).
- *Manage environmental risk* by avoiding costs associated with accidents, spills, consumer boycotts, and environmentally related lawsuits.
- *Redefine markets* by using several of these approaches simultaneously and convincing customers of their benefits ecologically and competitively (e.g., as BMW has done with cars that can be disassembled for recycling and are now in compliance with strict German "take-back" laws).[27]

Management systems are also keys to responsible environmental practice. Companies using proactive environmental management and cost accounting systems also emphasize pollution prevention and recycling, responsible purchasing policies, and new manufacturing strategies that reduce waste. In addition, community involvement is a critical aspect of a good environmental management system because communities are frequently impacted by environmental problems.[28] It is likely that in the future traditional and environmentally oriented accounting methods will be integrated as more companies are expected to account for all of their costs, rather than externalizing them to society.

Future Sustainability Practices

Simply trying to use the environment as a source of competitive advantage as many companies are currently doing, however, overlooks the fundamental problem of sustainability, as the data on ecological footprints of developed nations above indicate. Ultimately, balance demands a far broader perspective from leading corporate citizens and leaders of corporate citizens and the shift in perspective toward sustainability. This perspective takes into account not only economic but also societal and political considerations in determining the public good and ecological long-term sustainability on the broadest possible basis. This shift of perspective is the basis of much of the triple bottom line thinking now coming from Great Britain and the European Union, which emphasizes performance on economic, social, and ecological criteria and requires the postconventional levels of cognitive and moral development described in Chapter 4.

A number of emerging corporate practices can help move a company along the path toward sustainability.[29] One of these is product accountability, which along with life-cycle accounting applies the stewardship principle to all of the negative impacts of a product or service. Another is life-cycle management, discussed above with reference to life-cycle accounting, but here applied to the managerial practices along the entire value chain associated with developing, selling, using, and ultimately disposing of a product. A third approach involves spreading the costs among all emitting parties, thereby eliminating both free ridership and prisoner's dilemma situations (see Chapter 3). Some companies concerned with carbon dioxide emissions are also using benchmarking to compare their own performance with that of best practice firms in a fourth approach likely to become more popular as the ecology movement continues to gain the interest and attention of corporate citizens. Other leading corporate citizens are signing on to principles like those advocated by the Coalition for Environmentally Responsible Economies (see "The CERES Principles" and "The CERES Principles and Environmental Reporting" in the boxes that follow) to attest to their commitment to living up to high ecological standards.

ECOLOGY AND DEVELOPMENT

Developed nations, which leave a much larger ecological footprint than do less developed nations, account for about one of the six billion people populating the world. This one-sixth of the global population consumes about 57 percent of the world's energy and other resources, and creates most of the industrial, toxic, and consumer waste that is generated.[30] Population is expected to grow by approximately two-thirds to about 8.5 billion people by 2025, with most of that growth projected for less developed nations.[31] Combined with governmental policies, economic development, distribution of technological and land resources, and consumption patterns, this growth puts significant strains on ecological resources. Population growth, which some believe is at the crisis level, illuminates the need for bringing balance among the three spheres of human activity and the natural environment. This is an imperative that no human being or enterprise can afford to ignore any longer.

Economic development has many deleterious impacts on the natural environment, in part because as nations develop economically, people tend to make larger ecological footprints, consuming more resources in their daily lives and generating more waste and pollution. Factors that appear to result in this greater ecological impact include increasing urbanization and associated patterns of migration from rural to urban (as well as resource-rich coastal) areas.[32] Consumption of goods and services and energy tend to be higher on a per capital basis in urban than rural areas.

The CERES Principles

PROTECTION OF THE BIOSPHERE

We will reduce and make continual progress toward eliminating the release of any substance that may cause environmental damage to the air, water, or the earth or its inhabitants. We will safeguard all habitats affected by our operations and will protect open spaces and wilderness, while preserving biodiversity.

SUSTAINABLE USE OF NATURAL RESOURCES

We will make sustainable use of renewable natural resources, such as water, soils, and forests. We will conserve nonrenewable natural resources through efficient use and careful planning.

REDUCTION AND DISPOSAL OF WASTES

We will reduce and where possible eliminate waste through source reduction and recycling. All waste will be handled and disposed of through safe and responsible methods.

ENERGY CONSERVATION

We will conserve energy and improve the energy efficiency of our internal operations and of the goods and services we sell. We will make every effort to use environmentally safe and sustainable energy sources.

RISK REDUCTION

We will strive to minimize the environmental, health, and safety risks to our employees and the communities in which we operate through safe technologies, facilities, and operating procedures, and by being prepared for emergencies.

SAFE PRODUCTS AND SERVICES

We will reduce and where possible eliminate the use, manufacture, or sale of products and services that cause environmental damage or health or safety hazards. We will inform our customers of the environmental impacts of our products or services and try to correct unsafe use.

ENVIRONMENTAL RESTORATION

We will promptly and responsibly correct conditions we have caused that endanger health, safety, or the environment. To the extent feasible, we will redress injuries we have caused to persons or damage we have caused to the environment and will restore the environment.

INFORMING THE PUBLIC

We will inform in a timely manner everyone who may be affected by conditions caused by our company that might endanger health, safety, or the environment. We will regularly seek advice and counsel through dialogue with persons in communities near our facilities. We will not take any action against employees for reporting dangerous incidents or conditions to management or to appropriate authorities.

MANAGEMENT COMMITMENT

We will implement these Principles and sustain a process that ensures that the Board of Directors and Chief Executive Officer are fully informed about pertinent environmental issues and are fully responsible for environmental policy. In selecting our Board of Directors, we will consider demonstrated environmental commitment as a factor.

AUDITS AND REPORTS

We will conduct an annual self-evaluation of our progress in implementing these Principles. We will support the timely creation of generally accepted environmental audit procedures. We will annually complete the CERES Report, which will be made available to the public.

Source: http://www.ceres.org/about/principles.html.

The CERES Principles and Environmental Reporting

Over the past ten years, the Coalition for Environmentally Responsible Economies (CERES) has emerged as the worldwide leader in standardized corporate environmental reporting and promoting the transformation of environmental management within firms. Formed out of a unique partnership between some of America's largest institutional investors and environmental groups, CERES has pioneered an innovative, practical approach toward encouraging greater corporate responsibility on environmental issues.

Formed in 1989, the CERES coalition brought 15 major U.S. environmental groups together with an array of socially responsible investors and public pension funds. The latter represent more than $270 billion (in 2000) in invested capital, from the California and New York City public pension systems to an assemblage of more than 200 Protestant denominations and Catholic orders.

Companies signing on to CERES, which evolved out of the Valdez Principles developed after the *Exxon Valdez* spilled millions of gallons of oil in Alaska in the late 1980s, agree to the principles on the previous page and the following endorsement.

ENDORSING COMPANY STATEMENT FOR CERES PRINCIPLES

By adopting these Principles, we publicly affirm our belief that corporations have a responsibility for the environment, and must conduct all aspects of their business as responsible stewards of the environment by operating in a manner that protects the Earth. We believe that corporations must not compromise the ability of future generations to sustain themselves.

We will update our practices constantly in light of advances in technology and new understandings in health and environmental science. In collaboration with CERES, we will promote a dynamic process to ensure that the Principles are interpreted in a way that accommodates changing technologies and environmental realities. We intend to make consistent, measurable progress in implementing these Principles and to apply them to all aspects of our operations throughout the world.

ENVIRONMENTAL REPORTING IS PART OF CERES

According to CERES, corporate environmental reporting serves many different purposes for different stakeholders: It empowers people with the information they need to hold corporations accountable, and invites stakeholders more fully into the process of corporate goal setting. It permits investors to harness the power of the capital markets to promote and ensure environmentally superior business practices. It allows companies and their stakeholders to measure companies' adherence to the standards set forth in their statements of environmental principles, and their various goals and objectives. As an internal driver of change, it helps illuminate weaknesses and opportunities and set new goals. It will allow society to better understand the full implications of corporate activity, and thereby to design more sustainable local and global systems.

A growing number of companies are now voluntarily disclosing environmental information, both as stand-alone corporate reports and as special environmental or sustainability sections within corporate annual reports. However, if each firm utilizes its own format, indicators, and metrics, comparisons between these reports become impossible. Report users—investors, environmentalists, consumers, employees, other stakeholders, and other firms—have great difficulty in using reports to inform investment decisions, guide consumer product choices, and benchmark performance against comparable firms. The result is that the substantial resources firms spend on data development and analysis, report production, and report dissemination yield far less value than they could and should.

Among the companies that now issue reports based on the CERES Principles are:

- Arizona Public Service (follows the CERES Electric and Gas Utilities Form)
- Baxter International
- Ben and Jerry's Homemade Holdings, Inc.
- Coca-Cola, USA

- General Motors (follows Global Reporting Initiative Draft Guidelines)
- GreenMountain.com (follows the CERES Electric and Gas Utilities Form)
- Green Mountain Power Corporation
- HB Fuller
- Harwood Products
- Hughes Electronics
- Interface

- Polaroid
- PPL Corporation
- Sunoco, Inc.
- Timberland

Source: Excerpted from the CERES website: from pages, http://www.ceres.org/about/index.html; http://www.ceres.org/reporting/index.html; and http://www.ceres.org/about/principles.html.

According to futurist Hazel Henderson, population growth poses two critical issues for balancing the ecological impacts of human civilization. The first is that in industrialized societies, levels of consumption and ecological footprints are significantly greater than those of less developed nations, which as we have seen is inherently unsustainable. Second, there is a growing global consensus that one way to stabilize population growth is to educate and empower poor women, who serve as family educators, food producers, and family providers.[33] However, such empowerment is ideologically problematic for certain fundamentalists in more patriarchal societies and religious traditions.

From the perspective of sustainability, rather than purely economic or political perspectives, population control appears to be an imperative because of the human impact on all sorts of growth on the earth. Between 1700 and 1980, for example, forested areas of the planet were reduced by 20 percent, with continued deforestation of the rain forests that provide a heat sink, water resources, and much of the earth's supply of oxygen. More "advanced" farming methods, which have produced significantly enhanced yields to farmers during the 20th century, are now proving to be ecologically unsustainable. Soil degradation is estimated to have affected as much as 17 percent of vegetated land worldwide; since World War II the principal causes have been overgrazing, deforestation, and agriculture.[34]

Water wars may be the next big global ecological concern, as scarcity of water is predicted for many nations in the not too distant future. Energy consumption increased 100 times in the years between 1850 and 2000, with consequent increases in carbon dioxide emissions, creating the so-called greenhouse effect and possible global warming. Between 1950 and 1995, fossil fuel use and emissions accelerated some 3.6 times, with the United States as the largest producer (or consumer, depending on your point of view).[35]

The list of environmentally degraded resources could go on virtually endlessly. The real point, however, is that ecological sustainability must be married with societal- and community-based sustainability that balances political, social, and economic interests in a healthy whole.

BP Amoco: An Environmentally Conscious Oil Company?

At BP [British Petroleum] we're proud to be part of an organisation that does much to improve the quality of life of people everywhere. We believe our business should be competitive, successful and a force for good. Wherever we operate, we seek to conduct our business in a manner that is distinctive, responsible, and forward-looking. In everything we do, we try to make a difference—to be seen as part of constructive and innovative solutions to the world's growing needs for energy, materials, and services, and not as part of the problem. We believe our activities should generate benefits and opportunities, and our conduct should be a source of positive influence. We are committed to respect the rule of law and accept that we are accountable for our actions and the actions of those acting on our behalf.

Our policy goals are simply stated. First, excellent and ethical business performance. Second, benefit to the wider community—individuals and society—through our business performance. Third, no accidents in our operations, no harm to people, and no damage to the environment. To achieve these demanding goals we set measurable targets, submit the results to external verification, and publish reports of our progress.

A Good Citizen

We believe that our company should be a force for good in the world. This means contributing to the growth and development of the communities in which we operate through social investment programmes which complement and support our business presence.

http://www.bpamoco.com

John Browne, CEO of BP Amoco, takes a different view of the environment than many oil company executives. Moving BP Amoco toward enviromentalism has caused some critics to accuse him of having "gone soft" on climate change, as well as on other ecological issues of concern to many activists. BP Amoco not only has created a different rhetoric about its environmental responsibility than many other oil companies, but the company's website proclaims: "We aim to play a leading role in meeting the world's needs for oil, gas, solar power, and petrochemicals without damaging the environment." It is the latter statement that raises skeptics' eyebrows; for Browne, however, it has been a long-term commitment.

BP Amoco, a British company, is one of the world's largest petroleum and petrochemicals companies, with its main activities in exploration and production of crude oil and natural gas, refining, marketing, supply, and the transportation and the manufacturing of petrochemicals. With operations in Europe, North and South America, Asia, Australasia, and much of Africa, the company is truly global. It produces nearly three million barrels of petroleum daily, about 62 percent of which is oil and the rest natural gas.

Formed out of the merger of British Petroleum (BP), Amoco, and ARCO, BP has taken a leadership position as a corporate citizen by being one of the first oil companies to acknowledge the ecological issues associated with petrochemical production. As part of its commitment to responsible practice, the company issues an annual Environmental and Social Report, which is posted on its website: http://www.bp.com/.

Ecological responsibility, particularly for an oil company, needs to go well beyond such rhetoric, simply because the products the company produces are inherently not sustainable long term. As Browne stated in an interview with *The Earth Times:*

The approach of the company has to be not just one of rhetoric and debate, but of action and substance. When you have a joint venture with somebody in a country, you debate. Do you flare the gas? Or do you recycle the gas? . . . Do you encourage a government to make electricity through gas, or should they do it through coal? What should they do with waste water? Should they promulgate regulations to say the water should be as good as, if not better than, the water which was extracted and used? . . . We've been great proponents of clean development mechanisms, working with countries where the application of reasonably well-known technologies can improve enormously the local environment, both the local low level environment, as well as the high-level atmospheric activity. . . . We have made the environment a fundamental part of our business. I believe that is the right way to go.

Browne's vision of a sustainable petrochemical company, which he is attempting to instill in the company, takes what he calls a "wide sense of business," a perspective that involves inspiration, caring, and commitment as well as profitability. As he states:

The very wide sense of business, which is how do we create a business where people want to be in it, want to be part of it, want to be touched by it on a sustainable and growing basis? . . . I believe you have to do that with a systemic view. But also in the end, because you're dealing with people, . . . this is a very personal and human thing. The touching of people around the world. I'm filled with passion, because in the end, it's the passion that makes the difference.

Sources: Pranay Gupte, *The Earth Times,* January 25, 1999; http://www.earthimes.org/jan/business_investingjohnbrowne-jan25_99.htm; and http://www.bp.com.

INTEGRATING SUSTAINABILITY AND SOCIAL CAPITAL INTO ECONOMIC, POLITICAL, AND CIVIL SOCIETY

Sustainability is being used increasingly as a term that applies not only to the natural environment but also to communities and, indeed, whole societies. The rest of this chapter will attempt to broaden our understanding of society as a form of ecological system, and to form an integrated perspective on the linkages needed to build societies and communities that sustain themselves ecologically and are filled with meaningful relationships among their members. Business has an essential role to play in this mix, a role in which its power needs to be balanced with that of actors in the spheres of politics and civil society.

One of the apparent agents to bring about that balance is the presence of what is now called social capital—that is, relationships and linkages that connect people, communities, and businesses into relational networks. Social capital seems to be important in all three realms of human activity that we have been discussing throughout this book and to operate in related ways in each sphere. It forms a kind of social "glue" that can be used to generate decision-making policies aimed at long-term sustainability.

Political and Civil Society Spheres

Social capital, according to political scientist Robert Putnam, whose work was discussed in Chapter 3, "refers to features of social organization such as networks, norms, and social trust that facilitate coordination and cooperation for mutual benefit."[36] High levels of social capital are, as we shall see in reviewing Putnam's research, associated not only with healthy communities that seek and share a common good, but also with enhanced democratic government.

Putnam suggested that the benefits of high levels of social capital include the development of norms of reciprocity among individuals and groups, as well as trusting relationships. When trust exists, it is easier to coordinate, collaborate, and communicate within the network, especially as reputations are gained that establish the trustworthiness of others. Also, it is harder in such systems to engage in deceitful or opportunistic behavior, because others have developed expectations based on one's reputation. Finally, as Putnam noted, "dense networks of interaction probably broaden the participants' sense of self, developing the 'I' into the 'we.'"[37]

Putnam's research focused primarily on the levels of political and civic engagement of people in communities. He studied newly formed regional governments in Italy over a 20-year period to see if he could determine what made for more and less political success. Some of the regions were highly successful while others failed rather miserably. The differences in performance had little to do with affluence or prosperity, social stability, or political harmony, although that is what had been anticipated. Instead, the performance differences were associated with "strong traditions of civic engagement," which Putnam measured by looking at indicators like voter turnout, newspaper reading, membership in associational activities like choral societies, literary circles, Lions Clubs, and soccer clubs.[38]

Depending on their level of social capital, people seem to be either more or less involved in the democratic institutions of society, so governments appear to be more or less successful as a result of that involvement. More social capital results in higher levels of civic participation and better government, as the study of Italy's regional governments indicates. Putnam attributed the success to trust that other citizens will act fairly and obey laws, and to values of honesty and equality.

Additionally, social networks in the more successful regions appear to be—as they are in more successful companies today—horizontally, not hierarchically, organized.[39] In regions where civic engagement (i.e., civility and its attendant relationships) is highly developed, democracy appears to work best. In short, Putnam viewed these associational activities as essential to building not only successful communities (or civil society), but also successful governments. All of these associational activities also illustrate the importance and relevance of a strong and supportive civil society sphere if economic and political interests are to be balanced in the interest of long-term sustainability of society and, as discussed earlier in this chapter, the natural environment.

Civil Society, Ideology, and Corporate Power

One of the issues associated with corporate power in the modern world has to do with the impact of economic development—and multinational corporations in particular—on national and local communities; that is, on civil society or the set of relationships in which peoples and communities lives develop meaning. Local cultures are affected by forces that political scientist Benjamin Barber, in somewhat radical terminology, called "McWorld." McWorld's forces are those of globalization, represented by the homogenization of the world through look- and feel- and taste-alike McDonalds throughout the world to a set of simultaneous and countervailing forces he termed "Jihad." The forces of Jihad, in contrast to those of McWorld, are the countervailing forces of extreme localism, sectarianism, and, by implication, a zealous adherence to a local identify of some sort that excludes all who are not "inside" the particular system.[40]

Both of these contesting forces, according to Barber, represent threats to democracy or the political sphere, largely because they are indifferent to their impact on the state or community. Jihad arises in part from attempts to sustain cultural identity and, when not bound up in an extremism that excludes all who are nonbelievers or different, cultural identity is a significant and important aspect of the global village that most people agree should be preserved. McWorld represents a threat because of its homogenizing influences and because many global companies act as if they were without roots in any specific communities, hence ameliorating their connectedness and sense of responsibility for impacts. Lack of rootedness also lends itself to lack of consideration for the types of ecological concerns we have focused on earlier.

The Countervailing Power of Rootedness

Cultural identity and national ideology, as we have seen earlier in this book, are core elements of civil society. As billionaire financier George Soros pointed out in a controversial article, "Societies derive their cohesion from shared values. These values are rooted in culture, religion, history, and tradition." [41] Values and beliefs, Soros argued, are fundamental in shaping community life, conduct, and ultimately civil society, as well as democratic participation.

Healthy civil societies, as Putnam and others' demonstrated, have multiple layers of connectedness and a sense of community shared by members. This sense of community and connectedness develops out of shared beliefs that typically go beyond purely economic beliefs and that rest on shared assumptions about the nature of humanity, community, and society, about what is important and meaningful, and about how community members should live and work together.

Corporate citizens and their leaders need to understand and respect these values as they attempt to do business in the diverse communities that constitute the world. To do this well, corporations need to understand the communities in which they operate very well, respect local traditions and culture, and enter into a partnership that enhances, not detracts from, community life. Doing these things well ultimately requires that companies acknowledge localness as well as globalness and make some effort to become locally "rooted" to complement their globalism.

Rootedness represents acknowledgement of a sense of place, a home, and the sense of connectedness and community that develops from that sense of place. It respects local as well as global in the both/and logic we have argued is increasingly necessary for corporate success. Rootedness is also located within the natural ecology, since leading corporate citizens that acknowledge their rootedness know that they cannot exist when the earth itself is being unsustainably abused. And, as the work of Michael Porter discussed in the next section indicates, not only is this sense of global-localness—"glocalness"—important to communities and their governments (at whatever level of analysis), it also appears to be an essential element of competitive success.

Economic Sphere

Ironically, despite the forces of globalization and intense competition that characterize much of the modern economic sphere, local connections and a sense of the ecology of the whole of society connected with nature still appear to be vitally important to long-term economic (never mind societal) success. Innovative work by economist Michael Porter has highlighted this ecological perspective. In studying successful firms all over the world, Porter discovered that businesses are most successful when they operate in clusters representing critical masses of related businesses, not when they attempt to operate independently of such networks.[42] In what he termed the "paradox of location in a global economy," Porter found that long-term competitive advantage lies in creating localized advantages that rivals find hard to duplicate. The sources of these advantages, far from being low-cost outsourcing that has the potential of mistreating employees, turn out to be what some might consider to be the soft stuff of knowledge, relationships, and motivation.

Porter defined clusters as "geographic concentrations of interconnected companies and institutions in a particular field."[43] Clusters include an array of stakeholders: suppliers of inputs specialized to the industry or creators of industry-specific infrastructure; customers, particularly for business-to-business relationships and purchases; and manufacturers of complementary products and services.

Further, clusters can also include key educational institutions (e.g., Harvard or MIT in the Boston/Cambridge/Route 128 area, which provide talent for the local high technology cluster or Stanford and Berkeley in California's Silicon Valley) as well as governmental bodies and trade associations. All of these institutions can work collectively in a cluster to support the industry cluster in ways that a company acting alone would find impossible. These enterprises are found in all three spheres of activity that we have been discussing.

Clusters have interesting characteristics. They represent, at one level, an ecological system comprised of interdependent, symbiotic, collaborative, and simultaneously competitive organizations that take diverse forms. These are the very same characteristics of a healthy ecosystem. The boundaries of clusters can be determined by assessing the "linkages and complementarities across boundaries that are most important to competition."[44] Clusters are not necessarily bound by standard industry classification schemes because so many types of institutions are included, just as the effects of burning down large sections of rain forest go well beyond the boundaries of the forest itself and may well affect the global climate.

Interestingly, Porter viewed clusters as a new way of creating a value chain and, indeed, a new form of organizing without as much dependence on the hierarchical values associated with power aggrandizing. Clusters in their ecological formation are more emergent because they are self-organizing to a very large extent, with new businesses and other institutions springing from entrepreneurial roots as the need for them is recognized.

Healthy Clusters

Healthy clusters affect competitiveness in three ways, according to Porter. Clusters enhance productivity, drive innovation, and stimulate the formation of new businesses to serve cluster needs.

Productivity is enhanced because clusters offer better access to employees and suppliers locally as well as to other inputs, and because companies can source what they need without resorting to complex formal arrangements like alliances and joint ventures. Clusters also offer access to specialized information that grows up within the network of organizations operating within a specific cluster and provide for complementarities across organizations because each picks up its own piece of the business and serves others by doing so. They create pressures on local governments and communities to create access to public institutions and to public goods (e.g., infrastructure), that make doing business easier. And, because local rivalry tends to be high within clusters, they enhance motivation and measurement of results.

Innovation is enhanced by clusters for some of the same reasons that productivity is improved, and also because clusters tend to generate sophisticated and demanding buyers. Companies within clusters also tend to be more flexible, able to move quickly when necessary, and operate at lower costs because of their interrelatedness and constant mutual reinforcement of what is needed to compete successfully than companies outside clusters.

New business stimulation is enhanced because clusters have concentrated customer bases, which lowers risks and makes spotting opportunities relatively easier. As Porter pointed out, gaps in products or services are readily noted, while barriers to entry within a cluster tend to be lower for players already in the cluster (and even some from without). Additionally, local financial institutions know what to ask and seek in making loans and credit available. Overall, the perceived risk of investment is reduced within a cluster.

Glocal Companies and the Multiple Bottom Lines

Clusters create companies that management scholar James Post called "glocal." *Glocal companies* are simultaneously able to compete globally but remain strongly rooted in local communities.[45] Because they are local as well as global, glocal companies operating within clusters—arguably all companies—need to be actively aware of their multiple bottom-line responsibilities to the different primary and critical secondary stakeholders on whom they depend and who depend upon them. In part, this interdependence arises because glocal companies are deeply rooted in the local culture, community, and cluster. Such rootedness seems to be an important indicator of the potential for economic sustainability and even competitive advantage.

Tapping into knowledge that grows from numerous local interactions that enhance industry-specific expertise helps explain for the long-term development of localized human capital. Tapping into the relationships that exist among companies with local communities and their governmental bodies, and among employees argues for the enrichment of localized social capital. And motivation is frequently built on a combination of both human (intellectual or knowledge) and social capital, all built on a healthy ecosystem.

Long-Term Competitive Success and Social Capital

Porter's work on clusters highlights an important though frequently overlooked reality: One of the most important factors in successful economic development derives from the existence of trusting relationships and long-term connectedness among the entities that comprise his economically successful clusters. Ironically, it is this form of social capital, a cooperative and collaborative posture of interdependence, that arises as a key factor in success rather than individual action and cutthroat competition. Research on the relationship between economic and political development substantiates the notion that dense linkages among economic institutions provide a basis of success, as Putnam's work discussed above highlights. Examples include Asia's "network capitalism" and the industrial districts that develop when there is collaboration among workers and small entrepreneurs.[46]

Other research supports the link between plentiful social capital and economic success. Researchers at the American University found that high levels of trust were associated with strong economic performance.[47] The reasons given for these findings are that businesses operating where there are many positive social ties and a great deal of trust have incentives for innovation and capital accumulation because they are confident about the future. The findings are so powerful that international economic institutions like the World Bank have begun studying ways to promote social capital in less developed nations as a means of enhancing economic development.

Further, work in fields as diverse as education, urban poverty, unemployment, crime and drug abuse, and health care has shown that communities—civil society—too are more successful when there are strong social bonds.[48] Finally, as we have noted, Putnam's research on Italy's political districts suggests that governments are also more successful when there are rich norms of connectedness and civic engagement.[49] World Bank research corroborates these findings, suggesting that whole villages are better off if social capital is plentiful.[50] Economic prosperity appears to be complementary to a sense of community and place. Community and place need to be sustained as an ecology themselves and kept in balance with the natural environment on which we all depend.

PROMOTING HEALTHY GLOCALITIES

Companies that want to be leading corporate citizens must be "world class" in terms of productive capacity to meet the challenges of the modern economy. The natural environment demands ecological sustainability to preserve human civilization and leading corporate citizens are beginning to meet that challenge. Civil society requires healthy and positive relationships among all citizens in societies. "Glocality" means that companies may need to be located within healthy clusters as well as globally competitive and working toward sustainable development. Healthy clusters depend upon healthy civil societies supported by sufficiently strong and democratically based governments to meet the public interests identified by the people. Acting in the public interest to produce a balance among the three spheres suggests significant and important roles that government must play, not as an adversary of economic interests, but as ally or partner.

Porter identified some of the important roles that governments, local and national, need to play to foster healthy glocalities that generate active world class business clusters.[51] Through their educational institutions, governments need to ensure that citizens are well educated and able to take active roles in a knowledge-based economy. They must also develop local infrastructures, including transportation, telephone and electronic access, and other supports (e.g., water and sewage systems) that businesses need to survive and compete.

Modern governments hoping to support and enhance cluster development need to set appropriate rules of competition, particularly the enforcement of intellectual property and antitrust laws, to foster innovation and productivity. Finally, governments can, by working creatively and interactively in partnership with other institutions such as businesses, reinforce and build on emerging clusters through the provision of needed "public goods."

The combination of these needs speaks more than ever to the need to balance the three spheres of human activity, particularly to build in a positive and proactive role for government. Building a balance among the spheres of activity in human civilization, in effect, demands a sufficiently powerful and creative set of governmental organizations to establish and maintain rules of the game that balance resources, interests, and distribution of goods and services equitably.

LEADING CHALLENGES:
INTEGRITY—GAINING A SENSE OF THE WHOLE

Integrity, as was discussed in Chapter 4, means both honesty and wholeness. This sense of the whole—the systems perspective, and building a balance among individual and community interests—is operating in all three spheres of activity we have been discussing and which is based on a healthy ecology or natural environment. Thus, it is not only civil society but also economic productivity and the success of political or governing bodies that are enhanced when social capital is high that form a cornerstone of leading corporate citizenship. Because of the importance of social capital in all three spheres of human civilization and because a balance of the interests of human beings with those of nature is essential to humankind's long-term survival, corporate citizens need to think carefully about their roles, relationships, and impacts on the sustainability of societies and nature.

Integrity in leading corporate citizens also means being integrated; that is, integrating ecologically sustainable practices into corporate life on a day-to-day basis. Leaders of companies today need to be aware of the pressures of transparency and accountability all companies face with respect to their impacts on communities as well as on the natural environment. It is not enough for corporate citizens to operate as if they were in an "economic vacuum." Blinders no longer work in a world where the demands and pressures can change in the flick of a mouse and where unacceptable practices can be instantaneously broadcast around the world.

Rather, leaders need to take a systemic perspective on the ways that the practices of companies affect the communities in which they invest and the natural environment from which they draw resources. Operating with integrity means operating in the interests of the whole, as well as with honesty and forthrightness, and it means integrating principles into practices, as we discussed in Chapter 5. Doing so frequently requires adhering to increasingly important and widely accepted principles and standards, on which we will focus in the next chapter.

NOTES TO CHAPTER 9

1. Reported in Mathis Wackernagel and William Rees, *Our Ecological Footprint; Reducing Human Impact on the Earth* (Philadelphia: New Society Publishers, 1995); and Mathis Wackernagel et al., "Ecological Footprints of Nations: How Much Nature Do They Use?—How Much Nature Do They Have?" (ca. 1999). http://www.ecouncil.ac.cr/rio/focus/report/english/footprint/.

2. A hectare is a metric unit of measurement, equivalent to 2.471 acre or 10,000 square meters.

3. http://www.ecouncil.ac.cr/rio/focus/report/english/footprint/ranking.htm.

4. http://www.ire.ubc.ca/ecoresearch/ecoftpr.html.

5. One view of this transition is presented in Rogene A. Buchholz, *Principles of Environmental Management: The Greening of Business,* 2nd ed. (Englewood Cliffs, NJ: Prentice Hall, 1998).

6. Michael A. Berry and Dennis A. Rondinelli lay out this argument in "Proactive Corporate Environment Management: A New Industrial Revolution," *Academy of Management Executive* 12, no. 2 (May 1998), pp. 38–50.

7. See, for example, Stuart L. Hart, "Beyond Greening: Strategies for a Sustainable World," *Harvard Business Review,* January–February 1997, pp. 66–76.

8. Glen Dowell, Stuart Hart, and Bernard Yeung, "Do Corporate Global Environmental Standards Create or Destroy Market Value?" *Management Science* 46, no. 8 (August 2000), pp. 1059–74.

9. Berry and Rondinelli, pp. 38–50.

10. The developmental framework in the next paragraphs is derived from Hart, pp. 66–76.

11. Ibid., p. 71.

12. Dow's Public Report 2000 Update, at http://dow.com/dow_news/feature/05_18_00/index.htm.

13. Bill Schmitt, "Responsible Care: Making New Connections," *Chemical Week,* July 5–12, 2000, pp. 38–40.

14. Hart, pp. 1059–74.

15. Berry and Rondinelli, p. 5.

16. Ibid, pp. 38–50.

17. Amy Persapane Lally, "ISO 14000 and Environmental Cost Accounting: The Gateway to the Global Market," *Law and Policy in International Business* 29, no. 4 (Summer 1998), pp. 501–538.

18. William G. Russell, Steven L. Skalak, and Gail Miller, "Environmental Cost Accounting: The Bottom Line for Environmental Quality Management." *Total Quality Management* 3, no. 3 (Spring 1994), pp. 255–68.

19. Lally, pp. 501–538.

20. Russell, Skalak, and Miller cite the work of Carl Henn on life-cycle accounting. This discussion is developed from the Russell article.

21. Ibid.

22. Berry and Rondinelli, pp. 38–50.

23. Forest L. Reinhardt, "Bringing the Environment Down to Earth," *Harvard Business Review,* July–August 1999, pp. 149–57.

24. These covenants are described in Pieter Glasbergen, "Modern Environmental Agreements: A Policy Instrument Becomes a Management Strategy," *Journal of Environmental Planning and Management* 41, no. 6 (November 1998), pp. 693–709.

25. Ibid.
26. Reinhardt exemplifies this way of thinking, which comes from within the current set of management assumptions. The ideas in this and the next paragraph are derived from Reinhardt's article, "Bringing the Environment Down to Earth"; his ideas are more fully developed in *Down to Earth: Applying Business Principles to Environmental Management* (Cambridge: Harvard Business School Press, forthcoming).
27. From Reinhardt, "Bringing the Environment Down to Earth," pp. 149–157.
28. Russell, Skalak, and Miller, pp. 255–68.
29. These four are discussed in Glasbergen's conclusion, pp. 693–709.
30. Hart, pp. 66–76.
31. Hazel Henderson, *Building a Win-Win World: Life Beyond Global Economic Warfare* (San Francisco: Berrett-Koehler 1996).
32. Ibid. Data in this section are derived from this source.
33. Henderson.
34. All of the data in this paragraph are from Henderson,
35. Henderson.
36. Robert D. Putnam, "Bowling Alone: America's Declining Social Capital," *Journal of Democracy* 6, no. 1 (January 1995), p. 67. Benefits of social capitalism described in this paragraph are also derived from this article.
37. Putnam, p. 67.
38. Ibid. See also a summary paper by Robert Putnam, "The Prosperous Community: Social Capital and Public Life," *American Prospect,* Spring 1993, p. 13, at http://epn.org/prospect/13/13putn.html.
39. Ibid.
40. Benjamin Barber, *Jihad vs. McWorld* (New York: Times Books; Random House, 1995).
41. George Soros, "The Capitalist Threat," *Atlantic Monthly,* February 1997, p. 7; from http://www.mholyoke.edu/acad/intrel/soros.htm.
42. See Michael E. Porter, "Clusters and the New Economics of Competition." *Harvard Business Review,* November–December 1998, pp. 77–90. This discussion is derived from Porter's 1998 article; See also his book, *The Competitive Advantage of Nations* (New York: Free Press, 1990), and related article, "The Competitive Advantage of Nations," *Harvard Business Review,* March–April 1990, pp. 73–93.
43. Porter, "Clusters and the New Economics of Competition," p. 78.
44. Ibid, p. 79.
45. James E. Post, "Meeting the Challenge of Global Corporate Citizenship," Working paper, Boston College Center for Corporate Community Relations, 1999.
46. Putnam, "Bowling Alone," p. 65.
47. The work by Stephen Knanck of American University and Philip Keefer of the World Bank is cited in Karen Pennar, "The Ties that Lead to Prosperity," *Business Week,* December 15, 1997, pp. 154–155.
48. Putnam, "Bowling Alone," p. 65.
49. See Robert D. Putnam, *Making Democracy Work: Civic Traditions in Modern Italy* (Princeton, NJ: Princeton University Press, 1993).
50. Pennar, pp. 154–155.
51. The following discussion is taken from Porter, "Clusters and the New Ecomomics of Competition," pp. 77–90.

PART FOUR

Leading Corporate Citizens into the Future

CHAPTER 10

Global Standards—
Global Village

In my view Wal-Mart is a notable business success. . . . Wal-Mart adds a great deal of value to people in many of the towns it serves by providing a wide range of goods, employment, and investment opportunity. On the other hand, there are those who view the company quite differently. People who own or work in competing Main Street shops often experience Wal-Mart as an unfair bully, bent on destroying their livelihoods. . . .

Wal-Mart faces an important challenge, as do all firms when grappling with issues of value and policy. Wal-Mart is becoming a keystone species in many locales, as much of a fixture of the community as the local electric utility, the gas company, the major banks, or the local hospital. Wal-Mart's leadership must acknowledge and appreciate the extent to which others depend on it or feel vulnerable to it, as they do toward any greater establishment figure. . . .

. . . When a business ecosystem is powerful enough to reshape the social ecology of a local community, what responsibilities does it have? This question is by no means new to business leaders, but it is particularly relevant where companies pursue strategies based on boundary-making. . . . Ultimately, Wal-Mart's intent is to be the sole significant retailer wherever it does business, and it has the scale and efficiencies to do so. Companies that take this position in effect become the opportunity environment for many others, as well as operating in their own ecosystems. And because of their positions, they find themselves under the intense scrutiny of governments and activists who tend to apply much higher behavioral standards to these firms.

—JAMES F. MOORE, The Death of Competition:
Leadership and Strategy in the Age of Business Ecosystems

GLOBAL AND LOCAL STANDARDS

Since the end of World War II, the world has witnessed a virtual explosion of standards and principles intended to bring sustainability and ecological health within mankind's relationship to the natural environment. In addition, numerous sets of principles, codes of conduct, and international standards have been developed to foster respect for human dignity and rights, and better balance the three spheres of civilization: economic, political, and civil society. In part, this evolution of standards has occurred as a response to industrialization and globalization. Nations, non-governmental organizations (NGOs), Inter-Governmental Organizations (IGOs), and businesses alike have recognized the increasing power of transnational firms in view of their tremendous impact not only ecologically, but also on human societies. The emergence of standards is also a response by and for stakeholders attempting to find ways for their voices to be heard by powerful corporations and governments so that the balance of mutual yet different interests can be achieved. In effect, these standards and principles provide widely agreed-upon benchmarks for companies hoping to live up to the vision and values that they have articulated.

Many companies will want to—and should—develop their own codes of conduct, ethical principles, operating standards, and core values that reflect their unique purpose, customer groups, and internal values. In developing these internal principles, companies can define what they stand for and the standards of integrity they want to live up to. Yet it is clear that internally developed standards will have to satisfy the external scrutiny of increasingly sophisticated stakeholders like social investors, activists, as well as regulatory and standard-setting institutions. Thus it is helpful to have the global standards as a benchmark and, perhaps, a floor or minimum. To cope effectively with all these principles, companies need to ensure that their own standards are at least meeting the minimum standards set by various industry, governmental, NGO, and coalition groups.

The processes of globalization and the explosion of connectivity engendered by the World Wide Web have made obvious that some standards and principles of action need to be global in their scope. Further, implementation of these standards can help corporate citizens to avoid problems of free ridership, externalities, and prisoners dilemma that place some companies and countries at a disadvantage to others. The result is emerging standards and principles based on end values that attempt to ensure balance among the spheres of human activity and with nature and to provide for respect for basic human dignity.

Global standards and principles are typically arrived at through consensus-building processes established by international bodies, sometimes industry organizations and frequently coalitions of various interested stakeholders. Despite the vast diversity and pluralism of societies in the world, the emergence of these statements of principles and codes of conduct that powerful enterprises in society are expected to live up to is testimony to the fact that after all is said and done, we all live in one world.

To cope with the recent proliferation of standards and accountability measures, this chapter will explore the emergence of standards in all three spheres of human civilization and those that have emerged with respect to the natural environment. In this exploration, we will see that although global standards and accountability measures are still in the early stages of development, increasing agreement is being generated about what standards global companies—particularly because of the scope of their impact—will have to adhere to. We begin with the natural environment. We will then address the emerging expectations of activists in civil society with respect to human rights and labor standards for global businesses. Then we will explore the need for integrity in the economic system and the ways that standards, accountability, and transparency can provide a basis for building integrity. Finally, we will explore issues of corruption in the political sphere and the ways that businesses must operate with integrity even in systems where corruption is still common.

PROTECTING THE ECOLOGICAL SURROUND

This chapter begins with the natural environment on which we all, including businesses, depend for our survival, with the focus on moving toward sustainable economic and social practices as an imperative facing humanity today.

Respect for the Natural Environment: The Rio Declaration and Agenda 21

The United Nations has recognized the importance of environmental sustainability through development of its "Agenda 21" initiative, which was adopted at the first-ever global conference on the environment, which was held in Rio de Janeiro on June 14, 1992.[1] Agenda 21 is based in part on the principles of environment and development—the Rio Declaration—adopted at the conference.[2] Among the most important principles of which leading corporate citizens should be aware are the sovereign right of nations to use their own natural resources to meet the needs of future and present generations. The principles emphasize the need for sustainable development and its link to environmental protection through focusing on eradicating poverty, meeting the needs of developing countries as a priority, and paying particular attention to ensuring that the "voices" of vulnerable groups, such as women, youth, indigenous and oppressed peoples, are heard.

The Rio Principles also emphasize the need for global partnership in conserving and protecting the earth's ecosystem through an open and global economic system, with fair trade policies, discouragement of the transfer of environmentally harmful activities to more vulnerable or weaker nations, and internalization of costs. Nation-states are encouraged to promote countrywide initiatives to improve sustainability—scientifically and technologically—through citizen participation, effective environmental legislation, and active citizen participation in the enacting of national laws and regulations. The principles also encourage global intercountry cooperation in the interest of the environment and a spirit of collaboration and partnership.

Clearly, the Rio Principles are aimed at balancing the economic, political, and civil society spheres around ecological sustainability. They are further supported by the United Nations Environment Programs (UNEP) Agenda 21, a comprehensive document that sets forth an ambitious series of agenda items and goals linking economic and social development with ecological sustainability. Agenda 21 deals with the social and economic dimensions of sustainable development, including environment and development; and on the conservation and management of resources, such as atmosphere, land, forests, deserts, mountains, agriculture, biodiversity, biotechnology, oceans, fresh water, toxic chemicals, and hazardous, radioactive, and solid waste and sewage. It also focuses on strengthening the role of major groups, including women, children and youth, indigenous peoples, non-governmental organizations, local authorities, workers, business and industry, farmers, scientists and technologists. Finally, Agenda 21 emphasizes the means of implementation with respect to finance, technology transfer, science, education, capacity-building, international institutions, legal measures, and information.[3]

Agenda 21 covers many areas of concern to businesses that want to take leading citizenship roles. Agenda 21 focuses on combating poverty, changing consumption patterns, sustainability, and population/demographic shifts. It focuses on protecting and promoting human health while simultaneously promoting the integration of the environment and development into decision-making processes. Areas of environmental concern include the atmosphere, forests, and fragile ecosystems, including a focus on the increasing desertification of some parts of the world resulting from overpopulation and overuse of the land, and the creation of sustainable mountain, agricultural, and rural areas. Companies and nations need to learn to manage and protect biological diversity, and manage biotechnology safely. Pollution and waste management systems are aimed at improving the oceans and other bodies of water and the atmosphere, and reducing hazardous wastes and toxic chemicals, solid wastes and sewage, and radioactive wastes.

Responses from Business: CERES Principles, Responsible Care®, and ISO 14000

Businesses today are coming under increasing pressure from environmental activists, regulatory agencies, governments, and NGOs to respond to the move toward sustainable development. Some business groups are responding to these pressures by creating self-regulatory initiatives that focus their internal practices on more sustainable and acceptable practices.

One of the foremost business-oriented organizations in fostering collaborative relationships among the many parties interested in sustainable ecology has been CERES, the Coalition for Environmentally Responsible Economies. Comprised of more than 50 investor, environmental, religious, labor, business, and social justice organizations, CERES members worked together to draft a set of principles that were widely endorsed by companies and organizations at the end of the 20th century.

CERES Principles

The CERES Principles, which were presented in the previous chapter, came into existence following the tanker, *Exxon Valdez,* oil spill in Alaska's Prince William Sound in March 1989. The spill of more than 10 million gallons brought renewed activist and indeed global public attention to the need for an ecologically sustainable environment. Initiated in 1989 the CERES Principles were first called the Valdez Principles, then their scope and tactics were broadened toward influencing corporate strategies on the environment through the use of shareholder resolutions to initiate conversations with corporate directors about the company's practices.[4]

The CERES coalition views itself as successfully modeling cooperation and dialogue among investors, environmentalists, and companies, as a leader in standardizing corporate reporting on the environment, and as a catalyst for making measurable improvements in companies' environmental practices. CERES has accomplished much of this through its 10 principles detailed in the box in Chapter 9. These principles point to specific ways that companies can change their behaviors to achieve the ecological sustainability demanded by the four core principles of The Natural Step process discussed in Chapter 2.

As a result of CERES' efforts, many companies became interested in demonstrating their commitment to ecological principles. Among the current signatories are Sun Oil, Arizona Public Service Company, Bethlehem Steel, General Motors, H. B. Fuller, and Polaroid Corporation. By signing the CERES Principles, companies agreed to meet the 10 conditions although all of these companies clearly have a way to go before they are actually operating in sustainable ways.

As noted in Chapter 9, the principles revolve around protection of the biosphere and sustainable use of natural resources, including waste reduction, energy conservation, risk reduction, and safety. They also demand that companies actively engage with various external stakeholders in restoring damaged ecologies, providing information about internal corporate environmental practices to the public, and creating an annual environmental audit and report that can inform stakeholders about company environmental practice and performance. Additionally, the principles make clear the need for top management commitment in order to make the CERES Principles internally effective and truly valued throughout a company.

Commitment to the CERES Principles goes beyond regulatory or legal compliance and well into meeting high voluntary standards of environmental responsibility. The principles attempt to ensure that the principles of prudence and care, discussed in Chapter 2, are actually met in practice. Indeed, the commitment of major firms like those noted above has been somewhat controversial, especially because old-line companies involved in extraction industries such as oil and steel are clearly not yet meeting the standards. While the whole "movement" toward such environmentally sustainable principles is still rather small, it is important to note that by signing the principles, these companies have publicly committed themselves to a long-term *process* of continued improvement in their environmental practices.

Responsible Care®

Another example of an industry-led environmental effort is the Responsible Care initiative of the Chemical Manufacturers Association, which has received considerable public attention for its leadership (see the Dow Chemical box in Chapter 9). The chemical industry is, for obvious reasons, under significant pressure to improve its environmental performance. Like the CERES Principles, Responsible Care is a voluntary

TABLE 10.1. Responsible Care® Guiding Principles

Our industry creates products and services that make life better for people around the world—both today and tomorrow. The benefits of our industry accompanied by enduring commitments to Responsible Care® in the management of chemicals worldwide. We will make continuous progress toward the vision of no accidents, injuries, or harm to the environment and will publicly report our global health, safety, and environmental performance. We will lead our companies in ethical ways that increasingly benefit society, the economy, and the environment while adhering to the following principles:

- To seek and incorporate public input regarding our products and operations.
- To provide chemicals that can be manufactured, transported, used, and disposed of safely.
- To make health, safety, the environment, and resource conservation critical considerations for all new and existing products and processes.
- To provide information on health or environmental risks and pursue protective measures for employees, the public, and other key stakeholders.
- To work with customers, carriers, suppliers, distributors, and contractors to foster the safe use, transport, and disposal of chemicals.
- To operate our facilities in a manner that protects the environment and the health and safety of our employees and the public.
- To support education and research on the health, safety, and environmental effects of our products and processes.
- To lead in the development of responsible laws, regulations, and standards that safeguard the community, workplace, and environment.
- To practice Responsible Care by encouraging and assisting others to adhere to these principles and practices.

Source: Responsible Care ® website: http://www.cmahq.com/cmawebsite.nsf/pages/responsiblecare.

effort by chemical companies to commit to continual environmental, health, and safety improvements in a manner that is responsive to the public interest.[5]

Significant aspects of Responsible Care are that companies signing on commit themselves to continually improving environmental performance, collaborating to help each other improve, measuring progress, and gaining regular public input on their efforts. The effort operates through a set of guiding principles (see Table 10.1) and detailed guidelines for management practice in six operating areas important to chemical companies.

Notice that the Responsible Care initiative indicates a clear opportunity for input and concern for the public responsibilities of the chemical industry, as well as its relationships with key stakeholders, including employees, customers, suppliers, distributors, and local communities. All of these stakeholders might be affected by problems with the companies' products.

To further assure that environmental responsibility develops among chemical companies, the initiative has developed codes of management practice for six specific areas. In extensive detail, these codes cover management practices associated with (1) community awareness, (2) pollution prevention, (3) distribution, (4) process safety, (5) employee health and safety, and (6) product stewardship. Each code contains a statement of purpose and scope, details of how that code relates to the guiding principles, and guidelines for specific management practices associated with that area.

The stringency of the standards has resulted in favorable publicity regarding this initiative and for the Chemical Manufacturers Association as a leader in setting high industry standards and specific guidelines for corporate behavior and practices.

ISO 14000

Another set of emerging environmental standards to which many companies, particularly those operating in the European Union, are paying close attention is the ISO 14000 standards. Modeled in part on the International Organization for Standardization's ISO 9000 quality standards, ISO 14000 focuses the attention of companies on environmental management—that is, avoiding or minimizing the harmful effects of corporate activities on the environment. ISO 14000 and the related ISO 14001 auditing standards are largely industry driven and, unlike CERES, generally represent internally developed standards, rather than a more globally defined set of absolute standards and principles to which a company agrees to adhere.[6]

Like the CERES Principles, ISO 14000 emphasizes the operating policies and practices within a company, rather than the nature or use of products or services generated.[7] As mentioned, the goal of the ISO standards is to reduce the harmful environmental effects of the production process itself that occur from pollution and waste or from depletion of natural resources. ISO 14000 is actually a "family" of related standards that attempts to align businesses, industries, governments, and consumers around common ecological interests.

To deal with the complexity of the natural environment and the many ways production processes can harm it, ISO has created more than 350 standards to monitor various aspects of the environment. These aspects include air quality, water quality, and soil, and are intended to provide consistent, scientifically valid data to monitor the ecological impacts of economic activity. Generally, ISO expects companies to develop their own standards and environmental management system, in compliance with relevant legislation and regulations, and then audit their practices to assure conformance with internal standards. Companies operating under the ISO 14000 standards are also expected to focus on continual improvements in their environmental practices.

ISO 14000 standards emphasize several different aspects of environmental management, including corporate environmental management systems, environmental and related audits, environmental labeling practices, performance assessment, and life-cycle evaluation. As we will see below, many companies now must use the ISO 9000 quality standards to compete successfully simply because their allies demand it. It is very likely that a similar developmental cycle will occur for the ISO 14000 family of environmental standards and the CERES Principles, particularly with respect to more progressive companies hoping to partner with smaller companies or with government purchasing units, when the government is concerned about environmental quality. Hence it makes sense for companies that wish to be leading corporate citizens to begin moving toward meeting such standards.

Environmental Performance Standards

While the CERES Principles provide a set of general standards to which companies agree to adhere in terms of performance, the ISO 14000 series seeks to "balance socioeconomic and business needs with support of environmental protection and prevention of pollution."[8] In the sense that ISO focuses on conformance with internally generated policies while CERES and other environmental principles focus on external performance standards, CERES is a higher hurdle for many companies to achieve.

Nonetheless, significant environmental benefits could result from the voluntary acceptance of the ISO 14000 family of standards, as with the chemical industry's Responsible Care initiative. These ecological benefits include compliance with existing national environmental laws, external signaling of a commitment to environmental stewardship by participating companies, greater adherence to ISO standards because companies are part of the process of formulating the standards, and reduction of civil and criminal penalties associated with enforcement of environmental regulations.[9]

Coping with the complexity of managing environmentally will demand some degree of harmonization among the standards (e.g. CERES) now being promulgated internationally. Although ISO's environmental standards are currently company driven, one of the hopes of environmental activists is that ISO standards will move companies toward higher levels of sustainable practice over time, particularly if the international bodies interested in preserving natural resources can agree on a set of performance criteria and standards.

Other standards that involve business include the Montreal Protocol, which focuses on protecting the ozone layer, and the Business Charter on Sustainable Development, which comes from the World Business Council for Sustainable Development (see http://www.wbcsd.ch/). The latter organization is a coalition of more than 125 multinational companies united by a shared commitment to sustainable development and environment combined with economic growth.

Combined with consumer demand for greener products, reduced risk associated with environmental liability, and cost savings, the ISO and related sustainability standards are likely over time to improve environmental performance despite their lack of absolute performance criteria.[10] This improvement will come more quickly to the extent that powerful coalitions, such as CERES and the United Nations, agree upon the requisite performance criteria for sustainability in business practice.

GLOBAL ACCOUNTABILITY AND SUSTAINABILITY

Never has the need for sustainability been more apparent than it is today with the ecological or "natural" disasters that seem to be affecting humanity with increasing regularity. Sustainability of community and ecology is at the heart of much concern, as standards have demonstrated.

One fairly radical approach to business in the future has been offered by Amory B. Lovins, L. Hunter Lovins, and Paul Hawken, who have proposed a shift from the current capitalist paradigm to a new paradigm that they termed "natural capitalism."[11] Whether this model or other models of new economic thinking actually take hold, corporate leaders should be aware of the new demands by many stakeholders for transparency and accountability for corporate practices. Over time, the current definition of capitalism and its manifestations in practice will inevitably change as a result of these pressures and significant new expectations are likely to be placed upon businesses. Aware leaders will track such ideas to assure that their corporations can cope effectively as changes occur.

Below we will explore some emerging ideas about natural capitalism, as well as a new global reporting and accountability initiative that seeks standardized global reporting measures, particularly on corporate environmental matters, but also in other areas of responsibility and accountability.

Natural Capitalism

In their *Harvard Business Review* article, "A Road Map for Natural Capitalism," Lovins, Lovins, and Hawken argued that simple changes in corporate practices can provide significant benefits that will not only protect the natural environment, but also potentially be very profitable. If the idea of natural capitalism—sustainability— truly takes hold, and earlier chapters have provided a good deal of evidence that it might, becoming sustainable will require four dramatic shifts in business practices.

- Dramatically increase the productivity of natural resources by reducing wasteful practices, changing production design and technology, and stretching ecological resources significantly further than they are today.
- Shift to biologically inspired production models that are closed loop, as they are in nature, where all waste from one process becomes an input for another process so that nothing is wasted.
- Move to a solutions-based business model, where value is delivered as a flow of services rather than products, and well-being is measured by satisfying expectations for quality, utility, and performance of products and services.
- Reinvest in natural capital by restoring, sustaining, and expanding the planet's ecosystem.[12]

In part, this approach to natural capitalism is based not on the law of diminishing returns, which informs much current economic thinking, but a radically different perspective: the concept of expanding returns. This concept, which underpins approaches like lean manufacturing and whole system design, implies that big cost savings can actually cost less, or that saving a large amount of resources can be less costly than saving a smaller amount.[13]

The authors of this radical approach to capitalism argued that by thinking about the whole system—the closed loop—leaders can find numerous small changes that result in big savings, a point that Peter Senge called finding leverage in his important book *The Fifth Discipline*.[14] Kodak Corporation, for example, eliminated 700,000 pounds of landfill waste annually and produced yearly savings of $600,000 by developing a new process and material that wraps photographic paper waste.[15] By changing from a foil-coated paper that could not be recycled to a more environment-friendly wrapping, Kodak found that it would actually save money

TABLE 10.2.   Interface's Sustainability Model

The path toward sustainability we've chosen requires effort on seven ambitious fronts:

1. *Eliminate Waste.* The first step to sustainability, QUEST is Interface's campaign to eliminate the concept of waste, not just incrementally reduce it.

2. *Benign Emissions.* We're focusing on the elimination of molecular waste emitted with negative or toxic impact into our natural systems.

3. *Renewable Energy.* We're reducing the energy used by our processes while replacing nonrenewable sources with sustainable ones.

4. *Closing the Loop.* Our aim is to redesign our processes and products to create cyclical material flows.

5. *Resource Efficient Transportation.* We're exploring methods to reduce the transportation of molecules (products and people) in favor of moving information. This includes plant location, logistics, information technology, video-conferencing, e-mail, and telecommuting.

6. *Sensitivity Hookup.* The goal here is to create a community within and around Interface that understands the functioning of natural systems and our impact on them.

7. *Redesign Commerce.* We're redefining commerce to focus on the delivery of service and value instead of the delivery of material. We're also engaging external organizations to create policies and market incentives that encourage sustainable practices.

Source: Interface, at http://216.1.140.49/us/company/sustainability/seven_steps.asp.

and eliminate the landfill problem, as well as address ergonomic safety issues that were the original incentive for thinking about the change.

Taking such thinking even further, Lovins and his coauthors argued, that companies can rethink manufacturing processes entirely and create new products and processes that actually prevent waste in the first place. This technique, which requires shifting one's perspective away from looking only at production to looking at the whole system, is biologically based in the "waste equals food" concept attributed to Paul Bierman-Lytle of the Ch2M Hill architectural firm.[16]

In what they characterized as the third stage of progress toward natural capitalism, Lovins, Lovins, and Hawken identified Interface, formerly a carpet manufacturer and now a carpet service (lease) company, as shifting its business model entirely. Rather than focusing on producing and selling products, Interface's new sustainable business model—the one that natural capitalism argues for—views itself as a service-leasing business.[17] Instead of selling carpets, Interface now moves through what it calls its sustainability path, a path that has seven steps (see Table 10.2).

Interface's strategy is based in part on the ideas of sustainability expressed in Paul Hawken's innovative book, *The Ecology of Commerce.* Hawken suggested that certain goods should not be sold, but leased, assuring that responsibility is maintained by the manufacturer over the product's entire life cycle.[18] Radical as some of these ideas may sound today, the fact that such a mainstream and prestigious journal as the *Harvard Business Review* is paying attention to them suggests their importance and potential impact on business in the future.

RESPECTING HUMAN DIGNITY AND CIVILIZATION

In addition to developing a much better understanding of ecological principles and sustainability, the core of operating responsibly is respecting human dignity. As the globalization process continues, companies are discovering that they need to be careful to operate in accordance with principles that increasingly are being developed and applied. Failing to live up to emerging codes can subject companies to public criticism by human rights and labor activists, who can now easily spread their criticisms globally through the Internet.

Particularly for companies that source their products from developing nations, attention to the conditions in which those products are produced is becoming an imperative because of the rapidity with which activists can spread their criticisms and draw attention from consumers. The following sections will explore the standards of respect for human dignity that are generally agreed upon and which are increasingly applied to transnational as well as local corporations. While there is currently a decided lack of enforcement of many of these standards, the emergence of global activism is beginning to shift corporate responsiveness toward the implementation of standards to which they, in principle, agree.

Having explored principles related to human rights and human dignity, we will then turn to responsible operating principles that are emerging from the business community itself. In the political sphere, we will briefly explore the ways that companies operating multinationally can cope with problems of corruption.

CIVIL SOCIETY: RESPECT FOR HUMAN DIGNITY

Respect for human dignity and worth is at the core of all stakeholder relationships and certainly fundamental to the global principles around the basic human rights businesses are expected to employ. Below we will briefly explore some of the most important principles, and their promulgating organizations, to help provide a framework for the practices of leading corporate citizens with respect to stakeholders like employees, customers, and suppliers. Basic human rights can be found within the sphere of civil society, where we begin this exploration.

UN's Principles of Human Rights and the Environment

One of the most fundamental documents guiding today's understanding of human rights is the Universal Declaration of Human Rights, adopted by the General Assembly of the United Nations in 1948.[19] The declaration focuses on the freedom, equality, and inherent dignity of all human beings regardless of race, color, sex, language, religion, opinions, or national origin. It prohibits slavery, torture, discrimination, arbitrary arrest and detention, and forced marriage, and promotes equal recognition, justice, and due process before the law. The declaration also states that people should have freedom of movement within and without countries, the right to a nationality and belief system. It states that everyone has a right to free association

TABLE 10.3. Excerpts from the 1948 United Nations Universal Declaration of Human Rights*

ARTICLE 23

1. Everyone has the right to work, to free choice of employment, to just and favorable conditions of work, and to protection against unemployment.

2. Everyone, without any discrimination, has the right to equal pay for equal work.

3. Everyone who works has the right to just and favorable remuneration ensuring for himself and his family an existence worthy of human dignity, and supplemented, if necessary, by other means of social protection.

4. Everyone has the right to form and to join trade unions for the protection of his interests.

ARTICLE 24

Everyone has the right to rest and leisure, including reasonable limitation of working hours and periodic holidays with pay.

ARTICLE 25

1. Everyone has the right to a standard of living adequate for the health and well-being of himself and of his family, including food, clothing, housing, medical care and necessary social services, and the right to security in the event of unemployment, sickness, disability, widowhood, old age or other lack of livelihood in circumstances beyond his control.

2. Motherhood and childhood are entitled to special care and assistance. All children, whether born in or out of wedlock, shall enjoy the same social protection.

*Note that the language used in these articles reflects the time frame in which they were developed.
Source: UN Declaration of Universal Human Rights, 1948.

and peaceful assembly and it imposes the duties and responsibilities of citizenship on people as well.

The articles of the declaration most relevant to corporate citizens are numbers 23 to 25, which deal with the rights to work, a living wage, rest, and living standards (see Table 10.3).

ILO Conventions

The International Labor Organization (ILO), founded in 1919 to contend with inhuman and unjust labor conditions, has developed numerous "conventions" regarding labor standards and human dignity.[20] ILO considers seven of these conventions to be fundamental to the rights of human beings at work whatever the level of development of the country in which they are working. The seven fundamental rights (some of which overlap with the UN Declaration on Human Rights) and the rights they guarantee are listed in Table 10.4.

Most nations of the world are members of the ILO and subscribe to these fundamental conventions, as well as the numerous additional conventions issued by the ILO to sustain and support working people worldwide. But, as we shall see below,

TABLE 10.4. Fundamental ILO Conventions

Freedom of association
- Freedom of Association and Protection of the Right to Organization, 1948, No. 87. Establishes the right of workers and employers to form and join organizations of their own choosing without prior authorization, and lays down guarantees for the free functioning of such associations without interference by public authorities.

- Right to Organize and Collective Bargaining Convention, 1949, No. 98. Provides for protection against antiunion discrimination, protection of workers and employees' organization against interference by each other and promotes collective bargaining.

Abolition of forced labor
- Forced Labor Convention, 1930, No. 39. Requires companies to suppress use of forced labor, except for military service, supervised convict labor, and emergencies.

- Abolition of Forced Labor Convention, 1957, No. 105. Prohibits the use of forced or compulsory labor as a means of political coercion or education, punishment for free expression or ideological views, or workforce motivation or discrimination.

Equality
- Discrimination (Employment and Occupation) Convention, 1958, No. 111. Affirms that all people, regardless of race, creed, or gender, have the right to pursue both their material well-being and their spiritual development in conditions of freedom and dignity, economic security, and equal opportunity.

- Equal Remuneration Convention, 1951, No. 100. Calls for equal pay for equal work for men and women.

Elimination of child labor
- Minimum Age Convention, 1973, No. 138. Aims to abolish child labor, and stipulates that the minimum age for employment will be at least the age at which compulsory schooling is complete.

Source: ILO website, at http://www.ilo.org/public/english/50normes/whatare/fundam/index.htm.

the conditions imposed by these conventions and their underlying principles are not always met in all places, particularly where pressure on businesses to economize and to externalize costs are great. Too frequently, these economizing pressures create incentives for companies to avoid the humane principles embedded in conventions such as those issued by the ILO.

Following the United Nations conference on the environment in 1992, the UN also drafted a set of Principles on Human Rights and the Environment.[21] This declaration attempts to guarantee an ecologically sound environment following the principles of sustainable development to all people in the world. In March 2000 "The Earth Charter," an effort to promote fundamental values and ethical principles around the world, was released.[22] The focus of the Earth Charter, which was initially signed by more than 100,000 individuals and numerous civil society organizations around the globe, covers respect and care for the community of life, ecological integrity, social and economic justice, and democracy, nonviolence, and peace.

Unfortunately, as with many of these standards, charters, and declarations, few mechanisms for enforcement yet exist in the global arena. See the box below on

"Tough Going for Declarations." But other types of pressures, including negative publicity and pressure group activism, especially through the Internet, pose considerable new challenges for companies that would attempt serious worker exploitation, as will be discussed below.

Working Conditions: The Sweatshop Controversy

One of the important standards that companies who outsource much or all of their production to suppliers in developing nations have to face is how much to pay their workers. Forced in part by pressures from activist groups like United Students Against Sweatshops, Sweatshop Watch, Corporate Watch, UNITE, and the ILO (among many others), many companies now are paying much more attention to working conditions in supplier firms than they have in the past.

Companies such as Nike, Reebok, Liz Claiborne, and Phillips-Heusen, which have faced considerable controversy about their sourcing practices, have banded together to form a self-regulatory association called the Fair Labor Association (FLA). The American Apparel Manufacturers Association (AAMA), an industry trade group, has also created a less stringent set of standards for monitoring factories.[23]

Tough Going for Declarations

"All human beings are born free and equal in dignity and rights." So begins the first article of the Universal Declaration of Human Rights, proclaimed by the United Nations in 1948. The declaration goes on to list basic rights including asylum, association, and freedom of movement. The declaration was part of the UN mission to provide a moral force in world affairs: The theory was that signatory countries would be bound by its strictures and could be held accountable for violating them.

The idea of a guiding set of principles for the world proved so attractive that it has been replicated many times since. Particularly as we approached the new millennium, many thought the time was right for broad statements on the future course of human rights and development issues. The 1992 Earth Summit in Rio and the 1995 Fourth World Conference on Women's Rights in Beijing laid down courses of action for environmental protection and women's rights.

Now we've just seen the launch of the Earth Charter: signed by 100,000 people in 51 countries, including well-known personalities like Mikhail Gorbachev, it aims to "elaborate the moral and ethical values for a modern civil society." The Earth Charter sets out principles calling for democracy, nonviolence and peace, ecological integrity, and social and economic justice. A product of NGO collaboration, the charter is supposed to promote sustainable development worldwide.

But how useful are these lofty words? Do countries endorse them, and if so, do they stick by their words? Sadly, the truth is that declarations—however well-intentioned—often fail to meet expectations. [For example,] the Framework Convention on Climate Change had 150 signatories agreeing in general to reduce greenhouse gas emissions, with developed nations "aiming" for specific reductions. Yet global carbon dioxide levels have reached record highs, while U.S. emissions are projected for 2000 to be 13 percent above 1990 levels.

Source: Kumi Naidoo, Secretary General and CEO, Civicus, excerpted from e-CIVICUS, no. 90, Connecting Civil Society Worldwide.

UNITE (the Union of Needletrades, Industrial and Textile Employees), the Retail, Wholesale and Department Store Union, and the Interfaith Center on Corporate Responsibility are among the activists who believe that corporate-based regulation of suppliers' working conditions is mainly a public relations ploy, not a substantive move. Sweatshop Watch, which combines labor and community (civil society) interests, argues that the real solutions to sweatshop conditions must come not from industry self-regulation, but from implementation of enforceable labor standards and protection in international trade agreements and relatively standardized and enforced national and international laws.[24]

The companies forming the FLA hope that by regulating themselves, they will be able to avoid some of the negative publicity, activism, and associated diminution of their reputational capital and customer loyalty that accompanies activists' uncovering human rights and worker abuses in supplier companies. Companies in industrialized nations sourcing from developing nations naturally argue that if they were to pay prevailing domestic wage rates to workers in developing nations, they would lose the very competitive advantage and economizing benefits they had sought to gain in outsourcing production in the first place.

Human rights and labor activists, on the other hand, argue that working conditions and pay scales need to be monitored not just by industry groups like FLA and AAMA, who are likely to be biased in favor of the companies, but by external and more objective monitors. Activist groups have strongly criticized the formation of these industry-based monitoring organizations. One of them, Corporate Watch, converted its 1998 "Greenwash Award" into a "Sweatwash Award" to the FLA because activists feared that the creation of the FLA would mean that only cosmetic, rather than real, improvements in working conditions would be made.[25] Governments of developing nations, of course, argue that transnational companies bring much-needed jobs and economic development to their nations, thus they are sometimes willing to overlook transgressions of basic human rights and dignity in the interest of economic development.

Sweatshops

Sweatshop Watch defines a sweatshop as "a workplace where workers are subject to extreme exploitation, including the absence of a living wage or benefits, poor working conditions and arbitrary discipline." An excerpt from the Sweatshop Watch homepage describes conditions in sweatshops in the United States, where they say such conditions do exist, and in less developed nations:

> The overwhelming majority of garment workers in the U.S. are immigrant women. They typically toil 60 hours a week in front of their machines, often without minimum wage or overtime pay. In fact, the Department of Labor estimates that more than half of the country's 22,000 sewing shops violate minimum wage and overtime laws. Many of these workers labor in dangerous conditions including blocked fire exits, unsanitary bathrooms, and poor ventilation. Government surveys reveal that 75 percent of U.S. garment shops violate safety and health laws. In addition, workers commonly face verbal and physical abuse and are intimidated from speaking out, fearing job loss or deportation. Overseas, garment workers routinely make less

than a living wage, working under extremely oppressive conditions. Workers in Vietnam average $0.12 per hour, and workers in Honduras average $0.60 per hour. Sweatshops can be viewed as a product of the global economy. Fueled by an abundant supply of labor in the global market, capital mobility, and free trade, garment industry giants move from country to country seeking the lowest labor costs and the highest profit, exploiting workers the world over.[26]

Sweatshop conditions clearly fail to respect the basic human dignity of the workers who labor there. Companies that operate with integrity and hope to implement their vision and values through their stakeholder relationships, particularly with suppliers, need to be well aware of the conditions of work in those suppliers' operations. Integrity demands closely monitoring working conditions, and assuring that employees are treated with respect and dignity, including provision of a living wage even when economizing pressures push a company toward exploitative practices in the interest of a better financial bottom line. The values-driven company also pays attention to the social and ecological costs of its activities in, at minimum, a triple bottom line framework. See the box "Nike Just Does It" for an example of one company's response to activist pressure on sweatshop issues.

Nike Just Does It

Business Week made the initial proclamation: "After years of pressure to stop abusive practices in Nike's overseas plans, CEO Philip Knight has decided to revamp labor policies. In doing so, he becomes the one applying pressure—on other U.S. companies to match his new standards."[28] In a program the company calls "Transparency 101," Nike is working with external auditors from PricewaterhouseCoopers and Nike's internal compliance office to ensure that the company's foreign suppliers, which employ more than half a million workers are in compliance with the company's standards.

To cope with the plethora of criticisms directed against it, Nike instituted labor standards that included external monitoring, hiring PricewaterhouseCoopers to do its audits, providing financial assistance to factories, and improving environmental standards and working conditions in its supplier factories. Among the benefits Nike hopes to supply are increased overtime pay, new counseling programs, better safety procedures, new recognition programs, better ventilation, cleaner working environments, and enhanced training programs in its supplier factories.

Of course, it's not always that easy to ensure that standards are being met. But for years Nike experienced first hand what it is like to be targeted by human and labor rights activists unhappy with its practices—and the bad press that followed. Activist groups still keep a close watch on the company's activities in developing nations because even with the standards in place, compliance is not always assured. For example, after it instituted the new standards, Nike was subject to both mixed results and continued questioning of both its motives and performance by activists who found that auditors overlooked major problems.

Not only does Nike have to deal with the aftermath of all the bad press it received about its labor practices, but it also has to cope with competitive realities of shifting fad and fashion that have caused its sneaker sales to drop. The decline in sales occurred almost simultaneously with CEO Phil Knight's demand that the company "just do it" by meeting significantly higher labor standards while rebuilding the company competitively from top to bottom.

Knight was called to comment on the difficulty of meeting different and sometimes conflicting standards at the opening session of The Global Compact*, a meeting called by the United Nations Secretary-General Kofi Annan. At the session, Knight noted:

I believe the Global Alliance is an example of what we hope the Global Compact will inspire–cooperation among international and local companies, NGOs and other organizations to address the impact of globalization with real solutions. We know from experience that these partnerships can work. . . . We've learned that collaboration is difficult. It's hard work, takes a lot of time, and requires mutual respect and a shared vision.

As Knight rightly notes, it is not always the easiest or most comfortable place to be—on the cutting edge of new practices and performance standards when the whole world is watching—as it is with Nike.

* See p. 278.

Sources: Kelley Holland and Aaron Bernstein, "Nike Finally Does It," *Business Week,* May 25, 1998, pp. 46 ff; see also Louise Lee, "Can Nike Still Do It?" *Business Week,* February 21, 2000, pp. 12–28; http://www.nikebiz.com/labor/index.shtml. Opening Comments before The Global Compact by Nike Chairman and CEO Philip H. Knight, New York, July 26, 2000, http://www.nikebiz.com/media/n_compact.shtml.

The Living Wage Debate

One issue that is embedded in many of the discussions about fair labor practices in developing countries is what constitutes a living wage? There are numerous definitions and conflicting standards about this. Public attention to the issue, however, makes it imperative that each company that engages suppliers in developing nations ensures that the suppliers are indeed paying living wages. Further, the sweatshop controversy fosters attention to whether suppliers are operating their factories cleanly and with relatively high standards of human dignity lest the larger corporate ally be subject to extreme negative publicity and labor/human rights activism directed against the company's practices.

The criterion for wage payment that is rapidly evolving in the international community is the "living wage," which pegs the wage scale in any nation relative to the standard of living in that nation. Exactly how to calculate this living wage is yet undetermined (though Table 10.5 illustrates a sample calculation); however, there are multiple approaches, all of which attempt to assure that basic human needs for shelter, food, and clothing are met. For example, one coalition of activists, academics, and representatives of developing countries defined living wages in the global garment and shoe industries. The living wage is defined as a take-home wage earned by working within the country's legal maximum number of hours per week (but not more than 48 hours) that provides nutrition, water, housing, energy, transportation, clothing, health care, child care, and education for the average family, in addition to some savings or discretionary income.[27]

The Council on Economic Priorities has also attempted to define what is meant by a living wage in a way that accommodate the different standards for meeting basic needs in different nations. The method is presented in Table 10.5.

ECONOMIC SPHERE: RESPECT FOR THE ECONOMIC SYSTEM

In the economic sphere, respect is still the basic foundation on which various emerging principles and standards rest. In this sphere, however, respect for the integrity of

TABLE 10.5. Calculating a Living Wage

Defining a wage that meets basic needs in different countries:

1. Establish the local cost of a basic food basket needed to provide 2,100 calories per day per person.

2. Determine the share of local household income spent on food. Divide into 1 to get total budget multiplier.

3. Multiply that by food spending to get the total per person budget for living expenses.

4. Multiply by half the average number of household members in the area. (Use a higher share if there are many single-parent households.)

5. Add at least 10% for discretionary income.

Example: Assume the basic food basket costs $15 per week, 5.6 people per household, and families spend 40% of their income on food. A living wage would be: $15 × (1 ÷ 0.4) × 2.8 (half of 5.6 people) + 10% = $115.50 per week.

Source: Council on Economic Priorities Accrediting Agency, cited in *Business Week,* May 3, 1999, p. 188.

the economic system and generating trust in the integrity of the whole—without which the whole system would collapse—is critical. As with other standards, general standards relating business to the broader social environment tend to come from the business community itself, in part because business leaders frequently believe that by self-regulating they will avoid more intrusive governmental regulations.

By establishing high standards and operating principles and adhering to them, and, further, by engaging in dialogue about important issues with other stakeholders, business leaders can carve out a satisfactory economic agenda. If that agenda is to succeed long term, however, it must be aligned with the agendas of stakeholders in the civil society and political spheres, who now have access to communications technology that enables them to transmit information, ideas, and plans instantaneously around the globe. Thus, respect for the points of view of all stakeholders is gaining in importance, and corporate citizens increasingly need to carry out their responsibilities with integrity, transparency, and accountability to satisfy their many constituencies.

The Global Compact

At the World Economic Forum, held in Davos, Switzerland, in January 1999, UN Secretary-General Kofi Annan challenged world business leaders to "embrace and enact" a Global Compact in their individual corporate practices and by supporting appropriate public policies. The principles articulated by Annan include human rights, labor standards, and the natural environment (see Table 10.6). The Global Compact initially involved establishing a coalition of businesses, business associations, workers' or labor organizations, national governments, and other types of organizations that were attempting to establish standards for business and industry. Annan's goal was to establish a standard for corporate citizenship by developing global companies into model corporate citizens, who would voluntarily agree to op-

TABLE 10.6. Principles of the Global Compact

Kofi Annan calls for companies to live up to the following principles:

HUMAN RIGHTS

Principle 1: Support and respect the protection of international human rights within their sphere of influence.
Principle 2: Make sure their own corporations are not complicit in human rights abuses.

LABOR

Principle 3: Freedom of association and the effective recognition of the right to collective bargaining.
Principle 4: The elimination of all forms of forced and compulsory labor.
Principle 5: The effective abolition of child labor.
Principle 6: The elimination of discrimination with respect to employment and occupation.

ENVIRONMENT

Principle 7: Support a precautionary approach to environmental challenges.
Principle 8: Undertake initiatives to promote greater environmental responsibility.
Principle 9: Encourage the development and diffusion of environmentally friendly technologies.

Source: The Global Compact, http://www.unglobalcompact.org/gc/unweb.nsf/content/thenine.htm.

erate in accordance with a core set of principles that establish standards with respect to labor, human rights, and environmental practices.

Not everyone greeted Annan's attempt to galvanize corporate leaders with cheers. Indeed, many NGO leaders believe that the Global Compact puts the credibility of the United Nations at risk because it aligns the UN too closely with corporate forces.[29] In part, the critiques arise because the 50 or so companies that had signed the Global Compact by the end of 2000 had done so voluntarily. Additionally, there is little or no external monitoring of their activities on the three main areas covered by the principles and little enforcement power behind the standards. Clearly, corporations hoping to live up to the principles embedded in the Global Compact, as well as some of the other standards noted below, have a long way to go before their activities are fully transparent to nongovernmental organizations and activists and before they can be held fully accountable.

Other Emerging Business Standards

Other groups are also attempting to develop standards for business practices with respect to labor, human rights, environment, and ethics. Among the most notable of these is the Global Reporting Initiative (GRI); others include the Caux Round Table Principles, and the emerging principles for stakeholder relationships called the Clarkson Principles. While the GRI has received considerable press attention and involves numerous businesses and business-related organizations, the Caux and Clarkson Principles have received considerably less intensive attention from businesses.

The Global Reporting Initiative

Like the Global Compact, the Global Reporting Initiative (GRI) (see http://www.globalreporting.org/) is a voluntary initiative, in this case an international, multistakeholder effort to create a common framework for voluntary reporting of the economic, environmental, and social impact of organization-level activity. Unlike the Global Compact, however, GRI's mission is to elevate the comparability and credibility of sustainability *reporting practices* worldwide. In an effort to do so, the GRI incorporates the active participation of businesses, accountancy, human rights, environmental, labor, and governmental organizations.

Established in 1997, the GRI is attempting to develop global guidelines that companies can use to report on economic, environmental, and social performance—otherwise known as the triple bottom line (see Chapter 8). Convened by the founders of the CERES Principles, (see Chapter 9), GRI advocates working collaboratively with the United Nations Environment Program (UNEP) and includes members of the accounting profession to help build standards of reporting and accountability that can be used worldwide.

Aimed at providing reporting principles and practices, outlining the content of what can broadly be termed social reports, and setting standards for comparability and accountability of the companies issuing these reports, GRI presents specific and relatively elaborate reporting guidelines (standards can be downloaded at http://www.globalreporting.org/Guidelines/June2000/June%202000%20Guidelines%20A4.pdf). In 1999 the initial draft standards were field-tested by some two dozen companies; GRI leaders were clearly hoping to build on their initial success and acceptance to make GRI the acceptable "standard" for businesses operating globally in the future.

Caux Principles for Business

The Caux Round Table,* working in collaboration with the Minnesota Center for Corporate Responsibility, bases its principles for business on two basic ethical ideals. One ethical ideal is the Japanese concept of *kyosei,* which means living and working together for the common good, to enable cooperation and mutual prosperity to coexist with health and fair competition. The second ethical ideal is human dignity, which in Caux's usage refers simply to the sacredness or intrinsic value of each person as an end, not as a means to the fulfillment of others' purposes.[30]

The Round Table was founded in 1986 by Frederick Philips, former president of Philips Electronics, and Olivier Giscard d'Estaing, vice-chairman of INSEAD. Its purpose is to reduce trade tensions by enhancing economic and social relationships among participants' countries and focus generally on building a better world. The Caux Principles (see http:/www.cauxroundtable.org/english.htm.) attempt to move businesses and their leaders toward a perspective that says they should look first to their own actions and behaviors when they are determining the right thing to do.

---

*A coalition of European, U.S., and Japanese business leaders

TABLE 10.7.   Consensus Statement on the Stakeholder Model of the Corporation (Clarkson Principles)

- Corporations should routinely monitor the status of stakeholders, and take relevant stakeholder interests into account in decision making.

- Corporations should communicate openly and clearly with stakeholders, particularly about their respective contributions and benefits, and about the probability and severity of downside risks to which they may become exposed as a result of their contact with the corporation.

- Corporations should adopt processes and modes of behavior in dealing with stakeholders, that are accessible to relevant parties and appropriate in view of their commitments, contributions, and risks.

- Corporations should attempt to distribute the benefits of their activities as equitably as possible among stakeholders, in light of their respective contributions, costs, and risks.

- Corporations should avoid altogether activities that might give rise to unacceptable risks to stakeholders (e.g., Bhopal-type catastrophes).

Source: Clarkson Centre, http://www.mgmt.utoronto.ca/~stake/CBBE/.

Respect for Stakeholders Using the Clarkson Principles

The standards discussed above revolve around the need for businesses to respect the general condition of humanity and "play fair" to maintain the integrity of the business system as a whole. Another evolving set of standards focuses explicitly on the ways companies treat their stakeholders. Developed by the members of the Sloan Project on Reinventing the Corporation, these stakeholder principles are named for Max Clarkson, who was one of the leaders of the Sloan Project before his death in 1998.[31] The Clarkson Principles represent a consensus about the way companies should treat stakeholders—statements focusing directly on policies and processes that make sense when companies take a stakeholder perspective.

The fundamental premises of the Clarkson Principles, like those we have examined above, involve assessment and accountability for behaviors and impacts, transparency of corporate actions to key stakeholders, risk avoidance, and equity (see Table 10.7). The foundation of these statements is an assumption that the fundamental purposes of corporations are to create wealth through producing and selling products and services. In that wealth-creation process, some stakeholders will experience costs, make inputs, or put something at risk. Therefore, all of the stakeholders, not just shareholders, deserve to be treated with respect and have their interests fairly represented in the firm's wealth-creation process.

Accountability and Certification for Transparency

It must be clear by now that whatever standards emerge, companies will increasingly have to measure their progress toward meeting stakeholder and environmental demands. They will be subjected increasingly to public scrutiny from many different sources for their behaviors, and be compelled to create and implement reporting standards such as the emerging GRI standards. Leading corporate citizens need to be accountable not only for their decisions, but also for all of the impacts that their operations and activities have—economically and competitively, socially and politically. The very availability of information about corporate activities, the external assessments undertaken by numerous observers (some of which are described in Chapter 6), and the increasing pressure from stakeholders in multiple domains demand stricter accountability for impacts and far greater transparency of internal corporate activities for external stakeholders.

Electronic communications technology and greater stakeholder sophistication will only increase the demand for accountability. If companies hope to achieve trusting relationships with primary stakeholders, including customers and suppliers, and critical secondary stakeholders like communities, governments, and NGOs, they will need to verify publicly and even meet objective certification standards that they are living up to the principles they have themselves articulated. Fortunately for progressive firms, a number of new assessment techniques and certification standards are emerging that they can tap. Two of these will be discussed below.

SA 8000. SA 8000 (see http://www.sgsgroup.com/sgsics.nsf/pages/sa8000.html) is a set of social accountability standards and a certification process modeled to some extent on the ISO quality standards (see below) and ISO 14000 family of standards discussed earlier. The SA 8000 process and standards, established by the Council on Economic Priorities with input from corporations, unions, and NGOs, provide a comparative basis for corporate social performance. The key to SA 8000, which is used in the retail industry to cope with problems of child and sweatshop labor and to monitor working conditions, is an external certification process or audit. This audit looks at internal corporate practices to ensure that the company and its suppliers are in compliance with the SA 8000 requirements.

SA 8000 deals explicitly with supplier and subcontractor relationships and attempts to determine that a company and its allies are not using or supporting the use of child labor or exposing children or young workers to hazardous, unsafe, or unhealthful conditions. The standards also mitigate against forced labor—much as the UN Declaration on Human Rights advocates—and monitor compliance with reasonably high standards for occupational health and safety, including avoidance of workplace hazards, employee training, establishment of safety systems, and cleanliness. SA 8000 is also intended to determine that companies comply with international standards, such as the right to associate or bargain collectively, follow nondiscrimination policies, and avoid corporal, mental, or physical coercion and verbal abuse.

Further, companies are monitored for the number of hours employees work and compensation to ensure that they are in compliance with local labor laws. As of this writing, several companies have signed on to SA 8000, and the hope is that these standards will follow a developmental cycle similar to that originally followed by the ISO 9000 quality standards, and that is currently under way with ISO 14000.

AA 1000. In 1999 the Institute of Social and Ethical AccountAbility (see http://www.AccountAbility.org.uk/index.htm), an organization comprised of about 400 businesses, academics, consultants, and NGOs, issued another set of standards, the AA 1000 standard. AA 1000 provides a framework that companies can use to understand and improve their ethical performance and as a means for others to judge the validity of ethical claims made. AA 1000 builds on the work of SA 8000 and the GRI to focus explicitly on what constitutes best practice in accountability and performance measurement and evaluation. The new standard is intended for training professionals to perform the types of auditing needed to implement SA 8000 and GRI.

SUNSHINE STANDARDS. Truly progressive companies that adopt the principles of accountability and transparency may wish to go even further and use what are called the Sunshine Standards for Corporate Reporting to Stakeholders. Advanced by the Center for the Advancement of Public Policy, the Sunshine Standards are intended to provide guidance for progressive corporations that wish to communicate their impacts directly to stakeholders.[32]

The Sunshine Standards, like the others we have explored, rely on a set of principles to which corporations using them need to attend:

> All information should be provided that stakeholders may need to make rational, informed decisions in the marketplace, and to protect themselves from negative consequences of corporate actions; this disclosure must be complete, accurate, timely, objective, understandable, and public.[33]

The rationale underpinning this principle and the standards themselves is that this type of disclosure helps to support the free market system, is needed by stakeholders, and is ultimately the right thing to do. Among the stakeholders addressed by the Sunshine Standards are customers who need to know about regulatory actions, products, and what the standards call "social responsibility information," which is disclosure about supplier and vendor relationships. Employees need to know about employment security and stability, health and safety risks, employment data, grievances, anticipated technological impacts, pension programs, and the company's future plans.

Communities have detailed needs for information because companies have many impacts on communities. The information needs of communities include ownership information, legal and regulatory profiles of the firm, prior company performance related to special community benefits that have been granted, financial data, taxes paid, materials and waste, pollution emissions data, materials sourcing, facility construction data, vehicular activity, school impact data, investments, contributions, and lobbying and political action. Other stakeholders, such as suppliers, financial investors, lenders, and society as a whole, may also need various types of information, such as the amount and content of trade with nations where trade is officially discouraged, foreign exchange generated and used, and major government contracts.[34]

Transparency and Accountability

As with the movement in Europe toward the triple bottom line, the Sunshine Standards impose much higher expectations on corporate reporting systems than traditional financial accounting. While it is not yet clear which GRI system—SA 8000, AA 1000, or the Sunshine Standards—will come to be generally accepted, what is becoming increasingly obvious is that reporting will soon need to move significantly beyond the traditional bottom line and into, at minimum, the triple bottom line of social, economic, and ecological reporting. Very likely, the multiple bottom lines associated with all primary and critical secondary stakeholders will be part of reporting requirements in the future.

Quality Standards—ISO 9000

Customers are treated respectfully when companies deliver high-quality products that meet real customer needs in ways that establish trust and loyalty. Product quality is an essential component of developing customer loyalty, which has been addressed by many companies in recent years through implementation of continual quality improvement programs.

The International Organization for Standardization (ISO) (see http://www.iso.ch/welcome.html) originally addressed quality standards in the late 1970s and early 1980s and promulgated the first quality standards in 1987. Called ISO 9000, the quality standards seek to establish company-driven standards for product and process quality, continual improvement, as well as auditing or verification procedures for external use.

Pressures from the European Union, among other sources, drove many companies to implement the ISO 9000 quality standards because many European firms would not do business with companies not implementing these standards. Using the ISO 9000 standards became a source of competitive advantage for many companies and ultimately became the sine qua non quality standard for companies hoping to compete successfully internationally, since the ISO 9000 standards assured that minimum quality standards were met.

ISO's definition of quality is simply "all those features of a product (or service) [that] are required by the customer." Quality management, in ISO's terminology, means setting up a process of continual product and process improvement to ensure that products do indeed conform to customer requirements and expectations.[35] To help companies meet customer expectations and needs, ISO has developed an international consensus on what represents good management practice with respect to quality management for all types of enterprises.

ISO 9000 is an explicit set of requirements that quality systems need to meet, but companies are expected to determine how to meet those standards in their own unique ways. Like ISO 14000, ISO 9000 is actually a family of standards, some of which emphasize what constitutes an effective quality management system, while others give guidelines on different elements of quality management and management of a quality system. Additionally, the ISO 9000 standards provide for external audits of the quality system, which some customers find to be a useful way to ensure that their needs and requirements are being met.[36]

Quality systems like ISO 9000 and other continual quality improvement systems help companies develop the necessary trusting relationships with their customers. Companies operating with integrity know that this trust sustains the relationship and brings customers back.

POLITICAL SPHERE: RESPECT FOR THE LOCAL POLITICAL CULTURE

Companies operating in the global arena know that they must understand the ways that local governments operate in all of the countries where they have facilities, market products and services, or source materials. They need to be aware of local rules and regulations, as well as the ways companies are expected to operate in different cultures and with respect to governments. The different ideologies discussed earlier make for very different contexts, each of which must be individually analyzed and discussed by corporate leaders to ensure that integrity is maintained.

One of the serious issues facing companies when they operate outside their homelands is the apparently differing standard of integrity in different cultures. In some countries, business leaders face corrupt officials (and businesspeople) when they attempt to generate business or operate locally. What companies have discovered, however, is that difficult as it may be, sticking to their own internally developed values and standard of integrity with respect to their operating practices is, in the long run, the best practice. In this section we will focus on dealing with corruption when companies operate in the global arena, particularly as it applies to the political sphere of activity.

Pervasive Corruption

"Corruption is found, to some degree, in every society. As a sign that something has gone wrong in the relationship between society and the state, corruption is becoming a pervasive phenomenon."[37] So begins Transparency International's Source Book on National Integrity Systems.

Transparency International (TI) is a Berlin-based international nongovernmental organization (INGO) which has as its mission increasing government accountability and curbing national and international corruption.[38] Founded in 1993 by Peter Eigen, TI works by creating coalitions of people with integrity from all three spheres of activity—the political, business, and civil society—in all of the countries (and there are many) where TI has chapters.

Because corruption undermines the integrity not only of the business system but also the political and civil society systems, Transparency International has several purposes operating simultaneously (see Table 10.8). These purposes are to enhance civility or humanitarian aims, democracy, ethics, and trust in the free market system. TI view its long-term role as creating a "more effective, fair and efficient government" by reducing or preventing corruption and, fundamentally, increasing integrity. Its programs are aimed at developing national integrity systems that will accomplish these goals throughout the world.

TABLE 10.8. The Multiple Concerns of Transparency International about Corruption

Our movement has multiple concerns:

- Humanitarian, as corruption undermines and distorts development and leads to increasing levels of human rights abuse.
- Democratic, as corruption undermines democracies and in particular the achievements of many developing countries and countries in transition.
- Ethical, as corruption undermines a society's integrity.
- Practical, as corruption distorts the operations of markets and deprives ordinary people of the benefits which should flow from them.

Source: Transparency International, at http://www.transparency.de/index.html.

Using a systems perspective on each country, TI attempts to understand the causes, loopholes, and incentives that feed corrupt practices locally. Then TI attempts to determine what the main types of corruption are within the public domain in that country and where there are leverage points for change within that system. According to TI, the "policy response to combating corruption has several elements common to every society; the reform of substantive programs; changes in the structure of government and its methods of assuring accountability; changes in moral and ethical attitudes; and, perhaps most importantly, the involvement and support of government, the private business sector, and civil society."[39] Some of these areas for change can be addressed quickly, while others require longer periods of time.

According to Transparency International, reform efforts need to be both serious and concerted in order to be effective. TI has identified eight characteristics of successful corruption reform initiatives, which are listed in Table 10.9.

Transparency International points out five areas of reform that are particularly helpful in reducing corrupt governmental practices. These are public programs, government reorganization, law enforcement, public awareness, and the creation of institutions to prevent corruption. Each country's situation must be analyzed to determine what specifically can be done, in part because action in any one of these areas will have ripple effects to the others; that is, they are part of a whole system where change needs to be leveraged to have the greatest effect.

TI also produces annually a "Corruption Perceptions Index" that ranks countries on a scale from 10 (highly clean) to 0 (highly corrupt).[40] See Table 10.10 for a sample of the 2000 Index and go to TI's website for the index and annual updates: http://www.transparency.de/documents/cpi/2000/cpi2000.html#cpi. To create the index, Transparency International consolidates the results of 16 different surveys, requiring a minimum of three surveys for each country included, so as to assure validity of the results.

Transparency International's website (http://www.transparency.de/index. html) includes a great deal of information, including the Source Book, for business leaders interested in working against corruption in the countries where they do business. As

TABLE 10.9. Elements of a Serious Corruption Reform Effort

1. A clear commitment by political leaders to combat corruption wherever it occurs and to submit themselves to scrutiny.

2. Primary emphasis on prevention of future corruption and on changing systems (rather than indulging in witch hunts).

3. The adoption of comprehensive anticorruption legislation implemented by agencies of manifest integrity (including investigators, prosecutors, and adjudicators).

4. The identification of those government activities most prone to corruption and a review of both substantive law and administrative procedures.

5. A program to ensure that salaries of civil servants and political leaders adequately reflect the responsibilities of their posts and are as comparable as possible with those in the private sector.

6. A study of legal and administrative remedies to be sure that they provide adequate deterrence.

7. The creation of a partnership between government and civil society (including the private sector, professions, religious organizations).

8. Making corruption a "high-risk" and "low-profit" undertaking.

Source: Transparency International at http://www.transparency.de/index.html.

TABLE 10.10. Transparency International's 2000 Corruption Perceptions Index

(Sample results (top and bottom five countries and the United States)

Country/Rank	Country	2000 CPI Score	Surveys Used	Standard Deviation	High-Low Range
1	Finland	10.0	8	0.6	9.0–10.4
2	Denmark	9.8	9	0.6	8.6–10.6
3	New Zealand,	9.4	8	0.8	8.1–10.2
	Sweden	9.4	9	0.7	8.1– 9.9
5	Canada	9.2	9	0.7	8.1– 9.9
14	**United States**	**7.8**	**10**	**0.8**	**6.2– 9.2**
85	Angola,	1.7	3	0.4	1.6– 2.5
	Indonesia	7.7	11	0.8	0.5– 3.2
87	Azerbaijan,	1.5	4	0.9	0.6– 2.5
	Ukraine	1.5	7	0.7	0.5– 2.5
89	Yugoslavia	1.3	3	0.9	0.6– 2.4
90	Nigeria	1.2	4	0.6	0.6– 2.1

Source: http://www.transparency.de/documents/cpi/2000/cpi2000.html#cpi.

the next section suggests, doing business with integrity is increasingly critical in the global area, in part because organizations like TI are actively at work to expose in very public ways any instances of corruption and businesses that feed into or support corrupt systems.

Public Corruption and the Law

Despite what some managers believe, "corruption by public officials is explicitly or implicitly illegal in every country which has a legal system, and it should therefore not be an operation open to any private sector company."[41] All companies know that they need to operate within the laws and policies that a country has established as its rules of society. Companies operating with integrity work under a number of constraints on their behavior with respect to corruption. First, they must live up to their own articulated values and codes of conduct. If they themselves are "transparent," they may be producing responsibility audits for their stakeholders that will hold them accountable for the very standards they have set.

Additionally, companies are accountable within industry-level associations for self-regulatory practices that the industry demands of its member companies. To the extent that they are operating under any of the standards and principles already detailed above, they are accountable to those certification bodies or external groups assessing their practice. They are also accountable to the laws of their home country, which in the United States means adhering to the restrictions in the 1977 Foreign Corrupt Practices Act, which prohibits bribery by company officials.

Companies are also responsible to the laws of the country in which they are operating, many of which have anticorruption statutes, even if they are not enforced. One telling reality faced by a company leader thinking about engaging in an act of corruption is that she or he never knows when someone, somewhere will decide to enforce that law—and if laws are broken, jail is a likely consequence. Finally, as we have seen above, there is an emerging body of international standards to which businesses are increasingly being held accountable.

Bribery Is Now Outlawed Globally

To cope with corruption globally requires enforceable and consistent laws on an international scale. There are positive signs that corruption is becoming increasingly less well accepted globally. For example, not only has Transparency International made tremendous inroads into dealing openly with corrupt systems, but also some 34 nations signed in 1998 a new international treaty designed to outlaw bribery on a global scale called the Convention on Combating Bribery of foreign Public Officals in International Business Transactions.[42] Of these signatories, 29 are members of the Organization of Economic Cooperation and Development (OECD); that is, they are among the largest economies in the world. Prior to this treaty only the U.S. government outlawed bribery through the Foreign Corrupt Practices Act, which business leaders sometimes felt put their companies at a competitive disadvantage. With passage of this treaty, bribery becomes a criminal act in virtually every important economy in the world.

Transparency International points out that company directors and leaders need to understand and accept their responsibility for staying within both the letter and spirit of the laws in countries where they operate. Voluntary codes of conduct, accompanied by internal enforcement procedures, can help companies sustain their integrity in the face of potential lost business when a bribe is not paid. And, as TI points out, "grand corruption is the enemy of high standards and efficiency,"[43] and thus goes against business's core value of economizing in the long run.

LEADING CHALLENGES: MAINTAINING SYSTEM INTEGRITY

Operating with integrity wherever and whenever one does business has never been as important as it is today. This chapter has covered only a few of the numerous evolving sets of standards and principles to which business today is increasingly being held accountable. We can see that there are multiple interacting system holons, each of which needs to be healthy if society is to be healthy, and that the system as a whole needs to have integrity—both wholeness *and* forthrightness if businesses are to be trusted players in the global community.

For leaders of corporate citizens, the emergence of standards and continued demands for transparency and accountability pose significant new challenges—and new ways of doing business in the global context. Standards concerning labor practices, human rights, and the ways that environmental resources are used, as well as in dealing with governments, have gained great public awareness over the past two decades. This attention to making corporations accountable for their impacts is unlikely to diminish in an age where members of civil society who care about the ways that people are treated and about the health of the natural environment are now globally connected. Corporations will be held accountable for their actions and held to very high standards indeed if they hope to continue their global march.

For leading corporate citizens, the message is clear. Being "out in front of the wave" of potential global regulation means adopting high standards of integrity, treating stakeholders with dignity and respect, and allowing interested stakeholders access to information about what the company is doing in these domains is one way to achieve competitive advantage. Companies that attempt to hide behind veils of secrecy will only open themselves up to activism, protests, and negative publicity that damages their reputation and credibility. Leaders of corporate citizens who recognize the significant advantages to be gained by being forthcoming with and respectful of external stakeholders through adherence to high standards will truly put their companies into the lead.

The health of the ecological system is what we all depend on for our very breath and sustenance. The economic system needs to be healthy and the markets free, but it also needs to operate within the rules that societies establish to balance the interests of consumption and materialism with other values in society. The political sphere needs to operate with integrity, free of corruption and abuse, if people are to live freely and if democratic values are truly to spread throughout the world. And enterprises in civil society needs to be active participants in the economic and political systems, to carry a strong voice for the socializing effects of relationships, meaning, and values that bring civility to the world.

The principles and standards discussed in this chapter are among the most important features of the modern economic and social systems in which we live. We all need to learn to operate with integrity, individually and organizationally, and these standards provide a positive and proactive set of guideposts to help us along the way.

NOTES TO CHAPTER 10

1. The full text of Agenda 21 can be found at http://www.unep.org/unep/neworg.htm.
2. The Rio Declaration can be found at http://www.unep.org/unep/rio.htm.
3. From Agenda 21 at http://www.iol.ie/~isp/agenda21/watsa21.htm.
4. Additional information about CERES and the CERES Principles can be found at http://www.ceres.org/.
5. Information and the complete set of principles for Responsible Care can be found at http://www.cmahq.com/cmawebsite.nsf/pages/responsiblecare.
6. For an extended discussion of ISO 14000 and ISO 14001, see Amy Pesapane Lally, "ISO 14000 and Environmental Cost Accounting: The Gateway to the Global Market," *Law & Policy in International Business* 29, no. 4 (Summer 1998), pp. 501–538.
7. Additional information on ISO and the various sets of standards can be found at http://www.iso.ch/.
8. Suzan L. Jackson, "ISO 14000: Things You Should Know," *Production,* October 1997, p. 79.
9. See Lally for elaboration of these points, pp. 501–538.
10. Ibid.
11. Amory B. Lovins, L. Hunter Lovins, and Paul Hawken, "A Road Map for Natural Capitalism," *Harvard Business Review,* May–June 1999, pp. 145–158.
12. Ibid.
13. Ibid., p. 148.
14. Lovins et al., pp. 145–158. Peter M. Senge, *The Fifth Discipline* (New York: Free Press, 1990).
15. See http://www.kodak.com/US/en/corp/environment/1998/kodakPark/savings Recycling.shtml.
16. Lovins et al., p. 152.
17. See Lovins et al., and the Interface website on sustainability at http://216.1.140.49/us/.
18. Paul Hawken, *The Ecology of Commerce* (New York: HarperBusiness, 1993).
19. The full text of this declaration can be found at http://www.tufts.edu/departments/fletcher/multi/texts/UNGARES217A.txt.
20. See ILO's website at http://www.ilo.org/public/english/index.htm for general information and http://www.ilo.org/public/english/50normes/whatare/fundam/index.html for these fundamental conventions.
21. See 1994 Draft Declaration of Principles on Human Rights and the Environment, posted at http://www.tufts.edu/departments/fletcher/multip/www/1994-decl.html.
22. See http://www.earthcharter.org/ for a complete description.
23. See, for example, Aaron Bernstein, "Sweatshop Reform: How to Solve the Standoff," *Business Week,* May 3, 1999, pp. 186–190.
24. See http://www.sweatshopwatch.org/swatch/about/.
25. See http://www.corpwatch.org/trac/greenwash/sweatwash.html.

26. From http://www.sweatshopwatch.org/swatch/industry/.
27. From Sweatshop Watch website, see http://www.sweatshopwatch.org/swatch/newsletters/4_2.html#living_wage.
28. Kelley Holland and Aaron Bernstein, "Nike Finally Does It," *Business Week,* May 25, 1998, pp. 46 ff.
29. UNWire, "Globalization: NGOs Assail UN Ties To Corporate-Led Trend," *United Nations Foundation Weekly News,* September 7, 2000, http://www.unfoundation.org/unwirebw/archives/show_article.cfm?article=1173.
30. Details about the Caux Round Table and the framing of the two ethical ideals can be found at http://www.cauxroundtable.org/default.htm.
31. See the Clarkson Centre's website at http://www.mgmt.utoronto.ca/~stake/CBBE/.
32. See The Center for the Advancement of Public Policy's website at http://www.essential.org/capp/capp.html.
33. Ibid.
34. The Sunshine Standards can be found at http://www.essential.org/capp/sunstds.html.
35. From http://www.iso.ch/9000e/plain.htm.
36. Information on ISO 9000 standards can be obtained at http://www.iso.ch/9000e/9000pub.htm.
37. From http://www.transparency.de/documents/source-book/summary.html.
38. See http://www.transparency.de/index.html.
39. *TI Source Book,* Executive Summary, p. 2, from http://www.transparency.de/ documents/source-book/summary.html.
40. See, http://www.transparency.de/documents/cpi/2000/cpi2000.html#cpi for the full results of the Transparency International 2000 Corruption Perceptions Index survey.
41. *TI Source Book,* Part B: *Applying the Framework,* chap. 13: "The Private-Corporate Sector," 1998, at http://www.transparency.de/documents/source-book/b/Chapter13 /index.html, p. 1.
42. Information in this paragraph is from Skip Kaltenheuser, "Bribery is Being Outlawed Virtually Worldwide," *Business Ethics,* May–June 1998, p. 11.
43. *TI Source Book,* Part B, 1998, p. 3.

CHAPTER 11

Values Added:

GLOBAL FUTURES

. . . Mister! He said with a sawdusty sneeze,
I am the Lorax. I speak for the trees.
I speak for the trees, for the trees have no tongues.
And I'm asking you, sir, at the top of my lungs—
He was very upset as he shouted and puffed—
What's that THING you've made out of my Truffula tuft?

. . . So I quickly invented my Super-Axe-Hacker
which whacked off four Truffula Trees at one smacker.
We were making Thneeds
four times as fast as before!
And that Lorax? . . . He didn't show up any more.

But the next week
he knocked
on my new office door.
He snapped. I'm the Lorax who speaks for the trees
which you seem to be chopping as fast as you please . . .

I meant no harm. I most truly did not. But I had to grow bigger. So bigger
I got.
I biggered my factory. I biggered my roads.
I biggered my wagons. I biggered the loads
of the Thneeds I shipped out. I was shipping them forth
to the South! To the East! To the West! To the North!
I went right on biggering . . . selling more Thneeds
And I biggered my money, which everyone needs . . .

I yelled at the Lorax, Now listen here, Dad!
All you do is yap-yap and say, Bad! Bad! Bad! Bad!
Well, I have my rights, sir, and I'm telling you
I intend to go on doing just what I do!
And, for your information, you Lorax, I'm figgering
on biggering

*and **biggering***
and BIGGERING
*and **BIGGERING**,*
turning MORE Truffula Trees intoThneeds
which everyone, EVERYONE, EVERYONE needs!

And at that very moment, we heard a loud whack!
From outside in the fields came a sickening smack
of an axe on a tree. Then we heard the tree fall.
The very last Truffula Tree of them all!

No more trees. No more Thneeds. No more work to be done . . . .

—DR. SEUSS, The Lorax

SCANNING THE FUTURE: FINDING PATTERN IN CHAOS

Leading corporate citizens know that they need to think through the consequences of their decisions and actions carefully, lest we end up with "no more trees. No more Thneeds. No more work to be done" in the words of Dr. Seuss. They also need to understand very clearly the forces at play not only in their competitive/economic environments, but, also in their political and civil societal environments. And increasingly, corporate leaders know they need to operate in sustainable ways with respect to the natural environment because they are aware of the limitations of the ecological system in supporting life as we know it on earth. To do this we need to enhance awareness of what is likely to happen in the future.

We cannot predict the future. But we can understand its patterns and potentials if we study both the present and what is likely to happen carefully. Like many of the dynamics and relationships we have explored in this book, future trends, dynamics, and their implications are embedded in chaotic processes, the immediate outcomes of which cannot be known. What chaos and complexity theories tell us are that *we can seek patterns that provide significant insights.*

Using all of our leadership insights and our expanded awareness so that we can "hold" multiple perspectives (remembering the higher stages of development discussed in Chapter 4), we can explore what might initially seem to be a chaos (in the colloquial sense) of information, trends, and interrelationships. The "future" viewed prospectively actually exhibits large-scale patterns that can help us think through appropriate actions that provide significant expertise in coping with a changing world. To do this effectively, we need to know *how* to study the future, what data to look at, and how to think more creatively about possibilities.

Since the future as a chaotic process cannot actually be predicted, we seek patterns. To perform pattern seeking of the future, leading corporate citizens carefully monitor trends, the shifting dynamics and concerns of their multiple stakeholders, and the broader (and, importantly, more subtle) technological, competitive, and social shifts that take place throughout the various societies in which they operate. They do this monitoring not only because these forces and dynamics may pose problems, but also because they represent interesting and potentially profitable new opportunities for business development. If opportunities or challenges are overlooked or ignored by one company, they can result in a competitive advantage gained by other companies that pay closer attention to what is happening beyond their immediate short-term business concerns.

Once current trends, data, and patterns have been uncovered, a range of techniques can be used to project these patterns into the future and think about their potential implications for the enterprise. One such technique called scenario analysis has been used successfully used by Royal Dutch/Shell, among other prominent companies. Scenario development and analysis was particularly helpful in preparing Shell, for example, for falling oil prices, which some observers considered unrealistic but actually happened in the 1980s. Other techniques that companies can use to explore the future are future search conferences and open space meetings. We will explore these techniques at the end of the chapter.

Having a "futures" monitoring role in any corporate citizen is a critical element for all of the boundary-spanning functions discussed in Chapter 7, as well as for the organization as a whole. When the information gathered within functions is consolidated and used by the company to develop possible scenarios or "futures" for the company, the monitoring or scanning capability can be especially helpful in preparing the company for any of multiple possible outcomes.

This chapter will explore some of the current dynamics and trends that will shape the future. It will provide a basic framework for thinking about the ways in which leading corporate citizens can cope with the inevitable patterns of change and complexity they will face in creating and sustaining positive relationships with their stakeholders. The values are added, as the chapter title suggests, because we need to think not only about sustainability, but also about what is meaningful to people, to stakeholders, and ultimately to ourselves as citizens of organizations, of particular societies, and of the world.

THE SHAPE OF THE FUTURE

What is it that shapes our future? Although we as human beings have little control over nature, in many senses we do control our own destiny. We make decisions that impact our future on a daily basis, whether in our leadership capacities or within the companies we manage. For example, to the extent that we take "care" or steward-ship responsibility for our own impacts on the ecological environment, nature will reward us bountifully. Over the long term—to the extent that we provide for appropriate balance among the three spheres of activity in human civilization with respect to the natural environment and to each other—societies will be productive and meaningful places in which to live, work, and play. And it is the work of developing meaningful relationships within society and respecting all stakeholders, which we have argued throughout this book, that is the key to the long-term effectiveness of leading corporate citizens.

The world of tomorrow will continue to change rapidly, even chaotically, but, as we have learned from thinking about life processes organically and applying that thinking to our ideas of management, chaotic systems have their patterns which are, to a large extent, comprehensible and understandable. Understanding patterns and developing new ways of thinking about the implications of even potential patterns can help raise awareness of the implications of corporate decisions on stakeholders. Ultimately, it can also help us lead better lives as individuals in society and as corporate citizens.

Clearly, understanding future patterns may demand relatively high levels of cognitive, emotional, and moral development or we will, as developmental psychologist Robert Kegan put it, really be *In Over Our Heads.*[1] Tomorrow's leaders will need to work productively to develop a sense of what is meaningful to others and to think through the systems implications of their decisions to move themselves toward understanding the future. Such systems thinking, built upon understanding where the points of leverage are and what the interactions among different variables, issues, and relationships mean, also requires shifting perspectives to encompass data that might ordinarily be ignored or overlooked. Small shifts, as chaotic systems illustrate, can result in large changes down the road. As leaders of corporate citizens we need to be intensely aware not only of the larger patterns of society but also of the small shifts that can provide meaningful opportunity—or challenges—in the future.

This chapter presents some current data on the state of the world, then looks at some of the predictions that futurists—people who study the future—are making that are likely to affect leaders and leading corporate citizens in the future. Let us begin this exploration with some information about the current state of the world's social, political, economic, and ecological spheres. Then we will look at predictions of challenges and opportunities made by futurists that will inevitably shape global futures.

The State of the World

Some statistics about the current state of the world can help us to gain insights into the opportunities and issues that may develop in the future. For example, the United Nations Development Program (UNDP) reported some startling statistics in 1998 that set a context for potential and for problems.[2]

- The world's 225 richest individuals have wealth equal to the combined annual income of the world's *2.5 billion* poorest people—over $1 trillion. The world's three richest people have more wealth than the combined gross domestic product of the 48 least developed countries!
- The 20 percent of the world's population living in the highest-income countries account for 86 percent of total private consumption, while the poorest 20 percent consume 1.3 percent, down from 2.3 percent three decades earlier. The wealthiest 20 percent use 58 percent of the world's energy, consume 45 percent of all meat and fish, and have access to 74 percent of all telephone lines.

- Some 3 billion people live on less than $2 a day, while 1.3 billion live on less than $1 a day; 70 percent are women. Poor households typically spend more than half of their income on food.
- In 1996, 100 countries were worse off than they were 15 years earlier. Thirty years earlier, people in wealthy countries were 30 times better off than those in the poorest nations, where 20 percent of the world's population lives. By 1998 people in wealthy countries were 82 times better off—up from 61 times better in 1996.
- In the United States in 1995 the wealth of the top 1 percent of the population was greater than the *combined wealth* of the bottom 95 percent. The net worth of the top 1 percent of people in the United States is now 2.4 times the combined wealth of the poorest 80 percent.
- Between 1970 and 1990, the typical American worked an additional 163 hours more a year, equivalent to an additional month of work for the same or less pay.
- In the United States, average household debt is rising, net worth is falling, personal savings are falling, personal bankruptcy is rising, and the gap between rich and poor continues to widen.
- According to Pay Watch, *Business Week* reported that in 1999 top executives earned 475 times the average wage of a blue-collar worker, up from 326:1 in 1998 and 42:1 in 1980.

These statistics are startling enough, but evidence of the growing gap between the "haves" and the "have-nots" in the United States and the rest of the world continues to mount. This shift in the distribution of wealth has significant implications for the potential growth and prosperity of nations as well as of companies. Table 11.1 shows the shift in income distribution that disturbs many observers since it is occurring on a global basis.

Thinking about the differences between wealthy nations and their people and the less developed nations and their people suggests that there may be new business opportunities in serving less developed nations with ecologically sustainable products that still meet their needs, while attempting to close the growing gap between

TABLE 11.1. Global Income Distribution, 1960–1991

Year	Share of global income going to		Ratio of Richest to Poorest
	Richest 20%	**Poorest 20%**	**Ratio of Richest to Poorest**
1960	70.2%	2.3%	30:1
1970	73.9	2.3	32:1
1980	76.3	1.7	45:1
1989	82.7	1.4	59:1
1991	85.0	1.4	61:1

Source: http://www.globalpolicy.org/socecon/inequal/inctab.htm.

rich and poor. We have already recognized that economic development cannot continue apace without consideration of what is sustainable ecologically and socially in the long-term. Sustainability, in this case, also includes the sustainability of democratic institutions, free market economies, and healthy local communities in the face of enormous inequities in the distribution and use of resources. The wide availability of information has the potential to create significant disturbances among peoples with "less" if some moves are not made to close this growing gap. Sometimes this gap is manifested as what is called the "digital divide" (see the box on the digital divide). The gap exists between rich and poor in most if not all nations, as well as, generally speaking, between countries in the Northern and Southern hemispheres or, alternatively, developed and developing nations.

New, more ecologically sensitive and responsible practices are needed to serve the needs of the billions of people in the world whose living standards are below the poverty level. Businesses, obviously, have an essential role to play in developing the goods and services needed to close these gaps. What is true, however, is that facing up to these global realities means that some significant shifts in lifestyle and production processes may be needed, particularly for wealthier and more powerful citizens. For aware and innovative leading corporate citizens, significant opportunities may exist.

The Digital Divide

UN leaders, among others, are concerned about a growing "digital divide," the gap between those who are relatively well off and have access to information and communications technology (ICT) and those who do not. Even in the United States, the gap between technological haves and have-nots exists; some 80 percent of families with incomes over $100,000 a year have computers at home, while only about 25 percent of families earning about $30,000 a year have computers. Despite the reality of the gap in the United States, the United Nations Development Program (UNDP) report issued in 1999 noted that it would take the average American family only one months' income to purchase a computer, while the average family in Bangladesh would need eight *years* to do so.

Mark Malloch Brown, administrator of the UNDP, stated in July 2000 that while it was true that the information gap between rich and poor nations and within nations was vast and growing, ICT and the Internet offer new hope in areas ranging from health to education to business development. "If we fail to act now the Information Gap risks being widened into an uncrossable gulf that increases global inequality and leaves the poor further behind," he said. "But if we approach the matter with the same kind of urgency and application as the commercial 'dot-com' sector, then we have every chance of building a strong, new wired future that not only includes the world's poor but gives them an unprecedented opportunity to lift themselves out of poverty."

For businesses there are obvious opportunities in helping to "wire" those areas of the world that are now technologically disadvantaged. To bridge the digital divide the UNDP has launched a series of initiatives that include helping to develop policy frameworks and launch new networks in places where they currently do not exist.

Sources: Naomi Koppel, "Poverty Gap Is Widening with Technology, Report Says," *Seattle Times,* July 12, 1999, at http://seattletimes.nwsource.com/news/nation-world/html98/glob_19990712.html, and "UNDP Leader Warns G-8 Leaders of a Widening Digital Divide," UNDP Newsfront, July 21, 2000, at http://www.undp.org/dpa/frontpagearchive/july00/21july00/index.html.

Unilever and Sustainable Development

Being aware of future trends means changing today's behavior in significant ways and tapping into markets heretofore ignored or dismissed as unprofitable. How can a global corporation tap into the opportunity not only to develop new markets in less developed countries, but also to do so in sustainable ways? Awareness of the realities of life around the globe provides the change of perspective needed to bring new ideas to fruition. The British firm Unilever Corporation is one company that has begun to recognize the opportunities that exist in meeting the needs of poor people in sustainable ways and is beginning to act on them.

As a corporation, Unilever has committed itself to sustainable development in some interesting ways. A major player in the foods, personal care, and cleaning and hygiene products businesses, the company has developed a clear sense of corporate purpose and vision (see the box below) that helps guide its decision making.

Carrying out this vision involves operations in more than 90 countries in every continent to meet the needs of consumers for food, home, and personal care products. One of the most striking aspects of Unilever's commitment to its product and operating integrity is its emerging orientation toward sustainable development, which is in part a recognition of the need to close some of the gaps between rich and poor noted above, while recognizing the need for ecological sustainability.

Recognizing the future importance of ecological sustainability, Unilever has articulated a clear environmental policy and reporting structure.

> Unilever is committed to meeting the needs of customers and consumers in an environmentally sound and sustainable manner, through continuous improvement in environmental performance in all our activities.[3]

Unilever's Corporate Purpose

Our purpose in Unilever is to meet the everyday needs of people everywhere—to anticipate the aspirations of our consumers and customers and to respond creatively and competitively with branded products and services which raise the quality of life.

Our deep roots in local cultures and markets around the world are our unparalleled inheritance and the foundation for our future growth. We will bring our wealth of knowledge and international expertise to the service of local consumers—a truly multilocal multinational.

Our long-term success requires a total commitment to exceptional standards of performance and productivity, to working together effectively, and to a willingness to embrace new ideas and learn continuously.

We believe that to succeed requires the highest standards of corporate behaviour towards our employees, consumers, and the societies and world in which we live.

This is Unilever's road to sustainable, profitable growth for our business and long-term value creation for our shareholders and employees.

Source: http://www.unilever.com/.

Not only does Unilever have a clear line of responsibility for the environment, which is part of the top management team, but also the company regularly audits its environmental performance and reports publicly on that audit every two years. For example, Gessy Lever in Brazil, has made a commitment to the environment that has won it environmental awards numerous times. Not only does the company provide basic and adult education programs that help train and empower its workers (a civil society linkage), but also it implements a continually improving program of eco-logical responsibility. In the economic sphere, improvements range from better product formulation to emissions minimization, and include reduced packaging, in-creased recycling, and better waste management.[4]

Although Unilever, like many large corporations, has only begun its efforts toward sustainable development, it is clear that some of the necessary shift of perspective needed to incorporate the realities that exist in the developing world is taking place. In another example, the company's Algida ice cream factory in Turkey was the first site to be ISO 14001 certified (see Chapter 10). Selim Ergu, who is production and envi-ronmental manager at Algida, says "our people have realized that the ISO standard brings benefits: reduced costs, greater efficiency, better coordination of effort."[5]

Global Trends, Issues, and Opportunities

Unilever represents one example and Cisco another of companies that have tapped into some of the realities of the economic world we face (see box "Cisco Systems Takes its Academies Global"). Both are leading corporate citizens making an effort to develop those opportunities—while behaving responsibly. There are significant other trends, issues, and opportunities—some technological, some economic, others social and political—that make understanding the complexities of global dynamics an imperative for those leading corporate citizens today and that may provide sig-nificant business opportunities for creative entrepreneurs. Futurists can help provide understanding by identifying significant shifts in the world around us. The next two sections will briefly explore some of the major shifts already identified by futurists as likely to affect corporate citizens in the 21st century.

Cisco Systems Takes Its Academies Global

Making connections between a global organization and a local community in the developing world is challenging. For Cisco System (see the Cisco box in Chapter 3 for additional background) these connec-tions involve crossing North-South (developed-developing) country divides, income disparities, and cultural differences. Yet after only three years, Cisco's Academy network is already successfully connecting 5,000 institutions in 84 countries and training over 129,000 students. The primary goal of

the Academy Network is to teach students to design, build, and maintain computer networks and prepare them for the skills needed to compete in the 21st-century workforce. But doing this in developing nations presents its own set of complexities and challenges.

Cisco Systems, among the largest companies in the world, is sometimes called "the plumber of the Internet." Its products help computer users access and transfer information over the Web. Like other high-technology companies, Cisco has found that a major impediment to its growth is the availability of properly trained technicians.

The Networking Academy has developed a global "education ecosystem" to keep pace with the rapid evolution of information technology. The word "ecosystem" emphasizes the holistic and self-sustaining quality of the Networking Academy that Cisco considers essential. The core of the program is a 270-hour course, with major support delivered over the Internet and by teachers specially trained by Cisco. The online course prepares students to take the Cisco Certified Networking Associate exam, a certification recognized worldwide. The global system has been quickly built through a simple strategy: Find local institutions that can be partners wherever Cisco operates. These partners are mainly public and private education institutions, but business, government and community organizations around the world are also involved. (See the Cisco box in Chapter 3 for a description of the U.S. version of this system.)

Does this close relationship raise problems with commercialization of the education system—a sort of "buying educational time at public education institutions" approach? Most people say no for two reasons. "We've got a problem of high unemployment," says Mr. Simani, chairperson of South Africa's Houwteq Institute. "We saw an opportunity, and the Internet is the future." A 1999 analysis estimated that there would be demand for 600,000 more information technologists than are available in western Europe alone by 2002.

Cisco's interest in working upon disadvantaged youths as well as others is attractive—Houwteq is a postsecondary institution whose students are from traditionally black universities. With the need for employment, the demand for employees trained in networking technologies, and the problems of disadvantaged youth, the Networking Academy appears to be a win-win-win proposition. Program graduates obtain a globally recognized and sought-after certificate, Cisco has a source of trained employees in South Africa, and the country's technically trained labor pool is expanded.

Another reason most people are comfortable with the program is that Cisco's systems *are* the industry standard. Not teaching information technologists about them would be similar to refusing to teach about MicroSoft's DOS programs which are the backbone of about 85 percent of computers. Cisco provides about 80 percent of the equipment for Internet users.

Cisco has invested nearly $100 million in developing the Cisco Networking Academy Program. The majority has been spent on curriculum and software development which is constantly updated, training, assessment, equipment donations, translations, and staff who number 200 to 300. The staff is engaged in network building, curriculum development, and constructing the online teaching resource that is the backbone of the system. (For basic information see www.cisco.com/warp/public/779/edu/academy/). This includes a management system, learning assessment tools, and curriculum. Given its e-learning nature, improvements and updating to reflect the fast-changing nature of the information technology field are easy. "Just over the last year it has improved tremendously," says Nothemba Sonkwele, a teacher at Houwteq. "We now have really good simulations. [The program] is very well structured, the curriculum assumes no prior knowledge, and anyone can do it."

"Every country is different," explains Erin Walsh, Cisco manager of International Strategies and Partnerships, Worldwide Education, when asked about Cisco's network development strategy. When Cisco aims to develop a network in a new country, the government is an early point of contact. Attitudes of government and departments within a government toward the program, however, differ. Ministries of science and technology or communications might be most receptive in some countries, while ministries of education are always engaged in discussions. The period between initial contact and launch is often quite short; in the Philippines, for example, the launch of the new Academy took only six months.

Cisco's local partners include a variety of organizations. Information technology departments at universities often act as regional academies. Local high schools, colleges, and universities act as local academies. Although the program is designed for use at the high school level, given the inaccessibility to computers in many countries at that level, other arrangements must often be made. Often the program is placed at the postsecondary level. For example, at Houwteq the program is offered for holders of bachelor of science degrees.

One of Cisco's aims is to partner with organizations that have a particular interest in working with the traditionally disadvantaged. This was a core reason to work with IYF and BPD to develop academies in four countries, with the thought that the networks would allow more adventuresome and creative delivery strategies to poor communities than mainstream education institutions provide. Academies have been established in homeless shelters, prisons, women's housing projects, and community centers. In the Philippines, for example, the Ayala-Mitsubishi team's school had 127 students in its first year, 115 of whom were women, with an average household income of $650 per year. In South Africa the focus on the disadvantaged was one of the reasons that the first local academy was Houwteq, which concentrates on recruiting students from traditionally black colleges; almost all the students have been women.

Source: Steve Waddell, president, The Collaboration Works, senior researcher and consultant, Organizational Futures, 2000, http://www.thecollaborationworks.com; International Data Corporation, "The Internet Economy—An Employment Paradox," (Framingham, MA: International Data Corporation, 1999); S. Thurn, "How to Drive an Express Train," *The Wall Street Journal,* June 1, 2000, p. B1.

Trends 2005

The Center for Strategic and International Studies (CSIS) in Washington, D.C., has developed "The Millennium Project," which has attempted to identify the major trends in the world today.[6] Michael J. Mazarr, author of a report by this name, wrote of the current era:

> The basic transition . . . is from the industrial era of human society, around since the late 18th century, to a new age that goes by a variety of names—the information age, the postmodern era, and others. We call it the "knowledge era" because one way (though only one) of understanding it is as a time when the acquisition, diffusion, use, storage, and transmission of knowledge becomes the basic activity of human societies. This one fundamental shift will refashion all the institutions of our lives.

If Mazarr and the panel of experts that CSIS has put together are correct, leaders of corporate citizens have a lot to think about in determining how to manage responsibly their relationships in all spheres of human society and ecologically. The Trends 2005 report focuses on six major trends, which can be presented here only in the simplest terms. Citizens in all spheres of society, particularly corporate citizens, clearly need to be aware of these trends and know how to cope with them effectively if they expect to sustain a competitive advantage—and simultaneously build collaborative relationships with stakeholders essential to productive engagement in their worlds.

Mazzar and the other futurists identified several "foundations" as part of the first trend: demography, natural resources and the environment, and culture.

DEMOGRAPHY, ECOLOGY, CULTURE. Although the world's population *rate* is slowing, the population itself continues to grow and will do so until it levels off somewhere between 8 and 12 billion people. Trends of modernization, education, and expansion of women's rights reduce fertility and have tended to slow the rate of population growth. Because 95 percent of that growth will occur in less developed countries, the gap between rich and poor can be expected to widen and the processes of urbanization, already under way, will likely continue.

Although sustainable development is, as we have seen elsewhere in this book, gaining momentum, the population growth and many current organizational practices will continue to place significant strains on the natural environment. Although knowledge era businesses are less dependent on the ecology than industrial era businesses, significant ecological problems can be expected with respect to agricultural yields, increased demand for croplands, the intensity of modern farming methods—with resulting soil erosion, desertification, and overfarming—and a crisis in fisheries. Some 80 countries already face significant water shortages and this problem is likely to be exacerbated by continued population growth.

As we discussed in Chapter 2, culture and ideology are essential aspects of human life and one of the foundational elements of the Millennium Project's projections. As Mazarr pointed out, culture plays an essential role in determining a nation's economic prospects as well as its international relationships.[7]

SCIENCE, TECHNOLOGY, MODERNIZATION. An important factor in the dynamics facing corporate citizens, according to the Millennium Project, has to do with the push supplied by science and technology, which in turn contribute to the process of modernization. Among the technological and scientific shifts that can be expected are processes of miniaturization, biogenetic engineering, and continued revolution in information and communications technology (and the information thereby made available). The gap between rich and poor will intensify the gap between the information/technology rich and poor as well, as access to technological advances becomes essential to taking a role in the modern world.

Mazarr observed that "Richer countries tend to look the same—freer, more individualistic and less hierarchical, more concerned with the environment."[8] Not only does this "looking alike" tend toward greater homogeneity, but it also places considerable pressures for constructive (i.e., democratic) reform on repressive regimes. And, Mazarr noted, this process may well result in more peace and less war!

HUMAN RESOURCES AND COMPLEXITY. A third trend identified by the Millennium Project involves the move toward a knowledge-based economic system and the resulting increased attention to and value upon human resources—employee stakeholders. Mazarr identified four features of the "new economy" to which leading corporate citizens will need to pay attention:[9]

- Human capital is the key—because knowledge resides in human beings.
- Freedom and empowerment—because empowered people create and innovate.
- Disorganization trumps organization—companies using complexity and chaos theories as a base for organizing will outpace companies organized more hierarchically and traditionally.
- Networks and alliances—will become, as we have argued earlier, critical to organizational effectiveness and efficiency.

Mazarr identified the principles of the knowledge era as: speed, flexibility, decentralization, and empowerment. Using these principles implies that organizations trust their stakeholders, in particular their employees, and give them responsibilities that go far beyond traditional responsibilities. Ultimately, what these principles mean is that companies will have to design themselves in the ways we have been discussing throughout this book, so that the values of integrity and responsibility are embedded within all of their operations.

GLOBAL TRIBALISM. Although processes of globalism proceed apace on a global basis, much trading occurs within the three major trading blocs of Europe, the Americas, and East Asia, not between them.[10] Mazarr pointed out that this globalization process will demand increased global awareness, resulting from enhanced communications and the rise of the multinational corporation as a powerful social institution. But such ideological forces tend to erupt when threatened in forms of tribalism that political scientist Benjamin Barber called "Jihads." Thus we can expect continued attempts by various ethnic, religious, political, and cultural groups to sustain their identities in the face of global pluralism.[11]

TRANSFORMINGF AUTHORITY. Traditional institutions will face increased challenges to their authority in the knowledge era, where communications are instantaneous and information is widely shared, according to the Millennium Project. This trend is related closely to the political sphere of activity, because it foresees a trend toward greater levels of democratization throughout the world as information becomes more readily available and widely shared.

Among the factors that will influence authorities are tendencies to decentralize their organizations, creating "virtual" structures (as many companies already are doing), influencing people through knowledge and allegiance rather than coercion, and acquisition of power from competence and effectiveness rather than tradition.[12]

COGNITIVE, EMOTIONAL, AND MORAL DEMANDS ON HUMANS. As Robert Kegan, whose ideas we discussed in Chapter 4, noted, the many demands on human beings today place considerable strain on our capacity to understand and step into the perspectives of others, as well as to "hold" multiple perspectives in our heads simultaneously.[13] Mazarr, writing in the Millennium Project, also believes that the knowledge era will stretch the limits of human understanding. These demands will push the need for many more people to develop higher-level skills of cognitive, moral, and emotional development. The pace of change, the multiplicity of stakeholders and their numerous demands, and the complexity of coping simultaneously with technology, create the potential for what he termed the anxiety and alienation of individuals who strain to cope with all these demands.

LESSONS FROM THE GLOBAL TRENDS. Mazarr concluded his report on "Global Trends 2005" with three major lessons that strike to the core of what this book is all about.

> [T]he three most important lessons suggested by this transition are these: the decisive role of education, as the activity that equips people for success in the knowledge era; the primacy of moral values and social responsibility at a time when both are urgently needed; and the need for a "New Capitalism," a reform of some elements of capitalist theory to ensure that markets capture the true costs and implications of economic activities.[14]

TABLE 11.2. The Millennium Project's 15 Global Issues

1. World population is growing; food, water, education, housing, and medical care must grow apace.

2. Freshwater is becoming scarce in localized areas of the world.

3. The gap in living standards between rich and poor promises to become more extreme and divisive.

4. The threat of new and reemerging diseases and immune microorganisms is growing.

5. Diminishing capacity to decide (as issues become more global and complex under conditions of increasing uncertainty and risk).

6. Terrorism is increasingly destructive, proliferating, and difficult to prevent.

7. Adverse interactions between population growth and economic growth on the one hand and environmental quality and natural resources on the other.

8. The status of women is changing.

9. Increasing severity of religious, ethnic, and racial conflicts.

10. The promise and perils of information technology.

11. Organized crime groups becoming sophisticated global enterprises.

12. Economic growth brings both promising and threatening consequences.

13. Nuclear power plans around the world are aging.

14. The HIV/AIDS epidemic will continue to spread.

15. Work, unemployment, leisure, and underemployment are changing.

Source: http://www.geocities.com/~acunu/millennium/challeng.html.

Issues and Opportunities

The coming of the new millennium has challenged many thinkers and leaders to work together to try to predict the major issues and opportunities facing the planet. Another initiative, which is (ironically) also called the Millennium Project, has brought together more than 200 futurists and scholars from over 50 countries to analyze what issues, opportunities, and strategies are arising globally. This project was organized by the American Council for the United Nations University, in cooperation with the Smithsonian Institution, the Futures Group, and the United Nations University. Funded by the U.S. Environmental Protection Agency, the United Nations Development Program (UNDP), and UNESCO, the project's goal is to develop capacity to think about the future globally.[15]

The Millennium Project's "1999 State of the Future" report identified 15 global issues, 15 challenges, and 15 opportunities to which leading corporate citizens—and members of society and political leaders generally—need to pay attention in the next century. These issues and opportunities create potential new economic opportunities, as well as significant problems to be solved. The issues and challenges are reproduced in Tables 11.2 and 11.3.

The Millennium Project covered each of these potential threats and issues in great detail. Clearly, coping with these issues and opportunities demands collabora-

TABLE 11.3.   The Millennium Project's 15 Global Challenges

1. How can sustainable development be achieved for all?

2. How can everyone have sufficient clean water without conflict?

3. How can population growth and resources be brought into balance?

4. How can genuine democracy emerge from authoritarian regimes?

5. How can policy making be made more sensitive to global long-term perspectives?

6. How can the globalization and convergence of information and communication technologies be shaped in the human interest?

7. How can ethical market economies be encouraged to help reduce the gap between the rich and the poor?

8. How can the threat of new and reemerging diseases, and immune microorganisms be reduced?

9. How can the capacity to make correct decisions be improved?

10. How can shared values and new security strategies reduce ethnic conflict and terrorism?

11. How can the increasing autonomy of women and other groups be protected and promoted to improve the human condition?

12. How can organized crime be stopped from becoming more powerful and sophisticated global enterprises?

13. How can the growing energy demand be met safely and efficiently?

14. How can scientific and technological breakthroughs be accelerated to improve the human condition?

15. How can ethical considerations become more routinely incorporated into global decisions?

Source: http://www.geocities.com/~acunu/millennium/challeng.html.

tion among organizations from all sectors of society, including corporations who will have to meet the economic demands of the future and do so responsibly, with vision and values guiding the way. Significant creativity and capacity to understand the fundamental problems, while simultaneously maintaining respect for others' needs and differences, especially when they are in deprived economic circumstances or from very different cultures, will be necessary to find effective and efficient—or economizing—solutions to some of these issues.

Where there are issues, there are also opportunities, some for economic development and others for collaboration among the three spheres of human society, as the Millennium Project's list of 15 global opportunities indicates (see Table 11.4). There are significant business opportunities embedded in the opportunities listed for leaders who can understand how to tap into them. Of course, the future is much more chaotic and emergent than these neat lists of possibilities suggest. What future-oriented techniques (e.g., scenario analysis, future search or futures visioning processes, and "open-space" technologies) can do is help those who must cope with the future figure out the messy aspects and ways to cope, as well as creative approaches for handling the inherent uncertainty of the future.

TABLE 11.4.   The Millennium Project's 15 Opportunities

1. Achieving sustainable development.
2. Increasing acceptance of long-term perspectives in policy making.
3. Expanding potential for scientific and technological breakthroughs.
4. Transforming authoritarian regimes into democracies.
5. Encouraging diversity and shared ethical values.
6. Reducing the rate of population growth.
7. Emerging strategies for world peace and security.
8. Developing alternative sources of energy.
9. Globalizing the convergence of information and communications technology.
10. Increasing advances in biotechnology.
11. Encouraging economic development through an ethical market economy.
12. Increasing economic autonomy of women and other groups.
13. Promoting the inquiry into new and sometimes counterintuitive ideas.
14. Pursuing promising space projects.
15. Improving institutions.

Source: http://www.geocities.com/~acunu/millennium/isandop.html.

Because messy problems frequently cross sector and sphere boundaries, however, it may be that individual companies acting alone will be less successful in tapping into them than companies that know how to collaborate with enterprises from the other spheres. This blurring of boundaries means that the advantage will go to those companies, countries, and alliances that can cooperatively generate new ideas for dealing with the emerging issues and opportunities. The next section will briefly explore new research on such trisector collaborations.

Intersector Partnership and Collaboration

The interactions among enterprises in the civil society sphere,[16] the political sphere,and the business/economic sphere have typically been given scant attention in management thought. To their credit, many global business leaders have recognized the need to create strategic alliances and more cooperative strategies not only with each other, but also with governmental and nongovernmental organizations, as the burgeoning of social and trisector partnerships around the world attest.[17] Clearly this aspect of the pluralistic global economic and societal situation demands new skills of collaboration and mutual understanding of differences in perspective, culture, and ideology, among other factors, some of which shape the economic and political worlds as well as the relational world of civil society.

The kinds of problems briefly identified above suggest that old-fashioned single-sector solutions will no longer work. By their nature, these problems cross boundaries and are what scholar Russell Ackoff termed "messes"; that is, intractable and difficult problems for resolution of which various organizations, groups, and individuals are interdependent. Such unstructured problems require innovation and creativity that place significant demands on any one organization's knowledge, skills, and resource base, and thus elicit multisector approaches for their solutions.

When problems cross organizational and sphere boundaries, when stakeholders are interdependent in dealing with problems, and when there is a rich network of ties—or social capital—among the stakeholders, then multisector collaboration becomes a useful vehicle for effecting social change. Businesses have found this out in the United States, where for years they have been working with schools to help schools reform themselves. Increasingly, it has become clear that not only do businesses and schools need to be involved in these improvement efforts, but also, because education is at its root a social problem, all relevant stakeholders from all three spheres of activity need to be involved.[18]

Although establishing multisector collaborations is not easy, increasing information on some of the factors now makes such collaboration successful. First, there has to be some overriding reason why the actors should work together—a compelling shared vision, a common problem, a crisis to overcome, or a leader everyone wants to work with. Then, ways must be found so that the relevant actors and organizations can be brought together through networks and alliances or through a "brokering" or mediating enterprise of some sort (e.g., a grant or an organization that plays a mediating role). Finally, there must be sufficient mutual education about other stakeholders and their interests, and sufficient benefits to be gained by all to keep these parties, which typically may never interact, working together over time.[19]

In recent research on trisector collaborations involving organizations from the civil society, economic, and political spheres, Steve Waddell showed how these factors interact to make partnership feasible. For example, he studied a road maintenance project in Madagascar—an island country in the Indian Ocean off the coast of Africa—which had a weak governmental infrastructure but needed improved roads. So poorly maintained were the roads that anarchy and banditry were serious problems. To solve the problem, villagers formed nongovernmental organizations of "road users associations," and the government delegated its authority to those associations. By financing much of the improvement work with tolls, working with road contractors to improve their road-building techniques, and working on a peer basis with government officials, the associations brought villagers, government, and private contractors into a collaboration that has been largely successful in improving the roads.[20]

Such collaborative efforts will become more and more necessary in dealing with the global futures issues we have identified above. As one of the most powerful, perhaps the most powerful, institutions in societies today, corporate citizens will be increasingly looked upon as a resource for helping to resolve the significant problems, challenges, and opportunities facing societies.

Only if they operate with integrity, transparency, sustainability, and respect for stakeholders in all spheres of society, will corporate citizens be in a position to be effective in these emerging leadership roles, topics discussed at length in Chapters 8 and 10. Further, leading corporate citizens anticipate rather than react to future trends, issues, and problems and work interactively with the appropriate stakeholders in different spheres of activity to find solutions. They can do so best if they are engaged in continuing activities with their stakeholders to scan the future. Just how future scanning by leading corporate citizens in conjunction with stakeholders from other spheres can be accomplished will be briefly explored in the next sections.

OPEN SPACE, SCENARIOS AND FUTURE SEARCHES

Having scanned the current situation and sought out important trends, along with the weak signals that might become levers of dramatic change, how do companies cope with all of this information? One technique, called "open space technology," developed by Harrison Owen, can be helpful in determining what is going on and what needs to be changed in highly complex, emergent, and generally "messy" situations.

Two additional techniques are specifically aimed at helping decision makers anticipate and plan for the future: scenario analysis, which has been extensively used by Royal Dutch Shell, and future search conferences, which have been used by communities and others to assess what issues are likely to arise in the future. To conclude our look at the future, we will briefly explore some key aspects of each of these important techniques.

Open Space Technology

Open space technology is a technique, developed and written about by Harrison Owen (with, as he admitted, input from many others). *Open space technology* enables multiple stakeholders with widely divergent perspectives to come together around a problem of mutual interest to develop workable solutions.[21] Typically, an "open space" meeting is one in which interested parties work together in a "circle" on the problem at hand. Open spaces can be used to devise corporate citizenship strategies and competitive strategies, or to bring multiple resources to bear on a strategic, community-based, or technological problem. They might also be used effectively to deal with large-scale social problems.

An open space can be created anywhere that a circle large enough to contain as many participants—stakeholders—as are relevant to the problem can be formed. Owen believed that setting stakeholders in a circular format enables the type of interaction required to create the type of "third-way thinking" or boundaryless thinking that is needed to deal with complex problems. One of the first rules of open space, then, is to invite to the meeting "whoever cares"; a second important rule is that once the relevant stakeholders have been invited, "whoever comes is the right group." Open space has been used successfully with groups as small as 5 and as large as 1,000.

The time frame for an open space meeting also needs consideration. While they can be held for periods of less than a day, most successful open space meetings last between two and three days (at the outside) to give participants sufficient time to deal with the complexity of the issues at hand. While space prohibits a complete description of the open space technology, Owen emphasized that there are four principles and one law to any open space meeting:

Basically, the open space technique involves everyone present placing his or her ideas onto a board (typically using Post-its or some other method to attach notes).

TABLE 11.5.   Open Space Technology

The four principles of open space

- Whoever comes are the right people.
- Whatever happens is the only thing that could have.
- Whenever it starts is the right time.
- When it's over, it's over.

The one law of open space

- The law of two feet: If during the course of the gathering, any person finds him- or herself in a situation where they are neither learning nor contributing, they must use their two feet and go to some more productive place.

Source: Harrison Owen, *Open Space Technology: A User's Guide,* 2nd ed. (San Francisco: Berrett-Koehler, 1997).

Those present then organize the notes into activities on which those present will work, assuming that someone is willing to lead a session. Ultimately (within the time frame of the meeting) participants produce a report on that topic, and then allow those present to self-organize into a working group.

The basic idea is that if the key stakeholders have been invited to the open space, the important issues related to the topic at hand will be raised and organized by those present. Anyone interested in a particular aspect of the issue will then either post a "meeting" on that issue and run the meeting or attend one that someone else has organized. Each person then makes contributions to the way that issue is framed and develops possible resolutions and action steps. Small groups meet on particular aspects of the issue to consolidate their ideas and develop strategies and creative new approaches for dealing with that aspect. After each group meeting, those in attendance are expected to produce a report that can be combined, at the end of the entire meeting, into a book of action plans and projects that have come out of the open space meeting.

Although open space technology is not explicitly designed to deal with the future, it can provide a platform for understanding the complexities of the present and lead interested parties into designing a way forward into the future. In that sense, open space technology can be considered a useful "futures planning" tool.

Future Search

A related technique, but more explicitly futures focused, is the "future search conference." Developed by Marvin Weisbord and others, the *future search conference* brings together a diverse group of stakeholders interested in an issue, industry, community, or problem to share their views and wisdom about it.[22] The outcome of a future search conference is an action plan that stakeholders, who participate actively in identifying and analyzing the issues as well as developing the action steps, are expected to implement. The general idea is to get the relevant stakeholders together so they can devise workable solutions. As with open space meetings, future search conferences use emerging knowledge of how groups work to design the meeting so everyone's input is taken seriously in the process of devising solutions and a course of action.

The future search conference focuses on five tasks: reviewing the past, exploring the present, creating ideal future scenarios, identifying common ground among participants, and making action plans. A future search conference brings together groups of stakeholders from different spheres of activity who under normal circumstances might not interact or join in conversations. A future search conference—or similar "open space technology"—event can thus get people working together in new and exciting ways. Examples of the use of future search conferences include gaining citywide consensus on future city plans, bringing a union and management together for joint planning, and planning regional economic development, among numerous others.

Future search conferences, like open space meetings, need to bring all of the relevant stakeholders, that is, the whole system, into a common location to do the planning together. Future searches, also like open space meetings, use techniques to get the group to self-manage and tend to be organized in three-day blocks. The general idea is to get the gathered participants to think about the current reality and explore possible common futures.

Several ground rules apply to future search conferences. First, as with brainstorming techniques, all ideas are valid. Second, participants should record everything on flip charts (this creates a record that can be used later on). Third, they must listen to each other—remember the techniques of dialogue discussed earlier in the book? Fourth, all should observe established time frames, so that everyone's time is respected. Finally and importantly, participants should seek common ground and action rather than problems and conflicts.

The focus of a future search is on finding *common ground,* rather than differences, and is *future oriented,* rather than grounded in the past or present. In other words, participants will not dwell on current conflicts and problems, but on creative new ways of dealing with the problems at hand by thinking creatively about what values and goals they *share.*

The design for a future search conference involves getting stakeholders to sit together in "mixed" groups. In an economic development conference, for example, the stakeholders from the economic sphere should be mixed with those from civil society and government. The first step is to review the past by creating a timeline to the present about the relevant topic, a step Weisborg termed "recalling the past." The next step is to focus on the present: external trends affecting the relevant topic, a step termed "appreciating the present." In this step a complex diagram of the situation, called a "mind map," is generally created on large boards or walls using the input of everyone present. The mind map serves as an essential vehicle for creating a picture of the future: what is needed, what links exist between what is already present and what is needed, and where new ideas can be generated.

Four "rules" are essential to creating the mind map: All ideas are valid. The person who names the issue says where it goes. Opposing trends are OK. And "give concrete examples."

The critically important next step is to be "living the future"; that is, creating a desirable future based on input from all and creative ideas about what might emerge—in terms of common goals and ideas—from what is already present. Then the groups, if there are multiple groups at work, consolidate their ideas into the common themes and ideas, and move into an action planning stage.

Scenario Analysis

One other technique *scenario analysis,* which is a technique for developing narratives about different possible futures, has been widely used specifically to help companies plan strategically to cope with otherwise unforeseen events. It also has broad applicability for coping with multiple stakeholder interests. Groups interested in using scenarios undertake significant research on the topic of interest, seeking out all the available information and making sure that relevant stakeholders are participating in the process because all points of view need to be represented. The group gets together to construct alternative scenarios, or different descriptions of the future. Typically, several scenarios are constructed: a best case, worst case, and at least one radically different alternative where the unexpected happens.

By developing the scenarios as stories, planners can make them compelling and begin to think through the implications for a specific company and its vision, or for a group of stakeholders to a key issue or concern. One company that has had a great deal of success using scenarios is Royal Dutch Shell, which was able to prepare itself for the October 1973 oil shock and subsequent energy crisis using scenarios[23] (see also Chapter 1).

Scenario analysis is helpful because it provides for multiple different alternative futures and helps break leaders of the notion that simply extrapolating from the present is the only likely outcome of present trends. By asking for best- and worst-case scenarios and radically different alternatives, scenario analysis allows for possible discontinuities that make current projections meaningless—and helps prepare organizations for those potentialities.[24]

Scenario Analysis Process

Scenario planning is simple in its concept, although doing it well requires considerable research into current trends, gathering of extensive data, and synthesizing it into meaningful stories. First, a team of scenario analysts (anyone interested in a particular problem, issue, or strategy) gathers and discusses its perceptions of the key uncertainties around the focal issue. The topic might be, for example, the future strategy of a company, new competitive threats, or how to proceed with economic development for a region. The group should outline and define the relevant environment or issue, then determine key uncertainties and whether they are inside or outside of that group's control. The group should also consider the major constraints facing the planning group or company, because these define available strategic responses to the issue and determine what the major decision points might be with respect to the issue. The key issue is to determine how the future environment will be defined and constrained.

Next the group establishes a priority ranking with respect to the uncertainties identified, focusing on those with the greatest potential future impact and those that

TABLE 11.6. Guidelines for Future Responses by Scenario Analysts

Determine the applicability of potential decisions and action steps by asking:

- What are the "no brainers"—the actions common to all scenarios, that will be required in all foreseeable futures? These actions should be undertaken.

- What are the "no regrets"—the actions that may be valuable in some scenarios, less valuable in others, but not damaging in any way? These actions might be undertaken, but might be stopped if they become damaging in any way.

- What are the "contingent possibilities"—the actions that may be valuable in only selected scenarios?

- What are the "no ways!" scenarios—the actions deemed unacceptable? How should such actions be avoided?

Source: Eric K. Clemons, "Using Scenario Analysis to Manage the Strategic Risks of Reengineering," *Sloan Management Review,* Summer 1995, pp. 61–71.

are most poorly understood. The group then selects two or three critical uncertainties as the "driving uncertainties" and combines them for developing future scenarios.

Scenario development involves exploring the selected driving uncertainties and their implications in great detail. Typically, groups will create "stories" or narratives with an internal logic based on the driving uncertainties. Stories are compelling ways for leaders to begin to understand the implications of the uncertainties on the relevant organizations and stakeholders, especially if widely differing points of view have been incorporated into the different scenarios. As each scenario or story is written, different possible advantages and disadvantages, or implications, for the organizations and stakeholders emerge followed by possible strategic, development, or stakeholder-relationship responses.

The scenarios then are used to explore possible futures and to test out how different strategies for coping with the scenario will work. A critical test of a strategy, for example, is to see how it would work under vastly different scenarios. Doing such "testing" can help determine the robustness of a particular response. If a response to one scenario seems as though it might falter dramatically under another scenario, planners may wish to evolve a different strategy that would have a better chance of working under both scenarios. The key questions that should be asked—and answered—by scenario analysts are summarized in Table 11.6. These serve to guide decision making and future strategies by the stakeholders who have gathered to address an issue of relevance to all.

Common Ground on Planning the Future

Obviously, many more details go into planning a successful future search conference, open space meeting, or scenario analysis. It is clear, however, that all of these techniques use inputs from *all* relevant stakeholders, provide for sharing of concerns and ideas, use dialogical and brainstorming techniques, and demand that participants let go of preconceived ideas and agendas. Only in these ways can stakeholders to an issue work toward common ground—*and* analyze the possibilities and potentialities of the future without being biased by any one point of view. The general idea is to bring participants onto common ground, where fruitful new ways of working collaboratively can be developed, where there is open sharing of multiple points of view, and where reaching common ground and shared solutions is the goal.

Such techniques can be an important basis for generating not only innovative ideas but also actual commitments to carrying them out, especially when the issues and opportunities to be addressed are open-ended and ambiguous and when decision makers are present.[25] At some level these types of techniques also can help companies who want to be leading corporate citizens do far more than respond to the future: They can help companies, working with groups from the political and economic spheres, and interest groups representing the natural environment, create a common world that we can all live in. Futures assessments can also be helpful to companies and other organizations in avoiding significant problems that might otherwise arise because they are completely unexpected.

Not every group, however, favors the trend toward globalization of the economy and many are fearful of what the future might bring. An excellent example of these fears in action took place at the November 1999 meeting of the World Trade Organization (see the following box). Use of one of the techniques described above might have helped WTO officials anticipate—and better cope with—the protests.

Protest the Future

It was unexpected. But then again, was it? In November 1999 protesters cut short the meeting of the World Trade Organization in Seattle that was expected to foster continued globalization of the economy. In some respects, the disruption, which actually forced an early end to the meeting, was a clarion call to action for protesters of many stripes. Marching on the streets of Seattle were a mixed bag of activists focused on, among other things, trade deficits, job losses resulting from outsourcing and corporate mergers, international free trade agreements, labor rights, human rights, working conditions, sweatshops, and the environment. Generally, all were protesting continued globalization and its impacts on civil society and governments, impacts that they view as being imposed by powerful corporate forces without the consent of the societies affected.

Established in 1995, the World Trade Organization (WTO) is the only global entity that establishes the economic "rules of the game" regarding trade policies. The WTO creates negotiated international agreements around what is called the multilateral trading system, signed by member nations, that are aimed at helping international businesses produce, export, and import their goods and services. At the heart of WTO operations through treaties like GATT, the General Agreement on Trade and Tariffs, is breaking down trade barriers among nations, a process that citizens of some nations—and activists—feel may be threatening the uniqueness of their cultures and in some cases overriding national interests. Protest groups believe that WTO agreements have undermined environmental, labor, and human rights standards, in part because the agreements are created behind closed doors.

The protesters were seeking representation or "voice" in the closed WTO deliberations on globalization that will undoubtedly continue to impact civil society, governments, and the natural environment. None of their voices were supposed to be heard at the table in Seattle. And Seattle was only the beginning of globally spawned protests against continuing economic development and globalization with little input from those who are most affected by what might be called globalization without representation.

Protesters next disrupted the World Economic Forum meeting in Davos, Switzerland, in January 2000, claiming that world trade is basically undemocratic and driven by the need to maximize shareholder wealth without regard for other impacts of economic development. And that did not end the protests. In September 2000, World Bank and International Monetary Fund (IMF) officials, who provide loans to developing nations along with economic development requirements and restrictions, were forced to cut their annual meeting short after a week of protests, lobbying, and workshops against globalization in Prague, capital of the Czech Republic.

The protests were partly fueled by the capacity to mobilize activists on global issues in some respects by what one observer called "hactivism," Hactivism "blends Internet technology with the social protest producing new tools and methods that are not only annoying their targets—usually government and institutional websites—but also the ranks of traditional activists."[26] It also, ironically, uses the very results of globalization that are in some respects subject of the protests: the connectivity of advancing technologies.

Could the WTO, IMF, World Bank, and World Economic Forum have coped better with these protests? Even that bastion of the most conservative of business practices, *Business Week,* predicted the coming furor in an article titled "Bracing for a Battle in Seattle" two weeks before the first protests began. The magazine followed the protests with an editorial by Robert Kuttner (among others) claiming that "The Seattle Protesters Got It Right." Kuttner argued that global trade politics will never be the same and that

"however desirable cross-border trade may be, it is not the sum and substance of a democratic society."[27]

Kuttner outlined the key issues that need attention from these global trade organizations—and some alternative voices that could, with appropriate planning, be included in future talks:

Give poor countries some serious debt relief . . . In exchange, governments of authoritarian countries would have to embrace minimal standards of decency for their workers and citizens. Also, raise environmental standards, but accompany this with serious transfers of technology. Before Seattle, these ideas were not even debatable. Now they are getting a hearing."[28]

Arguably, WTO, World Bank, IMF, and World Economic Forum officials could have been better prepared and, if willing, could even have found ways to have included the excluded and avoided the protests that stymied them altogether. Of course, doing so would not only mean intensive scanning of the external environment, but also changing the current power structure to be more inclusive, exactly what the activists are demanding. In any case, perhaps now they will begin to consider not only external stakeholders but the ways in which the very processes of globalization that they themselves are fostering are impacting the capacity to protest against their policies.

Sources: David Moberg, "Everything You Need to Know about the WTO," *Salon.com,* November 29, 1999, at http://www.salon.com/news/feature/1999/11/29/wto/index.html; Julie Light, "Prague: The Aftermath," *Corporate Watch,* September 29, 2000, at http://www.corpwatch.org/trac/globalization/bretton/jl9-29.html; "Protests Mar Davos Summit, BBC News, January 30, 2000, at http://news.bbc.co.uk/hi/english/business/newsid_623000/623585.stm; Paul Van Slambrouck, "Newest Tool for Social Protest: The Internet," *Christian Science Monitor,* June 18, 1999, at http://www. globalpolicy.org/globaliz/special/internet.htm; Paul Magnusson and William Echikson, "Bracing for a Battle in Seattle," *Business Week,* November 8, 1999, pp. 38–39.

LEADING CHALLENGES:
WE CANNOT PREDICT THE FUTURE, BUT . . .
WE *CAN* CREATE RELATIONSHIPS

Leading corporate citizens cannot predict the future because it is an inherently chaotic process in which small changes can make large and fundamental differences. They *can,* however, prepare themselves and their organizations to cope with whatever happens by being aware of the changes that impact both internal and external stakeholders. They *can* implement dialogue and conversations with primary and critical secondary stakeholders who are capable of providing important input into the company's future plans, and they *can* continually scan the horizon for significant developments, whether technological, ecological, social, or political. By establishing these *relationships* with key stakeholders, companies can prepare themselves in an ongoing way for what the future is likely to bring.

Leading corporate citizens need not be surprised by technological advances, activism, or social changes that put their businesses at risk. As the sections on future search conferences, open space meetings, and scenario analysis indicate, there are numerous techniques available that companies can use on an ongoing basis to establish communication links with potential critics, key stakeholders, and social activists. Getting the kind of information that can only be gained when people with *different* points of view are brought together not only enhances a company's capacity to be a respected corporate citizen, but also it provides the basis for revealing new trends, competitive threats, and possible new opportunities. Many of these possibilities could never be discovered through traditional channels of market research and new product/service development.

By putting in place the types of dialogic processes with stakeholders that have been described above, by focusing on continually learning and incorporating that learning into constructive new stakeholder practices, leading corporate citizens can operate with integrity and be successful. They can also provide the means to achieve a better balance among the spheres in society and with the natural environment because the different points of view represented in these spheres will be better understood.

Is using these dialogic techniques easy? Of course not. They require a commitment to internal learning and change—and a commitment to real and recognized input from outsiders. They imply a willingness to listen to those who may be less powerful or have fewer resources than the company itself. But using such dialogue-based techniques to raise up the emerging issues, concerns, technologies, and problems, may be a better way of operating with integrity than to assume that economizing is all important. Business, after all, was created to serve society's interests, not vice versa. All of this, of course, suggests the need for a shift of paradigm in organizing and leading corporate citizens, which is the subject of the final chapter.

NOTES TO CHAPTER 11

1. Robert Kegan, *In Over Our Heads: The Mental Demands of Modern Life* (Cambridge: Harvard University Press, 1994).
2. Data are from http://www.globalpolicy.org/socecon/inequal/gates99.htm and http://www.globalpolicy.org/socecon/inequal/stats98.htm.
3. http://www.unilever.com/public/env/review/environ/public/17bra/71braco.htm
4. Ibid.
5. Quoted from http://www.unilever.com/public/env/review/environ/public/15turk/ 15turkfr.htm.
6. See, for example, http://www.csis.org/. Trends identified in this section are from Michael J. Mazarr, *Global Trends 2005: The Challenge of a New Millennium* (Washington, DC: Center for Strategic and International Studies, 1997). See also http://www.csis.org/gt2005/.

7. Ibid.

8. Ibid., p. 13.

9. Ibid., pp. 16–24.

10. Ibid., p. 25.

11. Benjamin Barber, *Jihad vs. McWorld* (New York: Times Books; Random House, 1995).

12. Mazarr, p. 31.

13. Kegan.

14. Mazarr, p. 37.

15. http://www.geocities.com/CapitolHill/Senate/4787/millennium/new.html.

16. This topic is discussed at length by Robert D. Putnam, *Making Democracy Work: Civic Traditions in Modern Italy* (Princeton, NJ: Princeton University Press, 1993); see also his articles: "Bowling Alone: America's Declining Social Capital," *Journal of Democracy* 6, no. 1 (January), pp. 65–78; and "The Strange Disappearance of Civic America," *American Prospect* 24 (Winter 1996), http://epn.org/prospect/24/24putn.html.

17. See my own work on social and public-private partnerships and Steve Waddell, "Market-Civil Society Partnership Formation: A Status Report on Activity, Strategies, and Tools," *IDR Reports* 13, no. 5 (1998).

18. See, for example, Sandra Waddock, *Not By Schools Alone: Sharing Responsibility for America's Education Reform* (Greenwich, CT: Praeger, 1995).

19. See, for example, Sandra Waddock, "Understanding Social Partnerships: An Evolutionary Model of Partnership Organizations," *Administration and Society* 21, no. 1 (May 1989), pp. 78–100.

20. Steve Waddell, "Business-Government-Nonprofit Collaborations as Agents for Social Innovation and Learning," paper presented at the Academy of Management Annual Meeting, Chicago, IL, 1999.

21. See Harrison Owen, *Open Space Technology: A User's Guide,* 2nd ed. (San Francisco: Berrett-Koehler, 1997), and *Expanding Our Now: The Story of Open Space Technology* (San Francisco: Berrett-Koehler, 1997).

22. Marvin R. Weisbord and Sandra Janoff, *Future Search: An Action Guide to Finding Common Ground in Organizations & Communities* (San Francisco: Berrett-Koehler, 1995).

23. For a good overview of how to perform scenario analysis, see Peter Schwartz, *The Art of the Long View: Planning for the Future in an Uncertain World* (New York: Doubleday Currency, 1996).

24. The description of scenario analysis presented below is derived from a combination of Schwartz and Eric K. Clemons, "Using Scenario Analysis to Manage the Strategic Risks of Reengineering," *Sloan Management Review,* Summer 1995, pp. 61–71.

25. To learn about future search conferences, see Weisbord and Janoff, *Future Search;* for information on open space technology, see Owen's *Open Space Technology* and *Expanding Our Now.*

26. Paul Van Slambrouck, "Newest Tool for Social Protest: The Internet," *Christian Science Monitor,* June 18, 1999, at http://www.globalpolicy.org/globaliz/special/internet. htm, p. 1.

27. Robert Kuttner, "The Seattle Protesters Got It Right," *Business Week,* December 20, 1999, p. 25.

28. Ibid.

Leading Global Futures:

THE EMERGING PARADIGM OF LEADING
CORPORATE CITIZENSHIP

Imagine a global economy that is healthy and self-governing. Imagine markets that are organized to empower people. Imagine an economy that is free, humane, competitive, profitable, decentralized, nonbureaucratic, and socially accountable. Imagine a global economy that operates for the common good, a market that develops local-to-global structures to build sustainable community.

This sort of economy is what we are talking about in civil development. It requires a new order of thinking about global markets characterized by freedom and accountability.

—SEVERYN BRUYN, A Civil Economy: Transforming the
Market in the Twenty-First Century

This remarkable statement synthesizes much of what this book is about: creating corporate citizens that have respect for human dignity and the natural ecology that supports it through a balanced approach to the three spheres of human activity that constitute civilization—economic, political, and civil society. All along we have been talking about developing managers into leaders who take their responsibilities seriously and proceed with their decisions wisely by consistently implementing a value and values added approach.

Past chapters have demonstrated that economic success results when companies treat stakeholders with dignity and respect, and when their practices match their rhetoric about vision and values. We have seen the need for balance among economic, political, and civilizing interests, all three of which are necessary to create successful and ecologically sustainable societies. We have seen the need for higher levels of awareness and development, both individually and organizationally to cope with the complexities and challenges of today and, particularly, tomorrow. In short, we have seen the need for and the beginnings of a shift of perspective on what it means to be a leading corporate citizen, both as an individual and as an organization.

SHIFTING PERSPECTIVES

This book has presented what I hope is a realistic but fairly radical perspective on the ways companies as citizens in the global village can be successful with, in, and of societies, not alongside or separate from them. The systems perspective presented through the three spheres framework, combined with the linkages among vision, values, and value added integrates responsibility, meaningfulness, and the energy and capacity of whole persons directly into organizational life.

By understanding that responsibility is integrated into all of the organizational practices that impact stakeholders and the ecological environment, organizations are discovering the power of vision to create meaning and purpose for the organization and its stakeholders, as well as the power of treating others with respect and dignity. Such a stance not only balances power among the three spheres of human activity but also tends to bring more equity and power balancing into relationships within organizations. When the full resources of individuals are tapped and people are treated as human beings, the tendency to treat people as mere cogs in the great machine of business diminishes. Respect and dignity are enhanced.

Transformation Based on Nature

Fully incorporating this emerging paradigm into the dominant management paradigm will require radical shifts in the current business model, in power dynamics, and in balance among the three spheres of human activity, which themselves must be put into sustainable *relationships* with stakeholders and the natural environment. Part of the needed wisdom can derive from principles embedded in nature itself, using what author David Korten termed a life-centered approach that taps the wisdom of nature and ecological systems. Certainly, if we hope to sustain productivity and use ecological resources wisely, a shift of balance in the powers among the spheres is needed.

Balancing power means that corporate activities can be undertaken on a scale accessible to human beings and with the best interests of all stakeholders kept firmly in mind and well balanced. Duly elected democratic governments can resume their rightful powers to determine the public interest and the common good. And the relationships fostered and sustained in civil society can nourish the spirit and the bodies of productive members of societies and productive corporate stakeholders.

Korten offered six lessens drawn from what is now known about self-organizing ecological systems that potentially help in rethinking the way that corporate life is currently scaled and operates (see Table 12.1).[1] To some extent, we can relate these to certain design elements that he developed for his visionary "post-corporate" world. Many of them are similar to ideas that we have been discussing throughout this book. Perhaps it is time to begin imagining different types of futures that provide inspira-

319

CHAPTER 12
Leading Global
Futures: The
Emerging
Paradigm of
Leading Corporate
Citizenship

TABLE 12.1. Korten's Lesson's of Life's Wisdom and Progressive Design Elements

Lesson's of Life's Wisdom	Progressive Corporate Design Elements
1. Life favors self-organization.	Human scale self-organization.
2. Life is frugal and sharing.	Renewable energy self-reliance. Closed cycle materials use. Regional environmental balance.
3. Life depends on inclusive, place-based communities.	Village and neighborhood clusters. Towns and regional centers.
4. Life rewards cooperation.	Mindful livelihoods.
5. Life depends on boundaries	Interregional electronic communication.
6. Life banks on diversity, creative individuality, and shared learning.	"Wild spaces" in nature and within organizations.

Source: Adapted from David Korten, *The Post-Corporate World* (San Francisco: Berrett-Koehler, 1999).

tion for human life in the midst of nature, where resources are equitably distributed among all of the peoples of the world.

SELF-ORGANIZATION. First, Korten said, life favors self-organization and companies would be wise to do so as well. Self-organization is the process of organizing that tends to emerge when people are together for a purpose. But self-organization is best suited to reasonably small-scale endeavors that are rooted locally, thus favoring human-scale enterprises that truly empower people, not just rhetorically, to self-organize. Human-scaled enterprises allow people to engage in a positive vision whereby they can achieve meaningful personal and company purposes.

FRUGAL AND SHARING. Second, Korten noted, life is frugal and sharing, values that are certainly found in the economizing values that underpin corporate efficiency. But from an ecological perspective, this also means thinking about operating in a sustainable manner for the long term, hence ecologizing, which effectively means wasting nothing.

INCLUSIVE, PLACED-BASED COMMUNITIES. Third, life depends on inclusive, place-based communities, what we earlier termed rootedness. Corporations need to be accountable to the communities that depend upon them.

RESPECTIVE BOUNDARIES. Communities do need to establish boundaries and local rules to sustain their culture and character. Leading corperate citizens operating within those communities respect the boundaries that communities attempt to erect. Communities develop on a human scale, not a global one, though technology clearly permits some global communities to exist electronically. It is not protectionism, in the negative sense, that exists when a community attempts to sustain its uniqueness and sense of place, but rather an attempt to free the human spirit with the sustenance of relationships, personal knowledge, and a shared sense of the common good found in community.

LIFE REWARDS COOPERATION. Fourth, life rewards cooperation. Symbiosis and interdependency strengthen the bounded organism, whether individual or community, in its attempts to "compete" for necessary life resources. Rather than fostering a dog-eat-dog hypercompetitive environment based on the accumulation of material goods, the whole human being is rewarded by helping others, each doing his or her bit to make the world a better place. This is not altruism but a belief in the goodness of the human spirit, a spirit fostered by what Korten called "mindful livelihoods," which earlier we have emphasized as finding meaning in work no matter where one works or what one does and being aware of imports.

LIFE BANKS ON DIVERSITY. Finally, life banks on diversity, creative individuality, and shared learning, just as successful companies do in the global environment. Only by tapping what Korten called "wild spaces" can this diversity of enterprise be maintained, but these wild spaces need to be based on more than the natural environment (though this is certainly important). Wild spaces allow for innovation and personal meaning making to develop within leaders throughout an enterprise. Organizational wild spaces turn everyone into leaders because they tap the richness of potentialities inherent in every human being and allow for that richness to be brought to bear in the context of shared vision and values to add value for all.

Wild spaces can be created through the types of dialogic practices discussed in the last chapter as part of the exploration of the future and by engaging regularly with stakeholders who have different perspectives than leaders of a company. Creating wild spaces in leading corporate citizens ultimately means hiring many different types of people from many different backgrounds, and tapping their insights and knowledge extensively. It means having the self-confidence—as a leader and as a company—to bring in diverse points of view and incorporate them into corporate values and operating practices. Doing so successfully may necessitate a significant shift of perspective.

Metanoia: A Shift of Perspective

Leading corporate citizens create meaningful and constructive visions and underpin those visions with operating practices that result in integrity in all senses of the word. Powerful and meaningful visions create a sense of higher purpose for the enterprise that brings everyone involved into a common vision and helps create a strong internal community and sense of belonging, where everyone knows what they individually have to contribute and how that contribution helps move the vision along. Such visions are underscored by constructive values that help stakeholders, employees in particular, know their place in the organization's efforts to make significant contributions to building a better world and sustainable future. The combination of vision and values meaningful to stakeholders results in the development of responsible day-

321

*CHAPTER 12
Leading Global
Futures: The
Emerging
Paradigm of
Leading Corporate
Citizenship*

to-day practices that allow the organization to add value in the by-product of profits and wealth generation. Combined, all of this means operating with integrity.

We have argued that leading corporate citizens with these characteristics will succeed in the complexities, dynamism, and connectedness likely to evolve in the future. They will do so in conversation with their stakeholders. Such corporate citizens also incorporate into their everyday activities not only objective data and information—that which can be observed—but also the subjective and intersubjective or more interpretive elements of life, such as aesthetics, emotions, and meaningfulness. They understand the need for ecological and community sustainability and are prepared to operate with issues of sustainability fully in mind. Developing corporate citizens that have these attributes calls for nothing less than a shift of mind. Peter Senge called this shift *metanoia,* which means a shift of mind, even transcendence toward a higher purpose.[2]

Metanoia takes leading corporate citizens away from thinking that their actions—as individuals or as organizations—can be taken in isolation. It moves them towards a more ecological or systems understanding of embeddedness, interconnectedness, and interdependence. It also asks them to think about the decisions they make as manager or leaders in an integrated way—that is, not only with their heads and analytical or scientifically based reasoning, but also with their hearts and spirits. *Metanoia* asks leaders to think about the meaning their decisions and actions have and the meaning embedded in the work that they and others do jointly—and then to create and tell "stories" that help them to share the meanings with others.

The new perspective thus asks leaders of and within corporate citizens to think deeply about the meaning and implications of *all* of the decisions they are making and what their impact is likely to be on the world around us. Leading citizens can do this because they explicitly recognize that there will be impacts and consequences of decisions. They know that all decisions are embedded with a set of values that either honors the relationships and stakeholders they impact or not. They are engaged in ongoing relationships with stakeholders and understand their perspectives, even when they are radically different than the company's internal perspective. This *metanoia* asks leading citizens to seek meaning and meaningfulness in decisions so that everyone can bring his or her whole self—mind, heart, body, spirit—to work (as opposed to "checking" their brains or heart at the door).

The changes in organizations and societies today also demand that leadership be distributed throughout the enterprise, rather than held closely in the hands of a few top managers. Effective and wise—or mindful—leadership means taking responsibility for the consequences of one's actions (and thinking through what those consequences are likely to be). It also asks most individuals to assume qualities like those of entrepreneurs, self-initiators, and leaders more than ever before, to be responsible for their own productive engagement with others and for the results that the decisions they make achieve. Leadership in this sense falls to everyone who takes part in bringing to reality the vision embodied in the higher purposes shared by individuals within the enterprise.

Ultimately, *metanoia* asks leaders of and within corporate citizens to seek *wisdom* and *mindfulness* in their work.[3] Mindful and wise leaders think through the consequences of their decisions to all of the stakeholders those decisions impact. Mindful leaders are aware that they do not and cannot know all that they need to know, but take seriously all of the responsibilities attendant upon their leadership. They continue to grow, learn, and develop and embed learning practices within their enterprises as part of the culture. They seek wisdom, knowing that, in the words of leading management thinker Russell Ackoff:

> *Wisdom is the ability to perceive and evaluate the long-run consequences of behavior.* It is normally associated with a willingness to make short-run sacrifices for the sake of long-run gains.[4]

Imaginization and the Leading Corporate Citizen

As difficult as the developmental task of achieving the emergent *metanoia* in real-world corporate citizens might be for some individuals and organizations, it is possible to imagine what an individual working in a new paradigm organization might experience. This task of what management thinker Gareth Morgan termed *imaginization* will be the subject of the next several sections.[5] Imaginization asks us to think in terms of metaphors and images of what might be, not necessarily what is. Imaginization is a technique for enhancing leadership and management creativity that helps leaders understand situations in new ways, find new images about organizing, create shared understandings, and link those capacities to personal and organizational learning and continued development. In this chapter we will adapt the technique of imaginization for our purposes, exploring in this chapter the vision, values, leadership attributes, individual and organizational work shifts, and structures that might provide leading corporate citizens with patterns for coping in the turbulent world of the future. Emerging new values and "logics" or ways of thinking, as well as societal implications of these logics, will be explored in our imaginary trip into a true leading corporate citizen.

Vision Shifts

The first stop in our imaginary trip into the emerging paradigm organization will be the implications of the new *metanoia* for vision (see Table 12.2 for the shifts that are likely to take place).

Imagine living and working with passion for your work and the purposes of your employing organization, a leading corporate citizen! Imagine a company with a vision embedded with bigger meanings and purposes that draw people in so that they can bring mind, heart, body, and spirit to work. Imagine that the vision was articulated clearly enough so that all relevant stakeholders understood it, acknowledged it, shared it, and valued it. Understanding the vision, primary stakeholders can live it because it is not just articulated but also is fully implemented—a lived, live, living, and lively vision. Imagine that this enterprise treated all of its

323

*CHAPTER 12
Leading Global
Futures: The
Emerging
Paradigm of
Leading Corporate
Citizenship*

TABLE 12.2. Vision Shifts Needed in Emerging Leading Corporate Citizens

Vision shifts from . . .	To . . .
Maximizing shareholder wealth without regard for other stakeholders.	Doing something important and useful for customers, using the full resources of employees in a way that treats all stakeholders with dignity and respect, and results in success and profitability.
General nonspecific core purpose.	Building a better world in some way, creating meaning and higher purpose, generating passion and commitment to that purpose and vision among stakeholders, especially employees.
Corporate vision and strategy are available only to top managers.	Corporate vision and strategy are shared by all primary stakeholders, are clearly articulated, and relate to higher purposes.
Business is separate from society.	Business is integral to society.
Responsibility is discretionary.	Responsibility is integral to and implicit in all practices that impact human and natural ecologies.
Stakeholder "management."	Stakeholder relationships.
Leaders direct through authority from the top.	Leaders generate meaning that guides core purposes and enables others to act in one's own and the enterprise's best interest

stakeholders, internal and external, primary and secondary, with dignity and respect and was rewarded with long-term success and profitability. This is what vision in the emerging paradigm for leading corporate citizens is.

Further, imagine that the organization is a business that sees itself and its impacts as an integral part of the broader set of societies in which it operates, so that it carefully acknowledges the inherent and unavoidable responsibility in all of its practices, decisions, and impacts. Imagine that top leadership is acknowledged as developing the core vision, a vision that demonstrates the higher purpose of the enterprise and benefited stakeholders and societies, and as guiding practice by enabling—truly empowering—others to act in their own and the enterprise's best interest. Imagine that everyone involved knows exactly what that vision is and what his or her contribution is to achieving it.

Imagine a company that understands—and acts upon—the need for balancing its own power, resources, and strategies with those of other stakeholders. Imagine that all relationships with stakeholders are engaging, dialogue based, and mutually respectful. Imagine that rather than "managing" the stakeholders, which implies an unbalanced power relationship, this company develops and manages its relationships carefully by respecting the interests, needs, and dignity of other stakeholders. Now imagine that responsibility is integral to and implicit in all of the multifaceted day-to-day operating practices the company develops. No longer is responsibility considered discretionary or something that is done after business is taken care of. Instead, business is undertaken responsibly, in a both/and logic that accepts the inherent tension and paradoxes of such a stance. Such is the nature of vision in the emerging paradigm organization.

Values in the Emerging Paradigm

The second part of our imaginization takes us to the realm of values. What are the values that underpin the leading corporate citizens compared to more traditional organizations (see Table 12.3 for a summary of the shifts in values accompanying the change to the emerging paradigm).

Economizing and power-aggrandizing values underpin all business activity as we know it today. Even as the new paradigm emerges, we can imagine that these values are likely to sustain business enterprise, but that they will be supplemented and complemented by the values that help balance the other spheres of activity. Thus, imagine economizing and power-aggrandizing values complemented by values of civilizing, which help to build community internally and externally, and ecologizing, which provides for community and ecological sustainability. Imagine that leaders of future corporate citizens are far more likely to operate with an understanding of the importance of community, relationships—civilizing— than most present day companies, to think relationally and systemically. In putting this understanding into operation, leaders create numerous means of engaging in mutually respectful conversations with stakeholders, some of which appropriately influence corporate practices. Simultaneously, imagine that current and future pressures from the resource constraints imposed by the natural environment heighten sensitivity to values of ecologizing, increasing attention to natural ecology and sustainable development.

Further, imagine that pushed by communications technology and the ready availability of information, the trend toward democracy in societies continues unabated and even enters the workplace. Imagine that the workplace itself has been transformed structurally so that many individuals in the company are expected (as they largely are today) to exert more entrepreneurlike qualities than they did in the past. The combination of entrepreneurial attitudes and independence among stakeholders may well move companies away from valuing hierarchy and dominance. Companies may move toward truly sharing power and empowering employees, but will likely sustain appropriate levels of hierarchy in the firm (some of which is likely to continue to be necessary as a structural element).

325

CHAPTER 12
Leading Global
Futures: The
Emerging
Paradigm of
Leading Corporate
Citizenship

TABLE 12.3.   Value Shifts in the Emerging Paradigm

Values shift from . . .	To . . .
Economizing and power aggrandizing.	. . . and including civilizing and ecologizing.
Imbalance.	Balance.
No respect or dignity for stakeholders.	Respect and dignity for all stakeholders.
Hierarchy.	Shared power, empowerment with appropriate hierarchy.
Dominance.	Partnership, equality.
Authority.	Democracy.
Competition.	Collaboration *and* competition.
Control through systems.	Control through goals and values.
Exclusive.	Inclusive.
Value the objective, scientific, observable.	Value the objective and subjective, interobjective and intersubjective.
Disconnected, fragmented, autonomous.	Connected, holistic, networked (linked).

Along with this shift, imagine that companies move away from stakeholder "management" toward developing stakeholder relationships because they value the mutuality inherent in the relationship itself. Even more radically perhaps, imagine that leading corporate citizens come to value the synthesis and generativity that is inherent in fostering collaborative as well as competitive relationships with stakeholders in all spheres of society. Values of collaboration and competition, rather than simple competition, might meld in a tension of opposite and paradox that will provide a basis for continual creativity and innovation in this world.

In organizations with clearly articulated vision and core values, where leadership involves creating meaning rather than directing through authority and hierarchy, we can imagine that controls through organizational systems will be supplemented by controls provided by the glue of common goals and shared values. Organizations thereby respect and value employees (in particular) and the contributions they wish to make toward accomplishing the organization's vision. And such enterprises are, we might believe, also likely to value the diversity of inclusive stakeholder relations in their primary relationships, whether with customers, suppliers, owners, or employees, rather than explicitly or implicitly generating exclusive tactics and policies.

Finally, we can imagine that there will be value for the holons (whole/parts) that corporate citizens recognize are always present in the connected, holistic, and networked system they call an organization. Individual stakeholders are holons that may form into groups that are themselves holons, which are part of larger organizations. All of these levels are respected as the wholes that they are, while recognizing that each is incomplete without the rest. Leaders in the emerging paradigm organization recognize the interrelatedness of the parts of the whole system and are careful about developing operating practices so that the integrity of each holon is maintained and negative ripple effects are minimized.

TABLE 12.4.   Individuals and Work Shifts in the Emerging Paradigm

Individual mind-set shifts from . . .	**To . . .**
Self-interest.	Self and other interests.
Contribute using body or mind.	Contribute using mind, body, heart, spirit.
Conventional reasoning, awareness.	Postconventional reasoning, awareness.
Single perspective held.	Multiple perspectives held simultaneously.
Mindlessness, lack of awareness.	Mindful, aware, fully conscious.
Do the job as structured.	Learn constantly, improve the job and its results.
"Instrument of the corporation," a tool.	Purposeful, self-directed.
Moral reasoning from society's demands.	Principled, care-based moral reasoning.
Emotionally immature.	Emotional maturity.

Developmental perspectives move from . . .	**To . . .**
Individualistic ideology.	Individualistic *and* communitarian ideologies.
Single-perspective stages of development.	Multiple-perspective stages of development.
Reactive, proactive stakeholder relations.	Interactive stakeholder relations.
One-way (top-down) communication.	Dialogue and mutual conversation.
Just do my job.	Constant scanning the environment for trends, opportunities, challenges.

Work shifts from . . .	**To . . .**
Meaningless.	Meaningful.
Powerless.	Empowered.
Individual gain.	Individual and community gain.
Not visibly connected to larger purpose.	Visibly connected to larger purpose.

Individuals Leading Corporate Citizens

Individuals operating within leading corporate citizens will need skills tomorrow that they can probably get away without today. Table 12.4 lists a few of the more obvious attitudinal (or mindset) attributes and developmental characteristics, as well as some implications for the nature of work in leading corporate citizens where, remember, we have argued that leadership needs to come from everyone at every level. Let us continue our imaginary trip into the leading corporate citizen of the future at the individual level. What would this organization be like for people and for working?

Imagine coming to work every day knowing that your best contribution is expected. That best contribution taps all of you. Of course your mind in this knowledge-based economy is a crucial part of doing your work. For some employees, physical labor

327

CHAPTER 12
Leading Global
Futures: The
Emerging
Paradigm of
Leading Corporate
Citizenship

is still demanded. But your contribution also involves thinking about the ways in which what you do and how you do it affects others in an emotional and aesthetic sense. You are also called upon to consider the ways your activities, especially in working with others, develop a meaningful and important contribution to making the world around you a better place, contribute to the organization's achievement of its vision, and enhance your feeling of being in a worthwhile community.

In coming to your job every day, you know that the organization (and life itself) has high expectations about the learning that you will do. You are expected to always be pushing the edge of your own learning to enhance the organizational vision and community, and to push yourself toward the higher stages of individual development demanded by an increasingly complex and dynamic world. You work at mindfulness—awareness of the implications of each decision and "presence" here and now—so that you are aware of what you and others do and are fully conscious of how others (other stakeholders) are affected by the decisions you make and the practices you develop.

Thus, developmentally you have moved toward the capacity to hold multiple perspectives simultaneously and are very skilled, when necessary, at taking the "other's" perspective (whichever "other" is relevant in a given situation). This skill helps you develop good relationships with important stakeholders whom your daily activities and work affect (or whose activities affect your work).

You personally and the company have moved away from simply reacting to external pressures, and have even moved beyond proactive strategies to forestall the actions of others, toward more consistently interactive strategies of being in dialogue with important stakeholders. This interactive posture helps you and the organization avoid nasty surprises from the external environment. In part, you can do this because you are constantly alert to any concerns from the stakeholders you interact with. In part, it happens almost naturally because your constant learning means that you pay attention to signals coming from outside (or arising inside) the organization. And because your opinion is as respected as any other, you know that when you voice an idea it will be listened to.

Your work has become meaningful and you have, in this transition to the emerging paradigm organization, become truly empowered, not only in rhetoric, but in actuality. Power is shared and the need for power aggrandizement, whether by individuals or the company, has diminished (while still present) in favor of focusing on a combination of individual person and company gain *combined with* gains for the larger communities that are relevant. You handle this somewhat paradoxical "both/and" well because you see how your work is connected to the larger purpose of the organization. You are connected to communities within and outside your organization and know exactly how your contribution fits in making these enterprises better.

TABLE 12.5. Structure and Practice in the Emerging Leading Corporate Citizen

Structures shift from . . .	To . . .
Rigid boundaries.	Overlapping, merging boundaries (boundary lessening).
Lead through authority.	Lead through vision and values.
High, relatively rigid structure.	Emergent, flexible, and adaptive structure.
Single, simple financial bottom line, financial capital.	Multiple bottom lines for stakeholders, including owners, employees, customers, and suppliers/allies, among others.
One dominant stakeholder (shareholder).	Multiple primary/secondary stakeholders.
Leadership at the top (top down).	Leadership is everywhere (top down and bottom up)

Practices move from . . .	To . . .
Economizing, power aggrandizing.	. . . and civilizing and ecologizing.
Exploitative practices, disrespectful.	Integrity in practices, respectful.
Reactive, proactive strategies.	Interactive strategies.
Objective, unemotional, meaningless.	Objective/subjective, emotional/meaningful.
Discretionary corporate responsibility.	Responsibility integral to operating practices.
Managing stakeholders.	Developing stakeholder relationships.
Fragmented functions.	Integral systems.
Operating instrumentally.	Operating with integrity.
Valuing contributions from and to owners.	Valuing contributions of all stakeholders.
Avoid accountability and transparency.	Necessary accountability and transparency.
Externalizing costs.	Internalizing costs.
Wasteful exploitative operations.	Ecologizing, nature-based operations.

Structure and Practice in the Emerging Leading Corporate Citizen

Accompanying the shifts in vision, values, and work in the new paradigm organization, leading corporate citizens will find themselves shifting both their structure and practices to accommodate improved relationships with stakeholders and more awareness of responsibilities. Table 12.5 lists some of the significant shifts in structure and practice that can be expected as we continue our imaginization.

Imagine an organization where there is consistent and regular interaction and dialogue between internal stakeholders and those who used to be outside, such as suppliers, customers, and community members. Because new paradigm organizations will likely structure themselves through collaborative alliances and partnerships of various kinds, the formerly clear and rather rigid boundaries separating different stakeholder groups have tended to blur. Overlapping and merging

329

CHAPTER 12
Leading Global
Futures: The
Emerging
Paradigm of
Leading Corporate
Citizenship

boundaries can be expected in areas such as customer relations where practices that tie one company's purchasing system directly to others' can be expected to increase, or in community relations where social partnerships created to solve community-based problems of mutual concern evolve.

Leadership through vision and values continues apace, creating the organizational glue and direction that provides structure, substituting emergent, flexible, and adaptive teams, ad hoc groupings, task forces, and project/process units for formerly readily identifiable (and permanent) structures and units. This adaptive structure, while complex and somewhat difficult to understand, allows the company to meet the needs of different stakeholders as they arise in what might be called an emergent structure or webs of connected groups that develop sustaining relationships over time.

The respectful and interactive stakeholder relationships point the company in the direction of being accountable to multiple stakeholders rather than to a single stakeholder. Indeed, the company has moved from "managing" stakeholders to a more respectful stance of managing stakeholder relationships and assuring their mutuality of interests. Thus, measurement systems and the relevant reward systems are geared to performance in the essential primary and secondary stakeholder domains. These include not only owners (financial performance and wealth generation), but also employee relations, customer relations, supplier relations, community relations, public and governmental affairs, and others. Multiple "bottom lines" are followed and reported upon externally so that the company's responsibility and practices are "transparent" to and accountable for impacts on key external stakeholders.

Imagine that internal corporate practices have also shifted, so that the dominant behaviors associated with economizing and power-aggrandizing values have expanded to include values of civilizing (relationship building) and ecologizing, assuring ecological and community sustainability over the long term. Because of the transparency of corporate actions to stakeholders, the company is clear that it operates in all respects with integrity in both of its definitions, honesty/straightforwardness and wholeness. Responsibility is considered integral to all operating practices; little is done without considering the stakeholder and ecological implications, thus accountability is built into the operating practices.

The close link of the company's vision and articulated higher purposes helps generate meaning for stakeholders who interact with the firm. Clear attention is paid to the corporate environment aesthetically, thus assuring that stakeholders are not only "satisfied," in the traditional sense of customer satisfaction and quality management, but also emotionally and aesthetically. To cope with the complexity of knowing that stakeholders are whole individuals, care is taken developing all relationships so that abuses and exploitation of stakeholders, wherever they are, are nonexistent. Stakeholder contributions are valued, wherever they come from.

Costs are fully internalized, with accounting systems incorporating the full product or service life cycle and all associated environmental costs. The company is an industry leader in advancing full costing processes globally. Operations are based on ecologizing and natural principles that indicate "no waste" practices.

New Logics across the Globe

Gaining the needed new perspective or *metanoia* involves incorporating into our thinking a new set of "logics" or ways of thinking and new values that accompany those logics.[6] Some years ago scholars Douglas Austrom and Lawrence Lad neatly synthesized these new logics and values that appear to be emerging globally (see Table 12.6). As has been discussed throughout this book, even Western thinking is rapidly moving from the fragmentation and atomization of the mechanistic Western view of science, nature, and the world at large, in part because of the influence of the new theories of chaos and complexity.

In many respects, progressive thinking about business in society is already generally moving toward a more integrated and holistic view that includes an ecological and systems perspective. It also is beginning to incorporate the nonobservable elements of emotions, aesthetic appreciation, and individual and collective meaning, sometimes characterized as creating meaningful work, at other times as spirituality in work. These new logics and values are manifesting themselves in many of the companies, research, and ways of thinking cited earlier in this book. The general movement is thus away from passive and toward engaged (interactive) behaviors,

TABLE 12.6.   New Logics and New Values

Prevailing Paradigm	Emergent Paradigm
BASIC WORLD VIEW	
Mechanistic, simple, linear	Organic, complexity, chaotic
Cartesian, Newtonian	Ecological, systemic
Atomistic, fragmented	Holistic (holons)
Objective	Objective, subjective, interobjective, intersubjective
Disengaged, passive	Engaged, active
"It" orientation	"I," "we," and "it" orientations
IMPLICIT LOGICS: PERSPECTIVES	
Focus on distinctions and separations	Focus on interdependence and interrelatedness
Either/or oppositions	Both/and relations
Dualities as opposites and contradictions	Dualities as paradoxes
Top down	Top down/bottom up
LEADING VALUES	
Self-contained individualism and agency	Communitarianism and community
Zero-sum game mentality	Positive-sum gain mentality
Win-lose orientation	Win-win orientation

Sources: This chart is adapted from Douglas R. Austrom and Lawrence J. Lad, "Issues Management Alliances: New Responses, New Values, and New Logic," in *Research in Corporate Social Performance and Policy*, vol. II, James E. Post, ed. (Greenwich, CT: JAI Press, 1989), pp. 233–355; with additions from Ken Wilber, *The Image of Sense and Soul: Integrating Science and Reason.* (Boston: Shambala, 1998; and the author.

331

CHAPTER 12
Leading Global
Futures: The
Emerging
Paradigm of
Leading Corporate
Citizenship

away from fragmentation and toward interdependence and interrelatedness, encompassing the logic of both/and rather than either/or. Paradoxes emerge in this both/and logic, necessitating a need for individuals and organizations to be able to cope with tensions of the opposites, such as in the top-down/bottom-up authority implied in the new logics.

Table 12.6 thus illuminates a decided shift away from mechanistic and inorganic perspectives on organizing and society, which foster dominance and rigidity along with a win-lose orientation. Movement is generally toward a more organic and holistic framing that incorporates a both/and rather than either/or logic. Although this emerging paradigm for leading corporate citizenship is fundamentally more complex than the older more linear and mechanistic approach, it can also be energizing and exciting because it asks leaders to think deeply about what they are doing and why they are doing it. The excitement comes in part because it based on a realistic assessment of the complexity of human life itself and because the emerging perspective is embedded in an understanding of the meaning of relationship—a fundamental aspect, as we have seen, of corporate citizenship.

Because the emerging paradigm is organic and holistic, it incorporates not only objective and scientifically observable phenomenon, but also the aesthetic, emotional, and appreciative, more subjective and intersubjective elements of living life within communities of various sorts, shapes, and sizes. Transformation in thinking—the *metanoia* we have been discussing—is thus needed in societies, too, a transformation that has implications for us all as human beings living in what we hope will be civil and democratic societies, with economies that are growing successfully, profitability, and sustainably.

Leading Corporate Citizens in Societies

The final stage of our imaginization is to assess what this *metanoia* might mean for the societies in which leading corporate citizens operate. Table 12.7 identifies just a few of the dominant social and political shifts that can be expected in our imaginary trip into the future.

TABLE 12.7. Societal Implications of the Emerging Paradigm

Social and political shifts from . . .	To . . .
Dominant economic sphere.	Balance among economic, political, and civil society spheres of activity.
Nonsustainable development.	Sustainable development.
Exploitative and abusive development.	Respectful development.
Uninformed, passive, voiceless stakeholders.	Informed, active stakeholders with voice.
Nation-state legal-regulatory framework.	International legal-regulatory framework.
Diminishing social capital.	Enhancing constructive social capital.
Few global standards, expectations.	Global standards and expectations.
Little enforcement capacity globally.	Global enforcement mechanisms.

Imagine that businesses act collaboratively with nongovernmental organizations (NGOs), international nongovernmental organizations (INGOs), and governmental organizations (GOs) to assure that the activities of each sphere are appropriately balanced with each other. Governments, tending toward democracy because of the power of information and its ready availability, rely on businesses to provide employment, economic development, and growth in the well-being and lifestyles of their citizens. All of this economic and social development is sensitively handled, keeping in mind the core cultural identity of each society and its distinctiveness so that citizens can develop a sustained sense of local community, bolstered by appropriate local, regional, and national infrastructure.

Development in the new paradigm is handled with ecological sustainability clearly in mind. INGOs have evolved that demand accountability and transparency from corporations, assuring responsible practices, and providing clear global standards to which all companies voluntarily adhere. When abuses in human rights, labor rights, or human and child welfare occur, companies as well as organizations from the political and civil society spheres are quick to act and compel the abuser to either change its practices or drive it out of business. Independent observers regularly audit corporate practices with audits then released publicly because international standards have created high expectations that such reporting will be standard.

The wide availability of information about these practices online makes retention of abusive practices difficult, especially as governments are clear about educating all citizens to a high enough level that democracy and free markets based on the biological principles articulated by Korten, The Natural Step, and others are followed rigorously. All market-based activities tend to support communities, rather than debilitate them, and citizens are encouraged to voice concerns so that they can be attended to by the appropriate corporate relations people, who are spread, in their leadership capacities, throughout companies.

An international legal and regulatory framework has been devised by all the nations of the world to foster sustainability, to provide opportunities for stakeholders to voice concerns, and to assure accountability in and transparency of all corporate activities. Enforcement mechanisms are strong, and sanctions are quickly imposed when necessary. Perhaps the most critical sanction is that of releasing negative reputational information about corporate abusers publicly, a type of sanction that tends to damage the company's reputation among its stakeholders to the extent that it actually prevents abuses.

LEADING CHALLENGES: LEADING CORPORATE CITIZENS IN THE NEW PARADIGM

Throughout this book, we have been discussing the shift to an emerging paradigm for leading corporate citizens. Admittedly, the book takes an optimistic rather than pessimistic point of view in suggesting that such a shift is taking place and will con-

333

CHAPTER 12
Leading Global
Futures: The
Emerging
Paradigm of
Leading Corporate
Citizenship

tinue to evolve in a constructive and positive direction. Clearly, power and resource inequities exist and not all corporations behave responsibly, pushed as they are by intense competition and demands from shareholders to increase value by economizing in sometimes-destructive ways.

Part of the agenda has been to look explicitly at what a new paradigm for leading corporate citizens would look like when it is more fully evolved. We have done this by using information, examples, and research that is already available as a guide to what might be in a world where balance, collaboration, and respect guide operating practices and, in this chapter, by imagining the possibilities.

Why does this optimistic scenario make sense? After all, problems abound in the economic, political, and civil society spheres that constitute human civilization, as well as in the ecological environment. Despite these problems and the inherent difficulties, dilemmas, and paradoxes in overcoming them, we have attempted to paint a picture of the way that companies *can* and very likely *should* act if they hope to become leading corporate citizens. And there are signs, as we have witnessed, that many leading corporate citizens are beginning to move in the directions articulated in this chapter.

Over the course of this book, we have looked at significant evidence that acting as a leading citizen not only results in effective behaviors, that is, doing the right thing with respect to stakeholders and the natural environment—but also economizes, resulting in practices that are efficient and profitable, that is, doing things right. Leaders of leading corporate citizens today have begun to understand this truly bigger picture and to act accordingly. Slowly but surely, they are moving their companies along this path toward this emergent and progressive corporate paradigm.

The evidence strongly suggests that the answer is yes to the question, Does this optimistic scenario make sense? Leadership and significant wisdom are required of leading corporate citizens to take steps that others might view as against the mainstream in a time of turbulence and great performance pressures. It requires courage to take responsibility for one's own impacts and those of one's company. It demands mindfulness and true wisdom to operate with respect for stakeholders and to engage with them rather than making assumptions about them and their needs.

Is taking this path always easy? No. Is it always more profitable in the short run? No. Will competitors still act in aggressive and competitive dog-eat-dog ways trying to outstrip companies acting in the paradigm of leading corporate citizens, which is far more collaborative in its orientation? Yes. But are companies that act with respect for stakeholders, with consideration for the full impacts of their decisions, with integrity and wisdom, successful? As we have seen, the answer is, yes!

NOTES TO CHAPTER 12

1. See David Korten's *The Post-Corporate World* (San Francisco: Berrett-Koehler, 1999); see also Fritjof Capra, *The Web of Life* (New York: Anchor Doubleday, 1995); and Stuart Kauffman, *At Home in the Universe: The Search for the Laws of Self-Organization and Complexity* (New York: Oxford University Press, 1995).

2. Peter M. Senge, *The Fifth Discipline* (New York: Currency Doubleday, 1990).

3. For a discussion of wisdom, see Russell L. Ackoff, "On Learning and the Systems That Facilitate It," *Reflections*1, no. 1 (1999), pp. 14–24 (reprinted from Cambridge, MA: Center for Quality of Management, 1996). Karl E. Weick discussed the relationship of wisdom with mindfulness in his talk "Educating for the Unknowable: The Infamous Real World," at the annual meeting of the Academy of Management, Chicago, IL, 1999.

4. Ackoff, p. 16. Italics added.

5. The term imaginization was developed by Gareth Morgan in *Imaginization: The Art of Creative Management* (Newbury Park, CA: Sage, 1993).

6. See Douglas R. Austrom and Lawrence J. Lad, "Issues Management Alliances: New Responses, New Values, and New Logics," in *Research in Corporate Social Performance and Policy,* vol. 11, James E. Post, ed. (Greenwich, CT: JAI Press, 1989), pp. 233–355.

References

ACKOFF, RUSSELL L. "On Learning and the Systems that Facilitate It." *Reflections* 1, no. 1 (1999), pp. 14–24; reprinted from The Center for Quality of Management, Cambridge, MA, 1996.

ANNAN, KOFI. "Business and the U.N.: A Global Compact of Shared Values and Principles." Speech delivered to the World Economic Forum, Davos, Switzerland, January 31, 1999. *Vital Speeches of the Day,* February 15, 1999, pp. 260–61.

ARGYRIS, CHRIS. *Knowledge for Action: A Guide to Overcoming Barriers to Organizational Change.* San Francisco: Jossey-Bass, 1993.

AUGUSTINE, NORMAN R. "Managing the Crisis You Tried to Prevent." *Harvard Business Review,* November–December 1995, pp. 148–58.

AUSTROM, DOUGLAS R., AND LAWRENCE J. LAD. "Issues Management Alliances: New Responses, New Values, and New Logics." In *Research in Corporate Social Performance and Policy,* vol. 11, J. E. Post, ed. Greenwich, CT: JAI Press, 1989.

BARNEY, JAY. *Gaining and Sustaining Competitive Advantage.* Reading, MA: Addison Wesley, 1997.

BARBER, BENJAMIN. *Jihad vs. McWorld.* New York: Times Books; Random House, 1995.

BELENKY, MARY FIELD, BLYTHE MCVICKER CLINCHY, NANCY RULE GOLDBERGER, JILL MATTUCK TARULE. *Women's Ways of Knowing: The Development of Self, Voice, and Mind.* New York: Basic Books, 1986.

BELLAH, ROBERT N., RICHARD MADSEN, WILLIAM M. SULLIVAN, ANN SWIDLER, AND STEVEN M. TIPTON. *Habits of the Heart: Individualism and Commitment in American Life.* New York: Harper & Row, 1985.

BERRY, MICHAEL A., AND DENNIS A. RONDINELLI. "Proactive Corporate Environment Management: A New Industrial Revolution." *Academy of Management Executive* 12, no. 2 (May 1998), pp. 38–50.

BETHKE ELSHTAIN, JEAN. "Not a Cure-All." *Brookings Review* 15, no. 4 (Fall 1997), pp. 13–15.

BIRD, FREDERICK B., AND JAMES A. WATERS. "The Moral Muteness of Managers." *California Management Review* 32, no. 1 (Fall 1989), pp. 73–88.

BORNSTEIN, DAVID. *The Price of a Dream: The Story of the Grameen Bank.* Chicago: University of Chicago Press, 1996.

BOYLE, THOMAS F. *At Any Cost: Jack Welch, General Electric and the Pursuit of Profits.* New York: Random House, 1998.

BRUYN, SEVERYN T. *A Civil Economy: Transforming the Market in the Twenty-First Century.* Ann Arbor: University of Michigan Press, 2000.

BUCHHOLZ, ROGENE A. *Principles of Environmental Management: The Greening of Business,* 2nd ed. Englewood Cliffs, NJ: Prentice Hall, 1998.

BURNS, JAMES MACGREGOR. *Leadership.* New York: Harper Torchbooks, 1978.

CAPRA, FRITJOF. *The Turning Point: Science, Society, and the Rising Culture.* New York: Bantam Books, 1983.

_____. *The Web of Life.* New York: Anchor Doubleday, 1995.

CARROLL, ARCHIE B. "The Four Faces of Corporate Citizenship." *Business and Society Review: Journal of the Center for Business Ethics at Bentley College* 100–101 (1997), pp. 1–7.

_____. "A Three-Dimensional Conceptual Model of Corporate Social Performance." *Academy of Management Review* 4 (1979), pp. 497–505.

CAVANAGH, GERALD F., DENNIS J. MOBERG, AND MANUEL VELASQUEZ. "The Ethics of Organizational Politics." *Academy of Management Review* 6, no. 3 (1981), pp. 363–74.

_____. "Making Business Ethics Practical." *Business Ethics Quarterly* 5, no. 3 (July 1995), pp. 399–418.

CLARKSON, MAX B. E. "A Stakeholder Framework for Analyzing and Evaluating Corporate Social Performance." *Academy of Management Review* 20, no. 1 (1995), pp. 92–117.

CLEMONS, ERIC K. "Using Scenario Analysis to Manage the Strategic Risks of Reengineering." *Sloan Management Review,* Summer 1995, pp. 61–71.

COLLINS, JAMES C., AND JERRY I. PORRAS. "Building Your Company's Vision." *Harvard Business Review,* September–October 1996, pp. 65–77.

_____. *Built to Last: Successful Habits of Visionary Companies.* New York: HarperBusiness, 1997.

D'AVENI, RICHARD. *Hyper-Competition: Managing the Dynamics of Strategic Maneuvering.* New York: Free Press, 1994.

DAVENPORT, KIM. "Social Auditing: The Quest for Corporate Social Responsibility." In James Weber and Kathleen Rehbein, eds. *Proceedings of the International Association of Business and Society* (1997), pp. 197–207.

DAVIS, STAN, AND CHRISTOPHER MEYER. *Blur: The Speed of Change in the Connected Economy.* Reading, MA: Addison-Wesley, 1998.

DE WAAL, FRANS. *Good Natured: The Origins of Right and Wrong in Humans and Other Animals.* Cambridge: Harvard University Press, 1996.

DEMING, W. EDWARDS. *Out of the Crisis.* Cambridge, MA: MIT Center for Advanced Engineering Study, 1982.

DERBER, CHARLES. *Corporation Nation: How Corporations Are Taking Over Our Lives and What We Can Do about It.* New York: St. Martin's Press, 1998.

DESSLER, GARY. "How to Earn Your Employees' Commitment." *Academy of Management Executive* 13, no. 2 (May 1999), pp. 58–67.

DILTZ, DAVID. "The Private Cost of Socially Responsible Investing." *Applied Financial Economics* 5, no. 2 (April 1995), pp. 69–77.

DONALDSON, THOMAS, AND LEE E. PRESTON. "The Stakeholder Theory of the Corporation: Concepts, Evidence, and Implications." *Academy of Management Review* 20, no. 1 (January 1995), pp. 65–91.

DOWELL, GLEN, STUART HART, AND BERNARD YEUNG. "Do Corporate Environmental Standards Create or Destroy Market Value?" *Management Science* 46, no. 8 (2000), pp. 1059–74.

DUBOFF, ROB, AND CARLA HEATON. "Employee Loyalty: The Key Link to Value Growth." *Planning Review* 27, no. 1 (January-February 1999), pp. 8–13.

EPSTEIN, MARC J., AND BILL BIRCHARD. *Counting What Counts: Turning Corporate Accountability to Competitive Advantage.* Reading, MA: Perseus Books, 1999.

EVAN, WILLIAM M., AND R. EDWARD FREEMAN. "A Stakeholder Theory of the Modern Corporation: Kantian Capitalism." In *Ethical Theory and Business,* T. Beauchamp and N . Bowie, eds. Englewood Cliffs, NJ: Prentice Hall, 1988.

FEIGENBAUM, ARMAND V. "Changing Concepts and Management of Quality Worldwide." *Quality Progress* 30, no. 12 (December 1997), pp. 45–48.

FELDMAN, STANLEY J., PETER A. SOYKA, AND PAUL G. AMEER. "Does Improving a Firm's Environmental Management System and Environmental Performance Result in a Higher Stock Price?" *Journal of Investing* 6, no. 4 (Winter 1997), pp. 87–97.

FISHER, DALMAR, AND WILLIAM R. TORBERT. *Personal and Organizational Transformations: The True Challenge of Continual Quality Improvement.* New York: McGraw-Hill, 1995.

FOLEY, MICHAEL W., AND BOB EDWARDS. "The Paradox of Civil Society." *Journal of Democracy* 7, no. 3 (1996), pp. 38–52.

FOMBRUN, CHARLES J. "Indices of Corporate Reputation: An Analysis of Rankings and Ratings by Social Monitors." *Corporate Reputation Review* 1, no. 4 (1998), pp. 327–340.

FREDERICK, WILLIAM C. *Values, Nature, and Culture in the American Corporation.* New York: Oxford University Press, 1995.

FREEMAN, R. EDWARD. *Strategic Management: A Stakeholder Approach.* New York: Basic Books, 1984.

FREEMAN, R. EDWARD, AND DANIEL R. GILBERT, JR. *Corporate Strategy and the Search for Ethics.* Englewood Cliffs, NJ: Prentice Hall, 1988.

FRIEDMAN, MILTON. "The Social Responsibility of a Business Is to Increase Its Profits." In *New York Times Magazine,* September 13, 1970.

GARDNER, HOWARD. *Frames of Mind.* New York: Basic Books, 1983.

GILLIGAN, CAROL. *In a Different Voice: Psychological Theory and Women's Development.* Cambridge: Harvard University Press, 1982.

GLADWIN, THOMAS N., JAMES J. KENNELLY, AND TARA-SHELOMITH KRAUSE. "Shifting Paradigms for Sustainable Development: Implications for Management Theory and Research." *Academy of Management Review* 20, no. 4 (October 1995), pp. 874–907.

GLASBERGEN, PIETER. "Modern Environmental Agreements: A Policy Instrument Becomes a Management Strategy." *Journal of Environmental Planning and Management* 41, no. 6 (November 1998), pp. 693–70.

GLEICK, JAMES. *Chaos: Making a New Science.* New York: Viking, 1987.

GLENN, JEROME C., AND THEODORE J. GORDON. *1999 State of the Future: Challenges We Face at the Millennium.* Washington: The Millennium Project, 1999.

GOLEMAN, DANIEL. *Emotional Intelligence.* New York: Bantam Books, 1995.

———. *Working with Emotional Intelligence.* New York: Bantam Books, 1998.

GRAVES, SAMUEL B., AND SANDRA WADDOCK. "Beyond Built to Last . . . Stakeholder Relations in 'Built-to-Last' Companies." *Business and Society Review* 105, no. 4 (2000), pp. 393–418.

GREIDER, WILLIAM. *One World, Ready or Not: The Manic Logic of Global Capitalism.* New York: Touchstone Books, 1998.

GREINER, LARRY E. "Evolution and Revolution as Organizations Grow." *Harvard Business Review,* July–August 1972, pp. 37–46; reprinted with comments, as HBR Classic, May–June 1998.

GRIFFIN, JENNIFER J., AND JOHN F. MAHON. "The Corporate Social Performance and Corporate Financial Performance Debate: Twenty-five Years of Incomparable Research." *Business and Society* 36, no. 1 (March 1997), pp. 5–31.

GRONROOS, CHRISTIAN. "From Marketing Mix to Relationship Marketing: Towards a Paradigm Shift in Marketing." *Management Decision* 32, no. 2 (1994), pp. 4–20.

GUERARD, JOHN B., JR. "Is There a Cost to Being Socially Responsible in Investing?" *Journal of Investing* 6, no. 2 (Summer 1997), pp. 11–18.

HALL, EDWARD T., AND MILDRED REED HALL. *Understanding Cultural Differences: Germans, French, and Americans.* Yarmouth, ME: Intercultural Press, 1990.

HAMILTON, SALLY, HOJE JO, AND MEIR STATMAN. "Doing Well While Doing Good? The Investment Performance of Socially Responsible Mutual Funds." *Financial Analysts Journal,* November–December 1993, pp. 62–66.

HAMMER, MICHAEL, AND JAMES CHAMPY. *Re-Engineering the Corporation: A Manifesto for Business Revolution.* New York: HarperBusiness, 1993.

HARDIN, GARRETT. "The Tragedy of the Commons." *Science* 162 (1969), pp. 1243–48.

HART, STUART L. "Beyond Greening: Strategies for a Sustainable World." *Harvard Business Review,* January–February 1997, pp. 66–76.

HAWKEN, PAUL. *The Ecology of Commerce.* New York: HarperBusiness, 1993.

HAYES, R. H., AND W. ABERNATHY. "Managing Our Way to Economic Decline." *Harvard Business Review,* July–August 1980, pp. 66–77.

HENDERSON, HAZEL. *Building a Win-Win World: Life Beyond Global Economic Warfare.* San Francisco: Berrett-Koehler, 1996.

HOFSTEDE, GEERT. *Cultures and Organizations: Software of the Mind.* New York: McGraw-Hill, 1991.

IHATOR, AUGUSTINE S. "Effective Public Relations Techniques for the Small Business in a Competitive Market Environment." *Public Relations Quarterly* 43, no. 2 (Summer 1998), pp. 28–32.

ISAACS, WILLIAM. *Dialogue and the Art of Thinking Together.* New York: Doubleday Currency, 1999.

JACKSON, SUZAN L. "ISO 14000: Things You Should Know." *Production* 109, no. 10 (October 1997), pp. 78–79.

KALTENHEUSER, SKIP. "Bribery Is Being Outlawed Virtually Worldwide." *Business Ethics,* May–June 1998, p. 11.

KANT, IMMANUEL. *Groundwork of the Metaphysics of Morals.* H. J. Paton, trans. New York: Harper & Row, 1964.

KANTER, ROSABETH MOSS. *World Class: Thriving Locally in the Global Economy.* New York: Simon & Schuster, 1995.

KAUFFMAN, STUART. *At Home in the Universe: The Search for the Laws of Self-Organization and Complexity.* New York: Oxford University Press, 1995.

KEGAN, ROBERT. *The Evolving Self: Problem and Process in Human Development.* Cambridge: Harvard University Press, 1982.

_____. *In Over Our Heads: The Mental Demands of Modern Life.* Cambridge: Harvard University Press, 1994.

KIDDER, TRACY. *The Soul of a New Machine.* Boston: Atlantic-Little, Brown, 1981.

KOHLBERG, LAWRENCE. "Moral Stages and Moralization: The Cognitive-Developmental Approach." In *Moral Development and Behavior: Theory, Research, and Social Issues*, Thomas Lickona, ed., Gilberg Geis and Lawrence Kohlberg, consulting eds. New York: Holt, Rinehart and Winston, 1976.

KORTEN, DAVID. *The Post-Corporate World: Life after Capitalism.* San Francisco: Berrett-Koehler, 1999.

_____. *When Corporations Rule the World.* San Francisco: Berrett-Koehler, 1995.

LALLY, AMY PESAPANE. "ISO 14000 and Environmental Cost Accounting: The Gateway to the Global Market." *Law and Policy in International Business* 29, no. 4 (Summer 1998), pp. 501–538.

LEAVER, ROBERT. *The Commonwealth Papers.* Providence, RI: Commonwealth Publications, 1995.

LENN, D. JEFFREY, STEVEN N. BRENNER, LEE BURKE, DIANE DODD-MCCUE, CRAIG S. FLEISHER, LAWRENCE J. LAD, DAVID R. PALMER, KATHRYN S. ROGERS, SANDRA A. WADDOCK, AND RICHARD E. WOKUTCH. "Managing Corporate Public Affairs and Government Relations: U.S. Multinational Corporations in Europe." In *Research in Corporate Social Performance and Policy,* James E. Post, ed. vol. 15. Greenwich, CT: JAI Press, 1993.

LIEDTKA, JEANNE. "Constructing an Ethic for Business Practice: Competing Effectively and Doing Good." *Business and Society* 37, no. 3 (September 1998), pp. 254–80.

LODGE, GEORGE CABOT. *Comparative Business-Government Relations.* Englewood Cliffs, NJ: Prentice Hall, 1990.

LODGE, GEORGE CABOT, AND EZRA F. VOGEL. *Ideology and National Competitiveness: An Analysis of Nine Countries.* Boston: Harvard Business School Press, 1987.

LOGAN, DAVID, DELWIN ROY, AND LAURIE REGELBRUGGE. *Global Corporate Citizenship—Rationale and Strategies.* Washington, DC: Hitachi Foundation, 1997.

LOGSDON, JEANNE M., AND KRISTI YUTHAS. "Corporate Social Performance, Stakeholder Orientation, and Organizational Moral Development." *Journal of Business Ethics* 16 (1997), pp. 1213–26.

LOVINS, AMORY B., L. HUNTER LOVINS, AND PAUL HAWKEN. "A Road Map for Natural Capitalism." *Harvard Business Review,* May–June 1999, pp. 145–58.

LYDENBERG, STEVEN D., AND PAUL KAREN. "Stakeholder Theory and Socially Responsible Investing: Toward a Convergence of Theory and Practice." *Proceedings, International Association for Business and Society,* Jim Weber and Kathleen Rehbein, eds. Destin, FL: International Association for Business and Society, 1997, pp. 208–213.

LYDENBERG, S., A. T. MARLIN, AND S. STRUB. *Rating America's Corporate Conscience.* Reading, MA: Addison-Wesley, 1986.

MACINTYRE, ALISDAIR. *After Virtue.* Notre Dame, IN: University of Notre Dame Press, 1981.

MACLEAN, TAMMY. "Creating Stakeholder Relationships: A Model of Organizational Social Identification—How the Southern Baptist Convention Became Stakeholders of Walt Disney." Paper presented at the Annual Meeting of the Academy of Management, San Diego, CA, 1998.

MACMILLAN, KEITH. "Managing Public Affairs in British Industry." *Journal of General Management* 9, no. 2 (1983–1984), pp. 784–90.

MAHON, JOHN F., AND SANDRA A. WADDOCK. "Strategic Issues Management: An Integration of Issue Life Cycle Perspectives." *Business & Society* 31, no. 1 (Spring 1992), pp. 19–32.

MAKOWER, JOEL. *Beyond the Bottom Line: Putting Social Responsibility to Work for Your Business and the World.* New York: Simon & Schuster, 1994.

MARCUS, ALFRED A., AND ALLEN M. KAUFMAN. "The Continued Expansion of the Corporate Public-Affairs Function." *Business Horizons* 31, no. 2 (March–April 1988), pp. 58–62.

MARENS, RICHARD, AND ANDREW WICKS. "Getting Real: Stakeholder Theory, Managerial Practice, and the General Irrelevance of Fiduciary Duties Owed to Shareholders." *Business Ethics Quarterly* 9, no. 2 (April 1999), pp. 273–93.

MARSDEN, CHRIS, AND JÖRG ANDRIOF. "Towards an Understanding of Corporate Citizenship and How to Influence It." *Citizenship Studies* 2 (1998), pp. 329–52.

MATURANA, HUMBERTO R., AND PILLE BUNNELL. "Biosphere, Homosphere, and Robosphere: What Has That to Do with Business." Available at http://www.sol-ne.org/res/wp/maturana/index.html.

MATURANA, HUMBERTO R., AND FRANCISCO J. VARELA. *The Tree of Knowledge: The Biological Roots of Human Understanding,* rev. ed. Boston: Shambala Press, 1998.

MAZARR, MICHAEL J. *Global Trends 2005: The Challenge of a New Millennium.* Washington, DC: Center for Strategic and International Studies, 1997; http://www.csis.org/gt2005/.

MCMILLAN, CHARLES, AND VICTOR V. MURRAY. "Strategically Managing Public Affairs: Lessons from the Analysis of Business-Government Relations." *Business Quarterly* 48, no. 2 (Summer 1983), pp. 94–100.

MEZNAR, MARTIN, AND DOUGLAS NIGH. "Managing Corporate Legitimacy: Public Affairs Activities, Strategies, and Effectiveness." *Business and Society* 32, no. 1 (Spring 1993), pp. 30–43.

MINTZBERG, HENRY. "The Fall and Rise of Strategic Planning." *Harvard Business Review,* January–February 1994, pp. 107–114.

———. *The Rise and Fall of Strategic Planning.* New York: Free Press, 1994.

MIRVIS, PHILIP H. "Transformation at Shell: Commerce *and* Citizenship." *Business and Society Review* 105, no. 1 (2000), pp. 63–84.

MITCHELL, RONALD K., BRADLEY R. AGLE, AND DONNA J. WOOD. "Toward a Theory of Stakeholder Identification and Salience: Defining the Principle of Who and What Really Counts." *Academy of Management Review* 22, no. 4 (October 1997), pp. 853–86.

MOHRMAN, SUSAN A., EDWARD E. LAWLER, III., AND GERALD E. LEDFORD, JR. "Do Employee Involvement and TQM Programs Work?" *Journal for Quality & Participation* 19, no. 1 (January–February 1996), pp. 6–10.

MOORE, JAMES F. *The Death of Competition: Leadership and Strategy in the Age of Business Ecosystems.* New York: HarperBusiness, 1996.

MORGAN, GARETH. *Imaginization: The Art of Creative Management.* Newbury Park, CA: Sage, 1993.

MORGAN, ROBERT M., AND SHELBY D. HUNT. "The Commitment-Trust Theory of Relationship Marketing." *Journal of Marketing* 58, no. 3 (July 1994), pp. 20–38.

NAHAPIET, JANINE, AND SUMANTRA GHOSHAL. "Social Capital, Intellectual Capital, and the Organizational Advantage." *Academy of Management Review* 23, no. 2 (April 1998), pp. 242–66.

NIGH, DOUGLAS, AND PHILIP L. COCHRAN. "Issues Management and the Multinational Enterprise." *Management International Review* 34 (Special Issue 1994), pp. 51–59.

NODDINGS, NELL. *Caring: A Feminine Approach to Ethics and Moral Education.* Berkeley: University of California Press, 1984.

O'HARA-DEVEREAUX, MARY, AND ROBERT JOHANSEN. *GlobalWork: Bridging Distance, Culture and Time.* San Francisco: Jossey-Bass, 1994.

OLSEN, MANCUR, JR. *The Logic of Collective Action.* Cambridge: Harvard University Press, 1965.

OWEN, HARRISON. *Expanding Our Now: The Story of Open Space Technology.* San Francisco: Berrett-Koehler, 1997.

_____. *Open Space Technology: A User's Guide,* 2nd ed. San Francisco: Berrett-Koehler, 1997.

PAVA, MOSES L., AND JOSHUA KRAUSZ. "The Association between Corporate Social-Responsibility and Financial Performance: The Paradox of Social Cost." *Journal of Business Ethics* 15 (1996), pp. 321–57.

PENNAR, KAREN. "The Ties that Lead to Prosperity." *Business Week,* December 15, 1997, pp. 154–55.

PETZINGER, THOMAS, JR. *The New Pioneers: The Men and Women Who Are Transforming the Workplace and Marketplace.* New York: Simon & Schuster, 1999.

PFEFFER, JEFFREY. *The Human Equation: Building Profits by Putting People First.* Boston: Harvard Business School Press, 1998.

PFEFFER, JEFFREY, AND JOHN F. VEIGA. "Putting People First for Organizational Success." *Academy of Management Executive* 13, no. 2 (May 1999), pp. 37–48.

PHILLIPS, ROBERT A., AND JOEL REICHART. "The Environment as a Stakeholder? A Fairness-Based Approach." *Journal of Business Ethics* 23 (January 2000), pp. 185–97.

PIAGET, JEAN. *The Psychology of the Child.* New York: John Wiley, 1969.

POARCH, MARIA. "Civic Life and Work: A Qualitative Study of Changing Patterns of Sociability and Civic Engagement in Everyday Life." Doctoral dissertation, Boston University, 1997.

POIRIER, CHARLES C., AND WILLIAM F. HOUSER. *Business Partnering for Continuous Improvement.* San Francisco: Berrett-Koehler, 1993.

POST, JAMES E. *Corporate Behavior and Social Change.* Reston, VA: Reston Publishing, 1978.

_____. "Meeting the Challenge of Global Corporate Citizenship." Series on Corporate Citizenship. Boston College, Carroll School of Management, Center for Corporate Community Relations, 2000.

_____. "Moving from Geographic to Virtual Communities: Corporate Citizenship in a Dot.Com World." *Business and Society Review* 105, no. 1 (2000), pp. 27–46.

POST, JAMES E., AND JENNIFER J. GRIFFIN. *The State of Corporate Public Affairs: Final Report 1996 Survey.* Boston: Boston University School of Management; Washington: Foundation for Public Affairs, 1996.

POST, JAMES E., EDWIN A. MURRAY, JR., ROBERT B. DICKIE, AND JOHN F. MAHON. "The Public Affairs Function in American Corporations: Development and Relations with Corporate Planning." *Long Range Planning* 15, no. 2 (April 1982), pp. 12–21.

PRAHALAD, C. K., AND G. HAMEL. "The Core Competence of the Corporation." *Harvard Business Review,* May–June 1990, pp. 79–91.

PRESTON, LEE E., AND JAMES E. POST. *Private Management and Public Policy.* New York: Prentice Hall, 1975.

PUTNAM, ROBERT D. "Bowling Alone: America's Declining Social Capital." *Journal of Democracy* 6, no. 1 (January 1995), pp. 65–78.

_____. *Making Democracy Work: Civic Traditions in Modern Italy.* Princeton, NJ: Princeton University Press, 1993.

_____. "The Prosperous Community: Social Capital and Public Life." *American Prospect* 13 (Spring 1993), http://epn.org/prospect/13/13/putn.html.

_____. "The Strange Disappearance of Civic America." *American Prospect* 24 (Winter 1996), http://epn.org/prospect/24/24putn.html.

ROYAL DUTCH/SHELL. *Profits and Principles—Does There Have to Be a Choice? The Shell Report 1998.* London: Royal Dutch/Shell Group, 1998.

RUSSELL, WILLIAM G., STEVEN L. SKALAK, AND GAIL MILLER. "Environmental Cost Accounting: The Bottom Line for Environmental Quality Management." *Total Quality Management* 3, no. 3 (Spring 1994), pp. 255–68.

ST. JOHN, BURTON, III. "Public Relations as Community-Building Then and Now." *Public Relations Quarterly* 43, no. 1 (1998), pp. 34–40.

SCHÖN, DONALD A., AND MARTIN REIN. *Frame Reflection: Toward the Resolution of Intractable Policy Controversies.* New York: Basic Books, 1994.

SCHWARTZ, PETER. *The Art of the Long View: Planning for the Future in an Uncertain World.* New York: Doubleday Currency, 1996.

SENGE, PETER M. *The Fifth Discipline: The Art and Practice of the Learning Organization.* New York: Doubleday, 1991.

SENGE, PETER M., CHARLOTTE ROBERTS, RICHARD B. ROSS, BRYAN J. SMITH, AND ART KLEINER. *The Fifth Discipline Fieldbook: Strategies and Tools for Building a Learning Organization.* New York: Currency Doubleday, 1994.

SHELLENBARGER, SUE. "Companies Are Finding It Really Pays to Be Nice to Employees." *The Wall Street Journal,* July 22, 1998.

SHRADER, CHARLES B., VIRGINIA BLACKBURN, AND PAUL ILES. "Women in Management and Firm Financial Performance: An Exploratory Study." *Journal of Managerial Issues* 9, no. 3 (Fall 1997), pp. 355–72.

SOLOMON, ROBERT C. *A Better Way to Think about Business: How Personal Integrity Leads to Corporate Success.* New York: Oxford University Press, 1999.

_____. "The Moral Psychology of Business: Care and Compassion in the Corporation." Business Ethics Quarterly 8, no. 3 (July 1998), pp. 515–33.

SOROS, GEORGE. "The Capitalist Threat." *Atlantic Monthly,* February 1997, http://www.mtholyoke.edu/acad/intrel/soros.htm.

STARIK, MARK. "Should Trees Have Managerial Standing? Toward Stakeholder Status for Non-Human Nature." *Journal of Business Ethics* 14 (1995), pp. 204–217.

STORBACKA, KAJ, TORE STRANDVIK, AND CHRISTIAN GRONROOS. "Managing Customer Relationships for Profit: The Dynamics of Relationship Quality." *International Journal of Service Industry Management* 5, no. 5 (1994), pp. 21–38.

TANNEN, DEBORAH. *The Argument Culture: Stopping America's War of Words.* New York: Ballantine Books, 1999.

TORBERT, WILLIAM R. *The Power of Balance: Transforming Self, Society, and Scientific Inquiry.* Newbury Park, CA: Sage, 1991.

VARLEY, PAMELA, ED. *The Sweatshop Quandary: Corporate Responsibility on the Global Frontier.* Washington, DC: Investor Responsibility Research Center, 1998.

VAUGHAN, DIANE. *The Challenger Launch Decision: Risky Technology, Culture, and Deviance at NASA.* Chicago: University of Chicago Press, 1996.

VELASQUEZ, MANUEL, DENNIS J. MOBERG, AND GERLD F. CAVANAGH. "Organizational Statesmanship and Dirty Politics: Ethical Guidelines for the Organizational Politician." *Organizational Dynamics,* Autumn 1983, pp. 65–80.

WACKERNAGEL, MATHIS, LARRY ONISTO, ALEJANDRO CALLEJAS LINARES, INA SUSANA LÓPEZ, FALFÁN, JESUS MÉNDEZ GARCIA, ANA ISABEL SUÁREZ GUERRERO, MA. GUADALUPE SUÁREZ GUERRERO. "Ecological Footprints of Nations: How Much Nature Do They Use?—How Much Nature Do They Have?" In http://www.ecouncil. ac.cr/rio/focus/report/english/footprint/.

WACKERNAGEL, MATHIS, AND WILLIAM REES. "Our Ecological Footprint; Reducing Human Impact on the Earth." New Society, Gambrola Island, BC, Canada, 1996.

WADDELL, STEVE. "Business-Government-Nonprofit Collaborations as Agents for Social Innovation and Learning." Paper presented at the Academy of Management Annual Meeting, Chicago, IL, 1999.

_____. "Market-Civil Society Partnership Formation: A Status Report on Activity, Strategies, and Tools." *IDR Reports* 13, no. 5 (1998).

WADDELL, STEVE, AND L. DAVID BROWN. "Fostering Intersectoral Partnering: A Guide to Promoting Cooperation among Government, Business, and Civil Society Actors." *IDR Reports* 13, no. 3 (1997).

WADDOCK, SANDRA A. "Linking Community and Spirit: A Commentary and Some Propositions." *Journal of Organizational Change Management* (Special issue on Spirituality and Work) 12, no. 4 (1999), pp. 332–344.

_____. *Not By Schools Alone: Sharing Responsibility for America's Education Reform.* Greenwich, CT: Praeger, 1995.

_____. "Understanding Social Partnerships: An Evolutionary Model of Partnership Organizations." *Administration and Society* 21, no. 1 (May 1989), pp. 78–100.

WADDOCK, SANDRA A., AND S. B. GRAVES. "Quality of Management and Quality of Stakeholder Relations: Are They Synonymous?" *Business and Society* 36, no. 3 (September 1997), pp. 250–79.

WADDOCK, SANDRA A., AND S. B. GRAVES. "The Corporate Social Performance— Financial Performance Link." *Strategic Management Journal* 18, no. 4 (1997), pp. 303–19.

WADDOCK, SANDRA, SAMUEL B. GRAVES, AND RENEE GORSKI. "Performance Characteristics of Social and Traditional Investments," *Journal of Investing* 9, no. 2 (Summer 2000), pp. 27–38.

WADDOCK, SANDRA A., AND NEIL SMITH. "Relationships: The Real Challenge of Corporate Global Citizenship." *Business and Society Review* 105, no. 1 (2000), pp. 47–62.

WARTICK, STEVEN L., AND JOHN F. MAHON. "Toward a Substantive Definition of the Corporate Issue Construct: A Review and Synthesis of the Literature." *Business and Society* 33, no. 3 (December 1994), pp. 293–311.

WARTICK, STEVEN L., AND DONNA J. WOOD. *International Business and Society.* Malden, MA: Blackwell, 1998.

WEEDEN, CURT. *Corporate Social Investing.* San Francisco: Berrett-Koehler, 1998.

WEICK, KARL E. "Educating for the Unknowable: The Infamous Real World." Paper presented at the Academy of Management Annual Meeting, Chicago, IL, 1999.

WEIGAND, ERIC M., KENNETH R. BROWN, AND EILEEN M. WILHELM. "Social Principled Investing: Caring about Ethics and Profitability. " *Trusts and Estates* 135, no. 9 (August 1996), pp. 36–42.

WEISBORD, MARVIN R., AND SANDRA JANOFF. *Future Search: An Action Guide to Finding Common Ground in Organizations and Communities.* San Francisco: Berrett-Koehler, 1995.

WHEATLEY, MARGARET J. *Leadership and the New Science: Learning about Organization from an Orderly New Universe.* San Francisco: Berrett-Koehler, 1992.

WILBER, KEN. *A Brief History of Everything.* Boston: Shambala Publications.

_____. *The Eye of Spirit: An Integral Vision for a World Gone Slightly Mad.* Boston: Shambala Publications, 1998.

_____. *The Marriage of Sense and Soul: Integrating Science and Reason.* New York: Random House, 1998.

_____. *Sex, Ecology, Spirituality: The Spirit of Evolution.* Boston: Shambala Publications, 1995.

WILLIAMSON, O. E. *Markets and Hierarchies: Analysis and Antitrust Implications.* New York: Free Press, 1975.

WILSON, EDWARD O. *Consilience: The Unity of Knowledge.* New York: Alfred A. Knopf, 1998.

WOLFE, ALAN. "Is Civil Society Obsolete? Revisiting Predications of the Decline of Civil Society in *Whose Keeper?*" Brookings Review 15, no. 4 (Fall 1997), pp. 9–12.

_____. *Whose Keeper? Social Science and Moral Obligation.* Berkeley: University of California Press, 1989.

WOOD, DONNA J., AND RAYMOND E. JONES. "Stakeholder Mismatching: A Theoretical Problem in Empirical Research on Corporate Social Performance." *International Journal of Organizational Analysis* 3, no. 3 (July 1995), pp. 229–67.

ZADEK, SIMON. "Balancing, Performance, Ethics, and Accountability." *Journal of Business Ethics* 17, no. 3 (October 1998), pp. 1421–41.

ZALEZNIK, ABRAHAM. "Managers and Leaders: Are They Different?" *Harvard Business Review,* March–April 1992, pp. 126–135.

ZECKHAUSER, RICHARD, AND ELMER SCHAEFER. "Public Policy and Normative Economic Theory." In *The Study of Policy Formation,* Raymond A. Bauer and Kenneth J. Gergen, eds. New York: Free Press, 1968, pp. 27–101.

Index